RIDING
ON THE
ETHER
EXPRESS

Riding

on the

Ether

Express

A MEMOIR OF 1960s LOS ANGELES,
THE RISE OF FREEFORM UNDERGROUND RADIO,
AND THE LEGENDARY KPPC-FM

Dave Pierce

Center for Louisiana Studies
University of Louisiana at Lafayette
2008

Chronology adapted from:
The New York Times. *The 20th Century: The Great Events from the Victorian Age to the Turn of the Millennium.* New York: Galahad Books, 2001.

Glennon, Lorraine, ed. *The 20th Century: An Illustrated History of Our Lives and Times.* North Dighton, MA: JG Press, 1999.

Center for Louisiana Studies
University of Louisiana at Lafayette
© 2008 by Center for Louisiana Studies
P.O. Box 40831
Lafayette, LA 70504-0831

Library of Congress Cataloging-in-Publication Data

Pierce, Dave.
Riding on the ether express / Dave Pierce.
p. cm.
ISBN 1-887366-77-6 (alk. paper)
1. Pierce, Dave. 2. Disc jockeys--United States--Biography.
3. Alternative radio broadcasting--United States--History. I. Title.

ML429.P55A3 2007
791.44'3--dc22
[B]

2007024196

Editor: Sarah Fox

http://cls.louisiana.edu

Printed in China by Everbest Printing Co. through
Four Colour Imports, Ltd., Louisville, Kentucky.

This book is printed on acid-free paper.

Ether (Radio) Waves continue to travel through space infinitely.
Therefore, all broadcasts, including the KPPC radio shows
are still out there, and could someday be recaptured.

Editor's Note

All characters are real, taken from the daily journal of the author. The journal, written during a time of revolution within our culture and political upheaval which began with Flower Power, love, and peace . . . and resulting in major changes in the society in which we now live and the music to which we listen, gives us an accurate accounting of the 1960s.

Extensive efforts were made to accurately credit writers and publishers. Any revisions or corrections will appear in future editions.

Contents

Foreword

By Dr. Michael C. Keith

> The radio was screaming "Power to the People—
> Right On!"
>
> — Hunter S. Thompson

Did they really happen—those long ago days of the purple haze? Someone once said (was it Abbie Hoffman or maybe Wavy Gravy?) that if you can remember, you weren't there. For those of us who were there, we can blame our failing memories on the nearly four decades that have since passed. However, while recollections are often blurred by the passage of time, the short-lived era of commercial underground radio remains quite vivid to many, especially to those who were a part of it, such as the author of this book. As these pages will attest, it was not a figment of the imagination or, in the vernacular of the times, a "trip," although in terms of its uniqueness in radio's programming history, it was something close to a dream.

Essentially the phenomenon known as commercial underground radio (also called progressive, alternative, and free form) was spawned by two key factors: a basic disdain for formula radio (specifically Top 40) by a handful of young and rebellious broadcasters (so called by members of the radio establishment at the time) and the cultural tumult and upheaval of the period. In the first instance, the highly formulaic hit music radio sound—featuring two-and-a-half minute doowop tunes and frenetic deejays—that dominated the AM airwaves had finally driven some radio aficionados to chart (no pun intended) a different course. What they had in mind was a radio station that focused on music not culled from the shallows of the major record label's "recommended" playlists and personalities who communicated with their listeners like real human beings not tobacco auctioneers or carnival barkers.

The movement, and it truly deserves to be called that, began on the East and West Coasts at about the same time (give or take a few months). In 1966, New York's WOR-FM broke the format mold by offering an unorthodox blend of album cuts and laid-back deejays, but the following year, it dropped the sound and returned to the standardized chart-toppers approach. Scott Muni and his defrocked collaborators at the fledgling underground station found another home in the form of WNEW-FM. The same year, the "non-format" format took hold on the West Coast as Tom Donahue expanded on Larry Miller's free form all night show at obscure Bay-area outlet KMPX-FM, located in a dingy warehouse along the docks. A few months later, Donahue headed south and implemented the underground sound at KPPC-FM. And the rest, as they say, is the stuff of legend. In the years that followed, dozens of stations around the country (KSAN, WBCN, KMET, WABX, KSHE, WHFS, KLOS, WPLO, WMMS, to cite a handful) would go to deep cuts and *au natural* voices behind the microphone.

This revolution on the radio dial found sustenance and inspiration in the counter culture movement that was sweeping the country. Rock music began to reflect the anti-establishment sentiments of the nation's youth, thus further fanning the flame of discontent that gave rise to commercial underground radio. At the core of the new programming paradigm was a profound dissatisfaction with the numbing status quo rampant in the industry and an appreciation for what was behind the ferment and clamor on the streets of a nation in serious flux. The underground radio movement quickly found a raft of enthusiastic adherents, among them Thom O'Hair, Scoop Nisker, Tom Gamache, Rosco, Ed Bear, Stefan Ponek, Dusty Street, Raechel Donahue (Tom's wife), Tim Powell, Vaco Cash, Dan Carlisle, Roland Jacopetti, Frank Wood, Charles Laquidara, Steve Segal, Les Carter, and this book's author, Dave Pierce, to name just a few.

It was radio oriented, "for the people," that gave the new programming genre its uniqueness and niche. Stations that espoused an anti-corporate and anti-government mindset did not exist on the commercial radio band. Audiences were not accustomed to hearing deejays speak out against the military industrial complex, big business, and social inequality while advocating free love and the use of mind-altering chemicals—indeed, a station (KSAN) encouraging listeners to send in their drugs to determine whether they were safe for consumption was not a common occurrence. Nor were listeners acquainted with radio that aired a broad spectrum of music (albeit, mainly rock) in thoughtful and evocative sets emphasizing quality and substance over quantity and banality.

The popularity of free form commercial radio continued to grow in the early 1970s, and as the war in Vietnam wound down and the drug culture turned hardcore, the companies that owned these outlets saw dollar signs. Soon underground radio was transformed into a more mainstream and diluted version of its former self, called Album Oriented Rock. One of the central figures behind the conversion was Lee Abrams, who implemented tighter playlists and a host of other programming strictures designed to attract a larger share of the ratings. (Ironically, in 2004 Abrams spearheaded the rollout of XM Satellite Radio as its chief programmer claiming that broadcast radio had become mundane and predictable.) Thus underground radio as conceived at stations like WOR, WNEW, KMPX, and KPPC was no more.

Fortunately, Dave Pierce keeps the memory of this singular event in commercial radio's history alive in his intimate, engaging, and revealing account. By fondly and cogently detailing his days at KPPC-FM, he provides readers with an inclusive and nostalgic chronicle of what underground radio represented and signified to its extraordinary practitioners and to its many loyal and devoted fans.

Dr. Michael C. Keith is one of the nation's leading scholars on electronic media. He has recently written a series of ground-breaking books which examine the use of the nation's airwaves by groups with strong social, political, and revolutionary messages and agendas. Some of his titles include *The Broadcast Century and Beyond*, *Voices in the Purple Haze*, *Waves of Rancor: Tuning in the Radical Right*, *The Hidden Screen: Low Power Television in America*, and most recently *Sounds of Change: FM Broadcasting in America* (with Christopher Sterling). Dr. Keith is Associate Professor of Communication at Boston College.

Introduction

Even while it was happening, I had the feeling that these were momentous times. Now, looking back on that tumultuous period between 1968 and 1971, there is little question that those four years represented the height and decline of the '60s revolution.

It took almost twenty years before America could begin to examine what happened, talk about it, write about it, and deal with it, in movies and on television. For most of us, the memories are etched as clearly as the days we lived them, colored only by the perspectives we've since gained.

The revolution was politics, of course, centering on the Vietnam War, but it was also lifestyles and music, civil rights and women's lib, and perhaps most important of all, the first seeds of the environmental movement. To be able to live in—and participate in this turning point in American history—I've always considered a happy stroke of being alive at the right time. To have witnessed it from the unique vantage point of an underground rock 'n roll radio station, I now know was a rare privilege.

KPPC-FM, Los Angeles' legendary Free Form pioneer, broadcast blasphemy against the state from the basement of the Pasadena Presbyterian Church. Its life cycle coincided with that 1968 to 1971 period.

Being on the radio amplified everything, made it bigger than life. So, it's understandable how the experience of those years still affects me today. I have the feeling, however, that I'm not alone in this. The times were bigger than life because it was so damned important. Millions of flower children out there look back, bittersweet, not just because it was their youth, but because of the dream of a better world...the dream that was worth having, worth fighting for, even if we only came up with a draw.

I wondered how my own personal experience correlated with my peers. How far back did you have to go into the '60s, '50s and even '40s, to plot the course that took us from all-American kids to longhaired, street-marching, dope-smoking, anti-government slogan spouters? All the time, asking, "Don't You Know Me, I'm Your Native Son?"

How did I make the journey from Cajun farm boy and student athlete to radical disc jockey? How did an FM station, broadcasting Sunday Church Services, mid-week devotionals, and classical music become an Underground Rocker playing a non-format of rock, blues, folk, bluegrass, gospel, country, comic bits, Cajun, classical and jazz, forgotten and obscure oldies by Dr. Demento, and featuring the Credibility Gap for a news team? Somewhere in there was a tale worth telling.

I lived and breathed America's music because I had the enviable job of playing it on the radio. But my fervor for rock 'n roll was no greater than the enthusiasm of the listeners I played it for. It was an age of music, the songs and the artists, the year and the month when they became famous, when the radio burned the lyrics into your memory banks. For the most part, the chronological correctness has been maintained, although there are some exceptions. This story is also about musicians and the music business, and the radio power plays of program directors that determine whose voice is heard. It's about the show biz fringes where the dreams of struggling young performers are crushed by the thousands every year in the City of Angels.

And it is autobiographical. Obviously, conversations are recreated from memory and the recall of the personalities of the real people in real events. We were possibly not quite as good nor nearly as bad as I have portrayed us. There was the risk of over dramatizing my life, sharing too much of that which is too personal to be publicly displayed, or offending friends and faces from the past. But in the end, I felt the only way to tell it was from my point of view and from the heart.

Today we accept the reality of mass manipulation by the media. There was a time in the late '60s when we saw first hand the power of music and broadcasting when it was out of control, when rock 'n roll burst onto the FM band and the consciousness of America was awakening. Anarchy raised its head in the streets and fascism fought back from high places. The music was the message. Real ideas were coming out of your radio speakers. For a brief time, the airwaves really did belong to the people. From out on the edge, the radical, reactionary, and rational voices were juxtaposed for all to hear and judge how much sanity was left on any side. Restrictions and broadcast rules were blown away in a flood of wailing guitars and reverberation. In the midst of all this turmoil were the underground disc jockeys who were *Riding on the Ether Express.*

South Louisiana Gulf Coast
1945

"Tinga, Tinga...Tinga, Tinga,
Clackety, Clackety...Clackety, Clackety."

At four years old I loved those sounds. The tinga, tinga of the steel triangle and the clackety, clackety of the spoons. I liked the fiddle, too, and the sounds that came out of the guitar and that Cajun squeeze-box were fascinating. There was something about the simplicity of the triangle and the spoons, seems like anyone could play them.

"Jole Blon,
Tu m'as quitte'
moi, tout seul
pon t'en alle
avec ta famille."

"Jole Blon"
(Joe Falcon and Cléoma Falcon)

The singer-accordion player belted out the classic Cajun love song. I understood enough French to know the song was about a pretty blonde girl. But, it was the *sound* that was in my blood, the chanka-chank accordion and the heartbreaking fiddle. The spoons and triangle keeping the beat.

A rotund lady with a box of soap flakes in hand weaved between the Cajun dancers, sprinkling the flakes on the wooden dance floor of Berro Bernard's Fais-Do-Do Club. Starting near the bandstand, I ran across the sixty-foot dancehall then went into a slide through the last dozen feet of soap flakes. I stopped just short of the group of men, laughing and joking while standing and drinking at the bar that was lit up by neon signs advertising Jax, Regal, Falstaff, Gobal, and Blatz beers. The young men wore cowboy hats. Some even had spurs on their western boots. Before the evening ended, there would be at least two or three fist fights, but after a while they'd talk it out, shake hands, and get back to drinking.

My mom and dad, Nellie and Casey Pierce, glided by as the dancers circled the dance floor. It would be years before I learned to appreciate the simple artistry of the Cajun two-step, or realize my dad was a master at it. I ran up to my parents and hugged them around their dancing knees. I was glad my dad was back from the war. He had been shot in Germany. He had a small bullet hole in his left shoulder with a six inch long scar next to it where they dug out the bullet. Dad also had a beautiful gold medal in the shape of a heart with a purple ribbon attached.

Mom tousled my hair. I ran off to join my sister and the other dozen kids between three and ten years old who were sliding across the soap-flaked floor. The youngest was Woodie Bernard. His grandpa, Berro, owned the place. When I slid into Woodie, knocking him down, he jumped to his feet. "Let's fight," he said. I laughed and ran toward the bandstand.

"'Jole Blon,'" I sang to myself, running and sliding through the two-stepping Cajun dancers.

Cajun Farm House
South Louisiana
1946

*"It was down in Mexico,
I met a senorita there,
Who wore the silver bells..."*

"New Silver Bells," Webb Pierce
(Webb Pierce and Owen Perry, Unichappel Music Inc.)

I was sitting on my seventy-year-old great-grandmother's lap. As the music ended, I heard the announcer's voice from the new radio, "That was Webb Pierce singing 'New Silver Bells.' Now folks, a great big Grand Ole Opry welcome to Cousin Minnie Pearl."

Cousin Minnie Pearl was her stage name of course, and though Webb Pierce was his real name, he wasn't kin to us either. Still, everyone on the Grand Ole Opry seemed like family. The roar of applause, hoots, and whistles spilled out of the cloth-covered speaker.

"How-Dee, I'm just so proud to be here," Cousin Minnie Pearl's famous opening line brought more applause and howls of laughter.

I slipped off Granny's lap and approached the radio. It stood against the wall, a foot taller than I was. Shiny brown veneer, one knob for turning it off and on and making it louder, another knob for tuning in the half-dozen stations it was capable of receiving.

"Maybe," I thought, "there is a little stage inside the radio, and Minnie Pearl in on that stage."

I squeezed my head against the wall and peeked into the back of the radio. No stage. No Cousin Minnie. Just strange looking glass and metal tubes and the backside of the speaker. And wires, lots of little ones and the big wire that plugged into that heavy battery that powered the radio. Too bad you couldn't see the singers.

My great-grandfather, David White and farm workers thrashing rice, early 1940s, Intracoastal City, La.

On horseback, 1942.

Cajun Farm House
South Louisiana
1947

"When the Yanquis come to Trinidad,
They find the young girls more than glad.
The young girls say they treat them nice,
And they give them a better price.
They drink rum and Coca-Cola,
Go down to Point Cumana.
Both mother and daughter
Working for the Yanqui dollar."

"Rum and Coca-Cola," Andrew Sisters
(Rupert Grant "Lord Vadar," Maurice Baron)

Now that song surely sounded different with the tinny sounding drums and the native island beat. I wondered where Trinidad was and why mother and daughter were working for the Yankee dollar. "Drinking Rum and Coca-Cola" was played a lot on the radio, but Dad liked it so much that he went out and bought the record that I was listening to now. My mom said Trinidad was farther south, past the Gulf of Mexico and "Drinking Rum" was a song that came out of the war. Dad talked a lot about the war and his face could get real bitter and mean when he talked about Franklin Roosevelt.

"If you re-elect me president, I'll see to it that your boys don't fight no foreign wars on no foreign soil."

"Franklin Roosevelt said that," Dad would say. "You can't believe what the government says on the radio. They'll lie to you. They'll lie to the whole country right there on the radio."

I knew Dad must be right. Damned old government; damned old dead Roosevelt. What did drinking rum and Coca-Cola have to do with the war? Funny about music, what makes them write a song.

"The boys all come to Trinidad," I sang to myself.

I examined the needle on the phonograph and decided to replace it. It was discarded alongside the other old needles strewn around the edge of the phonograph. I reached into the small yellow packet that contained fifty quality phonograph needles, pulled out a new one, and attached it to the big heavy arm located just underneath that shiny metal three-inch speaker where the sound came out. What an invention! I picked up the record and looked at it closely. It was big and heavy, and I was careful not to drop it, 'cause these records broke easily. I read the purple label in the middle, *Decca Records, Andrew Sisters, Drinking Rum and Coca-Cola. 78 rpm*. Wonder what 78 rpm was? I put the record back into place and cranked the handle until the phonograph was wound up tight. If it wasn't tight enough, the sound would start to slow down near the end of the song. I released the lever. That started the record spinning very fast. I eyed the first groove on the edge. You had to be careful not to let the needle fall off the edge, 'cause that ruined it. But, I played this phonograph many times. When the spinning record got up to speed, I laid the needle in the groove and the Andrew Sisters sang:

"When the Yanquis come to Trinidad,
They got the young girls all goin mad,
Drinking rum and Coca-Cola.
Both mother and daughter
Working for the Yanqui dollar."
(Ibid.)

1943

♦ While on tour in Trinadad in 1943, comedian Morey Amsterdam heard Lord Vadar's original calyso "Rum and Coca Cola." Back in the U.S., Amsterdam published the song and credited himself as the composer.

Casey Pierce, during WWII.

Nellie Pierce.

My sister Russie and me, 1945.

1947

♦ Les Paul markets a solid bodied electric guitar. The Gibson would become the standard for rock musicians.

1948

♦ At age 25, Norman Mailer publishes *The Naked and the Dead*, based on his WWII experiences. Its bitter cynicism gave readers another point of view about war.

♦ Composer Virgil Thomson wins a Pulizter prize for his score on the film documentary *Louisiana Story*.

♦ Dr. Alfred C. Kinsey publishes *Sexual Behavior in the Human Male*.

♦ NBC Texaco Star Theatre tranforms failed radio performer Milton Berle into "Mr. Television."

The Farm
South Louisiana
May 1949

"Hey, sweet baby, don't you think maybe,
We could find us a brand new recipe?"

"Hey, Good Lookin'!," Hank Williams
(Hank Williams, Acuff-Rose Music/Hiriam Music)

The singer was Whitney Lege, striding across the South Louisiana rice field, his hip boots pulled down around his knees, buccaneer style so that he looked like that picture of the pirate Jean Lafitte. I was forty feet up in the pecan tree behind our house. From up here I could see across a mile of marshland down the Vermilion Bayou to where it intersected with the Intracoastal Waterway. The shrimp boats were moving down the bayou, out to the bay, and on to the Gulf of Mexico. In a few days they would return, their nets hanging from the rigging. But today, my attention is on Whitney, sloshing through the six inches of water, shovel over his shoulder. The sun was getting hot on this late spring morning, but it was cool up in the gently swaying pecan tree. At this height, the southeast wind coming off the gulf always felt good. I watched Mom and Dad come out to greet Whitney.

"I just heard that Hank Williams' record on the radio," beamed Whitney.

"Is that what you're trying to sing?" Nellie asked.

"That's it." Whitney began singing again, "got a hot-rod Ford and a two dollar bill."

They'd all been to see Hank Williams in a show called the Hadacol Caravan, put together by local politician and patent medicine inventor, Dudley J. LeBlanc. Being 80% alcohol, Hadacol was a hot seller in Cajun South Louisiana and grossed 25 million nationwide. Coozan Dud knew country music could sell anything, so he hired Hank Williams. Dud's co-promoter was a fella named Colonel Tom Parker. The title of Colonel was bestowed upon him by Jimmie Davis, the governor of Louisiana and B movie actor, the same fellow who wrote "You Are My Sunshine, My Only Sunshine."

"Hank sure can sing good," Casey said.

"I like Hank Williams," I thought. "I'd like to see him make a record. I am going to do that when I grow up."

I looked out from my perch, across the miles of coastal marshland toward the Gulf of Mexico.

1950

♦ Muddy Waters releases "Rolling Stone" from which the British rock band and the U.S. magazine would later derive their names.

♦ Southern writer William Faulkner wins the Nobel prize stating, "If a story is in you, it has to come out."

♦ Lafayette Ron Hubard publishes *Dianetics: The Modern Science of Mental Health*.

♦ Charles Schultz creates *Charlie Brown*.

The Farm
South Louisiana
August 1951

"All around the water tank,
Waiting for a train,
A thousand miles away from home,
Sleeping in the rain."

"Waiting For a Train," Jimmie Rodgers
(Jimmie Rodgers, APRS)

I was pumping water by hand while the fifty head of cattle gathered around the water trough to quench their summer thirst. I'd been at it twenty minutes and was getting tired. But I did this chore twice a day, and was in shape for the task. Cattle and horses were in my blood. Before our Cajun ancestors were thrown out of Nova Scotia by the English, they were known as marshland dwellers and the keepers of beasts. When the Cajuns finally made their way to South Louisiana, they felt right at home. Under the nearby pecan tree, sitting in a swing, my dad, Casey, was playing guitar and yodeling the Jimmy Rodgers' song. I filled the trough to the brim and led my paint pony around to drink up.

"Don't let those animals waste that water," Casey said. "We could run out."

Casey was a fanatic about wasting water. How could you run out of water, I wondered. You might get tired pumping it, but there was plenty in the well and it was always raining.

I led my pony under the tree and began to loosen the girth. I had risen before daybreak, saddled up at the crack of dawn, and carrying my rifle in one hand, rode the half-mile through the oak trees and palmettos to the rice field on the edge of the marsh. There I tied my pony, climbed a ten-foot wooden scaffold, and began shooting rounds from my .22 rifle as the sun rose. That's when black birds began to swarm into the rice field. "Minding birds" was the job title. The whine of bullets kept the black birds from settling in and eating too big a share of the rapidly maturing grain. I would sit out there in the stark loneliness of the South Louisiana landscape watching the gulf winds make waves through the rice field and ripple on out into the saw grass in the marsh. I would pretend I was Roy Rogers or Gene Autry, or my favorite, the good guy who wore black, Lash Larue. I knew a lot of ten-year-old kids would envy me, shooting a gun and riding a horse. But the job got old by eight or nine in the morning. That's when the black birds moved off into the marsh for the day and I headed for home and breakfast. I would come back late that afternoon to do another three-hour shift till dark when the birds once again came in for a quick snack before roosting.

"Know who wrote that song, boy?" Casey asked, switching to harmonica to blow a few notes of the chorus.

Sure I knew. That was Jimmie Rodgers, the singing brakeman, the father of hillbilly music. Recorded that song in 1928, long before Hank Williams. Casey knew most of Jimmie Rodgers' stuff and I could always recognize the songs. Casey spent a lot of time in that swing under the tree picking his guitar, blowing his harmonica, and singing Jimmie Rodgers. He planted the rice crop and raised some hogs and cattle. But he didn't seem to have a lot of desire to get things done. Nellie said that he was still thinking about the war and how bad it had been. Sometimes he played "Lili Marlene" on his harmonica, that song about the German girl. He'd come back from Europe singing it six years ago and would sing and play it the rest of his life.

> *"I walked up to the brakeman,*
> *To give him a line of talk.*
> *He says, 'If you got money,*
> *I'll see that you don't walk.'*
>
> *'I haven't got a nickel,*
> *Not a penny can I show.'*
> *He said, 'Get off, you railroad bum.'*
> *And he slammed the boxcar door."*
> (Ibid.)

I had just turned my paint pony loose to graze when I saw them drive up in the brand new Buick. Two men wearing felt hats and neckties got out. Nellie went out to meet them and walked them around the back corner of the house to the pecan tree. Casey put down his guitar and leaned over to shake their hands when I ambled back within earshot.

"Mr. Pierce," one of them was saying, "we represent the Houston Oil Company of Texas and we want to talk to you about leasing your farm for the exploration of oil and gas."

"The country needs oil," the other man with the necktie picked it up. "This Korean conflict made us all realize that we're going to be fighting the communists from now on."

"What's a communist?" Casey asked, still sitting on the swing.

"What do you mean?" the first neck tie answered, still standing.

"I just got through fighting Nazis, now we're fighting communists. Who is this boy gonna have to fight when he grows up?"

"Sir, I don't know," one of them replied. "But we know you want to do your part and we'll pay you for the right to explore on your land."

"How much?" Nellie asked.

"Four hundred dollars now, and four hundred every year on this date for the next five years, or until we drill."

"Then what?" Casey asked.

"If it looks promising," the necktie continued, "we could drill a wildcat well. We bring it in, we'll pay you for every eighth barrel of oil we produce. How does that sound?"

"It sounds good," Nellie said.

"Who's going to count the barrels?" Casey asked.

"We will, of course," the man from the Houston Oil Company of Texas said. "Don't worry about nothing. We'll take care of everything."

"Bring us the papers and we'll sign them," Nellie said, escorting the men back to their Buick and thanking them for coming.

My mind was already racing ahead, wondering how many barrels of oil it would take to buy a black saddle with silver studs like Lash Larue rode on. Casey had never risen from the swing. He picked up his guitar and sang Jimmie Rodgers.

"He put me off in Texas,
A place I surely love...

I'm a thousand miles away from home,
Just waiting for a train."
(Ibid.)

1951

♦ Working on trains in Mississippi gave Jimmie Rodgers numerous stories and insights into traveling people. Being a musician, he empathized with people on the move. He also identified himself as a Texan.

Casey Pierce, Intracoastal City, 1948.

My pal Buster.

Cajun Farm House
South Louisiana
Late October 1952, 5:00 p.m.

"Tonight I heard the wild goose cry
Hangin' north in the lonely sky."

"The Cry of The Wild Goose," Frankie Laine
(Terry Gilkyson, Unichappell Music, Inc.)

Using pages torn from the old Sears Roebuck catalog, Granny was sitting in front of the fireplace wiping smoke and soot from the globes of the kerosene lamps. Next, she'd trim the wicks, then she would make sure there was enough kerosene in the base of the lamp to last the couple of hours of darkness until bedtime. This was her daily chore just before sunset.

In the kitchen, my sister Russie was helping with the dishes. Nellie was poking the wood fire back into life to prepare supper. She'd be warming up some of the garden-fresh vegetables left over from our noon meal. If there was any cornbread left from the batch she'd cooked up at sunrise, it would now be recycled into coosh-coosh by stirring the cornbread around in a black iron pot with a bit of oil. Served warm in a bowl of milk, it was a gourmet's delight. Nellie's cooking was recognized as some of the best, and when Cajun cooking finally gained national recognition, it was never as good as the simple dishes she turned out of a skillet on a wood stove.

As I walked outside in the yard, I felt the bite of the autumn air. I loved this time of year, so many smells, so much excitement in the air. I had already fed the chickens and picked the eggs, and now headed to the barn. Casey was finishing up some barnyard chores. He'd slopped the pigs and was doing the evening milking. He was good at it. He could fill a milk pail in a few minutes. Casey tried to teach me and Russie the right squeeze technique, so we could inherit his job. So far, I didn't have the hand strength or the desire and Russie was already daydreaming about Hollywood. Casey decided to keep on milking awhile longer.

Everyone had their chores, except great-grandfather David White, after whom I was named. At ninety, his activity had been reduced to reading. Paw-Paw Dave went through two novels, four magazines, and several newspapers, cover to cover, every week. He had vast knowledge on many subjects, which Nellie often discussed with him in long afternoon conversations while I listened. Born in 1862, he grew up in the post-Civil War South. To escape Reconstruction, his family moved down to Guatemala, but after four years of struggling they decided the mosquito coast of Louisiana was worth bending to the Yankee boot. He often said this country would not survive another internal conflict.

My interest was mostly piqued when he talked about the Old West. He'd read all the Zane Greys. He talked about how the Spaniards had come to California, the missionaries naming the towns along the coast, San Diego, Los Angeles, and all about the Gold Rush days.

These days Dave White mostly read, saddled his horse to ride to Berro's Bar for a drink or two at mid-day, napped on the hard wooden floor of his bedroom, and read till dark. At sunset, Nellie would bring him a glass of red wine to his rocking chair. He'd drink it, peel his own garlic, and wait for his evening meal to be served in his room. That regimen would keep him going another six months.

Dusk was setting in by the time I had the kindling box filled. To the east, across Vermilion Bayou, the moon rose slowly and looked down on the muddy brown water that sometimes shaded toward red. The Spanish had called it Rio de Los Lobos because wolves had prospered on the marshy prairie lands. The Cajuns came and called it the color they saw it, Vermilion. Less than a half-mile away, like silhouettes against the moon, the lights on the oil derrick lit up. Frank Godchaux #1, the first oil and gas well to be drilled in the Live Oak Oil Field was heading for thirteen thousand feet. The Godchauxs were one of the wealthiest families in South Louisiana. They certainly didn't need the money, but if Godchaux #1 came in big enough, maybe Houston Oil Company would cross the bayou and drill on our farm. It could happen. Fairy tales do come true. Then I could have...I could have...whatever I dreamed. I could be in western movies, not just watch them on Saturday afternoons. I could ride and shoot, like Lash Larue, Hopalong Cassidy, Gene Autry, and the Lone Ranger. I could see California, not just read about it the way Paw-Paw Dave did all his life.

The sound of honking geese pulled me out of the dream world back to the reality of the South Louisiana farmyard. I saw their V-shaped pattern flapping rhythmically across the red glow in the western sky. I carried the kindling box into the house. Granny had lit the lamps. Russie was carrying Paw-Paw Dave's plate. Nellie was bustling in the kitchen. Casey was already seated at the table, nibbling. A moment frozen in time.

On the old brown radio, the voice belonged to Frankie Laine.

"Wild goose, brother goose, which is best?
A wanderin' fool or a heart at rest.
Let me fly,
Let me fly,
Let me fly away."
(Ibid.)

My namesake, great-grandfather David White, at age 90.

The Farm
South Louisiana
Summer 1953

*"When other nights and other days
May find us gone our separate ways."*

"Moments to Remember," The Four Lads
(Robert Allen and Al Stillman, Charlie Deitcher Productions, Inc., Larry
Spier Music LLC)

I was humming the song I'd heard on the hit parade. Woodie Bernard was cussing. For a ten-year-old, Woodie had a pretty strong vocabulary. My mom said he was getting it from the comic books he was always reading. Woodie didn't necessarily like the activity at my house. There were just too many chores on a farm, but I also had a horse and a gun, and we'd become friends.

Recently Casey had purchased a John Deere tractor with a few dollars of oil lease money that the Houston Oil Company had so graciously sent along. In order to increase the farmable acreage, Casey had set out to clear the farm of oak trees and palmettos, starting with the first ridge at the edge of the marsh known as Coon Island.

Today we were pulling palmettos. Woodie and I were the roustabouts who pulled the chain back and hooked it around the three-foot diameter of the palmetto bush. Casey, on the tractor, pulled out the palmetto bush and dragged it over to a burn pile. Woodie and I unhooked the chain and got ready to do it all over again. Not a bad job, unless you're ten and eleven years old, beating off mosquitoes, dodging snakes, getting hung up on briars and stickers.

"Ga-ga-ga-got dam," Woodie stuttered. "How come we ga-ga-ga-got to do this in the middle of the—in the middle of the summer? I'm about to—about to sm-sm-smother. And last night shuh-shuh-shoveling cow shit. Your dad's a damn slave driver."

"We were making a smoke for the cows," I said, trying to explain the indignity of shoveling cow patties on to a blazing fire. "Cow manure makes a good smoke and keeps the insects off the cows. I build a smoke every night before dark."

The heat was oppressive today. And the mosquitoes were ferocious. But I was used to fighting both. There was no way to explain to Woodie that this was the way Casey worked. Offbeat jobs at oddball times.

Eventually the morning's torture ended, and we made our way back home to the noon-day shade of the old pecan tree. The smell of jasmine was tingling my nostrils.

"When you—when you gonna get a t-t-t-telephone and elec-electricity?" Woodie wanted to know.

"Soon, I hope," was the only answer I had.

"We don't have a phone and lights, but we don't have a phone bill and light bill, either," Casey lectured us. "You boys won't ever have it this good again."

Somehow that didn't make any sense to me and Woodie. The afternoon's tasks were less difficult. Casey drove the tractor, pulling an old farm wagon that only a few years earlier had been pulled by mules.

Attached to the rear of the wagon was a seed-planting device called a broadcaster. Its gears were linked to the wagon's right rear wheel so that as the wagon circled around the field, the broadcaster's seed trays spun rapidly, casting the seed in a broad path, twenty feet wide on either side of the wagon. Woodie and I rode in the wagon, pouring the fifty-pound sacks of lezpedeza seed into the hopper that trickled the seed down in measured amounts to the whirling seed trays. We were broadcasting. I didn't realize then, that the men who had invented radio years before had already borrowed this farmer's term for casting his seed, and used it to describe their technology for sending radio waves.

The next evening I spent the night at Woodie's house fifteen miles away in town, where the living was much easier...electric lights, telephone, and comic books...Batman, War Comics, Dick Tracy, Superman, Red Ryder and Little Beaver. Dozens of comic books, strewn all over Woodie's room. He had 'em all. I looked at a few of the Del Comics specials. Wonder Woman was rather shapely. But I tired of the comic books and spent a lot of time tossing the football with Woodie's fifteen-year-old neighbor. Woodie didn't come out of the house. The Comic Book Kid had his nose buried in the latest issue of War Comics.

1953

♦ Willie Mae "Big Mama" Thornton flies from Houston to New York City to record "Hound Dog" for Peacock-Duke Records. It sells two million copies and she is paid $500. Three years later, Elvis makes "you ain't nothing but a hound dog" an everyday phrase.

My best friend Woodie Bernard and me at
about age ten, Intracoastal City, La.

South Louisiana Country Road
August 1954

"While the Louisiana moon floats on high
And they wait for the day they can cry

Shrimp boats is a'coming,
There's dancing tonight..."

"Shrimp Boats," Jo Stafford
(Paul Mason Howard and Paul Weston, Hanover Music Corp.)

"Guess somebody knows we're here, even Jo Stafford is singing about us," I said aloud, staring at the white shell road winding through the oak trees, Spanish moss hanging. The glare from the hot August sun made me squint. The 1952 Dodge hit a pothole, rattling the doors.

"Hey, watch out," I told my sister. "I can drive better than that and I'm only twelve."

"Yeah, but I'll be fifteen this fall and get my driver's license. That's why Mom lets me drive to the store for practice."

"The Naughty Lady of Shady Lane," sang the car radio.

"What's your favorite song on the hit parade?" I asked. Then answered my question, "I like 'Shaboom,' myself. It's got a beat."

"The hit parade is dumb, you wanna hear a beat. Listen to this." Russie reached for the radio dial.

"It should have been me,
With that real fine chick,
Heigh, heigh, heigh, ho,
Driving that Dyna Flo."

"It Should've Been Me," Ray Charles
(Memphis Curtis, Anne-Rachel Music Corp.)

"Who's that?" I asked, getting excited.

"That's Ray Charles," Russie answered. "They call it rhythm and blues, and you should see how we dance it. It's called the dirty bump."

The announcer's voice came on. "Hey, all you cats and chicks, I've got the most requested song this week. This is Hank Ballard and the Midnighters."

"Work with me, Annie,
Uh ooh, uh ooh,
Work with me, Annie,
Let's get it   .
while the gettin' is good."

"Work With Me, Annie," Hank Ballard & The Midnighters
(Henry Ballard, Fort Know Music, Inc., Trio Music Co., Inc.)

"Boy, I like that," I said. "What do they mean, 'Work with me, Annie?'"

"They're talking about doing it, dummy, but don't tell Mom and Dad we're listening to that music; they won't let me go dancin'," Russie said, always looking for cover.

"Oh, I won't," I said, "but you gotta let me drive." She gave me a look, then pulled over to the side of the road. I knew I was going to learn to drive early. I got out of the car and walked around the Dodge to the driver's side singing to myself.

"It should have been me,
Driving that Dyna Flo."

"It Should've Been Me," Ray Charles
(Memphis Curtis, Anne-Rachel Music Corp.)

1954

♦ The phrase "Under God" added to the Pledge of Allegiance.

♦ In the first half of the '50s, America's teenagers began the underground grass roots movement of rock 'n roll. The sound was subversive in many subtle ways. Parents and teachers became angry and repressive in this era of comic book censorship and Red-baiting witch hunts. Churches organized bonfires to burn "evil" rock records and comic books. Hank Ballard threw fuel on the fire with his "dirty" lyrics, "Annie please don't cheat, Give me all my meat," in "Work With Me Annie."

♦ On October 16, Elvis Presley appears on the Louisiana Hayride broadcast live on Shreveport radio station KWKH.

Russie and me, Intracoastal City, 1955.

Nellie's first well.

Abbeville, Louisiana
April 1955

"Hearts made of stone,
Doo do wop, doo do wop,
Will never break,
Doo do wop, doo do wop."

"Hearts of Stone," The Jewels
(Rudy Jackson and Eddie Ray, Regent Music Corp.)

I walked out of the River Oaks Club and over to the shiny blue motor-cycle parked under the oak tree overlooking the lazy Vermilion Bayou. It was a sparkling clear spring Saturday. I was thirteen years old and had to keep pinching myself to make sure I wasn't dreaming. I straddled my new motorcycle, took a deep breath of the crisp sixty-five-degree air. The smell of wood smoke and barbecuing beef grabbed at my nostrils and sent anticipation signals to my stomach. This was real, all right.

When an oil company brought in an oil and gas well on a farmer's property, it was traditional for the landowner to throw a barbecue for the drilling crew. This was the second barbecue my family had staged in the past six months. Even though we had several friends among the oil work-ers, not everything was rosy with the oil company officials. Even after the oil began to flow, the company had taken its time about paying royalties. But the company made a mistake when it failed to send the annual lease payment in the interim period between initial production and the first royalty payments. Casey had taken offense at that lack of regard for a poor farmer and his family. With the help of a local attorney, he filed suit against the Houston Oil Company of Texas, and its new parent company, Atlantic Richfield. The attorney said it would take maybe five years, but sooner or later, the Louisiana Supreme Court would rule against Arco in a landmark decision. Arco would rue the day they didn't do all they said they would in the lease papers. Eventually, Casey, Nellie, and the attor-ney would split three hundred grand and never again would "big oil" take advantage of landowners in this same particular way. Casey said whatever happened, the oil company would steal it back over the years, anyway. He was more right than he knew. More than forty years later, a class action suit would accuse major oil producers of paying royalty owners at a lesser price than market value. After all, they were counting the barrels. Nellie said we should count our blessings. Without the oil company, we would still be fighting four hundred acres of marshland and mosquitoes. I was beginning to draw up my own image of what corpo-rate America was like. I noticed that as soon as the lawsuit was filed, the red tape holding back the royalty payments had mysteriously cleared up. The new blue motorcycle was tangible proof.

This motorcycle opened up a whole new world for me, including the possibility of playing football. With my own transportation, I could stay after school for practice, then eat the fifteen miles of shell road dust on the ride home long after the school bus had finished dropping off the other farm kids. My blue motorcycle became the key to the highway. Football was just the first step on the long run ahead.

Russie and three of her girlfriends came out of the River Oaks Club, arm in arm, Jax Beer cans in their hands, singing "Hearts Made of Stone." Their blue jeans were butt tight, rolled up on the calves, exposing white bobby socks. There were all talking about a young actor named James Dean. They'd just seen him in a film called *East of Eden*. I couldn't believe girls could be that silly. They were absolutely out of their heads about a guy who was just a shadow on the screen or a photograph in a movie magazine.

They completely ignored me, sashaying down to the bayou banks, hips rolling to the hit song by Otis Williams and the Charms.

"And they'll say
No, no, no, no, no!
No, your Daddy knows
I thought you knew,
Hearts made of stone."
(Ibid.)

The Air Port Club Dance Hall
Abbeville, Louisiana
December 1955

"Unchained Melody" was one of the biggest songs of the year. I had seen the movie starring my football hero Elroy "Crazy Legs" Hirsch. During one week in July, Les Baxter's version got to number four, Al Hibbler's vocal was number nine, and Roy Hamilton's recording was number thirteen on the National Charts. The haunting classic would be released by the Righteous Brothers in the '60s and that arrangement would later be used on the soundtrack of the movie *Ghost*, the key emotion driving millions of dollars in box office. In 1955, the picture painted by "Unchained Melody" was how most felt about love and life in the mid-50s.

The sound of black music was infiltrating white pop on the radio. A New York disc jockey named Alan Freed coined the phrase Rock 'n roll, and America's best poet was about to revolutionize the airwaves. In four years Chuck Berry would write thirty-five songs and his lyrics became part of our language. Black music was also steadily making its way into white clubs.

"Rum and Coca-Cola, please," I said leaning into the bar.

"How old are you, kid?"

"Eighteen...sir."

"You don't look it. Got any ID?"

"Just my draft card."

I fished out the draft card I'd paid twenty bucks for. If you were fourteen without a driver's license, you had to have a fake draft card.

"Here you are, sir."

"What about a drivers' license?" the bartender asked.

"Got suspended, sir, I was caught speeding," I said, a story that later turned out to be true.

"All right, one rum and coke coming up. That'll be fifty cents."

I peeled off the bar, sipping the rum and coke, and made my way through the darkened dance floor of the Airport Club. Fats Domino, the young R&B hit-maker from New Orleans, often played this club. So did Irma Thomas, and America's black Elvis Presley, Little Richard.

Tonight an all-black band called the Nighthawks was wailing on the bandstand. My attention focused on the twelve-year-old lead guitar player, the only kid in an adult band. That guitar sound was fantastic. Not just the rhythm and blues sound, but the sound of the guitar itself. Electric guitars were the greatest. Amplifiers made all the difference.

I sure would like to play a guitar like that black kid. I slipped out of the smoky Airport Club into the fresh night air. The full moon was high in the sky. It was closing in on midnight and I didn't want to push the curfew. After all, I was driving without a license.

I got into the '55 Mercury station wagon, which I'd already equipped with glass packed mufflers, dropped the tailgate window and gunned it up to forty or fifty, then slipped it into low and let that sound reverberate back into the wagon through the open tailgate window. It was sheer poetry.

I tuned the radio in to WLAC in Nashville, Tennessee. Disc Jockey Gene Noble was always on this time of night sponsored by Randy's Record Shop in Gallatin, Tennessee. Later, the Hoss Man, Bill Allen, would come on, followed by Wolf Man Jack. All the way from Nashville. Boy, there must be thousands of kids just like me out there listening! Playing records on the radio must be the most fun there is...all that music...and you get to pick your favorites. Wonder how you get a job like that.

"The moon stood still on Blueberry Hill,
And lingered until my dreams came true."

"Blueberry Hill," Fats Domino
(Vincent Rose, Larry Stock, Al Lewis, Chappell & Co., Inc., Larry Stock Music Co., Sovereign Music Co.)

1955

- Alex North wrote the music and Hy Zaret the lyrics for "Unchained Melody." The blind black singer, Al Hibbler, had the first vocal version which was used in the movie.

- "Blueberry Hill" was the first used in the 1940 western, *The Singing Hill* and was sung by the star, Gene Autry. Co-writer Al Lewis later portrayed Grandpa in *The Munsters*. Ron Howard, as Richie Cunningham, always sang "Blueberry Hill" whenever he found a date on *Happy Days*.

Abbeville, Louisiana
Summer 1956

*"I'm a'writing me a letter,
I'm gonna mail it to my local deejay.*

*You know my temperture's risin'
And the jukebox is blowin'a fuse..."*

"Roll Over Beethoven," Chuck Berry
(Chuck Berry, Isalee Music Publishing Co.)

Chuck Berry's distinctive voice was followed by the unique sound of that guitar. God, could Chuck Berry play guitar. I took both hands off the wheel to pantomime playing those lead licks from "Roll Over Beethoven."

"Gonna mail it to my local deejay," I sang as I wheeled my orange and white '56 Ford Crown Victoria through the park and around the swimming pool.

I gave my best James Dean look to three girls leaving the pool house, then drove over to the football practice field. I parked the Ford under the shade of one of four large oak trees that divided the entrance to the high school from the stadium area. At three p.m. in August, it was ninety-five degrees. I greeted my teammates and we entered the locker room under the stadium. We put on pads in silence, dreading the workout ahead. The assistant coach looked up from his desk near the dressing room door.

"You better get you a crew cut, kid, and get rid of them duck-tails. This ain't no beauty contest."

"Sure, Coach," I said, but I'd let him bitch a few more days, then trim a half-inch.

I liked my hair long. Everybody looks better with longer hair. As I jogged my warm-up lap, I was thinking how out of shape I was. I'd shown some promise as a freshman. The coach said that if I worked hard and didn't get mixed up with any chicks, I had a great future running with a football.

As a sophomore this fall, I needed to win a starting spot in the backfield. I loved to carry the ball. Didn't much care for blocking and tackling, and practice was a pain. Getting in shape in August was torture. But the smell of autumn was already in the air. Especially in the early morning before the sun got hot and reminded you it was still August. School would be starting soon. I'd be back in class and back on stage during the speech hour. I'd seen *Giant* six times that summer. I knew every one of Jett Rink's lines. Just thinking about James Dean made me ache. Dean had left a farm in Indiana to go to Los Angeles to study acting at UCLA. Maybe I'd go to Los Angeles.

I finished jogging the lap and joined the other players loosening up with stretches. Carliss "Fuzzy" Vincent, the big tackle, who sprang me loose several times on the freshman team, was singing as usual. Fuzzy had a good voice and it was one of my favorite songs, which always reminded me of the breeze coming off the Gulf of Mexico across the Louisiana coastal marshes.

"O the Wayward Wind is a restless wind,
A restless wind, that yearns to wander."

"The Wayward Wind," Gogi Grant
(Stanley Lebowsky and Herbert Newman, Universal Polygram International)

1956

♦ "The Wayward Wind" was also recorded by Eddy Arnold, Patsy Cline, Gene Vincent and the Blue Caps, Crystal Gale, Boxcar Willie, Neil Young, and Alabama.

Co-captains, myself and Carliss "Fuzzy" Vincent, Abbeville High School, 1958.

Annette Vincent and me in an Abbeville High School stage production, 1957.

Abbeville High School
Wildcat Stadium
November 1957

Our high scoring half-back, Fred Touchet, was singing the Little Richard hit as the running backs and receivers waited in line to run out for warm-up passes. It was the final game of the season. The stadium was spilling its sold-out crowd onto the sidelines. The archrivals from the west end of the parish had brought all their fans with them. It was a football Friday night in Eisenhower's America. It would never again be this innocent or this easy.

I scanned the stadium hoping to spot her. She'd moved into town last summer from south Florida, a little town named Cocoa Beach in a place called Cape Canaveral. She had a great tan. It reminded me of cocoa. Every guy in school had the hots for her. But she'd taken a shine to me, even though she was a senior and I was just a junior. I figured being a football star and an actor had done the trick. We'd been dating all fall, going to the movies, dancing, and parking at the drive-in. We'd gotten into some pretty heavy sessions, but we were usually double dating with Fuzzy or Fred, or my acting partner, Jimmy Chapman. Sometimes we put the third seat in the '55 Merc Wagon and triple dated. Anyway, I was beginning to get the feeling we could go all the way.

Then the last two or three weeks of the season she seemed to be getting restless. Today at lunch she said she couldn't meet me after the game 'cause her girlfriend from Florida was coming to visit.

I scanned the stands again. She was still nowhere around, but I did spot my mom, sitting alone in her burnt orange suit and matching hat. Nellie saw every one of our games, at home or on the road. She always wore that same thing. Her good luck outfit, she called it. Casey had seen a couple of games, but he didn't care much for sports.

"Hut-one, Hut-two," barked sophomore quarterback Reid Hebert.

The pass was overthrown and I couldn't quite reach it. I picked it up and jogged back, checking the stands. Then I spotted her, near the pep squad section, alone. I wondered why her friend from Florida wasn't with her.

"Come on, Pierce, get your mind on the game," the coach was yelling.

Maybe Coach was right, football and chicks don't mix.

Fuzzy's golden tones were coming from the showers. I had peeled off the shoulder pads and cleats, showered and dressed hurriedly, hoping to catch her before she left the stadium.

I rushed out of the locker room and headed for the main gate where the crowd was streaming out. I tried to be gracious and threw back a "Thanks, thanks a lot," for every "Great game, Pierce," "That's the way to put you head down."

We'd squeezed out a 7-6 win. Fred, Fuzzy, Reid, and I would make all-district this year. But now this game and this season were history.

The anxiety was welling up in my gut. The roar of the motors, beep of horns, and whistle of the traffic cops helping the flow of exiting traffic drew my attention to the parking lot. My focus locked on the two-tone green and white '57 Cadillac. It was Bobby Charles' car.

Bobby had written a song called "See You Later, Alligator." His recording had been covered by Bill Haley and the Comets as their second hit after "Rock Around the Clock." Bobby Charles had also co-written a song with Fats Domino. The Crescent City piano player would soon record the tune "I'm Walking To New Orleans" and add it to his string of hits. Bobby sent some of his tapes to Chess Records. They sent back a plane ticket to Chicago. When Bobby Charles arrived at the airport, he and Marshall Chess eyed each other for ten minutes before making contact. Chess didn't know what the swamp rocker looked like. He'd heard the tapes and was expecting a black kid. It was the beginning of blue-eyed soul. So Bobby had cashed in with a record contract and a tour. It seemed like he had all the money in the world. He damn sure had a Cadillac.

Bobby must have come to the game late because the Cadillac was parked in a good spot for a fast exit. The motor was running. The radio was turned up loud and Bobby was sipping on a flask. Then I saw her running across the parking lot. She jumped in the Cadillac, slid across the seat, put one arm around Bobby's neck and swigged long on the flask. I could see their laughter as the Cadillac moved into the honking line of brake lights hurrying into Friday night.

"Well I saw my baby walkin',
With another man today.
When I asked her 'What's the matter,'
This is what I heard her say."

"See You Later Alligator," Bobby Charles
(Robert Charles Guidry, ARC Music Corp.)

Frank's Drive-in
Abbeville, Louisiana
May 1958

It was lunchtime. Fuzzy, Reid, Mike Russo, and I were all piling out of Jimmy Chapman's Studebaker. Frank's Burger and Malt Drive-In, ten blocks from school, was a drive-in without curb service, so you had to get out of the car and go to the window to place your order. Mr. Frank and his wife were happy to serve the high school crowd, but they weren't known for their speed or efficiency. Kate Russo was at the window giving Mr. Frank hell. She had been wearing a cast on her left ankle for a couple of months now. She'd broken it, jumping off a roof on a bet with her brother Mike. She was only fifteen, but already a real Italian beauty with dark olive skin. When she walked with the cast on her foot, it gave an exaggerated twist to her butt. She was a sight to behold! Kate and Mike's dad, David Russo, owned the Falstaff Beer distributorship and the Four Club, where according to rumor, illegal gambling was taking place. Kate had also been seen driving a long black Cadillac through town. It didn't belong to her family. The license plate came out of the New Orleans district. I had seen her several times away from school with her mom and four younger brothers. The youngest, a blonde-headed four-year-old, was named Carlos, and rumor had it he was named after David Russo's friend, the Italian gangster and New Orleans crime boss, Carlos Marcello. Casey said they were all part of the same Mafioso family, and he strongly suggested I keep some distance from all of them.

But Mike Russo and I played football together. I liked Mike, and Kate was Mike's little sister. Right now she was on a tear.

"What the fuck do you think I ordered?" she was cursing at Mr. Frank. "I said a hot dog without this got-damned chili all over it?"

"Watch your mouth," Mr. Frank warned.

"Watch this," Kate came right back at him, throwing the chilidog through the window, splattering chili against the malt mixer machines. "Just stick the damn thing up your ass."

She wheeled around on the walking cast and headed for her car, butt twisting, still cussing a blue streak. Mike Russo seemed a little embarrassed.

"Well, that's my sister Kate," he said apologetically.

We collected our burgers and cokes, pushed Jimmy Chapman's Studebaker to get it started, piled in and started back for school, still laughing about the look on Mr. Frank's face. I had a feeling I'd be checking out Kate Russo's moves long after the walking cast was gone.

"He can run and kick and throw,
Give him the ball and
just look at him go."

"Mr. Touchdown."

In the town where Longfellow's Evangeline once lived, I was face down in the mud waiting for blockers and tacklers to un-pile. Inches from my nose the Dugas boy grinned at me and I grinned back. Dugas was a skinny, defensive back for the opponents. He was just another high school senior playing his last game. The college scouts in the stands hadn't come to see Dugas. They were watching me and my big left tackle, Fuzzy Vincent, both candidates for all state honors. But Dugas was playing his heart out, coming up to put a shoulder into me every time I crossed the scrimmage line. I was now a seasoned power runner. I outweighed Dugas by forty pounds and knocked him backward for extra yardage on every tackle. But all night long the skinny St. Martinville safety had held me to three, four and five yards. The exception was a forty-yard run that tied the score at 14-14 early in the third quarter. I was closing on two hundred yards in thirty-eight carries for the night. And Dugas and I were grinning at each other.

"Fourth and goal on the three-yard line with fifty-one seconds left in the game," droned the Announcer.

It had been a bruising no holds barred football game. In the bottom of one pile up, the opposing line backer had taken a bite out of Fuzzy's forearm. On the very next play, our right end threw a block from behind that left their line backer in a crumpled heap. He was carried out on a stretcher with a broken leg.

As I joined the huddle, I was aching. The big "32" on the back of my jersey was ripped completely out and my long hair hung down wet and muddy below the helmet line. I could hear the roar of the crowd and somewhere back there the pep squad was singing.

"They always call him Mr. Touchdown,
They always call him Mr. T."
(Ibid.)

"All right, huddle up," commanded Reid. "This is it, team, thirty-three on three, all the way this time. We don't get another chance."

The huddle broke and I glanced at the sideline. The majorettes were prancing, swinging their hips and holding their batons above their heads with both hands, then throwing them into the air and falling into a split as they caught them. My girl and Fuzzy's girl were among the prancers. A special treat was promised for tomorrow night if we won this one.

"I need this six points bad," I was thinking, as I lowered my battered body into the three-point stance.

I was behind Fred Touchet's 106 point 1957 scoring record. Tonight, after two touchdowns and two extra points, I had 105... I wanted the TD.

Thirty-three on three. The number three back going into the number three hole outside left tackle. No mystery here. Everyone in the stands knew where it was going. You might as well let the announcer call the play.

"Hut-one."

I was on automatic now.

"Hut-two."

The next few seconds would last forever.

"Hut-three."

Slow motion time. Reid fed me the ball as I leaned way over, shoulders down, both arms covering the ball, knees pumping. Fuzzy was moving the defensive tackle straight back. I would never forget this big guy as long as I lived. I put my shoulder against Fuzzy's butt and kept digging my cleats into the South Louisiana mud. Twenty-two players were converging onto this few square feet of turf. The forward motion was slowing and stopping, shy of the end zone. Head back, eyes scanning, operating on total instinct, I slid left as the hole opened and there to meet me at the goal line was Dugas.

I dipped my shoulder and slammed into the skinny defensive back. The crack of shoulder pads could be heard above and beyond the delirious crowd. My legs were still churning but there was nowhere to go. Dugas was on his knees in a heap. He had gone down but hadn't budged and more tacklers were reacting toward the ball. Now Dugas had his arms around my tangled legs and I knew it was the end of the line. With a last final effort, I spun to the left. The white striped goal line came up to meet me as I went crashing down. The ball was in my left arm and I flung it as far forward as I could. The ground was cold. The mud was blinding the vision in my right eye. The roar of the crowd was at once deafening, yet far, far away. Squinting, I saw the ball laying across the muddy white stripe. The referee had both hands in the air. Touchdown!

> *"I was the one who taught her to kiss,*
> *The way that she kisses you now..."*

"I Was The One," Elvis Presley
(Aaron Schroeder, Claude De Metruis, Hal Blair, and W. Andrew Peppers, Chappell & Co., Inc.)

Someone had punched up Elvis on the jukebox at the Candlelight Restaurant and Lounge. "Heartbreak Hotel" had gone to number one in April, 1956, but my favorite was still the "B" side, the song that was playing on the jukebox, "I Was the One."

"We understand you're interested in theater," the college football scout was saying as he cut into a blood rare Candlelight steak.

"That's right," I answered.

"You want to act?" asked the scout.

"Maybe. Maybe some radio or television."

"Well, I tell you, that game you played last night was straight out of a Hollywood script. That's the kind of dedication and effort we're interested in."

"Thanks," I replied, buttering up a baked potato.

I was just a little uncomfortable. Football had been fun, but there was an air of business about these steak dinners that made me uneasy. Besides, I wished the scout hadn't called tonight. That meant putting the rest of the evening on hold.

"How's your speed," the scout was looking straight at me.

"It could be better, I guess."

"You almost got caught from behind on that forty-yard run in the third quarter."

"I scored anyway," I said putting that first juicy bite of beef into my mouth.

"Yeah, you did. But another ten yards, he would have had you. We'll have to put the clock on you. We're looking for speed, you know."

"Yes, sir."

"You need to come visit the Louisiana State campus, look around the theater department. We have one of the best in the south. Paul Newman's wife, Joanne Woodward, studied there, you know."

I knew all the good theater schools. I also knew the film schools, like UCLA, but there weren't any Los Angeles scouts buying steaks down in Cajun country. We finished the meal, shook hands, and agreed to a visit and tryout in January. I walked out of the Candlelight and across the square to my '56 Ford. Five minutes later I was pulling into the Four Club Drive-In next to Fuzzy's '58 Chevy Impala where the girls and Fuzzy were parked and waiting.

"To know, know, know him
Is to love, love, love him,
And I do, and I do, and I do."

"To Know Him Is To Love Him," The Teddy Bears
(Philip Spector, ABKCO Music, Inc., Mother Bertha Music, Inc.)

The Teddy Bears were singing on the radio, the majorettes were snuggling sweetly, Fuzzy was driving and singing along. My mind, emotions, and hormones were all in the same turmoil. LSU, UCLA, acting, football, Los Angeles, the cool November night, the hot seventeen-year-old desires were all rushing my senses.

"So what's the big surprise?" Fuzzy asked.

"You'll see," his majorette answered, "just keep driving."

The Impala's eight-cylinder, twin four-barrel carbs had kicked in as we sped out onto the highway. David Seville and the Chipmunks came on the radio. Theodore, Simon, and Alvin were still going at it when we broke out of a long, hands-between-the-knees embrace.

"Turn here," Fuzzy's girl was saying excitedly.

I popped my head up from the back seat to see the blinking neon spelling out "The Ranch Motel."

The warm breath in my ear whispered, "Thought you might like to play cowboys and cowgirls at the ranch."

"And who learned a lesson
When she broke my heart?"

"I Was The One," Elvis Presley
(Aaron Schroeder, Claude Demetruis, Hal Blair, Andrew Peppers, Chappell & Co., Inc.)

South Louisiana State Highway 14
January 1959

The Cadillacs' song had been a favorite all through high school and Fuzzy had the words and melody down pat. He and Reid were in the back seat. Jimmy Chapman was riding shotgun, and I was behind the wheel of the '56 orange and white Ford Crown Victoria cruising at seventy-five miles per hour down the two lane highway. Mike Russo's taillights were up ahead, carrying the rest of the senior football team. Since the season ended, we'd all been hanging out a lot. Most of us would never play again and we were slowly drinking, eating, and smoking ourselves out of shape. With nothing else to do on a Thursday night, we had driven to the neighboring town to catch a basketball game. Now we were racing back to the hometown for more cruising. Later maybe we'd hook up with some of the girls when they returned on the bus. We were high on having fun, singing the "bop bop be-doo-be doop do-bies" behind Fuzzy's lead vocals.

When we neared the city limits, Mike Russo's '54 Ford slowed down from seventy-five to sixty as we blew by the posted speed limit of thirty-five. I was considering trying to pull out past Mike when the red flashing lights went on in the rear view mirror and the sudden wail of a siren cut Fuzzy off in the middle of a "speedo."

"Where in the hell did he come from?" Chapman asked.

"Oh shit, he's got us," Reid said, shrinking into the back seat.

The state police car sped past my '56 Ford, the trooper on the passenger side giving me a commanding pull over gesture as the flashing red lights pulled in behind Mike Russo and got right up on his rear bumper. That took the wind out of Mike's sails. He began to slow down and pull over to the shoulder, to face a hundred-dollar fine and possible driver's license revocation. Although it was also possible that Mike Russo, with his father's connections, could get a ticket like this fixed.

Was it fear, was it daring? I never knew what possessed me to make that snap decision. Instead of pulling over meekly behind Mike and the state troopers, I stepped on the accelerator and flew past the troopers just as they stepped out of their patrol car. The troopers were frozen in their tracks. The look on Mike Russo's face was incredulous. Inside the '56 Ford, no one could believe what was happening, least of all the kid behind the wheel.

"You lost your mind?" Reid was yelling.

"Turn here," Chapman started co-piloting, "get off on a side street."

I reacted, but found the '56 Ford was going up the wrong side of a boulevard. With cars approaching, the only choice was to climb the curb, cut across the grass in the median divider, dodge the oak trees, and get back on the right side of the boulevard. Reid was calming down and starting to get into the spirit.

"All right," he said softly, "we can't keep driving, they'll catch us. We've got to hide this car."

Suddenly Fuzzy spoke up.

"My house," he said, "four blocks away, hook another right."

Within a couple of minutes, the wanted vehicle was in Fuzzy's garage behind closed doors and the four of us were cruising in Fuzzy's Impala toward the Candlelight, our downtown soda hang out.

Standing outside the Candlelight, we were re-telling the story with Mike Russo's group when the state troopers drove slowly by, giving the whole bunch of loitering teens a very suspicious eye. The cops didn't seem to have a fix on faces. They were looking for an orange and white '56 Ford Crown Victoria.

The next day, the story spread like wildfire. In the gym at noon, Coach pulled me aside and began to lecture.

"What are you, some kind of juvenile delinquent?" he said. "Everybody knows you out-ran the state police last night. I'm sure your parents don't know about it, and I ain't going to tell them. But listen to me now. You were lucky. Don't think you can break the rules and get away with it. You get crossed ways with the police and you'll get your head busted. Do you hear what I'm saying to you?"

I understood. There was real fear in the pit of my stomach that I could still be caught. But there was also a very real high in escaping certain punishment. A bunch of kids had out-run and out-smarted the mighty state police. Authority was not absolute! There were holes in the armor. Surrender was not always the only choice; escape was possible! For the next several weekends, I left town to visit Woodie Bernard in his neighboring town. Meantime, the state police were cruising The Four Club, Frank's Drive-In and The Candlelight looking for an orange and white '56 Ford Crown Victoria. My parents wondered why I never wanted to drive that car again.

> *"Well alright so*
> *I'm being foolish*
> *Well alright let people know."*

"Well Alright," Buddy Holly
(Buddy Holly, Norman Petty, Jerry Allison, Joe Muldin, MPL Music Publishing Inc.)

Abbeville, Louisiana
February 1959

*"So I smile and say
When a lovely flame dies."*

"Smoke Gets in Your Eyes," The Platters
(Otto Harbach and Jerome Kern, Universal Polygram International)

She didn't want me to walk her to the door. No good night kiss, just "Good Bye," and slammed the car door. I watched the porch light go dark as soon as she entered her house. There was nothing left to do but pull up the collar on my red James Dean windbreaker and drive home. The last few days had been tough on us. Along with the realization that high school was really over in a few weeks, came more pressure from her for an engagement announcement and a tentative wedding date. Last week, I had reluctantly signed a scholarship to play football at the University of Southwestern Louisiana in Lafayette. The visit to LSU in Baton Rouge proved that college football was indeed a business, a scholarship being something you paid for with athletic ability, an obsession with winning, and a lot of pain. UCLA would have to be put on hold for at least two years, my parents making it clear that seventeen was just too young to go from La. to L.A.

Then she'd stepped up the demands, followed by a date with Reid, the quarterback, "Just to get a Coke and talk," she said. After all, if I couldn't commit to our future, maybe she should date other guys.

She definitely knew how to hurt a guy. Tonight had been one long argument.

It was 9:00 p.m. when I got home, feeling too low to want to attack that final English term paper. Sometimes I hated writing.

"Call Mrs. Berry," Mom sang out, "Something about the radio station needs an announcer."

My heart leaped from the bottom of my shoes right up into my throat. The phone call to the speech teacher verified that, indeed, the local radio station manager had called the high school and asked to send over a kid with a deep voice for some part-time work before and after school. Mrs. Berry figured I might be interested.

1959

♦ "Smoke Gets In Your Eyes" was written for the 1933 musical *Roberta* starring Ginger Rogers, Fred Astaire, Irene Dunne, Randolph Scott, and Lucille Ball.

Tuesday, February 10, 1959, 6:00 a.m.

"Listen to the jingle
The rumble and the roar
As she glides along the woodlands
Through the hills and by the shore."

"Wabash Cannonball," Bill Monroe
(Public Domain)

It was a foggy morning with that mild Louisiana winter temperature of fifty degrees. I was knocking on the front door of the radio station under the glare of the neon lights spelling out the call letters K-R-O-F. Bradley Meaux unlocked the door, smiling broadly.

"Come in, sha," he said in his thick Cajun accent. "Hurry up, my record's running out. Dere's de news machine. Tear off dat five-minute summary of de national news and come meet me in de studio."

I followed Bradley's hasty instructions and entered the open studio door just as the "On Air" sign lit up.

"Bonjour, mes amis, c'est Bradley Meaux, avec beau music. Ca c'est 'valse de Grande Texas! Comment ca va? Aujourd'hui Mardi, Mardi Gras, laissez le bon temps rouler."

Yeah, it sure was Mardi Gras Day. I was mesmerized the way Bradley Meaux was spitting out that Cajun. The "On Air" light went dark, the sound of chanka-chank Cajun music filled the studio and Bradley was firing off information. Thankfully, it was mostly in English.

"You take over at six tirty till eight, mon neg, here's de microphone switch. You start de turntable with dese switches and dese pots turn de volume up and off. Don't over amp you self. Keep de needle out of de red. Station breaks every half-hour. It's typed on dat card. Read it jes like it sez. Don't make nuttin' up. Give de time after every record, de temperature after every udder record. At 7:00 a.m. read you sef four minutes of national news and one minute of Louisiana news dat comes off de news machine at 6:55. Tu parle Français?"

"Not much," I said. "I understand a few words."

"Dat's too bad, dis would be a lot more simple if I could tell it to you in Franch. You follow dis log and read dese commercials. Dey're all in dis copy book in alphabetical order. Write down de exact time you played de commercials. Lucky for you, we don't have too many of dem. How much dey paying you?"

"I think they said a dollar an hour."

"Well, you'll never get rich being a disc jockey, anyway, unless you go to a big town. And you gotta quit by de time you tirty. I'm tirty-five. I'm already too old. It's a young man's game."

"Where's the records I play?"

"Six tirty to seven, you use de country stack. After de news you play dese popular records. From seven tirty to eight is "Navy Hour." You play de program off dis big record."

While Bradley took another break and spouted Cajun into the microphone, I looked at the oversized disk containing the "Navy Hour."

I fingered through the pop stack and quizzed Bradley when his mike went off, "Where's the rock 'n roll stuff?"

"We don't play no rock and roll and we don't play no nigger music. I don't mind it myself, but de station manager don't like it. Another ting he don't like is for us to cue de records."

"What's cue the records?"

"Dat's turning de record until de first part of de song comes on, den backing it up and cueing it up to de beginning, so you don't have no dead air. But, never mind, dey don't want us to do it. It wears out de needles, and dere's no money to buy new ones. Now practice readin you news and watch what I do, mon neg, you'll be by youself till dey get here at eight."

At 6:30 a.m. I sat behind the microphone. Bradley shot a "Bon chance, mon neg" over his shoulder as he hurried out the door, heading for his real job at the fire station.

When the chanka-chank from the Cajun accordion ended, I turned down the pot, opened the microphone, and heard my voice quavering in the headphones, "This is KROF, serving the rice, oil, and fur district of South Louisiana with one thousand watts from 960 on your AM dial in Abbeville, Louisiana."

I leaned over, started the turntable, turned up the pot, and clicked off the microphone. The record spun round and round at 45 rpms but there was no sound. So that's dead air. Finally the voice of Lefty Frizzell kicked in. I was off and running, pulling the Cajun record off the other turntable, and slapping on a Hank Snow, then taking it off and deciding to come back with the high lonesome bluegrass sound of Bill Monroe on "Wabash Cannonball." I choked up on the first live commercial and stumbled through the 7 a.m. news. I panicked once when I turned off the mike, then looked back to see an empty turntable spinning and realized I'd forgotten to put a record on it. But I pieced the sixty minutes together, hit the "Navy Hour" disk at 7:30 and walked out into the Fat Tuesday morning sunrise at 8 a.m. I had taken my first ride on the *Ether Express*. I knew then that I'd never again run with a football.

> *"From the Great Atlantic Ocean*
> *To the Wide Pacific Shore*
> *From the green and flowing mountains*
> *To the Southland by the shore*
> *From the hills of Minnesota*
> *Where the rippling waters fall*
> *You can Reach Your Destination*
> *On the Wabash Cannonball."*
> (Ibid.)

1959

♦ American folk song "The Wabash Cannonball" originated sometime in the late nineteenth century and was popularized by Country Music Hall of Famer Roy Acuff with his 1936 recording. During the Great Depression, it was one of the most recorded songs by Hillbilly artists. Story was, the 700-car train traveled so fast that it arrived at its destination an hour before its departure. Finally, the train took off so fast that it rushed into outer space and is probably still out there. Much like the ether radio waves.

Abbeville-Lafayette Highway South Louisiana
August 1959

"I'm going to Kansas City,
Kansas City, here I come
Got some crazy little women there
I'm gonna get me one..."

"Kansas City," Wilbert Harrison
(Jerry Leiber and Mike Stoller, Jerry Leiber Music, Mike Stoller Music)

It wasn't Wilbert Harrison's voice, but the jolt of tires veering from pavement onto the shoulder of white oyster shells and potholes that snapped me awake.

"Jesus, this is crazy," I said aloud, slapping my face to attention.

A full moon was setting in the western sky and the road was well lit. The clock in the dashboard said 4 a.m.

"Come on, kid, don't blow it. It's okay to play James Dean but you don't have to overdo it," still talking to myself.

The tan interior of the '59 T-Bird smelled new. It was my parents' graduation gift, a reward for a perfect 4.0 grade average. I'd really put some miles on it this summer. Like tonight. Woodie was in town, so we drove around Abbeville then made our way out to the Russo house, just past the Four Club. We were hoping to see Kate Russo, but when we turned into the driveway, two large men looking like body guards appeared from behind the black Cadillac with the New Orleans district plates and denied us entrance. None of the family was at home, they said, except Mr. David Russo who was in a meeting and did not want to be disturbed.

"We duh...duh...don't want to, want to disturb him either," Woodie stammered as we backed out onto the highway and headed for town.

Then we decided to drive forty miles over to Woodie's town, Rayne, to go out with a couple of his girlfriends. We'd seen a movie, had a burger, danced, drank and parked 'til 3 a.m. Now I was fading fast as I finally pulled into the KROF parking lot. I unlocked the front door and crashed on the couch in the lobby. The station had signed off at sunset and the only sound was the clacking of the teletype through the open door of the news machine room. In seconds I was asleep.

At 5:40 a.m., my eyes slammed open. I didn't need an alarm clock anymore. Six and a half months of morning shift made waking automatic. It also made me very tired, especially after a Friday night like this one. I'd been dreaming just before the inner clock went off. It was almost a nightmare in a way, a recurring dream that I'd had several times. A pretty basic dream, really. The record on the air was about to run out. I had to read some live copy, and I didn't have another record cued up and ready to go, which meant somewhere in there some dead air was coming up. A simple problem representing a common disc jockey insecurity.

I went about clearing paper from the news wire, firing up the transmitter. Even though I knew it was highly illegal, I went ahead and filled out the transmitter log in advance, faking the meter readings all the way up to noon. I was betting that if the FCC man ever walked in, it wasn't going to be this Saturday morning in Abbeville. By 8 a.m., I was finished with the boring parts, the Catholic rosary, the news in French (taped by

Bradley the night before), the farm report. I could quote the price of beef and hogs in my sleep. I'd played some country and western, which I really liked and brightened everyone's day with the "Navy Hour." Finally I could get down to playing some music.

Officially, there was still no rock 'n roll on the station, but the afternoon jock, Kirby Boudreaux, and I had conspired to sneak in some borderline ballads like "Lavender Blue, Dilly Dilly." The "Dilly Dilly" should have been enough to get it banned. So we figured maybe the format was loosening up.

Then the manager complained about The Drifters' "There Goes My Baby," and we realized nothing much had changed. Since Phil Phillips was from South Louisiana, the pressure from phone requests for "The Sea of Love" put that song on the play list. Of course, there were a lot of hits right now that nobody could argue with, "The Three Bells" by the Browns, Paul Anka's "Lonely Boy," and "The Happy Organ" by Dave Baby Cortez. So, it was possible to put together a pretty good radio show without breaking too many of the format rules. But we still weren't playing all the rock 'n roll we wanted. I was aching to play the records I heard on the big rockers out of Houston and on WLAC from Nashville at night.

This morning I led off with Martin Denny's "Quiet Village." That surely wouldn't offend anyone. Besides, I liked the song. I liked a variety of music, really, and was always listening for what could be the next hit. I got burned out fast on a song. I decided I couldn't stand to hear Johnny Horton sing out "Catch a Gator and Powder His Behind" one more time, so I slipped "The Battle of New Orleans" to the bottom of the stack.

Through the glass window that looked onto the lobby, I saw the station manager and his wife walk in. This was very unusual for a Saturday morning. Both were in their fifties, alcoholics, chain smokers, and mostly in a foul mood. They began opening mail and going over yesterday's log. Maybe they don't know its Saturday.

There would be no more cueing records while they were around. Kirby and I had been cueing on the sly and the station was sounding a lot tighter. But the manager knew we were doing it and called us both in for a tongue-lashing. We denied it and claimed we'd been eyeballing the grooves, and guessing at the cue.

I checked the news machine and came around to the lobby to get a drink from the water fountain. Smiling a friendly "Good Morning" got me back a grunt from the station manager's wife as she fired up another cigarette and continued to check the logs. The station manager never looked up from the mail. He was probably looking for checks that weren't there, paying for commercials he'd never sold. I headed back toward the studio.

"I thought I said belts were necessary," the station manager's raspy voice stopped me in my tracks.

I knew I was on shaky ground. We'd been down this road before.

The raspy voice continued the attack. "I don't mind blue jeans, but it just looks sloppy when you don't wear a belt."

I took a deep breath and tried to reply calmly, "I never wear a belt with jeans. No one wears belts with jeans."

"That doesn't alter what I just said."

Knowing I couldn't win, I swallowed his retort and went back in the studio.

"Silly, petty, mindless bull," I cursed to myself, as I fingered the forty-fives for the next record.

Then the yellow and white ATCO label caught my eye, Bobby Darin's "Mack the Knife." It was already getting airplay and we knew it was a hit. Bobby Darin had been banned from KROF because the station manager didn't like Darin's previous hit "Splish Splash I was Takin' a Bath." Too suggestive.

I had bought "Mack the Knife" yesterday, brought it in this morning, and planned to slip it in later.

"Oh, the shark, babe, has such teeth, dear,
And he shows them pearly white."

"Mack the Knife," Bobby Darin
(Kurt Weill, E. Bertolt Brecht, and Marc Blitzstein, Kurt Weill FNDT/
Music, Inc./WB, Weill Brecht Harms Co., Inc.)

The station manager was fuming when he hit the studio door.

"I threw that record away," he said.

So that's what happened to the station copy.

He continued, on the verge of exploding, cigarette smoke pouring out of his nose and mouth. "I said no Bobby Darin, that's a terrible song. More rock and roll trash."

"That song is from *Three Penny Opera* by Kurt Weill and Bertol Brecht," I countered, "and it's going to be the biggest song of the year."

"Don't argue with me. You trying to get fired?"

There was a long pause before I replied, "No, I'm trying to quit."

"Yes, that line forms on the right, babe..."
(Ibid.)

1959

♦ "Kansas City" first recorded in 1952 by Little Willie Littlefield, was also #2 in the UK that same year by unknown artist Richard Wayne Penniman, who called himself Little Richard.

My first ride on the Ether Express at KROF, Abbeville, La., 1959.

Lafayette, Louisiana
December 1959

*"One night a wild young cowboy came in,
Wild as the west Texas wind."*

"El Paso," Marty Robbins
(Marty Robbins, Mariposa Music Inc., Unichappell Music, Inc.)

I was in the sales room at KVOL, the premier station in south Louisiana. The studios were located only about eight blocks from my apartment across from campus. To a kid who had grown up on country and western it was really great to hear Marty Robbins break into the hot 100. This song was going to be a monster. It reinforced the cowboy image that every guy carried around with him. Everyone loved that song. It reminded me of *Giant,* and that west Texas was a sixteen-hour ride from here, halfway to California.

I looked down at the page of copy on the desk, trying to form the right sentences for this commercial. I hated writing. I hated it in high school, and English comp was still my least favorite subject in college. Now, here I was, stuck writing commercial copy as one of the chores at the radio station, when all I really wanted to do was disc jockey and act.

The job at KVOL came easy enough. I had walked right in and saw Evan Hughes within ten minutes. Evan was already fifty and silver haired, a radio legend around here. That morning in September he told me he'd hire me part-time, and he wouldn't pay me a dollar an hour, he'd pay me a buck and a quarter. I'd have to wait to get a deejay shift, however, until something opened up.

Meantime, I'd announce the football scores every Saturday afternoon, write copy for the sales staff, and sometimes co-anchor "The Noon News With Evan Hughes." I had worked on the election returns when New Orleans mayor deLesseps Morrison was defeated by the old dark horse, Jimmie Davis, who came back from Hollywood to do one more shift in the Baton Rouge governor's mansion. Election returns were a big production for KVOL. Evan loved to do the news as much as he disliked rock 'n roll.

"That kind of music is a passing fad," Evan insisted, "and KVOL is still number one because we don't play the stuff."

Adjusting to college life at the University of Southwestern Louisiana hadn't been easy. Speech Department rules kept freshmen off the main stage till their second year. My folks decided that I'd be better off my first year if I left the T-Bird at home. Then, the ultimate insult, the upper classmen had shaved my head. It was not a pretty sight. It wasn't that I had lumps exactly, but my skull was definitely not round and smooth. They'd never get clippers in my hair again. Of course, I'd have to beat the draft to make sure that didn't happen.

I'd just turned eighteen in October and registered with the Selective Service. Most young men in America were apprehensive about the draft. At least I wasn't carrying a fake draft card any more. This one was the real thing. My hair had grown back to crew cut length. If I could just get back to spinning records, things would start to level off.

When Jimmy Chapman left for the army, my cousin, Danny White, became my roommate. We were living in a small one-room duplex conveniently located at the corner of Johnston and University. Cross the street and you were on campus, although a class on the south side in "Little Abbeville" could be a tough hike on a rainy morn. Our neighbors in the apartments next door were Central American boys, attracted by the university's reputation and proximity. They were all very friendly, out going, and party loving. Andy Matuty from Honduras began cooking for us and we reciprocated. Then he followed me home to Abbeville for weekend visits with my family. In the years ahead he would become the epitome of the successful, politically connected Latin business man with interests in New Orleans and Tegucigalpa. For now we just had a rapport beyond our language barrier.

We all became familiar with the Blue Note Lounge, a few blocks from campus, one of several favorite college hang outs. The Blue Note would also attract the attention of a young songwriter on his way to Nashville. He'd pick his guitar and sing his compositions in the small dark club. His regular job was piloting for Lafayette-based Petroleum Helicopters, ferrying oil workers to their jobs on the Gulf of Mexico platforms. When he dropped a roughneck on the wrong platform his bosses pressed him for a choice between flying choppers or writing songs. Kris Kristofferson replied he "reckoned he'd rather write songs." Somewhere on one of his trips between Nashville and the Gulf Coast, the words "Busted flat in Baton Rouge" would burn into his consciousness.

I'd gotten acquainted with KVOL's broadcast board by watching the other jocks. My favorite local deejay was Floyd Cormier, a thirty-year-old Cajun who had a knack for cussing right up to the time he opened his mike. Then he went into his smooth deep-voiced delivery, "This is KVOL, the voice of Lafayette, 1330 AM on your radio dial."

Floyd would click off his mike and immediately start cussing again.

The board was rather antiquated. Cueing a record involved turning the pot up, switching it to the audition channel, turning the studio speaker to the audition channel, putting the needle in the groove, and cueing, then doing everything in reverse. Put the speaker back on program, pot down, and change audition channel back to program. Cueing the commercials was even more time consuming. All spots were on small reels about three inches in diameter. So you pulled it off the rack, threaded it through the reel-to-reel machine, reached down to turn the tape machine audition speaker on, play the tape up to the cue, stop the tape, back it up, turn the audition speaker off. Now do the same thing on tape machine two. With only two machines available to play back tapes and four taped commercials in each spot break, that meant you'd cue the last two commercials during the thirty seconds of the preceding spot. Close to a dozen separate moves for each tape. Possible in thirty seconds, but you had to move fast and stay organized. I was wondering how the whole thing could be done faster. Since I was having writer's block, I put off going back to the commercial copy by pulling some news copy from the AP machine. Senator Jack Kennedy from Massachusetts was going to announce his candidacy for president. First time I ever heard of him.

"All right, kid, you're through writing copy for the day," Evan had stuck his head in the door. "We just fired Chuck Hand. You're on the air. Hey, Ernie, break the kid in on the board."

With Ernie Alexander looking over my shoulder, I sat down at the board. The Top 30 at 1330's stack of records was at my fingertips.

At three minutes and forty-five seconds, "El Paso" was the longest record on the play list. Everything else averaged two minutes and thirty seconds. Some were two, fifteen, and a couple came in at one minute and fifty seconds. It didn't give a new jock much time to get the feel for it.

The Columbia label with Marty Robbins' name on it was spinning around. I reached for "The Big Hurt" by Miss Toni Fisher. That jet airplane sound knocked me out. "Phasing" they called it. I started to cue it up, but Ernie stopped me.

"Cue your record later," he said, "you're running out of time. Get your spot break cued up first. What's on the log?"

All commercials on the log were typed in red. With just a few days left till Christmas, the log was a sea of red ink.

"How many spots an hour are we running?" I asked.

"Maybe thirty-five units," Ernie answered, "close to twenty-five minutes an hour. Come on, now, hurry, get moving."

"Yeah, this is just great," I said, reaching for four taped commercials, thinking fast and moving quick.

> *"I picked a good one,*
> *He looked like he could run,*
> *Up on his back and away I did ride,*
> *...Out to the Bad Lands of New Mexico."*
> (Ibid.)

1960

♦ DJ Allen Freed charged with tax evasion.

♦ Berry Gordy launches Motown Records.

♦ Buddy Holly, Richie Valens, and the Big Bopper become rock's first martyrs.

A high school senior in 1959, and my "Sweet Little Sixteen," Kate Russo.

South Louisiana Gulf Coast
Summer 1960

*"I ain't got a home
No place to roam
I'm a lonely frog,
I ain't got no home."*

"Ain't Got No Home," Clarence "Frogman" Henry
(Clarence Henry, ARC Music Corp.)

Jimmy Chapman was home on leave from the 92nd Airborne. Boot camp behind him, he was rough and tough, macho and military. Ready to party, he called to set up a double date with his Italian girlfriend, Donna Lee Piazza and her cousin, Kate Russo. On Sunday we picked up the girls in the T-Bird, loaded the trunk with beer, and drove out to the boat landing. Mike Russo met us there in the speedboat. Within minutes, we were at David Russo's fishing camp on the edge of Vermilion Bay, a few miles from the Gulf of Mexico. We spent the day drinking, water skiing and generally having a good time. It was good to see Chapman again. He was full of war stories. I was definitely attracted to Kate. At seventeen, her sexy Italian body was blowing away her swim suit and her olive skin was tan to the max. Her don't-give-a-damn attitude was refreshing. She was an expert on water skis and did tricks all afternoon, most of the time with a Falstaff beer in one hand. I figured the family had probably put beer in her baby bottle.

As the shadows off the marsh grass began to slide farther into the water, we started packing the skis away and gathering up the empty beer bottles. That's when a fast moving speedboat pulled up to the camp with two people in it. One was David Russo, the other his driver, cook, and valet, a black man named Shabby. Russo was medium height, well built, early forties, and looked Italian. He immediately began issuing orders.

"Mike," he said, "you and Shabby get the groceries and supplies unloaded."

Looking at Chapman and me suspiciously, he added, "You boys help out. I got some beer and liquor needs to get inside the camp."

We didn't waste any time jumping into the task.

It was easy to see that Kate was the apple of his eye.

"Kato, my love," he said. "You and your friends will have to get going. I'm expecting company."

"Sure," she replied, "But Daddy, I need to go shopping."

David Russo chuckled, he enjoyed having her hit him up for money.

"Here's a couple of hundred," he said. "Don't spend it all in one place. Look, go put that "Cherry Pink" song on the record player, the one by that Cuban fella."

So the king liked Perez Prado. That's about right. He was known to like South Louisiana blues, too. When the Crescent City flash, Clarence "Frogman" Henry released a song called "Ain't Got A Home" a couple of years back, it went straight to the top. Mike Russo had bragged that his dad and some of his friends from New Orleans owned the Frogman.

Looking hard at us, David Russo complained, "Got damn, you fellas are slow."

The job completed, Mike's speedboat was loaded and we were about to board when a low flying seaplane came out of nowhere buzzing the camp. The plane made another pass, David Russo and the pilot waving at each other before the plane circled around to land in the water fifty yards away from the camp.

"You all might as well hang on a minute and meet the man," David Russo said to us.

Shabby and Mike moved the speedboats over to one side making room for the seaplane to taxi right up to the wharf. The pilot stayed at the controls. I recognized him as one of the local crop duster pilots. The door to the plane opened and a short stocky man about fifty stepped out. He and David Russo spoke in Italian while Kate ran up and gave him a big hug.

"Fellas, I want you all to meet my friend, Carlos Marcello," Russo was saying.

Marcello had graying temples, a friendly smile, a twinkling eye, and a limp handshake.

Jimmy Chapman and I exchanged looks while Kate grinned at us. Mike Russo fired up the twin motors on his speedboat and we all climbed aboard.

Kate, Donna Lee Piazza, Chapman, and Mike were all having one more Falstaff. But I'd had enough to drink. The roar of the motors didn't allow any conversation on the ride back to the T-Bird waiting at the landing. It was just as well. I was in deep thought.

I had seen Carlos Marcello's pictures all over the papers for the past several weeks. The Feds had been hounding him, trying to make any of several charges stick. Finally, they'd dug up an old marijuana possession charge from twenty-five years earlier. The judge had signed the order. Marcello was an undesirable non-citizen, or as Mike Russo put it, he was persona non son-of-bitch. Marcello was quickly deported to Guatemala.

That Sunday night at KVOL, between records, I prepared the 10:00 p.m. news summary. Right off the Associated Press teletype came the story. Carlos Marcello had dropped out of sight in Guatemala. No one knew where he was. The FBI people assigned to keep an eye on him were frantic. The recent publicity they'd gained by deporting this famous criminal would be blown to hell if he happened to sneak back into the country. I went on the air, read the story with a straight face, re-capped the weather calling for ninety degrees and clear skies along the Gulf Coast. Then I hit the record coming out at 10:05 p.m., smiling when the Frogman started to sing.

"I ain't got a home
No place to roam
I'm a lonely frog,
I ain't got no home."
(Ibid.)

*"Now, your daddy don't mind
And your mommy don't mind."*

"Stay," Maurice Williams and the Zodiacs
(Maurice Williams, Cherio Corporation)

"I want to stay, just a little bit longer," I was singing along with Maurice and the Zodiacs who were spinning around on the turntable in the production studio as I lined up the records for tonight's show, 7:00 to 9:00 p.m. Evan Hughes named the show *Teensville*, and I could play all the "rock" I wanted. Evan had figured out rock 'n roll was, in fact, going to be around for awhile, and *Teensville* was his attempt to gradually introduce rock into the Top 30 at 1330. Even though "Chain Gang" and "Georgia on My Mind" were by black artists they were on the regular play list right up there with "Please Mr. Custer, I Don't Want to Go" by Larry Verne.

I was also helping Evan put together the Wax to Watch list every week, so I listened to everything the record companies sent us. The production studio was my regular spot every night after 5:00 p.m. The old board was in there now. Since moving into the new studio in the summer, the latest equipment was being used in the broadcast booth. The new board allowed cueing the record by simply snapping the pot down to the cue position, one move instead of eight. But the real breakthrough was the tape machines, using cartridges the size of eight tracks, which were now self-cueing. The tapes inside the cartridge were seventy or forty seconds long for minute or half-minute commercials. They just looped around to stop on the cue tone at the beginning. It took the panic out of the twenty-three minute per hour commercial load. Disc jockeying was a lot easier now.

Casey bought me a two bedroom trailer made by the Villa Company. We set it up not far from the railroad tracks and right behind the "Roof Garden" on Jefferson Street which was the USL hang out. As convenient as that was, I was too busy and roommate Danny White was just plain anti-social. Late at night when the other college kids were drinking in the parking lot I would lie in my bunk and hear the train whistle heading west. Another KVOL disc jockey, Rod Wagner, from New Orleans, also lived with us for awhile. The three of us were spending a lot of time talking radio. We all believed rock 'n roll was the only way for a radio station to win the ratings race. All other formats were just imposters. Danny had my old job of announcing football scores on Saturday afternoon. Some nights, when no one was in the station, Danny came down to engineer and learn the board. The first step in being a disc jockey was learning the board.

We knew radio was the most fun there was and no one considered it work. Danny kept saying if he didn't get himself a disc jockey gig, he'd have to go out and find a real job.

Evan was still at his desk at 6:45 when I walked into his office.

"Hey Pierce, remember that instrumental record with the country-sounding piano thing you picked for the Billboard report?"

"Yah, Floyd Cramer's 'Last Date.'"

"Well, they sent this note today congratulating KVOL for being the first radio station in the country to pick Floyd Cramer for the top ten. Good ear, kid."

"You'd had to been deaf not to hear 'Last Date' was a smash by the fifth note," I said, avoiding Evan's gaze.

"You came to tell me you're leaving, didn't you?" the old man said.

"Well, not till next May, but I have made up my mind. How did you know?"

Evan's hair looked more silver than ever as he leaned back in his chair.

"After awhile you can tell when a disc jockey's ready to move on, even before he knows it himself. It's a small town, kid, but I've seen some good men come through. A few of them made it to the big markets. Most of them didn't, naturally. The competition in sheer numbers is ferocious. Multiply your own ambition by thousands all over the country and you'll get some idea of what I'm talking about."

"I know."

"No, you don't. You think you know. You're a gifted announcer, got a lot of talent, good voice. But so does everybody else. They're all good. They're all as confident as you are. Only a handful will make it. Those that the business don't beat, they beat themselves. The wrong woman, booze, or dope. They get hung up and beat themselves. So why the hell am I straining my voice. You're going anyway. Where?"

"Los Angeles. I've applied at UCLA."

"Listen, kid, you can't go directly from Louisiana to Los Angeles. You gotta work your way up. Go to New Orleans for a few months, then try to head up to Chicago or the East Coast and get close to New York. Or head west for Houston, then Phoenix, San Diego. You stand a better chance of getting called up from there."

"I appreciate your advice, Evan. I'm going to UCLA. That's in Los Angeles. I'll get a radio job. I know I will."

"Well, I'll write you a letter of recommendation when you go. Now get your ass on the air. Please don't play that Chubby Checker record again tonight. 'The Twist' is the silliest damned dance they've come up with yet. Another damned fad, it'll be dead and forgotten before the year's out."

I walked into the studio at 6:59 p.m., a stack of forty-fives in each hand. Connie Francis was spinning around on the turntable as the studio speaker belted out:

"Everybody's somebody's plaything
And there are no exceptions to the ru-u-ule."

"Everybody's Somebody's Fool," Connie Francis
(Howie Greenfield and Jack Keller, Colgems EMI Music)

On turntable two, I cued up the Ventures' "Walk, Don't Run," checked the log for red ink, and pulled four commercial cartridge tapes. The clock said just fifteen seconds shy of 7:00 p.m. I yanked the Ventures off and cued up another record. Connie Francis timed out perfect and I opened the mike straight up at 7:00 p.m.

"Hello, South Louisiana, I'm Dave Pierce on 'Teensville,' from the Happy Voice of Lafayette, KVOL."

The next sound they heard was Chubby Checker.

"Yeah daddy is sleeping
and yeah Mama ain't around.
We're gonna twist it, twist it,
'til we tear the house down."

"The Twist," Chubby Checker
(Hank Ballard, Fort Knox Music, Inc., Trio Music Co., Inc.)

1960

♦ New Innovations: Beverages in aluminum cans, felt tip pens, and heart pacemakers.

♦ First sit-in at Woolworth's all-white lunch counter in Greensboro, NC.

♦ Roy Orbison's "Only the Lonely" becomes international hit.

♦ Dave Brubeck Quartet's album *Time Out* makes jazz acceptable to the middle class.

♦ Paul Desmond's "Take Five" hits the charts.

♦ OPEC (Organization of Petroleum Exporting Countries) formed.

♦ John Updike publishes *Rabbit, Run* about American suburbia.

Kate, me, and niece Lisa Vaughn with an uncommon sight in south Louisiana, February 12, 1960.

The Villa
Lafayette, Louisiana
November 14, 1960

"Come all ye rolling minstrels
And together we will try
To rouse the spirit of the earth
And move the rolling sky."

"Rolling Minstrels," Fairport Convention
(unknow, Public Domain)

Danny White and I had been up till past midnight, strumming guitars. He was picking some fancy leads, while I was struggling to keep pace on the few chords I had learned to finger without the discipline to master. We often closed the day this way. With only the drinking crowd at the Roof Garden as neighbors, volume wasn't a problem. We were starting to join some of the Burke Hall actors for an occasional beer at the Roof Garden, and when the monthly student body meetings eliminated morning classes, we walked across the street to join the rest of the rebels to hold our own meetings.

Evan Hughes had a way of squeezing productivity out of his announcers, by scheduling multiple two-and-three hour split shifts every day. Mine were probably the most varied. On this morning I reported in at 5:45 to fire the transmitter and put the "Happy Voice" on the air. The clacking teletype told me Danny White and I were not the only ones up late the previous evening.

The Louisiana Legislature, in an after hours session, had closed all public schools in a futile attempt to prevent integration in New Orleans. With the day off from class, I visited Ernie Alexander and Kirby Boudreaux, who had all moved over to the new radio station KXKW. Then I checked in at Burke Hall.

Being a sophomore, I was having a better time of it at USL. I'd picked up the leads in the summer production of *Solid Gold Cadillac* and this fall's *Twelve Angry Men.* On the schedule was two of the greatest roles in theatre history, *Macbeth*, and the Marlon Brando role of Stanley Kowalski in *A Street Car Named Desire.* Striding the stage and booming my voice off the back wall of Burke Hall just came naturally. The USL campus with the quadrangle and Cypress Lake and the Cajun accents of the kids from Breaux Bridge, Carencro, and Mamou felt like home. But none of it mattered, I was itching to head west. Last week I was accepted at UCLA. I'd be there in ten months.

Woodie Bernard was on campus now. We'd meet at the Student Union almost every day for coffee. He said he'd come to the university to drink from the fountain of knowledge, but mostly he was just drinking. Since I had a fierce desire for my future, I figured he should too.

"What is it you really want to do?" I asked.

"I duh-duh-dunno, Da-David," Woodie replied, "ma-ma-maybe I read too many, too many Civil War novels. I really want, really want a chance to pr-prove myself. If a fight br-br-breaks out, I don't, I don't want to mi-mi-miss it."

Woodie was eager to leave school behind, join the military, and see the world. In the mean time, Woodie and Danny were taking turns borrowing the T-Bird while I was on the air at KVOL or on stage rehearsing at Burke Hall. Between the three of us the T-Bird had high visibility at Beverly's Lounge, The Blue Note, Dave's Top Hat, and The Skunk. We also dined regularly at Don's Seafood and Alesi's Pizza out past Four Corners. If I got off late, the Bowling Alley burgers would precede a game or two. Sometimes we bowled till three or four on the all-night special. Lunch was often an A&W Root Beer burger. Any meal could be complimented with large servings at the Borden's Ice Cream Shop.

Even with the college carousing, I went after the grade point average with a vengeance. With Kate helping do research, I'd win the Best Debater Award. I always found time to study at weird hours. Sometimes it was 8 a.m. before class, before or after tennis in the afternoon, or when no one would even think about cracking a book, like 2 a.m. Saturday night after a movie, drinking, dining large, and loving with Kate.

For a former athlete, college P.E. class was borderline degrading. I did enjoy the tennis and volley ball, but wrestling and tumbling weren't my game. As quarterback, I threw short side line passes to the kid with one arm, designed reverse hand offs, and boot leg keepers that consistently beat the athletically challenged opposition. Danny and I joined the Intramural League, led our defense, and missed the championship game loss to be at Burke Hall rehearsal. The P.E. coaches shook their heads and ragged me for not taking the football scholarship and being on the Varsity field with the big boys where I belonged. I didn't respond. These old jocks wouldn't understand my inner turmoil. They couldn't identify with speaking a playwright's words or opening a mic and talkin' radio talk.

Danny White had an off-beat sense of humor, and our activities were punctuated with a running commentary that denigrated authority and its rules. He was also a master at framing any current event in an old English literature context, so anyone from Beowulf to European Kings could appear as university Deans, professors, Burke Hall actors, or KVOL disc jockeys. He and I became students of local commercial radio, living in the wonderful world of pop music. When we weren't on the air, we visited other deejays and other radio stations. We often drove down to New Iberia to see thirty-year-old Les Lester, "The Boy Les," run his studio shift, or spin records for the real money at the highly publicized and wildly popular hops. Then late at night, inside the Villa, with the Roof Garden merriment and the train whistle as background, we'd strum those guitars. Our musical roots of lonesome country, black blues, and Cajun swamp pop rock would soothe us in Danny's raw vocals.

In a few months Danny White would end diplomatic relations with the university to start his own band, then pick and sing, and become a legendary country radio disc jockey among the rednecks in Central Louisiana. Unlike many of our classmates, Danny knew early on what he wanted to be.

"And to the rhythm of guitars
we hope you'll lend an ear
and the high notes come from you and me
for we will sing so clear.

Come all ye rolling minstrels
And together we will try
To rouse the spirit of the earth
And move the rolling sky."
(Ibid.)

Top, University of Southwestern Louisiana actors.
Bottom, in a USL production of *Twelve Angry Men* (Danny White, second from left).

"Somebody help me get out of Louisiana
...on a jet to the promised land."

"Promised Land," Chuck Berry
(Chuck Berry, ARC Music Corp)

After a long talk with Dr. Ellis, my director and mentor, I was cross-ing the Burke Hall stage, taking the long way from his office to the exit. Ellis had denied me the lead in *Macbeth,* throwing me an actor's bone as Banquo and saddling me with the tough task of make-up supervisor where I was up to my butt in beards and spirit gum. I also handled pub-licity, introducing the idea of promoting university productions on local radio. Our five-day run set records, filling Burke's 650 seats while turn-ing away over 300 every night. By midnight I would have the beards and wigs stashed away and the dressing room swept. Even though this effort would earn membership in the national theatrical fraternity, Alpha Phi Omega, I would never again accept the late shift on a Shakespeare pro-duction.

Ellis paid me back with the plum part of Stanley Kowalski in A *Street-car Named Desire.* With my buddy, big Norm Belleau playing Mitch, we were cast opposite two excellent actresses, Pauline Harding as Blanche and Genevieve Bernard as Stella. My actor's ego decided that some of my readings were as good as Brando, some better. And I didn't mumble, the back row could hear every word. If Dr. Ellis had been grooming me for two more years of lead roles, he didn't show any disappointment when I told him I wouldn't be back. Maybe he already knew. Like *The Streetcar,* I was ready to rumble on down the line.

By now the Burke Hall actors were a close social group, drinking and partying together. Pauline showed up at one event with a name tag that paraphrased her lines from Lady Macbeth, "To bed, to bed, Macbeth didn't heed, but Stanley did." One night Genevieve came over to the Vil-la, for beers. We were laying on the couch but were so loaded we rolled off the couch to the floor and spent the rest of the evening laughing.

Evan Hughes graduated me to the top spot of afternoon drive 4-7p.m. I was cookin' with Top 40 chops that I figured was worthy of the West Coast. After my show, I'd pick up a sweet little classmate named Sonya, we'd go to the Blue Note, dance and drink for two hours, then I was back at KVOL for the rest of the split shift, 9-10:30. Kate picked up on the indis-cretion and made me hurt till I promised to straighten up. She was pals with Hollis Gooch, local bad boy who had been busted, along with his compadre, Ted O'Neil, for siphoning gas from the chemistry teacher's car. Kate was winding down her senior year as a cheerleader and getting ready for high school graduation.

When finals finally came, the Burke Hall gang all sold our books and took the money straight to the Blue Note. It was supposed to be a few more weeks before I left town, but I was already poised at the exit. The show biz monkey was on my back.

*"Oh the biggest battle
Ever on the western Plains
When me and a bunch of Cowboys
Rode in to Jesse James."*

"Out On The Western Plain," Leadbelly
(Huddie Ledbetter, Folkways Music)

As Stanley Kowalski in a University of Southwestern Louisiana production of *A Streetcar Named Desire*.

California
June 1961

"You'll see Amarillo
Gallup, New Mexico,
Flagstaff, Arizona.
Don't forget Winona..."

"(Get Your Kicks On) Route 66," Bobby Troup
(Bobby Troup, Londontown Music; Troup London Music)

There wasn't much left of Route 66. At one time it was America's main street. Now most of it had already become Interstate 40, but the towns were the same. Kingman, Barstow, San Bernardino, just like Bobby Troup's song. We'd picked up the long cement river north of Dallas, had been on it for three days. The sun was beating down on the golden Thunderbird as it roared down from the high desert at eighty-five miles per hour. Traffic was moving at close to eighty, so we weren't passing that many cars. The trunk was loaded and the back seat was also piled high with the bare necessities a couple of nineteen-year-olds would need when moving to California, including a reel-to-reel tape recorder. In our wallets were fake draft cards saying we were 21, the legal drinking age in Los Angeles. Asleep in the passenger seat was Ron Adkins. We'd only met a month before. Word had gotten around USL that we were both headed west, so we met, liked each other instantly, and decided to team up. I had the car and Ron had a promise of jobs at Twentieth Century Fox. Ron was a big good-looking kid with a million-dollar smile and matching personality. It had definitely been fun on the road. Ahead, the brown haze that lives over Los Angeles could be seen oozing from the horizon toward the speeding T-Bird. This is it. California, here I come, the Promised Land, where the girls are really the most.

"Well, I'm goin' out west where I belong
Where the days are short and the nights are long
...Well, they're out there a'havin' fun."

"California Sun," The Rivieras
(Henry Glover and Morris Levy, EMI Longitude Music)

Two hours later, the T-Bird was creeping in bumper-to-bumper traffic on the San Bernardino Freeway. The mid-afternoon sun was trying to burn through the haze and smog. We could smell it now and our eyes were smarting. Ron was studying the map he held in his lap.

"Davey, it looks to me that this San Bernardino Freeway goes straight into the Hollywood Freeway, and that's where we're going."

"Turn the radio up, I want to hear this disc jockey," I said.

"Sure, you just drive and listen to the radio. Don't worry about nothing. Go ahead, leave it up to me to point you in the right direction. Just be ready to start swimming when you hear the Pacific Ocean lapping over your fender skirts," Ron was mumbling as he turned the volume up and went back to studying his map.

"That's the Shirelles," the disc jockey said, "with 'Dedicated to the One I Love.' Now here's a song that was first written by a Broadway musical team back in 1934. It was recorded by this group who cut their version in two takes at the end of a recording session. From there it went straight to the top of the charts a couple of months ago. It's still bouncing around this week at number 26. I'm Casey Kasem on KRLA in Pasadena, and these are the Marcels with their former number one song."

"Ba-ba-ba-ba, ba-ba-ba-ba,
Boom, a-boom, boom,
Blue Moon, you saw me standing alone
Without a dream in my heart."

"Blue Moon," The Marcels
(Richard Rogers and Lorenz Hart, EMI Robbins Catalog Inc.)

"Jesus, will you look at this mess," Ron said, as we crawled through the downtown Los Angeles interchange. "It must have been a Yankee who engineered this mother. There it is. Hollywood Freeway straight ahead."

"Yeah, I'll just stay in this fast lane," I said, seconds before stomping hard on the brake pedal when the car in front of us came to a squealing stop. The gridlock that was coming to every city in America was well underway here at ground zero.

It was speed up, slow down, and stop, but in just a few minutes Ron was pointing to an exit sign.

"That's it. Alvarado exit, one-half mile. We're here, good buddy."

The T-Bird peeled off at Alvarado and took a left onto a small side street named Waterloo. The Queen of Angels Hospital was looking down on us when we parked and climbed the rickety wooden stairs to a small loft in an old two-story building. This was home to Ron's cousin, Jim Bachman, who had been in L.A. for two years. A graduate of Chanard Art School, he was a set designer and had been working regularly in the movie industry. Bachman came in at 7:00 p.m. He and Ron exchanged family news while I sized him up. Bachman was about thirty, balding, had a full red beard, and he had a tendency to go off on tangents when he talked.

Bachman definitely had the scoop on the movie business. He had some good news and some bad news. The bad news was this was one of the worst years in history for Hollywood studios. *Cleopatra* was shooting in Rome and almost nothing was happening around Los Angeles. The jobs at Twentieth Century Fox would have to wait. The good news was we could stay for a few days in Bachman's cramped loft and sleep on the floor until we found an apartment.

That night I walked up to the Queen of Angels Hospital and called home. No, I wouldn't be back in two weeks like I had promised. Maybe I'd stay awhile longer. No, I didn't have a job at Fox. What would I do? Well, Bachman said there was a summer session at the famous theatre school, the Pasadena Playhouse. Maybe I'd check that out. There was another promise to come home before the summer was over, before UCLA in September.

Walking back down the hill from the Queen of Angels, I sniffed the cool Los Angeles air. The sultry Italian girl on the other end of the telephone line and the hot summer nights of Cajun country seemed like another lifetime, although it was only two thousand miles and three days away. Climbing those rickety stairs, the radio in the ground floor apartment was playing the Shirelles.

49

Two days later we moved into the sixth floor of an apartment building on Normandy, three doors up from Wilshire Boulevard and only a few minutes from Bachman. He'd already taken us to dinner at Musso Franks', the oldest restaurant in Hollywood, and filled our heads with a ton of Hollywood history. Bachman could talk nonstop for hours, although his thoughts weren't always connected. I loved it, getting a nice feel for the city and a gold mine of information from Bachman.

Ron scored a night clerk job at the front desk of the Beverly Wilshire Hotel and I was winding the T-Bird down the oldest freeway in the world to Pasadena. Parking in the fifteen minute green zone, I stepped out into the Spanish stucco-style of the Pasadena Playhouse courtyard. In the office, the admissions lady painted a rosy picture of what could be expected at the summer session, including the chance to compete for one of two full scholarships that fall. That is, if I was accepted. After all, standards were the highest. She showed the pictures of recent students including Earl Holliman, a favorite in the movie Giant. KRLA's newsman, Richard Beebe, had graduated in '57, Leonard Nimoy in '50. Names like Dustin Hoffman and Gene Hackman, who had been there just two years before, were still unknown.

"What were your grades like in high school and college?" I loved it when admissions people asked that question.

"4.0 in high school, Valedictorian. 3.5 in college," I smiled. "And don't worry about the scholarship, I've already committed to UCLA Film School in September."

Her ears visibly picked up.

"Oh, UCLA. Well, that's just fine. But, we'd like to have a student with your academic record here in our summer session. You'd have to pass the acting audition, of course, and it might be fun to compete for the scholarship, anyway. Here's an admission application explaining the rules and tuition costs. Why don't you take it with you? Classes begin next Monday. And you say you're a disc jockey. You might be interested in knowing that there's a radio station across the street."

"Is that where KRLA is?" I asked, thinking this was getting too easy.

"KRLA? No, I believe it's called KPPC."

"Do they play rock 'n roll?"

"Oh, no. No rock and roll. It's an FM station. They play classical music."

"Classical music?"

"Yes, beautiful classical music, except when the church service is on. The radio station is owned by the church, you know. They broadcast the service live on Sunday morning and the mid-week devotionals on Wednesday night."

"And the rest of the time they play classical," I said, losing interest quickly.

"Just walk across Colorado Boulevard and you'll see the Pasadena Presbyterian Church, the big beautiful building in the middle of the block. The radio station is in the basement under the church."

"So it's KPPC and it's owned by the Pasadena Presbyterian Church. I guess that's why they called it KPPC," I smiled politely.

"Yesss, I suppose so. It's FM, you know. You must have an FM radio to receive the signal. You should listen to it. They play beautiful classical music. Perhaps you could work there part-time while going to school at the Playhouse. Do you have an FM radio?"

"Not yet, ma'am, I'm afraid they don't play rock 'n roll on FM."

"Each night before you go to bed my baby,
Whisper a little prayer for me my baby."

"Dedicated To The One I Love," The Shirelles
(Ralph Bass and Lowman Pauling, Fort Know Music, Inc.,
Songs of Universal, Inc., Trio Music Co., Inc.)

Ready for Hollywood: me, my 'vette and the California sunshine.

San Bernadino Mountains
August 1961

"There was a time in this fair land,
When the railroad did not run
When the wild majestic mountains
Stood alone against the sun."

"Canadian Railroad Trilogy," Gordon Lightfoot
(Gordon Lightfoot)

David Crosby's fingers were dancing over the twelve-string guitar as he leaned back against the pine tree stretching sixty feet into the blue mountain sky. David Crosby had just turned twenty on August 14th. Within five years he and Roger McGuinn would electrify folk rock and Crosby would go into the pages of rock 'n roll history.

I looked out across Lake Arrowhead, where Danny Truhitte and I had gone sailing earlier that day. Hard to believe we were only three hours from the smog of Los Angeles. It was the last weekend before the summer session ended. The Pasadena Playhouse sponsored this recreation excursion. We had driven east to San Bernadino, then north up the winding road as the air got cleaner and thinner and the sky got bluer. California really was fantastic. Last weekend we were at the beach, today we were in the mountains. Big contrast to South Louisiana's bayous and mosquitoes.

"And when the young man's fancy
Had turned into his brain
...With many a fortune won and lost,
And many a debt to pay."
(Ibid.)

As soon as David Crosby strummed the last note, Danny Truhitte was talking to him, "That's a great song, who wrote that?"

"A fellow named Gordon Lightfoot," Crosby replied.

"I don't think I've heard of him," I said.

"Canadian folk singer," Crosby answered. "He wrote "Early Morning Rain," other good folk songs too."

"Folk songs, huh."

"Yeah, Pierce," Crosby said with a grin, "it's the closest thing you'll find to all that country and Cajun music you're always humming to yourself."

"I like what the song has to say," Danny Truhitte piped in. "It has a message."

Danny was from Sacramento, seventeen and totally idealistic. He followed me like a younger brother. He was also a hell of a dancer, with matching physique and all-American good looks.

David Crosby continued to finger the twelve-string.

"That song is called 'The Canadian Railroad Trilogy,'" Crosby said. "Here's another verse from it, slower rhythm."

"Laying down tracks, and tear up the trails
...Swinging our hammers in the bright blazing sun."
(Ibid.)

I wandered away from the group and hiked up the trail for a better view of Lake Arrowhead. Folk music, message songs. I'd never heard acoustic guitar played the way Crosby did it. I was hooked.

I was also facing a personal dilemma. The Playhouse authorities had called me in yesterday. They wanted to award me a scholarship, but knowing I was headed for UCLA, they had to know if I'd accept it before they made the announcement at the ceremony next Friday. I was surprised and amazed. The series of acting auditions all through the summer had felt good, still I had to think the 4.0 high school and 3.5 at USL was a big part of the decision. In any case, the problem was UCLA. In two years I could get a theatre arts degree from the Playhouse, but the UCLA Film School would be put on hold. I had to ask about the other scholarship. Although Danny Truhitte didn't know it yet, he was going to get the other one. I liked that idea a lot.

The tall pines swayed gently overhead. The crisp mountain air was the best I'd ever smelled. And David Crosby's melodic voice and twelve-string acoustic drifted up through the trees.

"There was a time in this fair land
When the railroad did not run
When the wild majestic mountains
Stood alone against the sun."
(Ibid.)

New Orleans
September 1961

With the scholarship locked up, I took an apartment in Pasadena and Ron Adkins went west on Wilshire into Beverly Hills. A flight home to South Louisiana brought congratulations from family and friends and publicity in the local newspaper. I felt like the conquering hero come home. My dad called me the prodigal son and promptly gathered up the fattest calf on the farm and staged a barbecue. When you've been a success all your young life, winning starts to come naturally. People expect it from you. You expect it from yourself. Hollywood was going to be easy.

Now it was time to face reality again. We were in New Orleans, the flight to the coast departed in one hour. We drove around Audubon Park one more time before I dropped Kate off at Dominican College. We had said enough good-byes. She understood California was something I just had to do, but she didn't want me to go. I'd seen this scene in the movies a hundred times. If I ever had to act it, I'd have the emotional part down tight.

"Don't you know that I danced,
I danced till a quarter to three
With the help, last night, of Daddy G.
He was swingin on the sax like nobody could,
...Blow Daddy!"

"Quarter to Three," Gary "U.S." Bonds
(Gary Anderson, Gene Barge, Frank Guida, Joseph Royster)

It was Friday night on the Pasadena Freeway. Danny Truhitte and I were in the back seat of Smokey Roberds' Eldorado. Smokey was behind the wheel with Gary "U.S." Bonds blaring from the radio. The rest of the Cadillac convertible was overflowing with Playhouse students. Gwen, Baby Caron, James Reader, Carol from Canada, and blonde brassy Jill Miani from Chicago. Smokey was from El Dorado, Arkansas, a Southerner, also a former athlete and disc jockey. After one three-hour bull session, Smokey and I knew we'd be friends for life. Two weeks earlier we became roommates and now my social life was picking up. At least I wasn't living alone anymore on El Molino up by the railroad tracks where that lonesome whistle brought back every Jimmy Rodgers' and Hank Williams' train lyric that I'd ever heard. I still missed home. Mostly, I missed the Italian girl.

Going to school at the Pasadena Playhouse was exciting. I liked it all, but wanted less class and more time on stage. One hundred and ten classmates were the highlight, all of them potential entertainers. The days and nights were filled with ad-lib scenarios, creative practical jokes, inventive imitations of characters, real and imagined, and the sense that we all were just months or weeks from breaking into show biz.

The Dovells on the Cadillac Eldorado radio played on.

"The kids in Bristol are sharp as a pistol,
When they do the Bristol stomp."

"Bristol Stomp," The Dovells
(Kal Mann and Dave Appell, Dave Appell Music, Kalmann Music, Inc.)

Back at our apartment on Los Robles, Smokey entertained the group until the wee hours. He looked like a young George C. Scott out of the Paul Newman movie *The Hustler*. A dancer, he had a well-built athletic upper body on his 5 foot 7 inch frame. When anyone remarked about his height, his standard retort was "I'm tall as anybody...in bed." He played folk and blues on his lyric harp, a wild looking acoustic guitar with angelic wing-like appendages along both sides of the neck, giving it a distinct sound. At 2:00 a.m. I slipped into the bedroom and made one more phone call to Kate's dorm at Dominican. In New Orleans it was 4:00 a.m. The phone rang nearly twenty times before I hung up.

She called Monday night after I'd been through a couple of miserable days. She'd gone to see an old boyfriend. She was getting itchy about being two thousand miles apart. Yes, she would sneak out of school and fly to Los Angeles for the weekend.

The fourty-eight hours with Kate in L.A. was a constant party, showing her the sights, introductions to the gang. Friday night to Sunday afternoon blew by in a flash and it was a painful drive out to Los Angeles International. We were ready to check her luggage when the schedule flashed "Delta Airlines flight to New Orleans delayed one hour." We looked at each other for a long time. I grabbed Kate's hand and we ran out of the airport to the waiting T-Bird. Six hours later, we were in the Las Vegas Court House applying for a marriage license. At eighteen, she was legal. But at twenty, I still needed parents' permission.

"What time does your shift change?" I asked the official.

"8:00 a.m.," was the stern reply.

At 8:15 the next morning, we walked back into the license office. Keeping my new California driver's license hidden, this time I pulled my fake Louisiana Selective Service draft card, showing I was twenty-two. Three hours later, we were standing in front of the proprietor of the Little Chapel of the Flowers. For ten dollars extra, we had the ceremony taped. For an extra five bucks, the proprietor's wife would have cried. That night, we were back in Pasadena. The next day, I was back on stage at the Playhouse, only now I had a wife.

1961

♦ Cameo/Parkway record executives Kal Mann and Dave Appell wrote "The Bristol Stomp" for a capella group the Dovells, singing about teenagers dancing a new step they called the stomp at fire hall dances in Bristol, a small industrial town near Philadelphia.

On stage at the Pasadena Playhouse with Smokey Roberds.

Pasadena
December 1961

We had the T-Bird loaded to the limit when we pulled into the Richfield gas station on Orange Grove in Pasadena. School was out for the holidays and we were driving home to Louisiana. Charles Laquidara came running up to the pump. He was six feet tall, thin, looking like a young Ben Gazzara. He was also Italian. Charles was a Playhouse classmate from Boston, with a heavy Massachusetts accent. Smokey always kidded him about it and Charles retaliated by knocking our southernisms. Everyone always mispronounced his last name and he always corrected them.

"Lah-Lah," Charles would say in phonetic detail, "Lah-kwi-dare-rah. Jesus Christ! Aren't there any Italians where you people come from?"

I didn't know Charles very well, yet. I'd seen him in class and envied the fact that after school Charles would always drive Jill Maina to the dorm on the back of his motorbike.

Kate leaned out and yelled, "Hey, Charlie, y'all got any regular gas?"

"Y'all? Do I have a frog in my pocket?" was Laquidara's reply.

"A frog in your pocket? What do I care about a damned old frog in your pocket? Just fill 'er up," she blasted back.

Kate was having trouble with Charles Laquidara's New England sense of humor.

"That's the trouble with you damned Southerners," Charles needled. "Not only can't you speak English, you're not very bright."

"What's his problem?" Kate asked when we drove away from the gas station.

"He's just a Yankee, that's all," I said.

After about a fifteen-minute drive through South Pasadena we merged onto Interstate 10, heading east. The Defense Department, under Ike's urging, had funded the Federal Highway Act, making the nation highly mobile for the next World War. During the '60s, I-10 would come together a few miles at a time, replacing Highway 90, the Old Spanish Trail. Slowly, the forty-hour ride would shrink to twenty-seven. On the radio Ray Charles was singing his hit song.

> *"Well I guess if you say so*
> *I'd have to pack my things and go (That's right)."*

"Hit The Road Jack," Ray Charles
(Percy Mayfield, Tangerine Music Corp)

Hollywood
March 1962

The Sensations were on KFWB when I took the Sunset on ramp to the Hollywood Freeway, in my brand new white '62 Corvette. I felt very much the Angelino. The top was off and I laid a little rubber from second to third gear, as the 'Vette merged into south bound traffic heading toward the interchange before taking the Pasadena Freeway.

At KFWB the interview had not gone well. The program director had given me only a couple of minutes. My audition tape was on the big Ampex in KFWB's production room less than thirty seconds. The tape was dated, almost a year old, but the PD was definitely not interested. There was no opening coming up, not even on the weekend. He suggested that I look for work out of town, go up to Ventura, or Santa Barbara, maybe down to Orange County, get some pace in my delivery. After all, KFWB was the home of B. Mitchell Reed, the fastest tongue in the west. The PD was right, of course, just as Evan Hughes had been right. You don't go from Lafayette, Louisiana, directly to Los Angeles and get a deejay job at a top rocker. It just didn't happen that way. Maybe I should blow off radio and stick with acting.

There was plenty of promise in that area. Jim Bachman was a valuable contact and steady source of encouragement. While he was working on the set of The *Ugly American* at Universal Studios, Bachman invited me over for lunch in the commissary where I wide eyed several recognizable performers. Then we strolled over to the sound stage to watch Marlon Brando go through his paces. I stood a few feet away as Brando mumbled his dialogue and kept calling for his lines while the director and crew worked take after take for America's finest actor.

Things were great at the Pasadena Playhouse. The director type cast me as a football player who feared gays in support of Jim Reader as the sensitive boy in *Tea and Sympathy*. Reader reminded me so much of James Dean it hurt. The Detroit Kid, Vince Donofrio, blew us all away with real animal magnetism playing Brando characters the way I wish I could. When the playhouse officials gave me a shot at the William Holden role in *Picnic*, I fell right into the emotion of every small town drifter who couldn't have the girl he really wanted. Last week Smokey Roberds and I played a scene from *The Defiant Ones* for a student body assembly. Smokey did the Tony Curtis part and I played the Sidney Poitier role. Knocked 'em out.

The school's talent scout had called us in for a pep talk. He said Smokey showed great emotional intensity, and my dark Cajun tan and characterization had been believable in a black man's role. He said we were the kind of exciting young talent the studios were looking for. Of course we were.

But I missed the turntables and microphone. The rock 'n roll hits just kept on coming. I wanted in.

"I-uh-I-uh-I (open up) hear music,
Let me in
Oh I heard it just then
Let me in, whee-ooh
(whee-ooh, whee-ooh, ho-ooh-oop-whee-ooh)."
(Ibid.)

With Betty Warrala in *Picnic*.

With Jim Reader in *Tea and Sympathy*.

With John Mcelveny in *Picnic*.

With Smokey Roberds in
The Defiant Ones.

With John Mcelveny, future senior production manager for the Academy Awards.

On Stage at the Pasadena Playhouse.

Pasadena
April 1962

We parked the 'Vette across Colorado Boulevard up on El Molino, Kate and I walking the half block down to the Pasadena Playhouse. Charles Laquidara, Smokey Roberds, and Danny Truhitte met us in the courtyard. Bud and Melonie Tedesco arrived in a couple of minutes and we all went up to the Balcony Theater. Bud Tedesco was from Riverside and a Playhouse student with a character face and an extremely dry sense of humor. Mel, like Kate, worked to help put her husband through school. She was pretty, long hair, thin as a rail, and had a three-pack-a-day habit. The single boys, Charles, Smokey, and Danny often had dates, but when they didn't, like tonight, the seven of us were a family.

A Playhouse graduate, now a Hollywood starlet, was playing at the Balcony in *Dream Girl*. The former Peach Queen from Yuba City in northern California, Charlotte Stewart, was blond, beautiful and talented. She'd already appeared on several TV shows, including *My Three Sons*, and was dating Tim Considine, one of the stars of that show. Over coffee after the show, the five Playhouse boys and two wives couldn't stop talking about her. I thought she was one "jole blon." Danny hoped he would find a girl like Charlotte Stewart to marry someday. Smokey wanted to get her phone number and ask her out that weekend. We all agreed it took that kind of talent to make it.

"She's so pretty, Lord she's fine.
I'm gonna make her mine all mine.
Hey, hey baby!
I want to know if you'll be my girl."
(Ibid.)

Charlotte Stewart

Pasadena
May 1962

"Oh, my little soldier boy,
I'll be true to you."

"Soldier Boy," The Shirelles
(Luther Dixon and Florence Green, ABKCO Music, Inc., EMI Longitude Music)

The top was off the Corvette. Charles Laquidara and I were cruising Colorado Boulevard near the Playhouse. The deejay told us the Shirelles' song was number one for the second week in a row. It fit our mood. The first year of the Playhouse was over. Besides being a nostalgic time of year, something else was on our minds: the draft. We were all on 2-S Student Deferments. One year from now when we graduated, we could be called in.

"You know there's a radio station down in the basement," I said, pointing at the Pasadena Presbyterian Church.

"You kidding, under the church?" Charles gave me his standard "you Southern boys are shitting me again" look.

"Seriously, KPPC. It's owned by the church."

"So, why don't you get a job? You and Smokey were supposed to be the big disc jockeys, or was that a lot of Southern bull, too?"

"It's an FM. All they play is classical."

"So what. You don't like classical?"

"I don't think I ever really heard that much," I admitted.

"I swear, you poor Southern bastards are so deprived when it comes to any kind of culture or education in the arts. Look, I've got a pretty good classical collection. We'll get together this fall and I'll enlighten you. Wait till you hear "Scherazade" or "Cappricio Español." You'll forget you ever heard a damned Cajun accordion."

"Sure, I'll listen, but I won't play it on the radio. I want a rock jock job."

"So, what are you gonna do for the summer, or don't you need a job," Charles said, like that would be undesirable.

"I need a job. I want to pay off this Corvette, so I went and got a job. I'll be counting money all summer for Bank of America. They think I'm gonna make it a career. Put me on their management training program."

"Oh, yeah. How did you get a job like that?"

"With my Southern education, that's how. When they found out I was in the top two percent in the nation in math, they gave me this test," I bragged, "so far, I'm the only kid in California who answered all twenty questions correctly."

"Get out of here," Charles jeered, "You can't make me believe that."

"Truth, every word."

"Yeah, sure. And I've just been named a star in Paramount's next feature."

As Charles exited the 'Vette, he put his hand out. I didn't respond.

"Okay, so I believe you. I didn't mean to bruise your ego," he apologized. "It's just that all that accomplishment stuff doesn't count as far as I'm concerned. Look, you and Kate have a good summer, okay."

"Sure, you too. See you in September."

The 'Vette left only a few yards of rubber going from first gear to second. I turned up the radio and headed for the summer of '62.

On August 5, 1962, Marilyn Monroe would die at age thirty-six of a drug overdose. Now the blonde image of Hollywood's pre-eminent sex goddess would become universal for all times. In the years ahead, Marilyn Monroe's memory, just like James Dean's, would seem more vivid and intriguing than real life, and dying on drugs would become the fastest exit for our heroes of the stage and screen, and the makers of music for the radio.

"Have a good time, but remember,
There is danger in the summer moon above."

"See You In September," The Tempos
(Sid Wayne and Sherman Edwards, Holly-Hill Music Publishing Co.,
Keith-Valerie Music)

1962

♦ Ken Kesey releases *One Flew Over the Cuckoo's Nest.*

♦ Helen Gurley Brown releases *Sex and the Single Girl.*

♦ Walter Cronkite becomes the first news anchor to use background music in his broadcast.

Pam McMyler, John Wayne's future co-star in *Chisolm.*

KPPC FM
The Basement
Pasadena Presbyterian Church
October 1962

I took the spinning 45 off Turntable One and glanced over at the LP that was on the air on Turntable Two. Dvorak went on forever. I moved the Turntable One lever back from 45 to 33 rpm. I didn't want to forget to do that. A Mozart LP would sound weird revved up to 45 rpm. I looked closely at the Little Eva hit on the Dimension Records label. "Locomotion," written by Goffin and King. Jerry Goffin and Carole King were pumping out hits, and gave this one to their babysitter. Although she'd never released a record, I'd heard Carole on a demo recording Smokey brought in from Hollywood. Loved her voice.

I usually brought a few forty-fives in for my shift at KPPC-FM. Playing classical music was dull, boring work. It was radio, but nothing like what I really wanted to do. So, while I beamed Beethoven and Tchaikovsky to the Pasadena area, I flipped the other turntable to the audition channel and played rock hits like Neil Sedaka's "Breaking Up Is Hard To Do," and "Sherry, Sherry Baby" by Frankie Valli and The Four Seasons, or the Crystals wailing out "He's a Rebel." Sometimes I felt like being a rebel and fade "The Monster Mash" in over Dvorak or maybe let "Ahab the Arab" play in faintly behind solo parts of a particularly dull classical piece. That ought to knock the little old ladies in Pasadena for a loop. I thought about it, but never did it.

Sometimes I questioned if I had the right attitude to be a rock 'n roll disc jockey, to do stunts like locking myself in the studio and playing "Old Rivers" by Walter Brennan until they kicked down the studio door and carried me out screaming, banned from the airways for life. Then I'd have to change my name to get a job. Maybe I'd call myself John-David like the great running back from Texas A&M. That would be a cool radio handle.

Dvorak was finally ending his symphony from the New World Fourth Movement. I turned on the microphone and called up my best deep classical announcer's voice.

"You're listening to Evening Concert on KPPC-FM in Pasadena, California, 106.7 on your FM dial. And now Wolfgang Amadeus Mozart."

Wolfgang Amadeus, now there's a great deejay name. Well, old Amadeus wasn't too bad. Some of his melodies I could recognize. But nobody could write like Jerry Goffin and Carole King.

Pasadena
May 1963

*"Little Jackie Paper
Loved that Rascal Puff,
And brought him strings
And sealing wax
And other fancy stuff."*

"Puff The Magic Dragon," Peter, Paul, & Mary
(Peter Yarrow & Leonard Lipton, Pepamar Music Corp-ASCAP)

Kate was singing to the seven-pound bundle that she held in her arms in the back seat of Charles Laquidara's 1938 Dodge. Driving home from Huntington Hospital, Charles and I were in the front seat, high with excitement. After nine months of waiting, John-David was here. We parked in the alley by the stage door of the Playhouse and went inside to show him off. "Panice and Son" was the song from the musical *Fannie*, currently being performed by some of the students. A big banner across the lobby of the Playhouse proclaimed "Dave Pierce and Son."

Two days later we christened John-David on a Sunday morning. That afternoon the Pasadena Playhouse commencement exercise was held. I received a degree in Theatre Arts, graduating *cum laude*. Jim Reader and Ed Kearney were *magna cum laude*. Charles was just happy to graduate. At the party later, Smokey lamented the loss of his 2-S student deferment. He figured he would probably join the National Guard. Charles wondered if he could fake a bad back if he were drafted. Danny Truhitte said he would fight if called. I was smiling inside. I knew that I'd just segued from a 2-S to a 3-A deferment. As a father, I would not be called to fight foreign wars on foreign soil.

With Hank Capps as Jesse James and Charlie Ford.

The cast of *Golden Goose*.

San Fernando Valley
Los Angeles, California
July 1963

"They all tell me,
Sing to him, swing with him,
And just do anything for him,
And tell him he's the one."

"Easier Said Than Done," The Essex
(Larry Huff and William Linton, EMI Longitude Music)

A group named Essex was blasting on KRLA and paintbrushes were swinging at 6416 Babcock in North Hollywood. Vince Donofrio, Jim Reader, and Charles Laquidara were all lending a hand to spiff up the duplex, purchased by my parents to solve our housing needs. My sister, Rus, would live in the other half of the duplex. She and her three children had come west to escape her bad marriage.

It was good-bye to Pasadena. Although I would have to drive the thirty minutes back to KPPC to do my classical shift, everyone figured North Hollywood was closer to where it was happening in Hollywood and the studios. Jim Bachman was now off Highland, below the Hollywood Bowl. Smokey Roberds was looking at a place in Laurel Canyon. Bud Tedesco had a job at ABC. And Vince Donofrio had been living in Hollywood ever since he got kicked out of the Playhouse the year before due to lack of respect for the Playhouse's official rules.

We all took a break for lunch, laying down our paintbrushes. Rus and Kate served foot-long hot dogs like the ones we always had at Dodger Stadium.

"Come here, David," Charles Laquidara was saying. "I want you to hear this."

The stereo was the first thing we had set up and the record collection was standing by in cardboard boxes. Charles was slipping a well-cared-for album out of the sleeve and onto the turntable.

"I listened to your classical show the other night, and it was dull, boring, nowheresville. You were playing Liszt, Bach, Sibelius, and Haydn, but you're leaving out all the good stuff," Charles continued.

"Hey, I never claimed to know classical music, but I'm starting to recognize a few titles. And I can pronounce most of the names. That piece sounds pretty good. What is it?"

"'Bolero,' David. Remember it. It's a fantastic piece by Ravel. You can play it as much as you want. Here's another one I want you to remember. 'Sabre Dance' by Kachaturian. Why don't you slide in some Gershwin, like 'Rhapsody in Blue,' or 'An American in Paris,' even Strauss' 'Blue Danube.'"

"I don't think KPPC has any Gershwin."

"So what, take my copy. It won't be the first time you sneak a record into a radio station," challenged Laquidara.

Now that was different, stretching a classical format might be real fun.

"Say, why don't you come down and do my shift with me," I said to Charles, "You could learn the board and engineer for me."

"Yeah, I could do that. We could ride together, too, if I lived nearby. You see, David, I'm not staying in Pasadena with all you guys moving toward Hollywood. I can get a job delivering pizza for Arnie's just around the corner."

"How are you gonna deliver pizza on a motorbike?"

"It can happen," he replied, "I'll have a bracket welded to the handlebars. I've already got that worked out. All I need is a place to stay."

"Well, there ought to be something in the neighborhood."

"How about with you guys? Look-it, you got a two-bedroomer here. John-David's only two months old. He and I could be roommates. Neither one of us would take much room. We'd both stay out of the way."

I paused for only a couple of seconds before replying, "Hey, I like it, but we gotta sell the idea to Kate."

"No problem. I'm Italian, she's Italian. I'll appeal to her sense of ethnic duty."

Vince Donofrio yelled from the kitchen, "Hey, Charlie, turn off that classical crap and get back on this paintbrush."

On KRLA Wink Martindale introduced the new number one song by Rolf Harris.

"Mind me platypus duck, Bill
And don't let him go running amok
...So we tanned his hide when he died, Clyde
And that's it hangin' on the shed!!"

"Tie Me Kangaroo Down, Sport," Rolf Harris
(Rolf Harris, Beechwood Music Corp.)

1963

♦ The Essex were five marines stationed at Camp LeJeune who recruited lead singer Anita Humes, who was the soul behind the sound in "Easier Said Than Done." They thought it was the "B" side and recorded it in less than 5 minutes. The Essex always appeared in full military dress.

"The Detroit Kid," Vincent Donofrio.

*"A young man rode
with his head held high,
Under the Texas sun."*

"In The Summer Of His Years,"
(Herbert Kretzmer and David Lee, Universal MCA Music Publishing)

"Hello, David, my name is Walter Reese. I have a film company called Rainbow Pictures with a studio in Coral Gables, Florida, and a contract with the Air Force to shoot a recruiting film at Lackland Air Force Base here in San Antonio. Your friend in Dallas, Ron Adkins, says you're the actor I need to play the recruit. We start shooting tomorrow morning. I'll expect to see you in Texas."

This was it, this could be the break I needed to get some film experience. In six hours Kate and I had all the bases covered. Charles would take my classical shift at KPPC. At midnight I flew out of LAX to San Antonio. By 7:00 a.m., I was having breakfast with Walter Reese a mile from Lackland at the Casa Mañana Motel where the film crew had set up headquarters. I looked the part, with one exception. The hair would have to go. Shaved down to GI length, with boot camp fatigues, I looked military. It bothered me a bit that this film was designed to entice eighteen-year olds to join the Air Force, something I would never do in real life.

"It's just an acting job," I kept saying. "I don't have to believe in it."

We shot for twenty-one days. I was getting a first-hand look at putting a film together and a real close-up of military life. Lots of structure, lots of discipline. No room for anything out of the norm. I was glad I was only acting.

The first ten days and nights got pretty lonely until Kate and John-David joined me at the Casa Mañana. Then the evenings brightened with Steve Allen on the tube and six-month-old "gah gahs" from my son in the portable crib.

"A shot rang out like a Southern shout."
(Ibid.)

There were only four days left to shoot, on Thursday, November 21, when President Kennedy flew into San Antonio to visit the Brooks Military Medical Facility. We watched it all on the evening news with the close-ups of the longish-haired young man with the beautiful wife. I slept badly that night as John-David whined. Kate thought she smelled gas from the kitchenette. The next morning I was exhausted and stumbled through my lines on the set at the radar shack. After lunch, while the crew was collecting footage of a military parade, I fell asleep in the director's car. As the band marched and played, I had fitful dreams. At 1:15 p.m. Walter Reese shook me awake with the words that burned into my consciousness.

"They killed him. They shot the president in Dallas."

"For a man shot down in a Texas town."
(Ibid.)

The longest weekend in history followed. The military panicked and Lackland was sealed tight. The film was on hold. The pall that gripped the world somehow seemed heaviest in that tiny motel room in San Antone. The black and white TV screen flickered out the images: LBJ swearing in, the flight back to D.C., Lee Harvey Oswald protesting his innocence, Jack Ruby in the basement of the Dallas jail blasting away the answers forever, the rider-less horse with the boot turned backward...the little kid's salute. The promise of JFK and Camelot was gone. The sixties had begun. In his corner of the world, John-David was spared the grief. He bounced in his crib and laughed. Somewhere in the next room, Peter, Paul, and Mary were on the radio, singing the words of a Minnesota songwriter.

"Yes, 'n' how many times
can a man turn his head
Pretending he just doesn't see?"

"Blowin' In The Wind," Peter, Paul, & Mary
(Bob Dylan, Special Rider Music)

East Texas
November 27, 1963

Trini Lopez hammered out his two-month-old hit on the Waco, Texas, radio station. The clock in the Cadillac said midnight. The highway sign read "Dallas, 100 miles." The speedometer needle was steady at eighty-five. John-David was snoozing between us on the front seat. We'd taken diet pills and our thoughts and conversation raced by faster than the darkened Texas landscape. Since November 22ⁿᵈ, Charles had gone into severe depression. Kate and I were worried about him.

As soon as we wrapped shooting at Lackland, Kate and I packed it up and sped out of San Antone, eager to put the Casa Mañana motel room behind us. We drove into Dallas at 2:15 a.m., and over to Ron Adkins' house. We talked till dawn, and then drove straight to Dealy Plaza.

We looked for the spot where the motorcade was hit. Ron showed us the Texas School Book Depository. He pointed out the grassy knoll and repeated the story floating around Dallas about other gunmen. That night we went into Jack Ruby's club and sat at the bar where Oswald had been seen.

The next week I'd be flying to Miami to finish the film at the University of Miami. I figured it was a matter of convenience for Rainbow Pictures located next door in Coral Cables. What I didn't know was the Army always shot their films there, and the University of Miami was headquarters for the Black Operatives, the largest domestic CIA station. Annual budget one hundred million dollars.

1963

♦ "Walk Right In" was one of the first pop-folk songs recorded with a twelve string guitar

---

Hollywood
January 1964

*"Yeah, you've got that something,
I think you'll understand."*

"I Want To Hold Your Hand," The Beatles
(John Lennon and Paul McCartney, Songs of Universal Inc.)

Grelun Landon pulled the Beatles' smash off the record player and sat, mesmerized for a moment. Smokey and I were sitting across from Grelun's desk in the RCA Records building in Hollywood.

"Phenomenal," Grelun kept repeating, "phenomenal."

At forty, Grelun had the graying temples to match his name, and an uncanny ability to talk a lot without giving you a clear cut picture of where he stood. We weren't exactly sure of what his position was at RCA, but he seemed to have contacts in talent development and was some kind of liaison between the record company and Colonel Tom Parker. At twenty-two years old, Smokey and I could use a guru in the music business. Grelun was it.

"You hear the high voice. Which one is the high voice?" Grelun asked.

Grelun couldn't get over the Beatles. Not only were the British Rockers the biggest thing since Elvis, but their success was revitalizing the whole record industry. Everybody smelled big dollars. Grelun began issuing orders.

"Smokey, you go by the Acuff-Rose Publishing office on Selma. Ask the secretary for the demo records for Jimmy Econimedes. He's producing a session for a new girl singer next week. Get over to Capitol Records, you put the demo in his hand, and make sure he hears it."

"What do I say to him?" Smokey asked.

"Tell him this is the hottest new song you've heard in a year. It's a definite smash. It's just right for his girl."

"Do I tell him anything else?"

"Play it by ear," was Grelun's standard reply.

Then looking at me he said, "Come on, Pierce, we're going to see the Colonel."

The ride over to Paramount was punctuated by Grelun button pushing his radio between KRLA, KHJ, and KFWB. It was important to know what they were playing. These Top 40 AM stations were the hit makers, and the Beatles were all over the three rockers. "*She* Loves You," "Please Please Me," "Can't Buy Me Love" were all getting heavy play and on their way to the top.

"You hear that high note? Which one's the high voice?" Grelun asked.

As we walked up to the receptionist seated in front of the Elvis poster, I asked why we were coming to see the Colonel.

"P.R.," was Grelun's reply.

The Colonel's office at Paramount was one large room overflowing with Elvis paraphernalia. Posters of Elvis' movies covered every inch of wall space. Stacks of Elvis records and sheet music, Elvis T-shirts, boxes of Elvis combs and pencil sets. Colonel Tom Parker was Elvis Presley's manager and reputed to own 50 percent of Elvis, making him one of the richest men in the country. He appeared to be around fifty, a somewhat rotund little man with a friendly face. He and Grelun talked in what seemed like circles. I gathered Elvis wasn't happy with his movie roles. Maybe we'd all have to go down to Long Beach in a couple weeks when Elvis would be giving away a yacht. On the way out, the Colonel reached into a crate full of apples with Elvis' picture pasted to it. He tossed an apple over, saying, "Here, kid, have a souvenir."

So this was P.R. We drove out the Paramount gate. When Grelun punched up KHJ, I realized no one had mentioned the Beatles.

"Close your eyes and I'll kiss you,
Tomorrow I'll miss you."

"All My Loving," The Beatles
(John Lennon and Paul McCartney, Sony/ATV Tunes LLC/Beatles)

1964

♦ "I Want to Hold Your Hand" was the first Beatles record to be made using 4-track equipment.

Christmas card from Elvis and his manager "Colonel" Tom Parker.

Hollywood
February 1964

Grelun Landon and I were at an ABC Studio rehearsal hall watching an English director put several country and western artists through their paces for a new show called *Shin-Dig*. What an Englishman was doing working on a country and western show seemed like a good question, but I never asked it. I didn't figure I'd understand Grelun's answer anyway.

Johnny Cash was over in one corner of the studio pacing nervously. Grelun edged over and I followed. Johnny greeted us. I shook his hand and he looked through me like I wasn't there. His eyes were empty. Nobody was home.

The loud music from the band on stage made it impossible to pick up on their conversation, so I watched the rehearsal.

After a couple of minutes Grelun spoke, "Come on, we're going back to the office."

I was about to do a "Nice meeting you" to Johnny Cash when I realized he was coming too. The six-block ride back to Grelun's office must have seemed like six miles to Johnny. Sitting behind him, I could see him twisting and turning in his seat, fidgeting, wiping his brow, and rubbing his hands together.

As soon as we got to the office, Grelun headed straight for his desk, pulled out a vial of pills, and handed Johnny Cash a cup of water. Johnny slapped a handful of pills in his mouth, gulped the water, and pocketed the rest of the vial.

"Yeah, thanks man," was all he said.

We all drove back to ABC and dropped Johnny Cash at the front door. His steps were springy. He was wired real tight.

As we drove away, Grelun said, "He's a good boy. He's just got a problem."

Back at Grelun's office I picked up my new T-bird, put the top down, and turned onto Sunset heading toward Beverly Hills. I was flipping the radio through the country and western stations, trying to catch a Johnny Cash song.

Hollywood
March 1964

"She could not leave the number,
But I know who placed the call."

"Memphis Tennessee," Johnny Rivers
(Chuck Berry, ARC Music Corp., Isalee Music Publishing Co.)

Smokey Roberds, Charles Laquidara, and I walked into the Whiskey-A-Go-Go on Sunset Strip. The crowd was elbow to elbow with little room to move about. The Whiskey would become the next hot club on the strip, but for now it was still the "in spot" for musicians and record company people to hang out. The main feature was quickly obvious. Hanging from the ceiling was a cage, slightly to the side of the bandstand, about ten feet above the dancing crowd. In it, one of several beautiful go-go girls, who worked out nightly, boogied to the rock beat. She was showing plenty of T and A through her skimpy costume. Naturally she wore go-go boots.

On the bandstand the boy from Baton Rouge, Louisiana, was breaking a sweat as he finished up "Memphis."

"That's our arrangement of the old Chuck Berry song," Johnny Rivers was breathing heavily into the microphone. "We hope to cut that one in our next recording session. Glad you like it."

"Like it? They love it!" Smokey said, as we worked our way through the crowd. "It's gonna be a got damn smash!"

Smokey had spotted Al Schmidt up on the balcony. So we climbed the stairs as Johnny Rivers cranked up the group into another rocker. The proximity to the go-go girl was maddening. When we sat down with Al Schmidt, Laquidara's total attention was riveted on the cage. Above the roar of the crowd and the music, Smokey quizzed Al about upcoming recording sessions. Our job was to place tunes with record producers and this was one of the ways you got it done. Al Schmidt would soon be producing Jefferson Airplane and he was already a comer. The music business was fast paced and a ton of fun. Smokey was writing songs and looking down the road at recording. I didn't have the same motivation. I wanted to be on the delivery end, slapping the finished product on the turntable and putting the needle in the groove. On this day, Charles Laquidara's ambition did not get past the go-go cage at the Whiskey.

"She's the only one
who'd call me here,
From Memphis, Tennessee."
(Ibid.)

"Baby take off your coat (real slow)
...Come over here, stand on that chair,
...They don't know what love is."

"Leave Your Hat On," Randy Newman
(Randy Newman, WB Music Corp.)

"Aren't you an actor?" Grelun Landon asked, knowing I would come out of my chair with excitement, "How would you like to be in a show at Melodyland?"

"Of course," I answered, "...where's Melodyland?"

"Anaheim, Orange County, next to Disneyland. Small part," Grelun tempered my enthusiasm, "but you'll earn a credit for your resumé."

"Right! What do I have to do?"

"Show up at this office on Fountain near LaBrea this afternoon at three. I understand Jerry Van Dyke is the star," Grelun said offhandedly, like it was no big deal.

"Oh, wow!" I thought, "Dick Van Dyke is the hottest comedian in show biz and I'll be playing with his brother Jerry. What a break! This could lead to something."

"Do I get paid?" I asked.

Grelun looked at me and smiled. "Play it by ear," he said.

The small audition office was crowded by a dozen young actors in their early twenties. We were all antsy trying to look cool and confident, but churning inside. The casting director, only slightly older than the actors, came out, looked us over, and pointed at six of us. The others were excused.

"All right you guys, here's the deal," the casting director said. "It's ten days rehearsal and a three week run. You'll all play soldiers in Jerry Van Dyke's platoon. Some of you may get a couple of lines, the director will decide. The pay is fifty dollars a week, enough to buy gas. Miss a rehearsal, you'll be cut from the show. You start tomorrow at 1:00 p.m. at Melodyland. Everyone in?"

The six of us all nodded. Then we all looked at each other as the casting director moved to the telephone for other more important business.

One of the actors was well built, good looking, dark haired, self assured, the qualities of a potential leading man.

"Anybody live in the valley?" he asked.

"I'm in North Hollywood," I said. "Hi, I'm Dave Pierce."

"Clint Ritchie," he said. "I'm off Ventura Boulevard, we should car pool. I can't afford gas. I got to eat on that fifty bucks."

Melodyland was huge with hundreds of seats surrounding the stage in the center. Jerry Van Dyke entered down one of the aisles, and worked the stage, trying to remember the lines he was supposed to have down cold by opening rehearsal. Jerry would be re-creating, for the stage, the film role that made Andy Griffith famous. I had never played in the round, with the audience totally surrounding the stage, and never in front of this many people. My small scene as a radio operator, counting down the big blast, was staged in the middle of one section of the audience.

The director was off the payroll after the final dress rehearsal. He said a few words of farewell and told us to break a leg.

No Time for Sergeants opened to a full house. Every night after the show, we'd party with the cast in Anaheim, then Clint and I would take the midnight ride up the Santa Anna freeway. The next night we'd do it all over again, one day driving in my new '64 Ford T-Bird convertible, the next day in his barely running old Ford convertible with the threadbare top. We got to know each other pretty well. Currently working in a garage as a go-fer, Clint Ritchie was determined to succeed as an actor. We both knew he had all the tools, including the most important one, he wanted it real bad. Clint was also very friendly and outgoing, a buddy with all the guys and flirting with the several girls in the cast and crew. One of the girls was a statuesque blonde whose only physical defect was her left eye, which seemed to wander when she looked at you. Otherwise she was perfect, and friendly. One midnight, when the after show party broke up in Anaheim, she slid in between Clint and me in the front seat of his old Ford and we headed north towards Hollywood. After a few minutes, our blonde friend had her head on Clint's shoulder and her hands in his jeans. I tried to stare straight ahead at the light freeway traffic. As we approached the downtown interchange, Clint whispered something in her ear. She turned to me, smiled, and reached for my belt buckle. The Capitol Records Tower was a blur as we sped by. Inside the ragged top convertible her long hair was all over my bare skin.

"You've never seen my pad," Clint said, driving right past my North Hollywood exit.

We took the Van Nuys off ramp, crossed Ventura Boulevard and drove a few blocks up into the hills. Clint's apartment was unbelievably tiny; a kitchenette, bath, sofa. We all three climbed the ladder to a loft big enough for a king-size mattress.

So this was the sex of the '60s. No fear, no long-term commitment, no guilt, no jealousy. Just doing what came naturally. Exercising your fundamental right as a human being. Following the program of your genes. Sexual adventure became the juice of life for the rest of the decade. Every generation has its own variation on the timeless art of relationships. For us in the '60s, in California, we thought we were inventing it for the first time. Perhaps it was only taking self-indulgence to a new low, or high, depending on how you looked at it, but Clint Ritchie and I were definitely on to a different kind of male bonding. Sharing a girl surely beat trading war stories.

When *No Time for Sergeants* closed, Jerry Van Dyke went on to a lack luster career, before finally landing the best role of his life on *Coach*. Clint and I stayed in touch for a while, his career creeping along. When George C. Scott came upon the death and devastation of a tank battleground in the movie *Patton*, and spoke the line, "God forgive me, but I do love it," the young wounded and dazed Captain up on the big screen with him was Clint Ritchie. Clint showed up in several films including the Western *Joe Kidd* with Eastwood, Duvall, and John Saxon.

For years I lost track. I couldn't believe that this guy hadn't been able to make it as an actor. Not being a fan of daytime television, I didn't realize that Clint Ritchie was in fact living his dream as a Buchanan on the soap opera *One Life to Live*.

*"Come over here, stand on that chair,
...They don't know what love is."
(Ibid.)*

North Hollywood
Memorial Day, 1964

"Please lock me away
And don't allow the day."

"A World Without Love," Peter and Gordon
(John Lennon and Paul McCarthy, Sony/ATV Tunes LLC)

Smokey Roberds was strumming his lyric harp and singing the Peter and Gordon song, which was already headed for the Top 10. We were all sitting around the patio at 6416 Babcock in North Hollywood. Kate and Rus were handling the barbecue pit. The guys were doing our cave man thing.

"Know who wrote that song?" I asked, already knowing the answer, since I'd heard Casey Kasem announce it last week on KRLA.

Danny Truhitte thought a minute. "Gee, I don't know."

"Come on, David, who cares. What is this, twenty questions?" Charles Laquidara complained, bouncing twelve-month-old John-David on his knee. Then he asked about the only question on his mind.

"Hey, Kate, when's that barbecue going to be ready?"

Vince Donofrio was playing tag with Rus' three kids. He didn't miss this opportunity to blast Laquidara. It was one of his favorite things to do.

"It's John Lennon and Paul McCartney," Vince yelled. "You're really out of touch, Charlie. In fact, sometimes you're really not cool, you know it."

Vince said our barbecues were bourgeois middle class suburbia. Kate said he could split any time it got too bourgeois for him. He always stayed.

Smokey continued to strum his lyric harp. He had just returned from several weeks of training, after joining the National Guard to escape the draft, but now he seemed highly programmed and had trouble relating to the rest of the group. His daily goal was to put a top-quality spit shine on all his shoes.

After awhile, Smokey had begun to get back to his music, but his bout with boot camp had put all of us closer to military life. Danny had just joined the Marine National Guard. Unlike Smokey, he really would have liked to go full-time, but his agent had convinced Danny he could get him a film deal if he stayed in town. Observing their reactions to the military indoctrination, I was piecing it together with what I had seen as an actor at Lackland in the Air Force recruiting film.

Back home in Louisiana, my dad was undergoing shock treatments. Casey had a nervous breakdown, seemingly for no reason. His life should've been going fine, but he stayed depressed and had nightmares. Mom had to seek treatment for him in a New Orleans hospital. Tying him down and turning on the juice was the standard treatment. I thought about the bullet hole and the six-inch long scar, and the gold heart with the purple ribbon. I wondered if there was a connection. I looked at John-David and thanked him for the 3-A deferment.

It was dark by the time Rus and Kate served up the barbecue. We wolfed it down. The party moved indoors and the television news showed some of the holiday's events, including memorial services from around the country.

Danny was visibly moved.

"I'd be ready to die for my country," he blurted out.

Vince was on him immediately.

"What are you, Danny? You some kind of nut or something? Die for your country? What's that supposed to mean?"

"It means he's not afraid to stand up and fight for his freedom," Smokey said, reaching for his lyric harp.

"Well, I'm not afraid, either," Charles piped in. "I'm not afraid to tell you I'm scared shitless! Whatever I got to do to get out of the draft, I'm gonna do it. I'll act queer if I have to!"

"You're already queer, Charlie," Danny was getting worked up. "You're some kind of fag commie, and you don't deserve to live in America. Why don't you move to Russia?"

"Why don't you move your ass outside, butthole, and I'll show you who's a fag," Charles said.

Danny sprang to his feet, flashing his dancer's poise as he moved into his karate stance.

"That's it, commie fag, on your feet!" Danny said.

Smokey quickly placed himself between Danny and Charles. Vince launched a verbal attack on Charles.

"That's really smart, Charlie. Can't you see Danny's been brainwashed. You're gonna get killed confronting a brainwashed zombie like that."

"You're the one who's brainwashed!" Danny screamed, ready to take the house apart.

I grabbed John-David and retreated to the kitchen, where Kate was cleaning up from dinner. She came storming back into the living room with a look on her face that froze the action.

"What the hell is going on in here," she demanded. "This is the twentieth century, fellas. You mean to tell me y'all can't have a conversation without trying to kill each other."

The boys looked around sheepishly; then Charles began to apologize. "Aw, it was nothing. I'm the butthole, ok. Sorry, Danny, I didn't mean anything."

He stuck out his hand. Danny would take longer to cool off, but he shook Laquidara's hand and went into the kitchen. After a moment, Vince began talking.

"You know, what we've just witnessed here is what's happening to this country. We're all running around spouting slogans and calling each other names and nobody's really listening to anybody else."

Smokey was strumming the lyric harp again and spoke up, "We've gotta have people willing to fight if we're going to contain communism. You guys don't know what's going on in Vietnam. We saw some film in boot camp. You wouldn't believe what the Vietcong are doing. America better wake up."

"What about what we're doing in Vietnam? What are we doing over there anyway?" Kate said; ready to mix it up now.

"And you know so much about Vietnam?" Vince asked.

"I know somebody who does," Kate blasted back. "My world history instructor at Valley State just got back from a year in Nam. The army is spending millions of dollars burning the jungle. As fast as they burn it, it grows up again. It's like trying to keep the grass mowed in Louisiana. While you're mowing the back yard, the front yard grows up to your crotch. Now they're starting to use chemicals. What's that going to do to the environment?"

I came in from the kitchen. Danny followed, carrying John-David on his shoulders.

"Hey, Charles," I said, changing the subject, "Mort Sahl is on at ten o'clock."

"Have you guys seen what Mort Sahl is doing?" Charles said. "He wants to reopen the investigation of the Kennedy assassination. He's got proof it was a conspiracy."

Danny dropped to the floor and lifted John-David off his shoulders.

"Listen everybody," Danny was smiling, "John-David says he wants to apologize for acting like a one-year-old just now. And if you all give him a chance, he'll try to grow up."

Smokey strummed his lyric harp and sang Lennon and McCartney.

"I don't care what they say,
I won't stay in a world without love."
(Ibid.)

1964

♦ "World Without Love" was the biggest hit written by John Lennon and Paul McCartney that was not released by the Beatles. McCartney went out with actress Jane Asher, which is how he met her brother, singer Peter Asher, of the duo Peter and Gordon. Peter Asher later managed James Taylor and Linda Ronstadt.

North Hollywood
July 1964

*"My boy, lollipop,
You make my heart go giddy up."*

"My Boy, Lollipop," Millie Small
(Morris Levy, Johnnie B. Roberts, Robert Spencer, EMI Longitude Music)

Kate was singing to John-David as he walked in circles around the living room floor. She was five months pregnant and starting to show. The new baby would have to be a little brother for John-David and was already referred to as Bruh. I was on the phone with Ken Rose, planning the next Cellar Theatre production. Ken had directed all of us at the Pasadena Playhouse. He was a very intense guy. We called him a mad genius. He was also from Lake Charles, Louisiana. Ken had opened the Cellar Theatre, a little Workshop Theatre on Cahuenga in Hollywood, in the basement of a six-story slum hotel called The Padre. Under Ken's direction, the Cellar was already getting a reputation for good work when Charles, Smokey, Bud Tedesco, and I joined the group. We were thinking about doing Gorky's *Lower Depths*, a Russian drama, boring as hell, but I had a shot at the lead. Smokey and I had gotten good reviews from the *Hollywood Reporter* for the previous show *Tiger at the Gates*. If you kept working at it in Hollywood, sooner or later, you'd be seen by the right people, or you'd luck into the right contact. True or not, that was the theory all beginning actors operate on. I was back on the air. In a state of shock over the Kennedy assassination, Charles had blown our classical job at KPPC while I was down in Miami last December. Charles had sneaked in a copy of *Camelot* and played it six days in a row before the complaints surfaced. The PD reminded Laquidara it was an FM station and therefore strictly a classical format. Then he gave him the boot.

Six months later, however, the church fathers were convinced they could bring more money into the church coffers by switching KPPC to a conservative pop format. My actor friend, Mike Stroka, sold the church on his general manager ability and I got the call for the 6:00 a.m. to 12:00 noon shift. I was behind the mic again, at 106.7.

A few days earlier, Bonnie Helmuth called me looking for a dancer to audition with her for a big movie that was coming up at Twentieth Century Fox. I called Danny Truhitte. Since the interview, Danny had missed his daily afternoon visits, so there had been no news. I figured something must be cooking. Around 2:00 p.m., just as we had John-David packed up for the beach, Danny burst through the door. His sandy brown hair had been bleached blond and his ear-to-ear grin told the story. He had gotten his break. He was signed to play the young Nazi soldier in *The Sound of Music*. We all piled into my '64 T-Bird convertible and drove out into the San Fernando Valley, then over the hill through Topanga Canyon to the beach at Malibu. Danny was talking nonstop. He had gone through several auditions, met the director, been screen tested, and walked off with the male juvenile lead.

Besides several excellent dramatic scenes, he would dance and sing Rogers and Hammerstein's "Sixteen, Going on Seventeen," with the film's

Ingénue. They were talking with the studio about a seven-year contract and he would leave in three days to shoot on location in Austria.

At the beach, we stretched out on blankets and watched the Pacific roll in. Kate warmed John-David's bottle in the sand, while Danny tried to show John-David the principles of building a sandcastle. We were all overwhelmed with joy by Danny's good fortune. Only three years in this town, and one of us had scored big. We just knew we all would. This show biz is a piece of cake.

"Under the boardwalk, down by the sea,
On a blanket with my baby, that's where I'll be."

"Under The Boardwalk," The Drifters
(Arthur Resnick and Kenny Young, Alley Music Corp., Trio Music Co., Inc.)

1964

♦ Little Millie Small was seventeen when producer Chris Blackwell brought her to England to record "My Boy Lollipop." Rod Stewart played harmonica on the session. The song helped develop the musical styles of Reggae and Ska. Blackwell later discovered and worked with Bob Marley.

Kate and "Bambino," John-David Pierce, 1963.

North Hollywood
October 1964

The clock alarm went off pulling me out of dreamland and putting on Wink Martindale's morning show from KRLA and Gale Garnett's hit song in my bedroom. It was Saturday. I had a rare day off from KPPC and had slept past the regular 4:30 a.m. wakeup time all the way up toward ten o'clock. I lay there for a minute recounting the last few days. Kate was still in the hospital recovering from the two-month premature delivery of baby Michelle. So John-David's little Bruh had turned out to be a girl. A tiny one. At only four pounds she would be in an incubator at least six weeks before she came home. Without Kate around, it was like a college boy's dorm. Smokey and Charles had been staying over, often coming in at dawn after chasing all night in Hollywood. They had been a help with John-David, Charles changing his diaper occasionally, and Smokey singing and playing the guitar for him. At seventeen months, John-David was "talking" a blue streak and was all over the house. I had attached a restraining accordion gate to his bedroom door. The result was he would trash his room if you didn't get to him as soon as he woke up.

Realizing it was about that time, I turned Wink's volume down. That's when I heard the sloshing from the bathroom. Moving quickly through the hall, I glanced into the other bedroom. Smokey and Charles were both out cold, their mouths wide open with slightly audible snores.

The room was trashed all right. Drawers pulled out, and clothes strewn about. Charles' arm hung to the floor, a diaper lay across it. John-David must have figured it was diaper changing time. Toys were scattered, and his little chair was pulled up next to the locked accordion gate. He'd made an escape. I reached the bathroom where the sloshing sounds were. There was John-David with an ear-to-ear grin, both hands in the toilet bowl. What could I say? I cleaned him up a bit, unlocked the obsolete gate, and changed the sagging diaper. Carrying John-David under one arm like a sack of potatoes, we headed for the front yard. I turned him loose to toddle around and harass the snails that collected in the flower-beds. Picking up the *Los Angeles Times* from the sidewalk, I positioned my lounge chair to greet the late morning sun and leaned back, October being as good as August for getting a year-round California tan.

L.A. Times had it all: a write-up on the Warren Commission's report that was only a few weeks old and drawing heavy controversy. Led by La-quidara's nearly obsessed belief in a Kennedy assassination conspiracy, we debated, almost nightly, the pros and cons with Vince and the gang.

The bottom of the front page read: "Cole Porter Dies." I played his songs often on KPPC. Sinatra, Ella Fitzgerald, they all sang 'em. Plus there were hundreds of big band and jazz instrumental arrangements. He had written a bunch. You could play Cole Porter anytime.

*"I get no kick from cocaine,
...Mere alcohol doesn't move me at all,*

"I Get a Kick Out Of You," Frank Sinatra
(Cole Porter, Warner Brothers, Inc.)

John-David looked up from his dirt pile play area as I sang aloud and flipped through the *Times*. Comedian Lenny Bruce was still getting arrested for vulgarity on stage. The police were having trouble with his act. Vince said it wasn't the dirty words, it was his ideas and attitude that was really bothering them. Whatever it was, Lenny was being viewed by the law as a distasteful component of society.

Here's more on the three civil rights workers who were killed down in Mississippi. It was hard for me to identify with what was going on in the South. Whatever racial problems we had in South Louisiana, they weren't the same as in Mississippi and Alabama. There just wasn't that much hatred in the Bayou Country. Perhaps some of the older Cajuns remembered being second class citizens themselves. Smokey and I were constantly telling Laquidara it wasn't quite that way in our hometowns. He accused us of not only being bigots, but also refusing to face the truth. Maybe he was partially right. But in Abbeville, Louisiana, and El Dorado, Arkansas, there weren't any crazy crackers burning down black homes like they were doing in Mississippi.

Flipping over to the editorial section, I found another article on Vietnam. "U.S. Says It Will Fight to Defend Asia." I wondered what that meant, exactly. I'll bet Vince Donofrio could give me an opinion about one hundred and eighty degrees from the writer in the *L.A. Times*. But then Vince was rapidly becoming a left-wing extremist. Barry Goldwater says extremism in defense of liberty is no vice. President Johnson wants to campaign on the plank against left and right extremists. Who're you gonna believe? Barry Goldwater or Vince Donofrio? Certainly not Lyndon Johnson.

"More Advisors Being Sent to Vietnam." "U.S. Planes Attacking North Vietnam Bases."

"It keeps heating up over there," I said to John-David and he grinned back at me.

I browsed through the sports section. Cassius Clay, now Muhammad Ali, says he won't be drafted. What a champ! Vince loves him. Boxing and baseball, those were a couple of things Vince still loved about America. Is that worth defending? I didn't know where I stood.

I picked up the sack-of-potatoes kid, brushing the squished snails out of his fingers. Turning John-David loose, I tuned in to Sam Riddle, who had just started his shift on KRLA, then I sat back to finish up the *Times*.

At UCLA Berkeley, Mario Salvo was still raising hell with the Free Speech Movement. Massive political protests were being organized. "The Haight-Ashbury District Heart of the Hippie Movement. Can you dig it? Kids everywhere with long hair. I like long hair, but this is wild. The miniskirts...girls are all wearing these short, short dresses. In no time at all, they'll be all over Los Angeles." I folded up the *Times*, turned up KRLA, and leaned back in the October sun. Sam Riddle, sounding about seventeen years old, introduced the number one song, and Roy

Orbison's magnificent and unique voice flowed over my corner of North Hollywood.

"I don't believe you, you're not the truth
No one could look as good as you."

"Oh Pretty Woman," Roy Orbison
(Roy Orbison and Bill Dees, Barbara Orbinson Music Co., Orbi Lee
Publishing, R. Key Darkus Publishing, Sony/ATV Acuff Rose Music)

1964

♦ Recorded for Monument Records in Nashville, "Pretty Woman" sold
more records in its first ten days in release than any other 45rpm
single in history.

John-David in the toilet bowl, October 1964.

"Her voice was soft and cool
Her eyes were clear and bright."

"She's Not There," The Zombies
(Rod Argent, Parker Music)

It was three o'clock in the afternoon. I'd worked my 6:00 a.m. to 12:00 noon shift at KPPC-FM and caught up on a couple of hours of sleep. Kate and I were walking out to go vote when Charles Laquidara drove up in a brand new convertible Volkswagen with the Zombies cranked up real loud on the radio. Charles had been very down. He'd tried to join the L.A.P.D., hoping that being a policeman would give him a draft deferment. He blew past the academics, the rigorous physical test, and the obstacle course. But he flunked the psychological profile. Charles just didn't have the killer instinct to be a cop. As the time to report for his draft physical got closer, he developed the idea of faking a bad back. He bought a back brace, but it looked brand new. In an attempt to age it, he had Kate wash it a dozen times. He picked at the threads to make it look ragged. In a last desperate attempt, he laid the back brace out on the driveway, and with John-David beside him on the front seat he drove the car back and forth over the brace for twenty minutes. He slept with it several nights to make marks on his skin. Then finally, this morning he had reported to the draft board. To his amazement, they said he really did have a back problem and would have a lot of pain in the future. That was the future. Today he was a free man and he ran out to celebrate, buying a new car.

That night Charles brought over Dr. Howard Richardson, author of a play called *Dark of the Moon* in which Charles had starred as Witch-Boy, the lead role. We talked theatre, then politics, watching Lyndon Johnson beat up on Barry Goldwater in a landslide. In New York, Robert F. Kennedy won his first election to a Senate post. Our immediate speculation was on the possible return of Camelot.

"Well no one told me about her,
The way she lied..."
(Ibid.)

Hollywood
December 1964

"Today while the blossoms still cling to the vine."

"Today," The New Christy Minstrels
(Randy Sparks, EMI Miller Catalog)

Nick Woods was singing lead onstage at the Troubadour. He was backed by two girls on tambourine and six other musicians, playing a variety of acoustic six and twelve-string guitars, mandolins and banjos. Randy Sparks' New Christy Minstrels were hot. A friend of Smokey's, Barry McGuire, had earned a spot in the group, and we had come down to see them. Nick Woods was knocking me out. It had been a great week. I'd received a call from MGM two nights earlier saying I had a day's work on *Dr. Kildare*. Only two lines, only minimum pay, but it was the easiest, most exciting hundred bucks I'd ever earned. Richard Chamberlain was courteous and professional. Meeting the guest star, Ed Begley, Sr., was a rare treat. Watching them work was a high. I'd met director Herschel Daughtery a few weeks earlier. He said he'd use me. His word was good. I now had my Screen Actors Guild card. It was a giant step. That's the way it works in Hollywood.

Friends were doing well. Danny Truhitte was driving a new GTO with some of his *Sound of Music* money. One of our classmates from Pasadena, Chris Conley, had a running part on *Peyton Place*, the new twice-a-week TV series based on the movie. Charles Laquidara and I had been to visit Chris on the *Peyton Place* set and met his co-stars, Ryan O'Neal and Mia Farrow.

At KPPC, General Manager Mike Stroka was working on *King Rat*, starring George Segal. Which meant no one was leading the station in any particular direction. We were just playing records. I knew all the standard big-band songs and every show tune. I liked the music, but it wasn't rock 'n roll. That's what I really wanted to be playing. Listening to the big Top 40 jocks in L.A., I began to wonder if I ever would get to be a rock jock. These guys were good, fast and witty, always sounding bright and happy. And cool. Like B. Mitchell Reed "the fastest tongue in the west." Big market sound. Could I do that? Did I still want to do that? Maybe I was too laid back, more like Casey Kasem. Filled with music biz info, I was already going in that direction, playing movie themes and show tunes, talking about who was in the movie, who directed it, and who wrote the song.

Maybe all I really wanted to do was act. The Cellar Theatre was going well. Ken Rose's brilliant direction was bringing out the best in his performers. We were all students of method acting, popularized by Brando and James Dean, but staying in character in the moment was not always a simple task. During rehearsals you could see Rose at the edge of the stage, then he'd disappear into the darkness, but he was there, maybe only a couple of feet beyond the lights. Just when you felt you had reached the depths of your character's soul, Ken would appear inches from your face.

"I been watching you," Ken would say, "and you lying to me. I can see it in your eyes."

Whipped, you started the scene again, and again, until Ken Rose said the words you craved to hear, "Good, I believed you that time."

It was all very time-consuming. I was often rehearsing until midnight, talking until one, going to bed at two, and getting up at 4:00 a.m., getting dressed while Kate fed tiny 'Chelle with an eye dropper. Then driving through Glendale to Pasadena, turning the transmitter on, putting KPPC on the air, and playing six hours of music I was only half excited about. While there was no obvious reason to be uneasy, there was an underlying unrest all about us. Not just me personally, it seemed to me the whole country was getting more uptight, certainly Los Angeles was. A couple of weeks earlier, during a Cellar rehearsal break, Bud, Charles, Smokey, and I were standing in the alley of the Padre Hotel, when a L.A.P.D. patrol car pulled in from the street. Two cops with guns drawn put us up against the wall and frisked us. We convinced them we were actors with a legitimate reason for hanging out in the Padre's alley. They claimed they were looking for robbery suspects in the neighborhood and we fit the profile. Back at home later, we had a laugh about the incident. But none of us forgot looking down the barrel of the L.A.P.D.

"Hey, brother Dave, where you at?" Smokey was asking, his glass held high for a toast.

"Right with you," I answered, raising my glass.

Tomorrow's battles belong to tomorrow. Tonight was our night...and Nick Woods'!

"I'll be a dandy, and I'll be a rover,
You'll know who I am by the song that I sing."
(Ibid.)

Tiger at the Gates with Leslie Dalton,
future Vegas "Gold Digger,"
at the Cellar Theatre.

Murray McCloud, Richard Redino, Peter Pastore,
Charles Laquidara, and Smokey Roberds at the
Cellar Theatre.

KPPC FM
Pasadena Presbyterian Church
January 1965

"I was born in Dixie in a boomer shack,
Just a little shanty by the railroad track.
Freight train whistle taught me how to cry,
Hum of the drivers was my lullaby.
I got the freight train blu-u-u-u-e-s."

"Freight Train Blues," Bob Dylan
(Jimmie Rogers, Jack Kingston, Marvin Rainwater)

The sound track from *My Fair Lady* was on the air at KPPC. On the other turntable in the audition channel was the young man from Hibbing, Minnesota, singing through his nose "The Freight Train Blues." I was leaning back in my disc jockey chair, reading the liner notes on the back of the Columbia album titled simply *Bob Dylan*. I'd heard a lot about Dylan, now I was really getting into him. The young singer-songwriter was twenty-three now, only five months older than me, and he had turned the folk world on its ear. Reading the liner notes, I learned that Dylan played harmonica like Sonny Terry.

Who was Sonny Terry? I wondered. Or Walter Jacobs, who played harmonica with Muddy Waters in Chicago. I knew about Muddy Waters. It says here that "Freight Train Blues" was adapted from a Roy Acuff disc. I figured if it was a train song, it had to go all the way back to Jimmie Rodgers. I could see Casey singing in the shade under that South Louisiana pecan tree.

"My daddy was a brakeman, and my Mammy dear,
Was the only daughter of an engineer."
(Ibid.)

Well, Dylan also listened to Jimmie Rodgers, Woody Guthrie, Jelly Roll Morton, Carl "Blue Suede Shoes" Perkins, and Elvis. No wonder Dylan sounded so good. He'd done his homework. Other names like Dave Van Ronk and Blind Lemon Jefferson were not familiar to me. There's a gold mine of information on liner notes. I wondered why disc jockeys didn't just put some of that information on the air instead of all that time and temperature stuff.

It was 10:00 a.m. I had flipped *My Fair Lady* to the second side and was listening to Bob Dylan sing Rick Von Schmidt's "Baby, Let Me Follow You Down," when General Manager Mike Stroka opened the studio door.

"Hey, Pierce," he said, "put a long record on, and come into my office. I want you to meet our new PD."

A new program director. That means one, you lose your job; two, you get a different shift; three, the format was in for a change; or any combination of the above.

Stroka's office contained several pictures of himself in various roles as an actor. He apparently had a day off from shooting *King Rat* and took this opportunity to bring in the new Program Director, Walt deSilva, a forty-year-old disc jockey who had been working at one of L.A.'s FM jazz stations. Walt was brief. There would be an evaluation of all air personnel. Some changes were probable. The air sound would be adjusted. We'd play sets of two or three records at a time. No more talk after every record or playing whole sides of show tunes. At least one song in every set would be instrumental, at least one song would be jazz oriented. That answers number three about the format change.

"Any questions?" Walt was asking in his best radio voice.

"Yeah. Will you be on the air?" I asked.

Walt hesitated and looked at Stroka.

"To show us how you want it done," I added quickly.

"We're still considering it," Stroka came back just as quickly.

So someone was going to lose his shift. Back in the control room, I checked on *My Fair Lady*. It had a few more minutes. Jazz, huh. Just when I finally knew all the movie themes and soundtracks. Jazz had always been a little foreign to my ear. Most of it was too far out. It didn't sound like music. It couldn't have that big an audience, but then I really didn't know that much about it. Why didn't we just move into a rock format, or at least folk? Two and three record sets, that sounded very interesting. Two Bob Dylan tunes back to back in a two-record set. Now that would grab some listeners. Stroka stuck his head in the door.

"Hey, you put us on the spot in the meeting. We weren't ready to let everyone know Walt will be on the air."

"Just interested," I said.

"Well, keep it to yourself, but the afternoon disc jockey is gonna be axed. Walt's got that shift. We're gonna fire the newsman and the weekend people, too. But don't worry, we want you to stay in the morning slot."

Answers to number one and number two.

"Well, thanks for letting me know, Mike. By the way, why jazz? This station doesn't stand a chance in hell in this market unless we rock. Why not be the first one in the country to play rock 'n roll on FM?"

Mike looked at me funny. I had his attention.

"We'll talk about it later," he said, making his exit. "For now, you listen to Walt deSilva."

Sure, I'll listen to Walt. I'll play jazz till my ears hurt. Someday, somebody is gonna do it right. I checked *My Fair Lady* and put Bob Dylan back on the audition channel.

"I got the freight train blu-u-u-u-e-s.
I got 'em in the bottom of my rambling shoes.
And when the whistle blows, I got to go."
(Ibid.)

1965

♦ Bob Dylan learned a great deal about harmonica playing by listening to Sonny Terry. Terry didn't play miked up electric blues but wrapped his big hands around the harp and could make it talk, sing, cry or laugh. Sonny and Brownie McGhee were the Sunshine Boys gone mad.

North Hollywood
February 1965

"But tomorrow may rain,
So I'll follow the sun."

"I'll Follow The Sun," The Beatles
(John Lennon and Paul McCartney, Sony/ATV Tunes LLC)

Ron Adkins had been back in L.A. for several weeks. His wife, from Long Beach, wanted out of Dallas. As soon as they got back to southern California, she left him. So he was hanging out at our house a lot. He'd drive up the freeway from Downey on Friday nights and we'd head up to Big Bear to snow ski on Saturday, then roll out to Zuma Beach on Sunday. Only in Los Angeles could you do that, and we Southern boys were still excited about that kind of recreational variety.

Ron was also babysitting for us often. He and John-David were big buddies. Tonight Ron brought over a stuffed monkey named Oscar. Ron had also developed a character voice for Oscar. It seemed Oscar had a fear of catching camel fever. The whole scene was driving twenty-month old John-David delirious with excitement. Oscar was real. The threat of camel fever was so real that John-David and Ron (and Oscar) were building camel traps out of chairs and sofa cushions. They were hoping to catch those camels coming out of the kitchen before they got to the living room and infected Oscar, and possibly the rest of us, with low-grade fever of the camel variety.

I was observing the fun while Kate sang a Lennon and McCartney lullaby to the tiny pink bundle named Michelle.

When the camel traps had all been set and John-David and Oscar got into their own thing, the adults started to talk radio. The jazz format had caused little excitement. A few little old Pasadena ladies had called KPPC to complain. They had liked my show tunes. They disliked the jazz as much as if it had been rock 'n roll. But actually it was too soon to evaluate the new format, and I was learning the music and the artists.

"Who gets paid the most money at a radio station?" Ron asked, leaning back against a camel trap.

"Well, the manager, of course," I answered.

"Naturally," Ron agreed, smiling his big Southern grin. "And who else?"

I was beginning to wonder where he was going with this.

"Well, probably the salesmen, except at KPPC, because they're not selling anything, but normally the salesmen do well."

"Is that right?" Ron was overly surprised. "Better than the disc jockeys?"

"Well, it depends. Top jocks in a big market do really well. Otherwise, I guess salesmen and managers carry out most of the dollars."

Ron took a dramatic pause before asking the question.

"So why aren't you selling radio instead of just playing records you don't like?"

"Because I'm a disc jockey. That's what I do. I'm not a salesman. I wouldn't know where to start."

"Nothing to it. Easiest thing in the world."

"Easy? Easy for you to say. You've sold insurance in Dallas. Now you're selling Goodyear tires and accessories to every brother in Downey. You've got the personality for it. I don't."

"I wouldn't mind selling radio," Kate jumped in. "That's damn sure where the money's at. It sure as hell ain't in playing jazz at KPPC or movie themes or whatever the hell you'll be playing next month."

"The money's in rock," I countered. "It's the only thing really worth doing."

The knock at the door was Smokey and Henry Capps. They were just coming in from a recording session in Hollywood and were really pumped up. Lorne Greene, the star of *Bonanza*, had gone to the top of the charts in December with a song called "Ringo." At tonight's session, he had recorded his next release, a song written by Smokey and Henry called "Pop Goes the Hammer." It was a real break for them as songwriters and would definitely open some more doors.

The conversation wore on. Midnight came and went. Finally by 2:00 a.m., everyone was leaving and I was able to drag into bed, only to have the alarm tear me out of it at 4:00 a.m. But now I was on to some little helpers...diet pills...available by prescription from your local M.D. A couple of times a week, when the sleep was scarce, and the coming day was long, I'd pop a gray and yellow. Of course there was a down side that hit you twelve to sixteen hours later, aching muscles, inability to sleep the next night. It took a day to get over it. But at 5:00 a.m., I'm driving into Pasadena feeling terrific. Besides a constantly dry mouth and a desire to talk a lot, it was going to be a great day. The memory of Johnny Cash gulping a handful sometimes crossed my mind, but I blew it off.

Like I'd done a couple of hundred times before, I walked down the steps of the church to the basement. Total silence, except for the sounds I made. The click of the door latch. Boots across the cement of the unfinished studio for the TV station that was never licensed. The rush of power as the transmitter came to life, the clacking of the teletype machine as I pulled stories for the 6:05 newscast. I sat in my squeaky chair, adjusted my headset. At 6:00 a.m. straight up, I hit the "Sign On" tape cartridge. I'm a disc jockey. This is what I do. It ain't glamorous, it don't pay much, it's a killer shift and it ain't rock 'n roll. But it was radio. I punched up "The Star Spangled Banner" cart while Lennon and McCartney lyrics rolled around in my head.

"But tomorrow may rain,
So I'll follow the sun."
(Ibid.)

With Kate, Ron Adkins and Jim Bachman, Hollywood Hills, early 1963.

Hollywood
March 1965

Woodrow Bernard, his brother Marion, and my dad, Casey Pierce, had all fought in World War II. Casey was wounded; Marion Bernard was killed. After the war, Woodrow worked eighteen years for Continental Oil Company. He was pro-business, pro-America, pro-military, and pro-religion. Casey was the opposite on all points. As I grew up in the '50s, I had watched Woodrow and Casey often debate those issues till past midnight.

Today Woodrow was up against a much more formidable opponent. His name was Vince Donofrio. The Italian rebel from Detroit, along with Charles Laquidara, had all come over to enjoy some of my mom's Cajun cooking. My parents and the Bernards were visiting us in Los Angeles and they were running head on into the beginning of the generation gap.

"Your problem, young man, is you have no knowledge or respect for history," Woodrow Bernard fired another round at Vince Donofrio.

"History tells me that it's the young men who do the fighting and dying, and you old guys who start the wars," Vince shot back.

"Let me tell you something. I fought in World War II and I'd do it again. My son, Woodie, is about to join the Green Berets and I'm encouraging him to do it. You, Dave, and this Laquidara boy all should join. You'd be doing yourself a favor. You'd be doing something for your country."

"Doing myself a favor?" Vince sneered. "This is still a free country and I'm free to decide when I'm doing myself a favor. And it sure as hell ain't going to be in Nam! If your boy is crazy enough to go to be a Green Beret, that's his choice. I can't believe you encourage him to go get shot at. Suppose he gets killed. How you gonna feel? Some father you are."

Woodrow jumped to his feet fuming.

"I'd feel proud knowing he defended his country against communism. But it makes my blood boil to know left-wingers like you wouldn't even appreciate it."

"Defend his country against communism? What's that supposed to mean?" Vince asked incredulously. "That's just another slogan they use to imprison our thinking so real ideas don't come out, so we can't see through all the lies and bullshit."

"Bullshit? What I see in front of me is bullshit. A worthless young man with a Beatle haircut. I'd like to see you with a shaved head taking orders from a drill instructor."

"Well, dream on, mister," the Detroit Kid stood up to face the older man, "'cause this is one poor bastard who ain't putting his ass on the line so your oil company, Lyndon Johnson, and the Brown & Root Construction Company of Houston, Texas, can pour some more cement and build some more airfields in Southeast Asia."

"You disrespectful son-of–a-bitch!" Woodrow could no longer contain his anger. "I ought to take you outside and teach you a lesson."

"Calm down, everybody," Casey interrupted.

"Yeah, y'all sit down," I suggested, "we're all just talkin' here."

Casey was still recovering from his nervous breakdown and several weeks in a New Orleans psychiatric ward. Getting over shock treatment was slow. He was on tranquilizers, but was methodically beating off addiction by breaking the tranks into pieces and taking only one-fourth of a pill at a time. His psychiatrist couldn't come up with a diagnosis or a reason for his depression. By now I was convinced it was related to World War II. War stories brought him to tears, which were welling up in his eyes now.

I grabbed Casey by the arm and we stepped outside to sit on the front step and breathe the smoggy San Fernando Valley air.

"The Germans now too
Have God on their side."
(Ibid.)

Inside we could hear the debate continue at a slightly less hostile level.

"It's all slogans," Vince kept up the needling, "like escalation. All of a sudden, that's the new operative word for Vietnam. They wouldn't come right out and say they're going to send a million more boys to Vietnam cause this whole country would go into a full-scale revolution. And I'm not just talking about a few disgruntled students. So instead of telling us the truth, the government invents words like incursion, pacification. They ship our boys out five and ten thousand at a time and call it 'escalation.' That's double speak. Straight out of fucking George Orwell. It's *1984*, twenty got damn years early."

"We'll send whatever it takes in men and material to kick their commie asses," Woodrow said with authority. "If we don't stop the reds in Southeast Asia, they'll be coming in our back door from Mexico."

Convinced that all Southerners were bigots, Charles jumped into the fray, attacking from a different direction.

"Mr. Bernard," he asked very politely, "what do you think of Martin Luther King marching in Selma, Alabama, this week? Do you think he's a communist?"

"No, I think he's a smart-ass Negro or a dumb Negro, depending on how you look at it," Woodrow Bernard replied. "I think he's being used by the communists. And, yes, there are communists in his organization. The NAACP is full of left-wingers."

"And those sympathy marches by whites all over the country, they're all communists, too?" Charles continued to quiz Woodrow.

"Maybe not, but they're misguided," Woodrow said, now back in control, "the same as some of you young people. You just don't understand the way whites and Negroes relate to each other in the South."

"Have you seen *I Spy* on TV?" Vince asked, not willing to let Woodrow off the hook. "You know, the one with Robert Culp and Bill Cosby. What would you classify them as, a nigger and a commie?"

"Look at your history, boys," Woodrow replied, "you'll learn something and you won't be so easily led."

"Well, I guess it's like Bob Dylan says, 'the times, they are changing,'" Charles offered.

"Well, times change, but reality doesn't, and the reality is a lot of boys died in the past so that you can have the freedom to speak out," Woodrow said, knowing he wasn't convincing these young men. "You think you could talk this way in Russia. Think about that. Freedom of speech wasn't earned by guys like you or this Bob Dylan character."

I looked at Casey and asked him if he wanted to take a walk. No, he was ready to go back inside. His fight was over. So was Woodrow's. The next fight belonged to Vince Donofrio, Charles Laquidara, Woodie Bernard, and me. And it wouldn't be only in Vietnam or Southeast Asia. It was going to happen right here in our homes. I would have to pick a side.

"If God's on our side,
He'll stop the next war."

"With God On Our Side," Bob Dylan
(Bob Dylan, Special Rider Music)

1965

- New innovations: soft contact lens and the Lava lamp.
- Jerry Garcia forms the Warlocks (later the Grateful Dead).
- U.S. report: cigarettes peril health.
- U.S. planes attack North Vietnam.
- Ernesto "Che" Guevara drops off the radar to organize guerrillas in Bolivia.

KPPC FM
Pasadena Presbyterian Church
Monday, March 29, 1965

"Every time I think that,
I'm the only one who's lonely,
Someone calls on me.'

"Along Comes Mary," The Association
(Tandyn Almer, Irving Music)

It was 5:45 a.m. I was thumbing through the jazz stack trying to find something familiar. Playing at least one jazz cut per set was a stretch for me, matching it up with another song so that the two sounded good together was a crapshoot. I had learned that a vocal by Mel Torme, Sinatra, Dakota Staton or Ella Fitzgerald usually worked coming out of a jazz instrumental. From there a big band sound could get you to the break. I'd discovered Brubeck and Paul Desmond's *Take Five* and sometimes played it two or three times per shift. The easy route would have been to mimic Walt deSilva, who sat back, grooved for five hours, and played nothing but jazz. To hell with what it sounded like. But not everyone at the station liked what Walt was doing, and I could feel a backlash starting to build.

In the teletype room, Charles Laquidara was clearing the AP machine. He'd woken me up when he came over at 1:00 a.m. and wanted to talk. So I climbed out of bed and made him a deal. We'd talk if he came down and helped me do the shift, run the board, clear the news machine. He'd done it a couple of times before and was mildly interested in what was happening at the radio station. He'd only been back in Los Angeles about a month after spending several weeks in Boston with his family. His mom had cancer. She didn't know it. Charles didn't think she'd last very long. He was right.

He seemed to have reconciled himself to the inevitable and was in better spirits. He was working part-time delivering food for a catering service. In contrast to most of the gang, Charles was drifting. His career was going nowhere.

"Hey, David, you ought to see all this stuff coming off the wire," he yelled over the clacking of the AP machine.

"What you got?" I yelled back, scanning the log, looking for commercials. There were none, only a few trades. The Pasadena Presbyterians had mucho assets, but how long did they want to foot the bill for this radio station? This was supposed to be a money making proposition.

"You have to read this story," Charles came into the control room excited. He was holding several pieces of news copy torn neatly to size, with one long piece trailing behind him. "The auto industry says there's no proof that smog in Los Angeles is caused by auto exhaust. Can you believe this shit?"

"The guy who said that must not live in the L.A. basin," I said.

"And listen to this. Ralph Nader in his book *Unsafe at Any Speed* is attacking GM cars. This is what Vince has been talking about. He says that the auto industry is just the tip of the iceberg. Large corporations and their bureaucracies all over the country are making money at our expense. You've got to put this on the air."

"Sure, Charles, I'll read the story, but at 6:00 a.m. in Pasadena, nobody's listening to KPPC. Here, give me the rest of that news summary. If you're gonna engineer for me, you better get set. The 'Sign On' and "Star Spangled Banner" carts are already set. After I read the headlines, you play the U.S. Savings Bond P.S.A., then give it back to me."

"Okay, I got it. Hey David, listen, I want to bring over a little surprise for you and Kate tonight, okay?"

"What is it?" I asked.

"It's a surprise. Something I just found out about with Vince. You'll see tonight."

"Alright. I can wait. Get ready. I want to go straight up at 6:00 a.m."

Charles punched up the "Sign On" cart, studied the board, and then looked at me. Headsets on his ears, an impish look on his face.

"Tell me again," he asked. "Which one is your microphone switch?"

"Now my empty cup tastes as sweet as the punch."
(Ibid.)

That night at 9:00 p.m., Charles arrived at the house. The kids were in bed and we were eagerly awaiting the surprise.

"Alright you guys, you got to promise you're gonna try this at least once," Charles was saying, as he laid out a pipe and some dry, greenish-brown looking tobacco from a small paper bag. He filled the pipe, using several matches before finally getting it lit. He smiled. "You're not gonna believe this," he said. "Now when you take a drag, hold it in awhile before you blow it out."

It didn't smell like tobacco. Charles took a drag and passed it on to Kate. She sucked on the pipe and immediately began coughing. It was my turn.

"Small drags, David," Charles instructed.

I took a puff, inhaled, and held it for a few seconds and passed the pipe back to Charles. It didn't taste like tobacco. Kate fared better her second try and then it was my turn again.

"What is this stuff?" I asked, inhaling.

"Pot," Charles answered, grabbing the pipe.

"Never heard of it," I said, exhaling.

"Here, one more time around," Charles said, taking his drag and passing it to Kate.

"I've heard of it," Kate said. "It's marijuana."

We were smoking marijuana. I was stunned.

"Marijuana is dope, reefers," I said aloud, my mind conjuring up all the bad things I'd ever heard about the evil weed.

"You can't believe all that bull," Charles reassured me, refilling the pipe. "How you feeling, Kate?"

"I feel pretty good. Give me another drag."

We circled the pipe a few more times and then put it away for the evening. I felt some effects, but nothing terrific. Charles said I was too uptight to get off. Kate didn't have that problem. She loved it.

We talked about it the next day. She and I decided if pot was marijuana, we could do without it. A conversation with Smokey revealed that he'd had some pot with a couple of musicians and thought it was cool. That Saturday night, along with Bud and Mel, we had a party at Charles' little house in the hills, across from the Hollywood Bowl. Smokey brought the pot and we rolled it up like cigarettes. Within a few minutes we were all sailing, tripped out for sure. Distortion of time, five minutes seeming like an hour, the Beatles on the stereo sounding fantastic, laughing, and eating. The whole gamut. Smokey and Kate ate about eighteen popsicles. Sometime during the evening, Bud Tedesco slipped a John Coltrane record on Charles' stereo. Suddenly I knew why Walt deSilva loved jazz.

Charles and his great dane "Hey"
(previously named Charles, but changed for obvious reasons).

Santa Monica, California
April 5, 1965

"Good luck will rub off,
When I shake 'ands with you."

"Chim Chim Cher-ee"
(Richard M. and Robert B. Sherman, Wonderland Music Company)

The best song and best score from a motion picture was being played by the orchestra after winning the Oscar at the Thirty-Seventh Annual Academy Awards Presentation in Santa Monica Civic Auditorium. The glitzy crowd of Hollywood royalty, complete with supporting cast, was enjoying the catchy melody that had zoomed up on the charts when *Mary Poppins* ran away at the box office. I was seated between Kate and Effie, all of us dressed to the nines, all fitting right in. Effie was Mike Stroka's girl friend and a real radio pro. She ran KPPC when he was out. Mike Stroka, always an actor on the hustle, was working the lobby between the major awards that kept going to either *My Fair Lady*, *Mary Poppins*, or *Zorba the Greek*. As GM of KPPC, Stroka scored tickets to Hollywood's biggest event by picking up the phone and speaking the call letters with an authoritative voice, an act he had down cold.

Bob Hope as MC was at his best. The glamour was so thick it was easy for us to wallow in it. When you haven't reached the top, rubbing elbows with those who have is the next best thing. It was one bitching evening.

Later we swung by Jim Bachman's to have dinner with him and talk about the awards. Bachman had insider info that amazed us. Even Stroka was impressed. Kate and I wound up the evening getting loaded with Effie and Mike at his place in Laurel Canyon. It wasn't long before we were talking radio. Mike was the complete opportunist. He understood the stroke that went with an L.A. radio station, especially if we could come up with a winner. Getting anywhere with the Pasadena Presbyterian Church fathers would be a never-ending problem. The only logical move was to try to buy KPPC. It would take a lot of groundwork to pull it off. Mike would begin laying it. Once we took over, we knew we could make it go, make it pay.

"No remuneration do I ask of you,
But my cap would be glad
With a copper or two."
(Ibid.)

On the way home, we drove north up Laurel Canyon to the peak at Mulholland Drive. The sky was clear and the San Fernando Valley was laid out, sparkling like a giant jewel. Bachman had told me the story of Mulholland. An L.A. politician, he had gotten rich building the curving roadway along the crest of the mountains from the Hollywood Hills west toward the ocean. The kickbacks that went with that much asphalt must have been enormous. I thought Huey Long paving Louisiana highways had invented the practice, but apparently Mr. Mulholland also knew how to get a road built. There are places along Mulholland Drive where you can look out one side of your car and see the Valley below you, a huge twinkling visual feast, then look out the other side and see the L.A. basin, stretching out to the south and east. Then let your eye follow Wilshire Boulevard from the tall buildings of downtown, as it snakes its way westward all the way out to Santa Monica and the Pacific Ocean. Whatever Mulholland paid himself, it was worth it.

It was 2:00 a.m. when we finally reached Coldwater Canyon, having one more look at the lights. Down to the left was some of the most expensive real estate in Beverly Hills. We turned right, then sped down the hill to North Hollywood. On KFWB, the news at the top of the hour was wrapping up the Academy Awards one more time.

I'd been playing "Chim Chim Cher-ee" a lot in anticipation of tonight. In four hours I'd really start working it. KFWB's all night jock (even he sounded great) was introducing the newest song by the Beach Boys. It would take almost two months, but that song was definitely headed for the top. Daylight belonged to the Sherman Brothers' Oscar winner, but tonight I was singing lead with California rocker Al Jardine.

> *"And I know it wouldn't take much time*
> *For you to help me Rhonda,*
> *Help me get her out of my heart."*
>
> "Help Me, Rhonda," The Beach Boys
> (Brian Wilson, Irving Music)

*"In the jingle jangle morning
I'll come following you."*

"Mr. Tambourine Man," The Byrds
(Bob Dylan, Special Rider Music)

The transmitter was warming up. The sign-on cart and Star Spangled Banner were in place and ready to go. Dylan was in the audition channel singing his song that the Byrds had taken to number one. David Crosby and Gene Clark with Jim McGuinn on a twelve-string Rickenbacker guitar had forever united folk and rock. *Tambourine Man* had played till 2:00 a.m. at my house while we smoked pot and debated. I felt like hearing the song some more as I scanned the AP news copy, editing, trying to put my own slant on some of the stories coming from a very conservative press.

Heavy bombers from Guam were pounding the VC in South Vietnam. University teacher sit-ins were protesting administration policy in Southeast Asia. Lyndon Johnson was going to ask Congress to double the draft.

We had covered it all last night. Bonnie and Cameron Helmunth were over to watch McGeorge Bundy on TV defending Johnson's policy. Bonnie, a former Pasadena Playhouse classmate, was thin, blonde, waifish, and sexy. Cameron, her new husband, was a good-looking Ivy League type, handsome enough to become a fashion model in national publications in a few years. But for now he was still a student, one of many who felt that the U.S. needed to maintain a presence in Vietnam at all costs. When Vince and Charles arrived, the debate had risen to new heights and finally deteriorated into a cloud of smoke. I didn't have a clear view of where I stood. By that time of night only Dylan's "Mr. Tambourine Man" made any sense.

*"I'm ready to go anywhere,
I'm ready for to fade."*
(Ibid.)

The lyrics continued to haunt me as I shifted in my squeaky chair, put on the headsets and punched up another broadcast day on KPPC-FM.

"Wait only for my boot heels, to be wandering."
(Ibid.)

By 10:00 p.m. that evening, I was thinking about turning in early to catch up on badly needed sleep, when Smokey blew in with an entourage in tow. One of them was Murray McCloud, his new song writing partner. They had just completed writing both sides of a new single for a young English actor named Davey Jones. Bachman and I had seen Jones on stage at the Biltmore Theatre in downtown Los Angeles. He was exciting to watch. But to Davey Jones, all of this was just a warm-up until he became one of the Monkees.

Smokey was hanging out with another Playhouse grad, Stuart Margolin, who was hustling acting parts while keeping one eye on the music business. Later he would create the role of Angel, James Garner's street-wise sidekick on the TV series, *Rockford Files*. Tonight Stuart led an old black man into my living room and sat him on the sofa.

"Hey, everybody," Stuart announced, "I want y'all to meet Sonny Terry."

Now I knew who Sonny Terry was and who Bob Dylan had listened to for harp licks. They had all been at a recording session in Hollywood where Sonny was blowing harmonica. They were swapping jokes with Sonny and he was telling old bluesman stories. When the session broke up, they had to bring him along. As usual, the party moved to my house. They all knew they could find a late night snack in Kate's kitchen. Tonight she was serving blueberry cheesecake. Everybody dug in, including Sonny Terry. He polished off two big slices with a lot of gusto, then downed a cup of coffee. He never missed a beat, never dropped a crumb. Not bad for a blind man. Kate never figured out that Sonny couldn't see. When I told her later, she thought I was making it up.

Smokey told me how Sonny Terry performed with Brownie McGee, who was crippled. They made a memorable entrance onstage when they did a show, two old black men, one limping and leading the other one, who was blind. But when Brownie fingered his guitar, and Sonny blew his harp, you knew they weren't handicapped. Having seen them play a particular song several times, Smokey wondered why they seldom changed chords in the same place, yet always in unison. Asking for an explanation, Smokey said to Sonny, "I know you're not counting."

"Course not," the old black man replied, without explaining exactly how the two bluesmen were so in tune, "you never count when it's happening."

Murray pulled out the Devil weed, and Sonny fished out his harmonica and began to sing, play, and do field hollers on a song that was a lot older than any of us. I forgot about sleeping. It was going to be another night with the show folk.

> *"Good morning, Mr. Devil,*
> *I thought I'd chain you down,*
> *Every time I move*
> *You knock my rider down.*
>
> *You, the mean old devil,*
> *Make me weep and moan,*
> *You, the mean old devil,*
> *Make me leave my family and my happy home.*
>
> *I was at home doing very well,*
> *Now you got me here,*
> *Now I'm catching hell."*
>
> "Good Morning, Mr. Devil," Sonny Terry

KPPC FM
Pasadena Presbyterian Church
July 1965

"Eight days a week
Is not enough to show I care."

"Eight Days a Week," The Beatles
(John Lennon and Paul McCartney, Sony/ATV Tunes LLC)

Charles Laquidara had come down to engineer for me and we had the latest Beatle hit cranked up in the studio at 5:45 a.m. while we set up. Although there were probably no farmers in earshot, on Saturday mornings we did the agricultural news on KPPC. I suggested Charles take the pile of news stories in his hand and read off the five minutes worth of farm price reports live at 6:15. Not one to turn down a challenge, he read through the pork belly futures in his best Boston accent. He engineered the rest of the morning as we strung our jazz sets together till noon. By 1:00 p.m., we were back at home in North Hollywood, where nine-month-old 'Chelle was crawling on the floor. She was still tiny, about the size of a baby half her age. Her thin, silky blonde hair was like the Christmas bow on a perfectly wrapped package. She had everybody charmed, including John-David. And of course, Charles, her Italian godfather, was putty in her doll-sized fingers.

Danny Truhitte's GTO was in the drive when we drove up. But he wasn't in the house. Kate answered my inquiring look with a nod toward the back yard. I crossed through the kitchen and found Danny sitting on the patio. He was staring out over the six-foot high brick fence that separated us from the alley behind Joe's Liquor Store.

The Sound of Music had just opened. Danny's performance was excellent as the young German boy who slowly gets indoctrinated by the Nazis till he finally has to make the wrong choice. He had told me he was in love with Gabrielle, the Austrian girl who worked on "Sound" as a stand-in for Charmean Carr, the Ingénue lead. He was hoping to marry her soon. Other film opportunities were certainly on the horizon.

"You all right?" I asked.

"I'm worried," he answered.

"About what?"

"You, Kate, Charlie, the kids, this pot smoking."

"It's no big problem. It's not bad for you."

"It could be bad for you. You don't know that."

"Hey, don't worry about it."

"Okay, I won't. I was just leaving anyway," Danny said, as he exited the patio into the house.

"We're going to the beach. Come with us," I hurried after him.

"No, I gotta go see my agent," he threw back over his shoulder.

In the living room, Charles was swinging John-David in circles by one arm and one leg. He stopped Danny in his tracks when he said, "What's the matter, big shot, you ain't got time for your friends anymore?"

Danny paused for a minute.

"Not friends who are doing what you are, following left-wingers like Vince, smoking reefers."

"Hey, you gone completely Nazi on me?" Charles was up in arms too. "You must still be in character, young Mr. Nazi. This ain't Austria here. This is Los Angeles, California, United States of America."

"If you want to talk about my character in *The Sound of Music*," Danny leveled back, "you're the ones getting sucked in by the party line. You're making the same mistake he did."

He turned smartly on his heels, stepped crisply to his car, fired up the GTO, backed onto Babcock, and peeled out the half block up to Victory Boulevard. We could hear the bark of second gear rubber from in front of Joe's Liquor as he sped off toward Hollywood.

We loaded Charles' VW convertible. On the drive out to Malibu, Charles was silent for a long time. On the radio, the KHJ disc jockey, Scotty Brink, was doing his best time and temperature act.

"It's one-thirty on a million dollar weekend. Ninety-two degrees in Hollywood and I'm mighty hot this afternoon."

Then he hit Sam the Sham and the Pharaoh's month-old hit, *Wooly Bully.*

"You know, David, he might be right," Charles said suddenly, turning the radio down, so he could be heard over the San Diego Freeway traffic.

"About what?"

"About getting sucked in by Vince."

"He might be," I replied, turning Sam the Sham back up to high volume.

At the beach, 'Chelle snoozed in her shaded bassinet while Kate read. Charles, John-David, and I chased all the seagulls until they gave up and left our area. John-David made tiny footprints along the edge of the water as he ran after Charles.

Kate couldn't resist the beat. She put down her book and began to boogie in the sand when Doug Sahm from San Antone came on the radio, cashing in on the British invasion sound with a blend between Tex Mex and the Beatles. The producer promoter genius who invented the Sir Douglas Quintet was Huey P. Meaux who grew up fifteen miles from my home in Vermilion Parish in the '30s and '40s and went on to the Houston recording studios to help create the swamp pop sound of South Louisiana with Dale and Grace, Tommy McLain, Rod Bernard, T.K. Hulin, Freddie Fender, and Warren Storm. When they pulled out of Port Arthur heading for Houston, Huey was riding in the back seat with disc jockey J.P. Richardson as the "The Big Bopper" wrote the "B Side" for that night's session. He called it "Chantilly Lace," and coined the phrase, "Oh baby that's a what I like."

Huey was known as "the Crazy Cajun" and said to have the best ear in the South. He correctly identified one of the elusive but easily copied elements of the Beatles, which was that the beat was on the beat. Easy for Huey P. Meaux, growing up on the Cajun two step where the beat is on the beat. As soon as he figured it out, he put Doug Sahm in the studio and climbed the charts with "She's About A Mover." Out on the Pacific Ocean at Malibu, Kate was dancing in the sand.

*"Well, she was walkin' down the street
lookin' fine as she could be
Hey, hey! Yeah, what I say!
She's about a Mover."*

"She's About A Mover," Sir Douglas Quintet
(Doug Sahm, Crazy Cajun Music)

The KPPC staff, 1965.

North Hollywood
August 20, 1965, 4:30 a.m.

Black spokesman Malcolm X was dedicated to the Muslim cause "No Revolution Without Bloodshed." Malcolm X would die in a hail of assassin bullets. KKK activities in the South were at an all time high. In southeast Los Angeles, in a black community called Watts, six thousand residents had been rioting for three days. They were burning down their own homes and stores. Twenty thousand troops were called in. Some of the violence had spilled out of Watts and onto the freeways. There was fear it could spread to the white sections of Los Angeles.

Ron Adkins had driven up from Downey to spend the night. I got up every morning at this time. He didn't have to be up, but he was. On this morning in North Hollywood, Ron Adkins handed me a .38 caliber revolver.

"You never know when the brothers from Watts might decide to come north," he was smiling broadly. "You wouldn't want to run into any of them while driving through Burbank."

"What am I supposed to do with this gun?" I asked.

"Keep it under your seat. Go ahead, take it," Ron said, with his Southern Adkins grin. I put the gun next to my albums and he continued, "You know, I've been thinking about joining the National Guard. I ain't a coward. And I ain't a communist. But I don't love old Lyndon enough to want to get shot at."

"I know how you feel," I agreed with him. "Do it like Smokey did, a few months in boot camp, then you're back in L.A."

"I'm not coming back to Angel Town," he said. "Hell, if I'm in the Guard out here, I might have to fight the brothers in Watts. I don't mind selling them tires, but I don't want to shoot at them. I just as soon fight the Cong. No, I'm going back to Texas. Lots of opportunities around Dallas for a guy like me whose neck is just a little bit red."

"I envy you in a way," I said.

"Don't feel like you gotta stay here. I know that you came out here to accomplish something, but life ain't like that."

"Yeah, I'm beginning to realize that. When you going?"

"Christmas. It'll take me till then to get loose. Hey, will you do me a favor?" Ron asked.

"Sure, name it."

"Jim Bachman, look out for the old red head, I'm gonna miss him."

The brothers from Watts never got as far north as Burbank or Glendale or Pasadena. I made it through my morning of jazz. Newsman Bob Mayfield was on a tear, talking about how we all better do something about the "black problem." Bob was a Californian, had never even been in the South, but he was the biggest racist I knew.

At 7:00 p.m., I was down at the Cellar Theatre for another performance of *Involution* written and directed by Stuart Margolin. A two-character show, it starred Charlotte Stewart and Smokey Roberds. Charlotte played an actress in an on-again, off-again romance with her boyfriend. When she was down and out, she leaned on Smokey's character for support. He, of course, was in love with her. In real life, Charlotte was now engaged to Tim Considine, after going out together for several years. Charlotte was really playing herself. The character Smokey was playing was really Stuart Margolin. It was a showcase part for both Charlotte and Smokey. The whole production had good reviews. When the stage manager quit in a dispute with Ken Rose, I volunteered to take over and found myself in the light booth cueing up the closing music, the current hit from the Rolling Stones. On stage, Charlotte kissed Smokey good-bye and ran out to meet her boyfriend. Smokey, milking it for all he could, looked at himself in the mirror, pulled a joint from his pocket, fired it up, and crossed the stage to the radio. When he touched the switch, I punched up the Stones. As I pulled down the lights, Smokey boogied his way back across the stage. The last thing the audience saw was a puff of smoke as he danced with himself in the mirror. In the booth, I sang along with Smokey and Mick, thinking that Mick Jagger and Keith Richards could have also written this song for the brothers in Watts.

> *"But he can't be a man*
> *'Cause he don't smoke*
> *The same cigarettes as me."*

"(I Can't Get No) Satisfaction," Rolling Stones
(Mick Jagger and Keith Richards, ABKO Music, Inc.)

1965

♦ "Eve of Destruction" writer P.F. Sloan also wrote the Johnny Rivers hit "Secret Agent Man."

Smokey Roberds and Charlotte Stewart.

Beverly Hills
October 23, 1965

Charlotte Stewart and Tim Considine were married in a beautiful ceremony at the Belaire Church on Mulholland. Ken Rose was bending my ear during the reception that followed.

"Tim has a guest shot on *Bonanza*," Ken informed me, as he sipped steadily on a glass of bourbon. "His and Charlotte's careers should take off."

Ken and I were less optimistic about our own theatrical careers. I had gotten a day's work each on two more *Kildare* segments. Another single liner speech on one. No lines, only a close-up on the other. Not much to write home about.

Ken, who lived in a depressed state, was even more down than usual. While being a great creative outlet for him, the Cellar Theatre was a constant harassment.

"Davey, boy, I been thinking," Ken edged up close to me, speaking in a low voice. "Maybe not right away, somewhere down the road, I should take on a partner at the Cellar. If I do, you'd be the kind of guy I'd want to talk to."

"Sure, Ken, I'd like to talk some more about it," I said. "There's a lot going on with me, maybe not in acting, but I've got a broadcasting career, too."

The possibility of buying KPPC was very much alive, according to Mike Stroka. He was pushing hard on the church fathers for them to either spend the money for a tall tower and bigger transmitter or sell the station. With those two choices, he figured they'd sell. There was also a small FM station down in Orange County, call letters KTBT, in Garden Grove that was for sale. We thought we could put together the money for that one, but you couldn't own the L.A. radio audience from Orange County. You could from Pasadena. Besides, who'd want to drive an hour one way to Garden Grove? Not me.

Meantime, life was kind of a drag watching Ken Rose agonize over small details at Cellar rehearsals till midnight. The fun was staying up late to wind down and groove till 2:00 and 3:00 a.m., smoking pot three and four times a week. Bud, Mel, Charles, Vince, Smokey, Murray, Bonnie, Cameron and the non-smokers Jim, Ron, Danny, or any of the above in any of several combinations were all part of our group, and usually at my house. Since Don Adams was a hit in *Get Smart* on television, most statements were preceded by "Would you believe?"

Los Angeles disc jockey, Bob Crane, made good in the World War II P.O.W. comedy, *Hogan's Heroes*, strengthening my belief that a radio and acting career was a good mix. The war in Southeast Asia continued to occupy most of our conversation at our group gatherings.

U.S. bombers had cut rail lines from Hanoi to Red China and the news see-sawed back and forth like two college football teams gaining and losing momentum in the biggest game of the year.

"After he took from you
everything he could steal."
(Ibid.)

Kate and I were driving to Las Vegas on an occasional weekend to catch Wayne Newton at the Flamingo and Rowen & Martin at the Sahara.

Kate had worked three weeks at KPPC filling in for Effie in the traffic department. She was a fast learner and an even faster worker. If we ever had the opportunity to run a radio station, we knew the ins and outs.

Charles was now the regular KPPC-AM announcer on Wednesdays and Sundays, the only two days that the AM was on the air. On those days the Presbyterians broadcast the Sunday service and midweek devotionals, but stayed on the air additional hours, enough for Charles to play what he knew best, classical music. We were overlapping shifts on a Wednesday when he came out of the AM studio over to the FM studio where I was putting together another three-record jazz set.

"Jesus Christ, David, I've got the hiccups," he gulped. "What do I do now?"

"I don't know. There's nothing more worthless than a disc jockey with hiccups."

"This isn't funny, David. I'm blowing my mind here. I've got a break in two minutes."

"Tell you what you do. You keep your hand on the microphone switch, start talking. When you feel a hiccup coming on, turn off your mike, wait for the hiccup, then turn your mike back on and keep going."

"There could be a lot of dead air waiting for the hiccup."

"So what? You'll sound like a real professional classical announcer. Those guys love dead air. Now get out of here. I've got to back announce this set."

Charles was slowly becoming more of a leftist. It wasn't just Vince's influence anymore. He was drawing his own conclusions and being very vocal with his opinions. At KPPC, newsman Bob Mayfield hated Charles with a passion.

I kept listening to both sides of the Vietnam issue at the nightly gatherings. Dragging myself out of bed at 4:30 a.m., I drove eighty miles an hour down the eastbound Burbank leg of the 134 Freeway, timed the red lights through Glendale to Colorado Boulevard in Pasadena, drove past Los Robles, U-turned just before El Molino, parked in front of the church, and looked up at the building's architecture reaching into the dark pre-dawn of the smoggy San Gabriel Valley. The click of the lock, the clack of the news machine. And while I thumbed through the jazz LPs trying to second-guess Walt deSilva's disapproving ear, Bob Dylan played on the audition channel.

"How does it feel,
To be on your own?"
(Ibid.)

West Texas
December 1965

We drove out of Los Angeles heading east on Interstate 10. Our '64 T-Bird loaded for Louisiana, followed by Ron Adkins with all his worldly possessions, packed into his aging Chevy. Two days later we were a couple of hundred miles east of El Paso, where Interstate 20 sliced off to the northeast. We followed it through Pecos, Odessa, Big Springs and finally to the outskirts of Abilene. We pulled over to the side of the road. Ron kissed Kate and the kids good-bye. Then he and I stood looking out at the distant mountains of the New Mexico Badlands, the West Texas wind blowing through our hair and rustling our shirtsleeves. When we'd first arrived in Los Angeles four and a half years earlier, we saw Marlon Brando and Karl Malden in the classic western movie, *One Eyed Jacks*. Ron had learned to mimic Brando's Kid Rio mumble. We knew most of the lines from the screenplay and used them often. This was the perfect setting and I knew what Ron would say before he started to talk.

"Dad," he said, squinching his nose to get the proper Brando nasality, "you remember that time down in Sonora when you got drunk and shot that lady's goat?"

"You're a One-eyed Jack around these parts, Kid," I replied, playing my part and feeding him the lines, "but I done seen your other side."

"Take it easy, Dad." Ron gave me one last grin. "Maybe we'll get together sometime and transport some gold for the government."

Then he was gone, heading east to Dallas. We spent a couple of days with the Bernards in Abilene. Woodie was in from his first round as a Special Forces paratrooper. That was all he could talk about.

We were home in the Bayou Country for the Christmas holidays. My younger cousin, Ted Cessac, was getting ready to report for boot camp. High school buddy, Jimmy Chapman, was in town. After six years with the 82nd Air Borne, he was military from his boots up. His conversation was light years away from anything Vince and Charles talked about. The whole town was like reading a World War II novel, when all the young men were getting ready to go off to war. The headlines kept the backdrop held up in everyone's sight line: "U.S. Jets Smash a Big Power Plant in Haiphong."

Everyone in our hometown felt the same, turn our boys loose and these gooks would be out of business by next Christmas, then all our friends could come home.

Trying to explain my career to David Russo was an impossible task. He wanted his daughter, Kate, back home. My lack of definitive progress was the club he liked to use on me. I met with Russo and Carlos Marcello one night over dinner. They had some friends on the coast. They'd use their contacts to get me some acting work. I went away thinking they'd follow through and help me out. I was mistaken.

On New Year's Day, I sized up the past twelve months and decided this was how life beat up on your ambitions. One year at a time. Years like 1965. I was uneasy in the old hometown and anxious to hit the road for California. We loaded up, did the family farewells. I walked down to Granny's room that looked out on the lazy Vermilion Bayou, flowing by under a darkening winter evening. In the corner next to the window was that same old oversized radio with the brown veneer wood. No Amos and Andy, no Grand Ole Opry. Just a relic of the past. Granny was past eighty now. She looked up from her rocking chair, at the man I'd become. She took my hand. We said good-bye.

"And a time to every purpose under heaven.
...a time for peace,
I swear it's not too late."

"Turn, Turn, Turn," The Byrds
(Pete Seeger, Melody Trails, Inc.)

1965

♦ "Yesterday" was part of the Northern Songs Publishing Catalogue that was sold by John Lennon and Paul McCartney prompting them to later write "If You're Listening Late at Night, and the Words Don't Come Out Right...It's Only a Northern Song."

The Family, Barbara and Dave Russo with "Uncle Carlos" Marcello, Louisiana mafia boss.

"He hands you a nickel,
He hands you a dime
He asks you with a grin,
If you're havin' a good time."

"Maggie's Farm," Bob Dylan
(Bob Dylan, Special Rider Music)

I reported in at KPPC for my first shift of the New Year. I was half asleep, half high, and not at all interested in the music I was playing. At 10:00 a.m., Walt deSilva walked in and broke the news. Mike Stroka had been axed as GM of KPPC-AM and FM. So the Pasadena Presbyterians had exercised a third option not factored in by Stroka. They weren't selling, they weren't spending more money for better coverage. They simply told Mike to go away.

"Who's the new GM?" I asked.

"I'll be acting GM for the interim," Walt replied. "I've hired a new sales manager, Al Herion. This jazz format is just starting to catch on. There's a lot of talk about us around Hollywood. If we can just get our sales off the ground, we can get some respect. Dave, you need to concentrate on this music and really get behind my format. I feel like you're holding back."

Ignoring his overture, I congratulated him on being the acting GM. Then I asked the only question I wanted answered. "With your extra duties as GM, Walt, you'll probably need to get off the air. These early mornings are killing me. I'd like your afternoon shift."

"No chance," Walt stiffened. "That's my slot. I need to stay on the air to show you guys how to do it."

Walt told me all I needed to know. One, he wasn't at all secure as acting GM with the church people. And, two, as long as he was around, I'd only sleep two to four hours a night. David Russo had an expression that seemed entirely appropriate at this moment.

"Let the hair go with the hide, Walt."

"What?"

"I quit. Good-bye. Include me out. This is my notice. Count me down, two weeks and I'm out of here."

I'd blown his mind. He didn't realize that for me KPPC wasn't just another gig. It was my shot at the top. I didn't believe Walt knew which way to get there.

"Alright," he replied slowly. "But look, think about staying on for a weekend shift. It'll keep you in shape till you get another job."

"Fair enough," I said, counting myself lucky that I'd have a place to keep my audition tape updated.

At 1:00 p.m., I drove into Hollywood to meet Smokey and Murray. They had an office just below Sunset Boulevard down between Gower and Vine. Smokey had formed a publishing company, EPI, El Dorado Publishing, named after his hometown in southern Arkansas. They had added a third partner, Stuart Margolin. Smokey and Murray had both gotten parts in a series last fall. Good parts. They'd just learned that the series didn't sell. They were not happy campers. The office was a shambles. Sheet music, dubs, tape, guitars everywhere, in no particular order. They were having trouble getting organized.

"What you guys need is an office manager," I offered.

"Well, brother Dave, where would you look for such a person?" Smokey asked.

"Right over here," I replied. "Take me on as a partner. I don't need 25 percent. Give me ten, 15 percent. Whatever."

"We're not making money now," Murray said. "We're all pitching in to pay the rent."

"I know that. But you guys are gonna get a hit record any day now. It's no gamble on my part."

"We could be the fastest growing company in this town!" Smokey said, getting excited.

"Sure," Murray smiled. "All we have to do is keep taking on partners."

Back home in North Hollywood, I was feeling real good about the day's events. I hugged John-David and 'Chelle, went straight to the stereo, and put on some Bob Dylan.

"He asks you with a grin,
If you're having a good time."
(Ibid.)

"Music Man" Smokey Roberds with singer Andy Williams (above), with Bill Justis, producer of Kris Kristofferson's hit "Why Me Lord" (top, right), and with Al Delorean, producer of several Glen Campbell hits (bottom, right).

North Hollywood
February 1966

*"Don't say I never warned you,
When your train gets lost."*

"It Takes A Lot To Laugh, It Takes A Train To Cry," Bob Dylan
(Bob Dylan, Special Rider Music)

Now that I was no longer getting up at 4:30 a.m., we were getting high almost every night and staying up till 5:00 or 6:00 a.m., then sleeping till noon. "Gorging ourselves with life" was the way Smokey described it. Charles said we were on a fast track to Hedonism. Grass was cheap and plentiful if you had a connection. We had one. Pop Banks was his name. Pop wasn't a dealer. He was Dave Banks Jr.'s dad, who was kind enough to share his stash. He was in his late fifties, the prototype of the old-time head, more hip than the hipsters and beatniks from his era, but too old to be a part of this pre-hippie age. All presented in a statuesque frame, with golden voice to match.

Pop Banks had been around the radio circuit. At one time he worked the New Orleans giant WNOE. He told me, "Pierce, radio sales is a great life. You sign up a retail businessman to advertise with you and the two of you become partners. Every morning he opens his doors to the public and works all day long. All you do is mention his name a couple of times a day between records. At the end of the month, he sends you your cut."

Pop lived in an upstairs courtyard apartment in Hollywood. The first time I went to his apartment for a ten dollar bag, I rediscovered the fear I had that night seven years earlier when four Cajun kids ran from the state police. I walked out onto La Brea Avenue, the bag bulging in my blue jeans pocket, taking forever to cross ten yards of sidewalk to my car. I just knew the place was under surveillance and I'd wind up in the bottom of a cellblock in Alcatraz, or I'd get stuck in Folsom Prison, or even get deported to Guatemala like they did Carlos Marcello. The long arm of the law never reached for any of us, but sometimes late at night at home in North Hollywood there would be trouble at the lounge next to Joe's Liquor Store. Then the flashing red lights on Babcock sent us scurrying to the bathroom, ready to flush the evidence. The icy paranoia would crawl up our spines and we knew we were lawbreakers, pure and simple.

Timothy Leary lectured on LSD in Hollywood one evening. Kate and Smokey were there. They came home telling about a filmed experiment where the doctor handed a subject the powerful hallucinogen with the words: "I believe it's time for your lysergic acid." For several months afterwards, we always found an appropriate moment to tell someone, "I believe it's time for your lysergic acid." So far it was all for laughs only.

At the EPI office the creativity was flowing. Ideas for songs, lyrics, and melodies were constantly churning. Some of it good. Some of it off the wall. Smokey wrote a lyric to the old "Streets of Laredo" melody, something to the effect of "Groovy Go Go Girls Should Carry My Fender." EPIC Records thought it was brilliant.

Disc jockey Scotty Brink did an interview with us and broadcast it on KHJ. More publicity like that and the town would beat a path to our door. It was blowing my mind.

My once a week Sunday shift at KPPC was 1:00 to 10:00 p.m., so partying till dawn was no problem. One Saturday evening we were all at my house. Stuart Margolin was a superb comic and kept us entertained with his sharp-witted style. Stuart was describing how he'd snowed a casting director at Twentieth Century Fox. Murray McCloud was doing an impromptu blues guitar. About that time Smokey arrived with Charlotte Stewart in tow. The Dream Girl was back in the gang for good.

> *"Let me tell ya about my baby*
> *She make ya feel alright,*
> *And her name is G-L-O-R-I-A."*

"Gloria," Them
(Van Morrison, Hyde Park Music)

The Pierce family, North Hollywood, 1967.

Hollywood
March 1966

"And if I kiss you in the garden,
in the moonlight, will you pardon me."

"Tip Toe Through The Tulips With Me," Tiny Tim
(Al Dublin and Joe Burke, Warner Brothers, Inc.)

It was 10:00 p.m. I was just wrapping a rehearsal from playwright Arthur Miller's *Memory of Two Mondays*, my best part yet at the Cellar Theatre. Ken Rose had cast me as nineteen-year-old Burt, the kid in the machine shop on his way to college and a better future. Peter Pastore, another Pasadena Playhouser, was playing the thirty-year-old machinist-philosopher who would never fight his way out of the life in which he was trapped. Pastore worked as a barber daytime and acted at night. Arthur Miller could not have found anyone whose real life fit this character better than Peter Pastore. For me it was an opportunity to act in a strong emotional role, playing a young appealing character. Ken Rose knew how to cast a show.

Kate and the kids were at the theatre waiting for me to finish up. The Padre Hotel was the permanent residence for a group of midgets who worked in films. Evenings they mingled in the lobby of the Padre. While I rehearsed in the basement, John-David and 'Chelle played with the little people in the Padre alley between the hotel and the Cellar Theatre. There was something kind of strange about watching kids and midgets play together, but they all seemed to be having a good time.

Before we drove out to the valley, we circled by the EPI office to pick up some paperwork. Smokey and Murray were working on a song. The sound of Margolin's old Porsche pulled up out front and was followed by Stuart entering the office, a wild look in his eye.

"You won't believe this guy I just saw," Stu was saying. "What a freak!! At first I thought he was snowing me and the whole audience, but he's for real. He calls himself, would you believe, Tiny Tim."

"Is he a kid?" Murray asked.

"No, he's a grown man. At least I think he's a man. At first I thought maybe it was a woman. He sings in a high falsetto."

"What does he sing? Does he play a guitar?" Smokey wanted to know.

"He plays ukulele."

"A uke," Smokey was incredulous. "Nobody plays a uke."

"I know," Stu said. "It's too wild. He sings all these old songs, like 'Tip Toe Through the Tulips.'"

"Can he sing? How does he sound?" Murray asked.

"No, he can't sing. He sounds horrible. He's terrific. I'm telling you, we gotta go see this freak, put him under contract. He's playing a storefront off Fairfax called The Cabaret Theatre."

The next night we were at The Cabaret. The lights dimmed and the spot came up on one of the strangest humans we'd ever seen. In half song, half narration, he said, "Welcome to my dream, and how are you? Brush off that stardust. Where have you been? Don't tell me my rainbow was late getting in." He segued into a country and western arrangement of the George M. Cohan song titled 'Then I'll Be Satisfied With Life,' a song I remembered Casey singing fifteen years earlier. He also did a weird rendition of 'I Got You, Babe,' doing both Sonny and Cher's parts in high and low voice, all the time strumming on a uke that was in bad need of tuning. After the show we told Tiny Tim how much we enjoyed his performance. He seemed genuinely humble, a real person trapped in a weird characterization.

It was only a few hours later at the EPI office when Stuart came up with the idea of a midnight musical review every Friday and Saturday in Hollywood. The Strip was loaded with young freaks every weekend. We'd give them a show on stage that would be even freakier than what was happening on the streets. We'd start with a couple of straight acts like folk singer Donna Washburn from the Playhouse. Next we'd send on a large black girl blues singer we were trying to manage, perhaps a couple of comedy acts, and an off-the-wall hip rap from a young actor named David Kent. Then we'd out-freak them all with Tiny Tim. We grooved on the idea for a few days. We rented a theatre, negotiated with Tiny Tim. He came over to the EPI office carrying a bag full of bananas which he nibbled on while we talked. Tiny Tim lived in New York at the time and was ready to get back to the city. The four-week Cabaret gig had been a disappointment to him. Only a few people had come to see the show, and apparently, we were the only ones who had offered him any encouragement. On face value, he was totally lacking in talent. The real essence of Tiny Tim was going way over the heads of his small audience. Stuart was convinced Tiny Tim could be a major act. He said the times demanded a star with Tim's look and personality. But Tiny Tim was homesick. We drove him and his bag of bananas to L.A. International. The entertainment world and Tiny Tim had a couple more years to wait on each other.

Without Tiny Tim to headline, our musical review went into low gear for a few days. *Memory of Two Mondays* opened to great reviews. Peter Pastore and I were both singled out for praise. All it would take is one casting director, one agent, one director, one producer. If any of the above saw us, we could get a break. But, like Tiny Tim, we were left waiting night after night.

At KPPC, I continued doing Sunday afternoons and evenings, 1:00 to 10:00 p.m. Nine hours was much too long to keep your energy up and do a competent job the whole time. I was also discovering that not working everyday was a sure way to rust a disc jockey's skills.

In early April, Walt deSilva was fired as PD. He immediately showed up as a weekend newsman at KHJ, a tribute to not only his great voice but also his connections as a pro. I envied Walt. I would have gladly read the news anytime day or night just to get into the number one rock 'n roll radio station in Los Angeles. With Walt gone from KPPC, the jazz influence faded rapidly, although I still played a lot of Brubeck.

Smokey, Murray, and a singer/songwriter named Jerry Riopelle all took LSD one weekend. Smokey talked at length about the experience. He couldn't decide if the acid trip had been more enlightening than frightening. He was pretty spacey for a few days. He didn't seem eager to do it again.

Stuart kept talking about the midnight music review. One day he walked into the EPI office like a bad kid with a new idea for mischief.

"I'm gonna blow your mind," he announced. "First of all, I found an act to headline the show. They are booked at the Whiskey A-Go-Go in a few weeks and they're going to be hot. Listen to this, man, this is the groovy part. Know what we're going to name the show? The Groove Corp. Is that outta sight? The freaks will love it. It'll be designed especially for the pot-heads. Lights, loud music, multi images projected on a screen."

"Who's the group?" Murray asked.

"Lead guitar, drums, and a cooking organ. The keyboard guy is named Ray Manzerak. I think he's got a degree in music or something. They're all UCLA people. The singer's real sultry, bluesy. The chicks love him. Jim somebody. Dig this, he's a theatre arts major. They call them-selves The Doors."

We put the show together in less than a week. Stuart directing re-hearsal from 9:00 p.m. to 3:00 a.m.; Pop Banks' son, David Banks, was the tech director. They knew their stuff and had it whipped into shape by the weekend. Smokey, Murray, and I printed up flyers announcing the Groove Corp. opening. We tacked them to every light post on Sunset Strip. Opening night, we parked Laquidara's '38 Dodge on the street to attract more attention.

Stuart stood out on the curb in flower power garb with dark glasses like a carney barker, yelling, "Come on in. Experience the Groove Corp. It's a happening."

The crowd was modest the first weekend. The second weekend more freaks came. So did the police. Just looking around, checking everybody out, directing a little traffic. They didn't go inside, didn't bust anybody. Monday morning Stuart was in a panic. The cops' presence was disturb-ing him. He figured that for every uniform we saw there were three or four undercover. The paranoia level was running deep. The freaks off the street who came in were loaded with dope. If the customers got busted, we as promoters might be implicated. Nobody's career needed that ag-gravation. We decided to close the next weekend. On Saturday night, Stuart, Smokey, and Murray all had somewhere to go. I went down to pay off the acts. We had barely broken even. I watched The Doors run through the last show. Someone had come up with the idea of putting a dancer/stripper in one number. Jim Morrison was having too much fun singing the old Willie Dixon blues song, "I'm Your Back Door Man, The Men Don't Know Me But the Little Girls, They Understand." Morrison kept the stripper on for his last song, one written by guitarist Robbie Krieger called "Love Me Two Times, Babe, I'm Going Away."

When The Doors finally got their amps off the stage, it was past 4:00 a.m. A few freaks were straggling off into the night. The undercover cops were still standing around. They were easier to recognize by now. Their worries were over for the time being. The EPI entrepreneurs would not be the ones to give the emerging underground a focal point. Our timing was off. The Groove Corp. was just a few beats ahead of the music.

"You know the day destroys the night
Night destroys the day
Tried to run, tried to hide."

"Break on Through," The Doors
(John Paul Densmark, Robert Krieger, Raymond Mazarek, Jim Morrison,
Doors Music Company)

1966

♦ The name The Doors was Morrison's idea. The name came from the
book *The Doors of Perception* by Aldous Huxley, which was inspired
by a line of poetry written by William Blake. When The Doors' first
album was released, The Beatles promptly bought eight copies.

Arthur Miller's *Memory of Two
Mondays*, Cellar Theatre, Padre
Hotel, Hollywood.

With Peter Pastore in *Memory of Two Mondays*.

KPPC FM
Pasadena Presbyterian Church
May 23, 1966

"Stopped into a church
I passed along the way
I'd be safe and warm
If I was in L.A."

"California Dreamin'," The Mamas & The Papas
(John and Michelle Phillips, Universal MCA Music)

I was in the basement of the church putting together an audition tape. Along with "California Dreamin'," the recent smash by The Mamas and The Papas, I had a couple of Beatle albums and two current hits, "The Ballad of the Green Beret" and Nancy Sinatra and Lee Hazelwood's "These Boots are Made for Walking." My tape would be up to date. Working once a week was a crutch keeping me from going after a full-time deejay job. The music business and EPI was a ton of fun, but it was really Smokey and Murray's career, not mine.

Bob Mayfield was now the PD at KPPC. He wanted me to work Sundays, 6:00 a.m. to 2:00 p.m. instead of the 2:00 to 10:00 p.m. I had gotten comfortable with. That was the final straw. I decided to break away completely.

I finished my tape. On the way out I bumped into Al Herion, the new sales manager. He told me he liked my air work and wanted me to stay. He promised to get the station moving. He had plenty of ideas, none of them new.

On the drive home, I listened to Richard Bebe do the news on KRLA. Bebe was also a Pasadena Playhouse alumni and Ken Rose's student. Maybe I should concentrate on news. I was a good reader. But once you did news, it pretty much killed your chances as a deejay in the same market.

Back in the valley, the party was on for John-David's third birthday. A big Batman fan, he was delighted when he got a Batman suit. He was flying around the back yard, his cape flowing in the breeze. Charles dressed up as the Joker. The dozen kids at the party were all knocked out by his characterization. Charlotte Stewart Considine was also at the party. She looked fantastic and I had hungry eyes all over her. She and Tim invited us to watch the Indy 500 on Memorial Day via closed circuit at Grauman's Chinese Theater. I was excited about the invitation.

When the kids o.d.'d on the birthday party, and finally went to Batman dreamland, Charles, Smokey, Charlotte, Kate, and I lit up and grooved.

The next day I took my audition tape to the only two radio stations that had an opening for a full-time deejay. One was KNOB, the jazz station in Hollywood. The other was KTBT FM Garden Grove, fifty miles away in Orange County.

"Did you ever have to finally decide?
Say yes to one and let the other one ride."

"Did You Ever Have To Make Up Your Mind," The Lovin' Spoonful
(John B. Sebastian, Alley Music Corp, Trio Music Co.)

Program Director Frank Ernest had called. They liked my audition tape. I drove for an hour, south on the Hollywood Freeway then down the Santa Ana Freeway past towns I didn't know existed and finally into Garden Grove and KTBT.

Frank showed me the news machine, introduced me to the morning man, and asked me to sit down and do a couple of hours, starting with a noon news cast. I read the story about our Surveyor soft shot landing on the moon, and sending back photographs. The Soviets had beat us to the moon, but we were catching up.

"This is KTBT-FM, 94.3 from the heart of Orange County," I said, punching up the Cyrkle's "Red Rubber Ball." I had found the number one hit song in a stack of unopened albums and was digging for more when Frank raced into the control room.

"We don't play that kind of music," Frank Ernest said, as straight faced as a guy with that name would.

"What would you like me to play, Frank?"

"Well, you know Mr. Berliner owns a Latin publishing company, and he likes the disc jockeys to play some Latin artists."

"Fine," I said, fishing out a copy of Perez Prado's "Cherry Pink and Apple Blossom White." David Russo and Carlos Marcello would be right at home here in good old Orange County. I'd have to send them a postcard.

"By the way, Frank," I asked, "what station were you with before you came to KTBT?"

"Oh, I wasn't in radio," he answered. "I worked at the bank. I handled Mr. Berliner's account. This is my first radio job."

"That's about right," I thought. "A banker for a PD. This is some kind of zoo."

Oliver Berliner had inherited a fortune. His grandfather invented the Berliner microphone. Oliver must have figured the best way to promote his Latin music was owning a radio station and playing Latin until people bought it. The idea was right. But nobody seemed to know how to execute it. I guessed I could do Latin. Sleeping till 9 a.m. and deejaying noon to six could certainly fit right into my lifestyle.

After a couple of hours on the board, I met the manager, Michelle. She was thirty, blonde, beautiful, only a bit stocky, and very congenial. She was also Oliver Berliner's girlfriend. They were ready to hire me and pay just about enough to make it worth the drive. I asked about KTBT's future. She showed me the plans for the new broadcast booth and the showroom.

"What showroom?" I asked.

"The video showroom," Michelle answered. "Oliver owns the distributorship in Orange Country for Sony and Panasonic video tape machines and cameras. Isn't that exciting?"

"You bet it is," I said. "I'll take the job. I love driving the Santa Ana Freeway, and the two hours commute everyday will be fun. I'll be on the air tomorrow at noon. Before I go, though, would you be kind enough to tell me a little bit about Latin music. I've always been interested in it, and

I just need to know who the artists are. And by the way, what's the name of Mr. Berliner's publishing company?"

"He found a promoter who nearly fell off the floor
He said I never engaged in this kind of thing before
But yes I think it can be very easily done.
We'll just put some bleachers out in the sun..."

"Highway 61 Revisited," Bob Dylan
(Bob Dylan, Special Rider Music)

AS I.Z. IT

By IRWIN ZUCKER   PROMOTION IN MOTION

6515 SUNSET BLVD.
HOLLYWOOD, CALIF. 90028
(213) HO 6-9594

H'WOOD & (GRAPE) VINE! -- I'll go out on a limb to predict huge "Tarzan" disk success for the Marketts.... Roger Gordon back from Hawaii where ex-L.A. dj Earl McDaniel is now doing a TV sports show.... Record Merchandising -- Larry Ray hobbling with foot injury, Don Grierson "lucky to be alive" after 2 wks. of summer camp.... Local Chesterfield label releasing a Buck Owens classic, "Leavin' Dirty Tracks," penned by Virginia Richmond.... Jim Dyk produced the Dick Michaels "Goodbye" for Banyan banner.... Multiple-voice man Paul Frees has touches of Lorne Greene & Mike Douglas in his Hanna-Barbera gem, "A Girl".... Paul also produced H-B's new find, Peter Harcourt, debuting with "Sneaky Pete".... Betty Spector moved her pencil & pad to A & M's.... Maria Korda to star in Roy Orbison movie, "The Fastest Guitar Alive".... Guy Ward & Bill Harris ravin' 'bout Walt Reo's "What'cha Want Me to Do?" platter.... Big seller at Al Arden's Record Rendezvous in Vegas is Burl Ives' Decca LP, "Something Special".... Larry Larson, promo branch for the Family Tree, info's "Prince of Dreams" coming into hit reality for Mira.... Week's best bet -- Bert & Bill's beauty, "A Different Time" (Vanguard).

DOWN RADIO-TV ROW! -- Ask Alene McKinney to get you a Gary Owens (KMPC) Failure Card.... Don Elliot scooted KFXM for production job at KBLA.... From up Oregon way, Jay Hamilton of KASH sez The Smoke Rings are afire with "Love's the Thing" (Prospect Records).... Don Hillman & KWACrew tossed a Get Well Party for ailing dj Bill Woods.... Ye olde KRLA dj Roy Elwell joined KLAC.... KTKT dj Frank Kalil & ad exec Jay Taylor cooked up comedy LP for Capitol.... Ex-KBLA personality Henry May has a swingin' record shop in Pacoima.... Johnny Darin named mus. dir. at KMEN.... It's a male dj, Hal, for Doug & Adele James (of KGIL).... David Pierce of KTBT, new FM stereo station in Garden Grove, is a look-alike for Paul Anka.... Belated Happy 5th Ann'y for the Jim (KDEO) Prices.. Cheers to KRLA's Jim Steck for his groovy hosting of KCOP-TV's "Teenscope".... Tho Jack (KCBQ) Hayes programmed nuptials with Bev Hockin, he's available to do indie programming for Top 40 stations.

LATE FLASHES! -- 'Twas Happy Birthday Aug. 26 for society maestro Lester Lanin, my Dee Zucker, Bob Stern's Kitty and Luis Fields' mate, Jane.... Chapman Dist. in orbit with Gemini Records, swinging with "Where Are You Bound?" by His Majesty's Coachmen.... Signs of Royalty -- the Count Five, cashing with "Psychotic Reaction," dubbed their mgr. Sol Ellner as King Solomon.... The K Squad -- Ed Kassner & Danny Kessler -- whizzed in to kick hot wax by new British group, Hat and Tie.... Folk-singer Kriyananda penning a book, "Yours -- the Universe".... Good luck to TV producer Yale Farar & frater Sim on formation of new management firm.... Record execs scrambling to ink Jim Loss, 17, singer-writer. Their Loss would be their Gain, too.... Maria Metlova penned a dandy piece on Capitol teenstar Debbie Burton for Valley Green Sheet.... Don't miss Pat Morgan's bash Sept. 17 at the Shrine. One of the surprises will be Little Gary Ferguson, age 7.... Era prexy Herb Newman inked a true Mr. Talent in Howlett Smith. Dig the album, "Smitty." Rates a mitty.

Laurel Canyon
Late June 1966

They'll stone ya
When you're trying to make a buck.
They'll stone ya
And then they'll say, 'good luck.'"

"Rainy Day Women #12 & 35," Bob Dylan
(Bob Dylan, Dwarf Music)

If there was one guy in L.A. who was a bigger Bob Dylan fanatic than me, it was Tim Considine. Kate and I were often up at the Considines' house. While she and Charlotte became closer friends, Tim and I were listening to track after track of Dylan. I genuinely liked Tim, but beyond our interest in folk rock, our backgrounds were extremely diverse. I was a Cajun farm boy trying to make it in the city. He was an Angelino rich kid with show biz lineage and early success on *My Three Sons*. He had decided to leave the hit TV series to segue into movies. It was the big gamble that most TV actors at some time feel they have to take. He would get some movie roles, but never the one he needed. Worse, he got a part that probably contributed to the decline of his career. In the movie, *Patton*, George C. Scott slapped a cowardly soldier, was reprimanded, and forced to apologize. The actor playing the dirty little coward was Tim Considine. Sometimes Hollywood is a crapshoot.

Danny Truhitte was back in town. He had been on the road several weeks as a dancer working opposite Juliet Prowse. The kid was quite taken by her, talking constantly about Prowse, her dancing ability, great legs, and sexy face. Meanwhile, he'd missed a good supporting role in *Sand Pebbles*, shooting in the Philippines and starring Steve McQueen.

One weekend in late June, we helped Smokey move into a house overlooking Laurel Canyon. To get to it, you had to make a one hundred and eighty degree turn onto a gravel driveway that climbed fifty yards at a steep angle. At the top was the house, complete with deck and surrounded by trees and vegetation, the structure hanging out over the canyon more than a hundred feet below. Smokey was an ace at finding a dynamite pad, then giving it an appropriate name. He called this place "The Hideout."

The next Friday I finished my shift at KTBT, feeling good about the progress. By now I knew how to pronounce Tito Puente and was trying to figure out a format of pop, big band jazz, and Latin that would make some kind of sense. On the drive back to Hollywood I was listening to the new KHJ disc jockey, "The Real Don Steele." No question this guy was going to be the top jock in town.

We all met at the EPI office, then went over to EPIC Records recording studio to cut Smokey and Murray's "Groovy Go-Go Girls Should Carry My Fender". Stuart and I clapped and sang on the chorus. It was a real high. By midnight we figured we had a hit in the can. A half an hour later, Charlotte and Kate, Smokey and I were at the Hideout. We went up on the deck, got loaded, and watched the third quarter moon come up and hang low over the City of Angels. We grooved on the summer night and each other till the early morning chill set in. Then we went inside, lit the fireplace, and smoked some more. Smokey and I laid back on the two big sofas while the girls whispered in front of the fire. By the time dawn was breaking through Laurel Canyon and the fire had burned itself out, the two girls had taken turns on both sofas.

"I once had a girl,
or should I say,
She once had me."

"Norwegian Wood (This Bird Has Flown)," The Beatles
(John Lennon and Paul McCartney, Sony/ATV Tunes LLC)

1966

- The National Organization for Women (NOW) formed.
- Masters and Johnson's *Human Sexuality Response* published.
- Truman Capote wrote *In Cold Blood*.
- Frank Zappa released rock's first two-disc album *Freak Out*.
- Supreme Court upholds the right to remain silent in *Miranda vs Arizona*.

Hollywood
July 1966

My day started at 10:00 a.m. at the EPI office in Hollywood, taking care of paperwork, on to Garden Grove to do an easy shift on KTBT. There weren't many commercials on the log, although these guys were fairly adept at trading. The sales manager had a trade with the Tokyo Spa, an Anaheim massage parlor, a stone's throw from Disneyland. I was back in Hollywood at 7:00 p.m. stopping by Charles' apartment. I had been helping him with his personal accounting since '63. He couldn't balance a checkbook and was always running behind on his bills. Today was no different.

"Jesus Christ, David," Charles was saying, "how does the average poor bastard like myself keep up? Suppose I had a wife and kids like you? I couldn't support them on what I make."

"Just try to keep going," I encouraged. "Something will break for you."

"Yeah, maybe someone in the gang will make it really big and give the rest of us working class stiffs a break. I know I would if I could."

"Sure you would, Charles. Any of us would."

"Sometimes I'm not sure about all of us," Charles said.

I could tell he was starting to grow a thin, bitter edge.

"One of the guys at work said I should declare bankruptcy," he said, staring at the brown vegetation on the Hollywood hillside. "I don't want to lose my car, but I might have to."

> *"And everybody yeah, tries to put my Sloopy down*
>
> *Hang on Sloopy, Sloopy hang on."*
>
> "Hang on Sloopy," The McCoys
> (Wes Farrell and Bert Russell, Morris Music Inc.)

I left Laquidara pumped up as I could get him, then back to EPI to meet Stuart, Murray, and Smokey. There were two other people at the office. One was a guy named John Linxwyler from El Dorado, Arkansas. He knew Smokey from high school, had heard he was doing well in Hollywood, and came out to get into acting and producing.

"Howdy, Dave," he grinned broadly when we were introduced. "I'm Link Wyler."

Link had already shortened his name for the marquee. He was 100 percent hick, looking something like a young Slim Pickins. Probably didn't have a shot in the world. But anybody who changes his name the first day in town bears watching.

Link moved in with Smokey. Tim Considine introduced him to a producer friend. Link went dove hunting with the producer. In six months Link Wyler was working regularly on *Gunsmoke*.

The other guest at the EPI office was a beautiful young brunette actress who had just won a talent contest in her hometown of Sebastopol, California. Her distinct voice quality and fresh sexiness said "All American Girl Next Door—Cast Me." One of thousands who came to Hollywood every year, but this girl was different. Her name was Karen Valentine.

I spent a few minutes with my EPI partners. They had several big projects working, including the management of new talent. Karen and Link were both possibilities. I excused myself, heading for my next stop, the Cellar Theatre.

"Sorry, guys, I gotta run," I said. "We're trying to get rehearsal going on *La Ronde* at the Cellar. Ken's been agonizing a lot lately. He's in a foul mood."

"Brother Dave," Smokey said, "we're going to have to name you 'Trouble Buster' from now on."

"Trouble Buster, huh." I liked that. Good name for a guy on the move. Accurate description of what I like to do.

At the Cellar, a dozen actors were standing around waiting. Ken Rose hadn't shown up.

"What's cooking?" I asked Bud Tedesco.

"Bad news," Bud said, looking glum. "Pete's on the phone now over at The Padre. Ken beat up his wife. He's in the can."

Pete Pastore arrived with the details. Ken had been drinking all day and finally had blown up, manhandling Patty Rose till she called in the cops.

"He needs bailing out, five hundred dollars. Where are we going to get that kind of money?" Pete asked.

"I'll handle it," I answered. "That's my job. That's what I do."

At the downtown L.A. lockup, I laid five C notes on the counter and they gave me Ken. He was remorseful, apologetic, and feeling awful.

"Davey," he said, "I can't handle it by myself any more. You gotta be my producer on this show. Take some of the pressure off me. Don't worry about your money. I'll pay you back."

"Sure, Ken," I said, knowing the five hundred in long green would have a short memory, "No problem."

Producer. There's all kinds of ways to make it in this town. I'd just discovered another one.

"Look out, kid,
They keep it all hid."

"Subterranean Homesick Blues," Bob Dylan
(Bob Dylan, Special Rider Music)

1966

♦   The McCoys were a small rock group from Ohio that never guessed their "Hang on Sloopy" would become the Ohio State fight song.

Hollywood
August 1966

"Doesn't seem to be a shadow in the city."

"Summer In The City," The Lovin' Spoonful
(John Sebastian, Steve Boone, Mark Sebastian, Alley Music Corp., Trio Music Co., Inc.)

The Real Don Steele had just punched up the Lovin' Spoonful's smash, "Summer in the City." If there was anyone in L.A. hotter than Don Steele, it was John Sebastian, singing lead and chalking up hits with The Spoonful.

Stuart had scraped enough money together to rent a camera. He was shooting his "Involution" script on 16mm with Dave Banks, Jr. as his producer. His crew included Murray and Link as grips and lighting men. Smokey and Charlotte were recreating their Cellar Theatre roles for the camera. The shoot was happening days at the Hideout. At night, on the same set, Kate and I were partying with Charlotte and Smokey.

Karen Valentine had been invited to join the CBS Actor's Workshop. She asked Smokey, Kate, and me to attend one of their presentations. She was going after her career full speed.

One hot August night, we went to a Hollywood Bowl performance with Mike Stroka and Effie. Josh White opened with his big booming voice and acoustic guitar. The headliner was a new folk singer named Judy Collins. She sang, "Hey, Nellie, Nellie," a Civil War traditional, and a driving composition by Papa John Phillips, called "Me and My Uncle." It was the first time I had heard either song. Mike Stroka was on his way to New York to try his luck acting on the soaps. Within months, he would score a starring role in *Dark Shadows.* Effie was leaving KPPC to run the traffic department at KADS, a new L.A. radio station with the outrageous concept of wall-to-wall want ads, a solid twenty-four hours every broadcast day. Kate would replace her at the bottom of the church as operations manager under KPPC Sales Manager Al Herion.

I came away from the Bowl thinking about Judy Collins' blue eyes, golden voice, and driving guitar. Folk music was my answer in Orange County. I stayed up till 2:00 a.m. composing a letter to Michelle, KTBT's manager. I outlined the need for a flow of new music from the record distributors in L.A., the timely introduction of new releases into our format, and the organization and maintenance of a record library. Since I was the only employee living in L.A. with proximity to the music distributors I was a natural choice for the job. But I needed the title of program director to make my official rounds with the record people. Since Frank Ernest was PD, the situation called for some diplomatic maneuvering. Simple. Make Frank the assistant manager where he could exercise his executive skills.

The next day before my shift, I presented the letter to Michelle over coffee. She listened politely. Said she'd talk to Berliner. Two days went by while Frank Ernest gave me snide looks. Then Michelle asked Kate and me to join her and Berliner at a Kingston Trio concert in Ontario, fifty miles east on the San Berdu Freeway. While the Kingstons sang "Hang Down Your Head, Tom Dooley," Berliner flirted with Kate and gave me the job of PD. I told him how excited I was to be a part of the empire he was building in Orange County, and how folk groups like the Kingston Trio and Judy Collins were the best way to attract an audience. Berliner said folk was okay, as long as I played his Latin and stayed away from rock 'n roll.

As the Kingston Trio sang, Michelle and I kept accidentally touching knees under the table.

"If it wasn't for Sheriff Grayson,
I'd be in Tennessee."

"Tom Dooley," The Kingston Trio
(Frank M. Warner and Alan Lomax, Ludlow Music, Inc.)

The next day I was all over the record distributors. A call to my old mentor, Grelun Landon, gave me the names and numbers. One of them was Doug Cox at Atlantic Distributing. He seemed like the nicest guy in the world and went out of his way to get me the record company product. It would be five years before I really got to know Doug Cox.

Most of the distributing houses were on Pico Boulevard below Wilshire on L.A.'s south side, so I stopped by on my way to Orange County. I was trying to move into a folk, pop, jazz, Latin format. I was listening to a ton of music, auditioning albums, track after track, till the wee hours. One Saturday afternoon, Smokey pulled me away from a stash of records with a phone call.

"Hey, brother Dave," he said, "why don't you and Kate get a babysitter and come on up to the Hideout. We'll turn on and get a little scene going. A friend of ours says she wants to see you guys."

"You got lots of friends, you old double dealing devil. Who are you talking about?"

"Here, I'll let you say a word to her," Smokey said.

"Hey, Dave, why don't you and Kate come on up?" said the voice on the phone. My heart was pounding double time. I would have recognized that voice in a windstorm. It was Karen Valentine.

"And babe, don't you know it's a pity
the days can't be like the night."

"Summer In The City," The Lovin' Spoonful
(John Sebastian, Steve Boone, Mark Sebastian, Alley Music Corp., Trio Music Co., Inc.)

Hollywood
Orange County
September 1966

In Louisiana, as in most of the country east of the Rockies, you can feel the coming of autumn. You actually get a premonition on a cool August morning, when a deep breath tells you there's a sniff of football in the air. In southern California there's little distinction between the seasons. This year fall sneaked up on me with her running mate, nostalgia, and once again, I had no defense. On Labor Day, we had gone to a drive-in movie with 'Chelle and John-David to see the new Batman movie. Jim Bachman was getting ready to head south for Dallas and Louisiana. He'd spend several weeks scouting locations for a new movie to star Faye Dunaway, Warren Beatty, and Gene Hackman titled *Bonnie and Clyde*. Charles Laquidara was still in a rut. He took us to see the movie, *Years of Lightning, Days of Drums*, as more conversations and controversy centered on the JFK assassination plot. When a television special with David Suskind interviewing Bobby Kennedy and Pete Seeger aired, Charles made sure we all watched it.

On September 8, NBC premiered a new show called *Star Trek* starring young William Shatner as Captain Kirk and Leonard Nimoy was cast as Spock in the only role he'd ever be able to play.

At KTBT we were airing the old *Lone Ranger* radio serial on Saturday evenings. John, the sales manager, put together a promotion with a tract home developer for the Lone Ranger and Tonto (including horses Silver and Scout) to spend Sundays giving horseback rides to kids while their parents toured the new homes. John cast himself as the masked man. I was a Cajun actor with a suntan. I got the job as the Indian. It was a real kick playing Tonto. I mastered talking the halting speech I'd heard from J. Silverheels, the Tonto of screen and radio. I spent a lot of time practicing my quick draw, so I was handy with a gun. Riding a horse was as natural as driving a sports car. All I needed was a part in a Hollywood western. The small children who came out to see the Lone Ranger and Tonto at the track homes were thrilled. So was I.

I was now driving to Orange County seven days a week. I tried to talk Smokey into doing my Saturday afternoon deejay shift, but he could feel himself closing in on a hit record.

After playing music all day at KTBT, I was hustling back to Hollywood to put the EPI office and books together, then stopping in at the Cellar to do my producer's job. I was definitely on a fast track and I was worn out. But I was also high on the job, the music, and Valentine. We were all spending a lot of time together. Even when her mother was in town, Karen asked us to join them for dinner. Kate was beginning to feel jittery about the direction we were going.

128

In late September, Smokey and Karen came out to the valley to have dinner, smoke, and party. When Kate and Smokey fell asleep, Karen and I talked till day break, watched the sun rise, then made breakfast for John-David and 'Chelle. We were both aware it was autumn. Changes were coming down.

For San Francisco, the summer of love was 1967. In Los Angeles, we started a year early.

"Gather round all you clowns
Let me hear you say-ay-ay."

"You've Got To Hide Your Love Away," The Beatles
(John Lennon and Paul McCartney, Sony/ATV Tunes LLC)

KTBT
Garden Grove, Orange County
October 1966

"All that summer we enjoyed it
Wind and rain and shine
...By August she was mine."

"Bus Stop," The Hollies
(Graham Keith Gouldman, Bramsdene Music Corp.)

I only flashed on Valentine a couple of times when KRLA disc jockey Reb Foster played the Hollies' top ten song, as I drove the Santa Ana Freeway to Orange County. After four months at KTBT, I couldn't see much progress. The morning man, and especially Bernie, the night jock, played the Latin cuts dutifully, and both seemed to have a better feel for it than I did. I was still playing catch-up, learning which were the most playable tracks. Of course, the artists like Vince Guaraldi on *A Taste of Honey* or any of Sergio Mendes and Brazil 66 was easily workable. I needed to just relax into it. Radio was radio. Sure, the music was important, but being on the air and working regularly was more important. Afternoons really agreed with me. Even a five-hour shift was relatively easy. The air checks told me it was my best work yet. Keep working and learning, I'd get my shot. The right opportunity was just ahead, somewhere. Meantime, I would concentrate on playing the right songs. The right song has power, no matter if it's folk, rock, jazz, country and western, or even Latin. So how do you pick the right song before it hits the charts? Just as important, how do you precede it and follow it, especially playing a two- or three-record set? Is there really a correct time of day to play a particular record? What about rotation? How often? Program Directors wrestled with these questions, each developing their own particular format. But that's all formula, not the real thing. The real knowing is the instinct to pull the right sound at the exact moment. You just know or you don't. You can pick hits or you can't. Your own taste, that's all you have, right or wrong. If you want to capture a big piece of the market, you have to be in tune with the times and the city. Putting the right sound together is an elusive business.

Arriving at KTBT early, I spent a few minutes quizzing Frank Ernest on the progress of the new On Air booth that would look out onto the video showroom. Then I auditioned albums for an hour. At KTBT I was building a good folk section, and ran across a group that would fit right in. The group name was catchy. The Stone Poneys. The "more folk than rock" sound was well produced. But the lead singer was really dynamite. Linda Ronstadt was knocking me out. A tone-deaf sales manager could have heard "hit maker" all over her voice.

Rather than pay me back the five-hundred dollars of bail money, Ken Rose offered me half ownership of the Cellar Theatre, if I threw in an additional five hundred dollars. I put the money in his hand the next day. On October 12, I turned twenty-five. A PD of an Orange County FM station, producer and part owner of a workshop theater in Hollywood, and a partner in an up-and-coming music business company. A long way to the top, but a fair start on grabbing a small piece of this town by the ass.

I was worried about Charles. His obsession with JFK kept him in front of every Mark Lane TV show. The military buildup continued in Vietnam, and a numbed response was settling in on all of us.

When our parents came to town, Russie drove Casey into Hollywood to see the EPI office. Lounging around talking with Smokey, Casey picked up the harmonica that Donovan had left behind on an earlier visit. He began to blow "Lili Marlene," the one-time German military march turned plaintive theme for the boys of World War Two, on the same harp that Donovan blew protest in "Universal Soldier."

John-David and 'Chelle were attending Montessori's Learning School. We knew the teaching style was right. The kids progressed at their own pace in a very loose setting. 'Chelle at two was still a baby trying to put sentences together. Three-and-a-half-year-old John-David was developing his social skills, a sense of humor, and a somewhat offbeat personality. For his art class Halloween party, he went dressed as a hobo.

"When I say we'll be cool,
I think that you know what I mean
We stood on a beach at sunset,
Do you remember when?"

"Sunshine Superman," Donovan
(Donovan P. Leitch, Peer International Corp.)

1966

♦ "Bus Stop" was written by Graham Gouldman who also wrote "Heart Full of Soul" and "For Your Love" for the Yardbirds, and "No Milk Today" for Herman's Hermits. He later formed the band 10cc who had the hit "I'm Not in Love."

♦ Donovan was good friends with the Beatles and originally subtitled "Sunshine Superman" (for John and Paul). Jimmy Page played lead guitar on this recording.

North Hollywood
November 1966

It took eight weeks for "Last Train to Clarksville" to get to be number one. By that time nobody cared that Davey Jones, Mickey Dolenz, Michael Nesmith, and Peter Tork were more actors than musicians, playing a part on a TV show about rock 'n rollers. Over four hundred actors and singers had turned out for Monkee auditions, including would-be stars like Stephen Stills and Paul Williams. Smokey Roberds and Murray McCloud were among them. With the year winding down, 1966 hadn't lived up to its promise. Smokey came down from the canyon into North Hollywood one Saturday afternoon.

"Brother Dave," he said, "we're going to have to close the EPI office. I hate like hell to admit it, but none of us can afford the rent."

"Let's hang in awhile longer," I said. "You guys are writing great stuff. You and Murray are a good team, and the hits are there, I know it."

"I know it, too, partner, but Stu and Murray want out by Christmas. We'll keep working; we'll just have to go underground for awhile. Take a low profile."

"What about the Tiny Tim tapes?" I asked.

Stuart had succeeded in putting Tiny Tim under an EPI manager's contract. We raised enough money to go into the studio for a session.

"The whole town laughs," Smokey answered. "Tiny Tim is just too weird for them."

The coming demise of EPI didn't stop me from wanting to enhance my image with a new set of wheels. In southern California you are what you drive. Atlantic Richfield was still counting the barrels of oil back in Louisiana, but I was getting a piece. So one night John-David and I drove into Hollywood and bought a 1967 black 912 Porsche. He could barely contain himself. Neither could I.

On November 8, Charles and I sat down in front of the TV to watch the election returns. All over the country, Republicans won big. California Governor Edmond G. Brown was beaten by an ex-actor, Ronald Reagan.

Hollywood
December 1966

It was 9:00 p.m. at EPI. Smokey, Murray, Stuart, and Link Wyler were all packing up the boxes of tapes, sheet music, and a myriad of personal items that had gravitated to the Hollywood address over the past year. The office was being closed, but there was only optimism in the air. We were all harmonizing on the Beach Boy's song that had entered the charts at number eighty and moved steadily up to number one in a month and a half. The boys at EPI sounded real good. Except for Link, everybody was real stoned.

Smokey had a part in a movie called *The Cat*. All were either working as performers or had something coming up. I left them to finish the packing. The black Porsche climbed the Vine Street on-ramp heading north on the Hollywood Freeway for the last leg of my fourteen-hour day. At home in the valley, my boyhood pal, Woodie Bernard, had just finished up his last stateside dinner with Kate and the kids. He was shipping out the next day from Los Angeles for Okinawa and Southeast Asia.

"Well, I'm sure going to remember-going to remember, this meal," Woodie stuttered. "From now on, it's monkey meat for me."

Despite his slight speech impediment, Woodie had always been a talker and a storyteller.

"You wanted to go to Nam, didn't you?" I asked.

Woodie cocked his head to one side and grinned. "Wanted to go?" he replied. "Ever since this war st-st-started out, I've been trying-I've been trying, to figure out how to ge-ge-get there. That's when I de-de-decided on the Green Berets, but they almost-they almost side-tracked me."

"What happened?"

"Hell of a story," Woodie said, leaning back. "I'm punching-I'm punching sixteen thousand foot hu-hu-holes in the Gulf of Mexico for the oil company and I'm having a ga-ga-good time, right? So I ge-ge-get this-I get this wild hair to be a Beret. They put me through a year of training. I ga-ga-got outdoor living skills to match-to match an Aborigine. They drop me off in the Okefenokee Swamp down in Georgia, ge-ge-give me a knife and a piece of string. The Captain sez go ge-ge-get it Cajun boy, you still alive in a week, you'll be a Green Beret. When they picked me up I'd ga-ga-gained four pounds. I had been studying the political history of Vietnam for six-for six months. All of a sudden they tell me I'm not-I'm not going to Nam, I'm going to Panama."

"How did that happen?" Kate asked.

"Well let me tell-let me tell you. It seems the Berets have a de-detachment in Panama that's responsible for digging-for digging water wells for the populous. They pulled my records, see I du-dug for gas in the gulf. They figure, they figure I can di- di-dig for water in Panama."

"Most guys we know would have called that a streak of luck," I said.

"Me, I'm-I'm pissed," Woodie replied. "So I go-I go to my sergeant-major and tell him my problem. He says, 'Go ge-ge-get two bottles of Johnny Walker Red. So I-so I do that. The sergeant-major keeps one bottle of Johnny Red for himself. Me and him ta-ta-take the other bottle to the guy in personnel, who makes a few changes on my record and assigns me to Okinawa. 'I want to- I want to go to Nam,' I say. 'Ta-Take Oki,' he says. 'They'll send you to Nam, but since you're ba-based in Oki, they ga-ga-got to pay you extra Travel Duty Pay for every day you're in Nam.' So it cost me two bottles of Johnny Red, but I'll see all the Nam I want. And every da-da-day the sun comes up over the jungle, I'll be TDP money ahead. But if, if anybody dies and leaves me a fortune, se-se-send it to my address in Oki."

"What will it be like in Vietnam?" Kate wanted to know.

He proceeded to tell us what he was prepared to do. He would be flown by chopper to an area in Vietnam. While the chopper hovered, he'd climb down a ladder into the jungle. He would link up with other Green Beret operatives and the native Montagnards. After an incursion lasting days or weeks, he'd be pulled out of the woods for awhile, then be sent right back. Woodie was honed to a sharp edge. Tough and confident, he was ready. We talked till midnight. It was the last long conversation we would have for a whole lotta years. Kate told him to write. He said he would.

At KTBT I kept playing more folk and less Latin. Frank Ernest would lurk around the deejay booth to let me know he was listening.

"Don't forget, Mr. Berliner likes to hear his records played," Frank would say, with his "I may have to turn you in" tone of voice.

I let Frank and Michelle know that I wanted to be program director in function as well as title. When a part-time disc jockey didn't like his schedule, he took his complaint over my head to Frank. The next day I axed the disc jockey. Berliner backed me up. He liked that kind of action.

"Winchester Cathedral" by the New Vaudeville Band was a big hit and totally safe for our format. For once, L.A.'s top rock jock, The Real Don Steele, and I were playing the same song. I was feeling at home in Orange County. One night when I got off the air, Kate and I, Danny Truhitte and his new Austrian bride, Gabrielle, all went over to Melodyland to catch *Les Girls*, a big production number with dancing and costumes galore. It was right down Danny Truhitte's show biz alley.

On December 15th, Walt Disney died. The next Saturday at KTBT I worked 6:00 a.m. till 12:00 noon, while Kate, John-David, and 'Chelle picnicked and played in the video showroom among a quarter million dollars worth of cameras, recorders, tripods, and sync generators. Then we were off to Disneyland, which had gone all out to pay tribute to the founder. For the kids it was Disney characters, color, and spectacle. They didn't even hear the man's voice in the crowd behind us, who was moved to say, "God bless Walt, he sure did a lot for us," as Mickey Mouse and Goofy led the parade down the facsimile of main street America.

The year was coming to a fast close. Charlotte and Tim Considine dropped by North Hollywood to give us a ride in Tim's new Mercedes. Tim was really loosening up. Vince had disappeared. Charles said he was on a Zen trip, studying with the Roshi, a Zen master in south Los Angeles. Charles was watching Mart Sol on TV, who continued to blast the Warren

Commission. Link Wyler, after finishing up a shoot on *Gunsmoke*, came into Hollywood with us for the Christmas parade. We stood with the crowd watching the celebrities' floats go by. 'Chelle on my shoulders, John-David on Link's.

We made our annual visit to Cajun Country at Christmas time. Two-year-old blonde 'Chelle was trying to talk. Santa brought her a talking doll. The child and the toy were very much alike. John-David had freeway fever. All he wanted to do was roll. Saint Nick left him a bat-cycle.

On New Year's Eve, we attended a party. Familiar high school faces were there, including Hollis Gooch. Hollis was a borderline bad kid in school, siphoning gas from the teacher's car, cherry bombs in lockers. He was now an agri-pilot, or crop-duster. From dawn to dusk, he wrestled several tons of World War II vintage, bi-winged, single-engine aircraft. The kind of airplane the Royal Guardsmen sang about in *Snoopy Versus the Red Baron*. Diving out of the sky and dodging power lines, he'd skim over rice fields to spray herbicides and fertilizers, then pull up hard before smacking into a line of oak trees, the G-force flattening the flesh on his face. I was not surprised to learn he'd grown up to be a daredevil. We had a drink together and talked about southern California. The crowd was slow dancing, rubbing tummies as the band's lead singer emoted Johnny River's lyrics: "Welcome back, baby, to the poor side of town."

Everyone in town drank, heavily. It was part of the *joie de vivre* of Cajun Culture, the *bon temps rouler*, let the good times roll. It was also what was left over of the '40s and '50s lifestyle. At festival or holiday time the booze flowed faster than the bayou after a flash flood from a thunderstorm. The marijuana that was sweeping the West Coast had not yet infiltrated the South. Kate's younger brothers and their friends were smoking, but they had a connection. It wasn't something you talked about. You never knew who was a smoker and who wasn't. Our old friends in their mid-twenties were all getting drunk. Many of them would never get high on pot. They would swear grass was communist-inspired as they drank themselves into alcoholism.

Around midnight Kate and I stepped outside in the foggy December air to fire up a stick of Acapulco Gold. We drifted away from the sound of "Auld Lang Syne" to the far side of the parking lot. Before we could strike a match, the sweet smell of marijuana came drifting through the mist.

"Well, I'll be damned," said the voice from behind a pickup truck. "I figured y'all were heads. Come take a puff of this stuff Bobby Charles brought back from Nashville." The voice belonged to Hollis Gooch.

"Electrical banana...
Is bound to be the very next phase."

"Mellow Yellow," Donovan
(Donovan P. Leitch, Southern Music Publishing; Peer International Corp.)

1966

♦ On "Mellow Yellow" Donovan gave a nod to his friend guitarist, Bert Jansch, who was part of the very successful British folk rock group Pentangle. At the recording session it is rumored that Paul McCartney whispers the "quite rightly."

Hollywood
January 1967

*"I thought love was only true in fairy tales
Meant for someone else but not for me."*

"I'm A Believer," The Monkees
(Neil Diamond)

I left Louisiana on January 2nd to get back on the air at KTBT. Kate and the kids stayed behind to lengthen the visit. Tonight I was maneuvering the Porsche through heavy traffic on Santa Monica Boulevard while the Monkees sang "I'm A Believer," the Neil Diamond composition and their second major hit. By my side was Karen Valentine. Karen was very serious about her acting career. It was the only thing that meant a great deal to her. She was interested in joining the Cellar Theatre's acting group, but doubted if we could keep her busy. Ken Rose had fallen into a pattern of doing a couple of shows a year, then the rest of the time agonizing about picking the right script and perfect cast that would uphold our reputation for quality work. Karen felt the Cellar was moving too slow. She wasn't the only one who felt that way.

One night after a particularly frustrating evening at the theatre, Bud Tedesco and Pete Pastore cornered me.

"Let's go talk," Pete said.

Over coffee at the Two Guys From Italy Pizza Parlor, Bud picked up the conversation.

"We can't be so damned afraid to fail," he said.

"If I have to listen to one more night about our got damn high standards, I ain't coming back," Pete added.

"Me neither," Bud said. "The whole company is ready to walk out."

"I agree with you guys," I said. "Every two months we should have a new show on the boards and another one in rehearsal."

"Yeah, give more actors a chance to work," Bud was speaking in low tones, but from the way his teeth were grinding, you could tell he was getting pissed.

"Well, it's up to you," Pete said finally.

"I'll see what I can do," I said. "But Ken's not going to let me run the group. As long as he's a part of it, we'll have to do it his way."

"You got to do it," Bud said, almost under his breath, looking me in the eye.

"Do what?" I asked.

"Whatever it takes to get Ken out," Pete answered.

"Wait a minute, guys, this is his theatre. He built it. He's our director."

"Not any more," Bud argued. "You own half of it. We do all the work. I can direct. Or Laquidara will direct. Get Ken out of here, so we can get moving."

"Yeah," Pete repeated. "Ken's out, or we're out. We'll start a new group."

I thought about the proposal the two Italian actors had made. I knew it was an offer I couldn't refuse. How to enact it would take some planning. I didn't believe Ken Rose would accept an offer to buy him out. Several days later I telephoned Ken. I told him my work schedule was too heavy. I was resigning from the group. On the other end of the line, I could hear Ken take a deep breath.

"Davey, I understand what you're doing," he said. "The Chinese have a saying for it. It's called killing the chicken in order to frighten the monkey."

Late the next evening, Ken called back and said he was ready to throw in the towel. Suddenly I was the sole owner of the Cellar Theatre, climbing to the top, Hollywood style, but I didn't like way it had all come down.

"...will there be not a trace left behind,
I could have loved you better,
Didn't mean to be unkind."

"The Last Thing On My Mind," Tom Paxton
(Tom Paxton, Deep Folk Music, Inc.; United Artists Music Co., Inc.)

KTBT
Garden Grove, Orange County
January 27, 1967

"Yeah, you know it ain't but one thing,
This black man he did was wrong,
That's when I moved my wife and family,
I move them down on Mr. Tom Moore's farm."

"Tom Moore's Farm," Lightnin' Hopkins
(Sam Hopkins and Mack McCormick, Traditional Music; Early Recordings,
Vol. 2 Arhoolie)

I was listening to "Tom Moore's Farm," by Sam "Lightnin'" Hopkins, as he took this eat-your-heart-out blues guitar ride. Sam Hopkins had spoken and I had heard. It had only been a few nights earlier when we were playing Dylan songs, that Tim Considine pulled out a stack of blues records and introduced me to Lightnin' Sam.

Today, I was on the air at KTBT and a Latin record was blasting out over Orange County. But inside the booth, on the audition channel, I was listening to Lightnin' Hopkins, because he fit my mood. I got up from the control board, walked out of the broadcast booth, and wandered through the video showroom, looking through the viewfinder of a Panasonic camera. Ahh, television. Magic! Sight and sound. Color. Motion. Emotion. One of these days I want a television station. But I'll start with a couple of these Jap cameras down at the Cellar. I'll have the first theatre in Hollywood to train actors in camera technique using video tape.

Through the door of the teletype room I could hear the clanging of the bell, notifying newsmen and disc jockeys all over the country that something was coming down.

"URGENT, URGENT, URGENT," clacked the teletype, then slowly, methodically, it spelled out the message. "Astronauts Grissom, White, and Chaffee were killed today at Cape Kennedy when an accidental fire engulfed their capsule as they sat waiting to go through a pre-countdown test."

I stood stunned for only a moment before hurrying back to the broadcast booth. Quickly pulling the headset over my short-billed Beatle-style cap, I read the story into the microphone. As soon as I could fire off another Latin record, I called Laquidara on the phone. He was taking everything too seriously. I wanted to get to him before another wave of depression grabbed him. He was shocked by the tragedy. It was the first major NASA accident, and it occurred at a time when we were all beginning to feel invincible in space. I talked Charles up and we firmed plans to see a movie that evening.

The film starring Burt Lancaster was titled *The Professional.* It showed how a group of professional hit men could have assassinated JFK. We were convinced that this is what actually happened. On the way home from the movie, we stopped to talk with Bud and Mel. Once again we rehashed the assassination.

One of the evolving theories pointed at New Orleans and Carlos Marcello. Kate rejected that possibility since she knew "Mr. Carlos" and believed him to be like her father, David Russo, basically a good family man. Charles didn't think the mob had the power to assassinate the President unless aided by the CIA. We were convinced the country was being lied to about the Dallas murder and the conspirators were out there going scott free. We were being sold a bill of goods. Laquidara swore it would be his life-long mission to expose the truth.

> *"I told him, 'No, Mr. Moore, who-o-ah,*
> *Somebody's got to go.'*
> *'Yes,' he said, 'If you ain't able to plow,*
> *Sam, stay up there and grab your hoe.'"*
> (Ibid.)

Carlos Marcello and David Russo.

Hollywood
February 1967

"Finally made contact,
She touched my soul and I
Felt the full impact,
And the night stood still.

Then I kissed her eyes with mine,
And she knelt before me,
Poured the wine,
And told me her story.
We lit a fire
And watched it grow higher,
Sunshine girl, won't you stay with me?
Sunshine girl, won't you stay with me?"

"Sunshine Girl," The Parade
(Fred Roberds, Murray MacLeod and Jerry Riopelle, Inevitable Music/ Good Sam Music)

When Smokey met Raula, a honey blonde twenty–year-old model, I knew it was all over for him. Smokey called me in a few days, his voice dancing with excitement. With in a few hours, he was in our living room in the valley, Raula by his side, his Martin guitar in his lap, singing the lyrics of the hit song we always knew would be coming.

A couple of weeks later, I was driving in from KTBT at 8:00 p.m. I peeled off the Hollywood Freeway and drove to the A&M Studios. Inside, they were laying down the tracks for "Sunshine Girl." It was Murray and Jerry Riopelle's melody. All three were on the vocals. The new group was called The Parade. Laying down the lead acoustic guitar was a quiet skinny kid named Jimmy Messina. From here he would go on to produce Buffalo Springfield's final album. Then he would form Poco. In the '70s, he would team up with Kenny Loggins for six years, produce eight albums and numerous hits, like "Mama Don't Dance," "Angry Eyes," "House at Pooh Corner," and "Vahevala," as Loggins and Messina became household words.

But tonight Jimmy Messina was still a kid with quick fingers on an acoustic guitar, playing lead for The Parade. Jerry Riopelle had been a producer for Phil Spector. Every one knew something about cutting hit records.

Stuart Margolin and I stood in the control room looking out into the studio with all that talent. Stuart had already developed some of the personality of Angel, the character he would become on *Rockford Files*. He had a grin six inches wide. You could feel the excitement. This song was going to be big. Anyone with half an ear could have told you that.

"Magic all around,
Like I never felt before,
And the only sound,
Was the crackling fire,
Then all at once,
The day was melting the nighttime,
Shades of dawn burst into sunshine.
I took her hand and ran through the morning.
Sunshine Girl, won't you stay with me?
Sunshine Girl, won't you stay with me?"
(Ibid.)

Jerry Moss, head of A & M Records, signs "The Parade;"
here with Murray McCloud, Jerry Riopelle, Smokey Roberds.

North Hollywood
Early March 1967

"You can't see the
Forest for the trees."

"Different Drum," Linda Ronstadt & Stone Poneys
(Michael Nesmith, Screen Gem-EMI Music)

Cameron and I had been playing tennis together for six months. We'd sometimes bring the families along, Bonnie and Kate playing singles in the adjacent court while the babies, John-David and 'Chelle, and their daughter, Heidi, played on the gym set a few yards away. Today, only the guys were out. John-David accompanied us and was playing with his trucks on the cement court. He was loading and unloading imaginary sand, gravel, and fill dirt, perhaps building that new leg of the Hollywood Freeway that would cloverleaf at Victory Boulevard two blocks from our home, cutting thirty minutes off our daily round trip drive from North Hollywood to any and all points south, east, or west. John-David was working away on his construction project with all the confidence and bravado of a macho four-year-old.

John-David was simply reflecting what he'd been observing from the two tennis players on the court. Cameron and I went at it like it was Wimbledon.

I really liked Cameron. He was the epitome of cool: good looks, great intellect, sense of humor and a hell of a tennis player.

Kate and I were spending a lot of time with Cameron and Bonnie. There was a heavy sexual undercurrent going on in the relationship. Swinging had hit Hollywood. The four of us were toying with the possibilities.

To spice up our game, Cameron and I were teasing each other with a bet. Winner of the match would get the other guy's wife for an evening. We played the best tennis of our lives, split the first two sets, and as the sun was setting somewhere west of the Encino, I took the final set 7-5. I didn't expect Cameron, or Bonnie, to honor the bet, at least not right away. We were only kidding of course. But the ego rush that went with the winning, and the fantasy, was better than any drug high. We had a good laugh, loaded John-David and his armada of trucks into the Porsche and headed for home. What I didn't know at that time was that Cameron had already collected his winnings every afternoon for the past three weeks while I played disc jockey an hour's drive away in Orange County.

The #42 song on the Billboard Hot 100, "Sunshine Girl" by The Parade had been four weeks on the national charts, breaking in at #87. In Los Angeles, "Sunshine Girl" was even hotter, bubbling under the top ten on KHJ, KRLA, and KFWB. California Rockers all up and down the coast were giving it heavy play. Smokey Roberds' "Ode to Raula," and the spring of 1967, had struck a chord that was reverberating all across the nation. Anyone in the music business lives for this moment, when you know you have a stone cold hit.

"Finally made contact...
She touched my soul and I,
Felt the full impact."

"Sunshine Girl," The Parade
(Fred Roberds, Murray MacLeod and Jerry Riopelle, Inevitable Music/
Good Sam Music)

We all sang as I wheeled Cameron's car up Laurel Canyon toward the Hideout. We'd driven out to the Malibu to watch the sun go down over the Pacific. Smokey and the Sunshine Girl were in the front seat next to me. Cameron was seated in the back between Kate and Bonnie. He was too stoned to drive, so I took control of the wheel and the buttons on the radio. We hung around the Hideout for awhile before hitting the streets again for dinner. We cruised Hollywood first, then crossed over the canyon into North Hollywood and Van Nuys, punching up the 40 AM Rockers to see how many times we would hear "Sunshine Girl." We got to sing along a half dozen times between 9:00 p.m. and midnight.

"And the night stood still,
Then I kissed her eyes with mine
As she knelt before me,
Poured the wine
And told me her story."
(Ibid.)

We dropped in on Charlotte for a drink and smoke. Tim Considine was playing national guard for the weekend. President Johnson had announced plans for a draft by lottery. Nineteen-year-olds would be called first. All deferments would be cut by January '69. Anyone not in the guard was scrambling to cover his ass. Mohammed Ali would not serve in the army because it was against his Muslim religion. We could all get behind that. Killing or getting killed wasn't anything I wanted to do either.

Back at the hideout, Charles had arrived. We spent the rest of the night singing and smoking.

"And the night, it's so groovy,
Magic all around like I never felt before,
And the only sound was the crackling fire."
(Ibid.)

Smokey and Charles debated Zen issues. Charles dubbed Smokey "Reverend Roberds." At dawn we walked out onto the hillside, barefoot in the wet grass. With a red Indian blanket wrapped around him Buddhist style, Reverend Roberds stood outside a small maintenance building on the hillside. The building had an open window looking down fifty feet to the bottom of Laurel Canyon. Stating that he believed he could really fly, Smokey stepped into the building. As we stood aghast, we saw Smokey run through the building, pass the open door in full view of all of us. Then he leaped out the open window toward eternity. Actually what went out the window was Smokey's red Indian blanket, while he slid down out of sight below the window. In our sleep-deprived, stoned-out state, the split second was too real. It was as close to a real Zen trip any of us had ever been.

> "Then all at once the day,
> Was melting the night time.
> Shades of dawn burst into sunshine.
> I took her hand and ran through the morning.
> Sunshine Girl, won't you stay with me."
> (Ibid.)

Allen Roberds and Raula (the Sunshine Girl).

North Hollywood
March 26, 1967

"To try to pull the reins in on me."

"Different Drum," Linda Ronstadt & Stone Poneys
(Michael Nesmith, Screen Gem-EMI Music)

"I'm going to the beach," Kate said, getting out of bed at six a.m.

"It's Easter Sunday. The sun's not up yet. What are you talking about?" I asked incredulously.

"I got to go get my head straight."

"Well wait a minute. We'll wake up the kids and we'll all go," I said.

"I want to go alone. I'll see you later."

The next sound I heard was the front door slamming and the Porsche firing up in the driveway. What, in my mind, was a super marriage and a fantastic relationship had been rapidly deteriorating over the past few weeks. Kate was moody and distant. My attempts at digging for the cause were met with denials of any problems or vague references to not being happy.

Bonnie told us she was sure Cameron was seeing someone. He was asking her to iron his shirts before he went to class. So my buddy was getting some on the side. Too bad about what it was doing to his wife. I couldn't figure out my own problems, so I responded by working harder, leaving home at 9 a.m., being a program director, deejay, music producer, and actor/producer until returning at midnight.

Kate returned from the beach in a somewhat better mood. We loaded the kids, picked up Charles, and went to Elysian Park. Twenty thousand people had gathered for one of the first love-ins in southern California. The sound of flutes and drums and the smell of incense and marijuana was overpowering.

The flower children were beginning to band together and celebrate their lifestyle in public. All over America they were abandoning society's rules tuning in and dropping out. The revolution was under way. On this Easter in Elysian Park, it was peace and love, children and dogs, and flowers in your hair. It would soon escalate to clubs and rocks, tear gas and bullets.

Hollywood
Tuesday, March 28, 1967

On the way in from Orange County, I made my nightly exit at Cahuenga Boulevard, stopped at the Cellar Theatre to confer with Peter Pastore and Bud Tedesco, then headed up Laurel Canyon for a meeting with Smokey at the hideout. He met me at the door.

"Partner, you better get back down to the Cellar," Smokey said. "Tedesco just called, the Padre Hotel is on fire."

I gunned the Porsche back into Hollywood and arrived on the scene to find the L.A. Fire Department fighting a blaze in that section of the Padre Hotel that stood right above the Cellar's basement theatre. Smoke was pouring from the roof. Pete and Bud were looking grim. There was no danger to the Cellar other than water and smoke, but the writing was on the wall. The fire-damaged portion of the Padre would be condemned within two weeks. The remainder of the building would be razed. The stage where we had created laughter and suspense would be six feet under asphalt. In a few months, it would all be just another L.A. parking lot. We were jobless actors without a theatre. My tenure as a producer was short-lived.

The changes around me were coming too fast. Kate became progressively colder. On the morning of April 4, I packed some of my clothes, hugged John-David and 'Chelle, and told her I was moving out. I would stay away until Kate decided what she wanted, or what she wanted me to do.

"You have to decide," was all she said.

The day's work of spinning records dragged on, then it was time to go...somewhere. I had dinner with Bachman, talking videotape, then finally at midnight, showed up at the Hideout, where Charles was already rooming with Smokey.

"Sorry to show up so late," I said to Smokey, who met me at the door in his shorts, with his guitar in one hand and a joint in the other.

"Come on in, brother Dave," he said. "You know how it is when you're family, it don't matter what time of night it is. When you knock, we got to get up and let you in."

Charles was in the corner, sitting in a Yoga position, meditating. He came out of it long enough to say, "We've been expecting you."

The next week was like a bad dream. Unable to sleep, I found myself in Barney's Beanery with Charles, shooting pool at 2:00 and 3:00 a.m., or smoking until dawn with Smokey, getting up three hours later and dragging ass down the freeway to KTBT. By Friday night I was exhausted and fell asleep on the living room floor at midnight. Somewhere around 4:00 a.m., I woke up to Charles' voice.

"Has he been there all night?" he was asking.

"Yeah, he's worn pretty thin," Smokey said.

"Poor bastard, he still doesn't know, does he?"

"I guess not."

"Who's gonna tell him?" Charles asked.

"He'll figure it out, sooner or later," Smokey replied.

Figure it out? Figure out what? My mind was racing as a knowing ache started in the pit of my stomach. I pretended to be asleep for an hour until Smokey and Charles went to bed. Then I slipped out of the Hideout and drove into the valley at daybreak. The lights were on at Babcock. I unlocked the front door. John-David and 'Chelle were having breakfast around their little table. They ran to me with excited shouts.

"Daddy, Daddy, you're home," 'Chelle exclaimed, hugging my knee.

"I missed you, where you been man?" John-David said.

"I missed you guys terribly, too," I said. "Sorry I left, I guess that's just one more mistake I made. Y'all up a little early, aren't you?" Then looking at Kate, I asked, "Just coming in?"

She looked at me briefly then went back to pouring milk for the kids.

"Where is he?" I asked.

"On the patio," she answered.

It was barely daylight, but close friends are easy to recognize. Cameron grinned sheepishly.

"It's all over, pal," I said.

"I know," he replied, then stopped me as I turned to go back inside. "I didn't want to hurt you," he said, "it was just one of those things. I couldn't help myself. I'm sorry."

"Sure," I said. "It happens in the best of families."

Inside, Kate followed me into the living room.

"How long?" I asked.

"A while."

"A while?"

"A few weeks, does it matter."

"I guess not."

"We were just coming in to change baby sitters," she said. "I'll be back tonight."

"I'll be here. I want to start over," I said.

"I know," she replied.

"To try and pull the reins in on me."

"Different Drum," Linda Ronstadt & Stone Poneys
(Mike Nesmith, Screen Gem-EMI Music)

KTBT
Garden Grove, Orange County
April 1967

"Look out kid
Don't matter what you did."

"Subterranean Homesick Blues," Bob Dylan
(Bob Dylan, Special Rider Music)

On April 10, the city of Los Angeles sent an eviction notice to the Padre Hotel. We had already salvaged the dimmerboard, a few seats and some other essentially worthless equipment. We began the frustrating search for a new home for the Cellar Theatre.

On April 16, the leaders of the anti-war movement staged a rally in New York City. One hundred thousand people attended. Draft cards and flags were burned.

On April 24, Oliver Berliner called a 2 p.m. meeting of the staff of KTBT. It was the middle of my shift so I put on the longest Latin record I could find and stepped out of the booth. Something was in the air. Frank Ernest was even more snide than usual and Michelle wouldn't look me in the eye. Berliner beat around the bush a bit. The video department was off to a slow start, but he was really optimistic about the future. The Latin publishing firm was going great, carrying the load for the other companies.

"Here it comes," Bernie, the night jock, muttered to me under his breath. "Bend over and kiss your butt good bye."

"Only KTBT is a big disappointment," Berliner continued. "It isn't Frank and Michelle's fault, and certainly isn't the fault of our on-air staff, but sales are just not keeping up with our expenses and we're forced to make some cuts. Frank has come up with some answers. We're going to do what many small stations are doing. We're investing in automation equipment. Of course that means we'll no longer need the services of our disc jockeys. It doesn't mean you're fired. The automation won't arrive for another two and a half weeks. So, you'll have at least that long to find other employment. We appreciate your loyalty and effort. That concludes this meeting."

So Frank Ernest had evened the score, in a left-handed sort of way. What else could you expect from a banker in a radio station? You might as well have an accountant selecting the music. I had been reading about automation. I wasn't totally surprised by Berliner's decision. Somewhere along the line, I knew a robot would get my job. In a way I guess I was thankful it was this job at KTBT, and not a radio show on a station that could have taken me all the way to the top in the ratings. The other jocks were devastated. I was numb. I'd been on automatic for a month now. I was on a fast train heading downhill. Charles said I was back-feeding my problems with negative energy. Smokey called it a king-size bummer.

KTBT
Garden Grove, Orange County
Early May 1967

I was on the air at KTBT, totally bored with it, all enthusiasm gone. Just marking time until the automated equipment got hooked up and made my skills obsolete. Charles Laquidara was in the video showroom, talking with the salesman about the equipment. This was his third trip to Orange County with me to check out the video gear. He was excited about it and trying to fire me up too.

At Charles' urging I mortgaged my furniture and Kate's VW, raised a thousand dollars, and bought a basic video rig: camera, tripod, and VCR deck. What was left of the Cellar acting group began meeting at Bachman's house. It was centrally located below the Hollywood Bowl, just a few blocks from where the old theatre had burned. Bachman was glad to have us around, excited by our efforts and felt we were headed in the right direction. We'd meet twice a week, perform scenes in front of the camera, then critique the tape. Tim Considine and I had several meetings about the use of video in acting workshops. He thought Charles and I were on to something. I was ready to link up with him which would have been a good move for both of us. We even found a site near Hollywood High School. But Charles was cool to the idea. He was holding out for a facility large enough to rebuild the Cellar stage, and eventually the timing for Tim and me passed us by.

In San Francisco Ralph Gleason and Jann Werner formed a new magazine to write about the emerging counter culture. They called it *Rolling Stone*. A disc jockey named Tom Donahue, having built KYA into "The Boss of the Bay," was Mr. Radio. And all across America, Aretha Franklin was burning up the airwaves.

Hollywood
Mid-May 1967

"And you're sick of all this repetition,
Aw, won't you come see me, Queen Jane?"

"Queen Jane Approximately," Bob Dylan
(Bob Dylan, Special Rider Music)

By mid-May, "Sunshine Girl" was #25 nationwide, and Smokey was a staff writer at A&M Records. I auditioned for a rock station in Palmdale, fifty miles north out in Antelope Valley, but nothing happened. I just didn't seem to have what they were looking for in a Top 40 jock. May 12th was mercifully my last day at KTBT and I was once again without a microphone. On May 15th, I drove my Porsche up to the unemployment office and filed for benefits. Then I looked up Vince Donofrio.

"The past is but a dream," Vince was saying. "The future doesn't exist, 'the eternal now' is all there is. Live in the present. Live the moment with all your being."

For several months Vince had been studying Zen Buddhism with the Roshi, a Zen master residing in East Los Angeles. Unlike Charles, who went down every morning at 4:00 a.m. to meditate in the Roshi's presence, then going about his daily life like the average Angelino, Vince had actually moved into the Roshi's quarters, devoting twenty-four hours a day to his spiritual enlightenment.

The recent reversals in my family, business, and career had devastated me. I was borderline distraught. I was ready to listen to anyone. Vince had the truth according to Zen. I could have done worse.

"Too much greed, too much graft," Vince continued. "It's like this crazy Vietnam thing. Under the guise of being the world's policeman, we're fighting the communists but it's all meaningless. A million souls will perish and nothing will change. Only more billions of dollars line the pockets of the military industrial complex and the defense establishment. We should be policing our environment. We're too caught up with catching the boogey man to look around and smell the air. The real aggression is in the corporate board rooms of America." There was a lot of radical left in this Zen student. Then Vince began to personalize the lecture and hit home where I lived.

"So what happens if you and Smokey and Charles ball half a dozen starlets per night?" Vince continued. "You're not any better or worse off. What happens if through hard work or luck, you're able to build the #1 rock 'n roll radio station in this town? Nothing will change. You'll still be you, in the eternal moment of the majestic flow of life. You must experience ego death, the giving up of yourself. Then you can really live life, experience it, and be in it. You must die to be born again and live. But you see, I'm preaching to you, using words and ideas to describe what can only be experienced. Drinking water is only understood by drinking water, not by reading or hearing about it. There is no scripture in Zen. It is the wisdom of the absolute mind. Man, beyond all creatures, has the ability to reflect on life, we objectify it. That's when we lose our absolute wisdom. Through the study and practice of Zen principles, we strive to regain this wisdom. Once you've done that, then you can become a new human being and able with this knowledge to live in the eternal now."

What Vince was saying was making a lot of sense, except that I couldn't believe that building the #1 radio station in the City of Angels wouldn't make some kind of irreversible change in one's being. I went home and put the *Revolver* album on the stereo. I skipped to the last cut on side two. It sounded to me like Vince Donofrio and John Lennon were on the same trip.

> *"Turn off you mind,*
> *Relax and float downstream...*
> *Lay down all thoughts,*
> *Surrender to the void."*
>
> "Tomorrow Never Knows," The Beatles
> (John Lennon and Paul McCartney, Sony/ATV Tunes LLC)

1967

♦ "Tomorrow Never Knows" was the Beatles' first psychedelic song, which Lennon was inspired to write after reading *The Psychedelic Experience* based on the *Tibetan Book of the Dead*.

Vince Donofrio

North Hollywood
Late May 1967

"What can you do with a woman
When she got a back door friend?
She just prayin' for you to move out
So her back door friend can move in?"

"Back Door Friend," Lightnin' Hopkins
(Sam Hopkins and Stanley J. Lewis, SU-MA Publishing Co.)

From an introduction to Zen, we segued right into psychodrama. I learned that my problems and Lightnin' Hopkins' were basically the same. A few thousand years of the sexual double standard was coming to an end. The sisters were fixing to even the score. In psychodrama, I came face to face with Kate's point of view as she told it, no holds barred, to an actor friend playing my part. My words and attitudes, spoken by him, often sounded hollow, indefensible. We acted it all out in front of the video camera, then played it back and studied it. While the sexual revolution was sweeping the country eastward like a hot Santa Ana wind, we were already wading through the fallout of failure, searching for answers, carrying a video camera.

Deciding to take this enlightenment even deeper, we started setting up the camera in the living room at parties. Charles, Kate, Vince, and I took turns as camera operators, recording what was going on with the subjects in front of the lens, and also revealing a great deal about what trip the camera man was on. Our favorite activity became having dinner while the camera sat stationary, locked down on a wide shot. Eventually, we would forget it was on, then forget to be cool, forget to act. We decided you could learn everything you needed to know about a person, be it yourself or someone else, by watching him dine.

"Don't you work as hard as you play
Make-up, break-up, everything you shake up,

...Good Vibrations and our imaginations
can't go on indefinitely
And California dreaming
Is becoming a reality."

"Creque Alley," The Mamas and the Papas
(John and Michelle Phillips, Universal MCA Music Publishing)

1967

♦ "Creque Alley" tells the story of the formation of the Mamas and the Papas. It references John Phillips' friendship with Scott McKenzie ("If You're Going to San Francisco"), along with the beginnings of the Byrds and the Lovin' Spoonful.

"One day the Princess Delores
Found herself lost in the forest.
She was very frightened, of cour-us
Of the witch which was in the sky.
She stumbled down to the river.
Midnight dampness gave her a shiver.
A snake bet the old frog a fivver
She'd never make the other side..."

"Frog Prince," The Parade
(Fred Roberds, Murray MacLeod, Stuart Margolin and Herman Neilds,
Inevitable Music/Good Sam Music; Irving Music)

"Sunshine Girl" was at #12 on the Billboard, a breath under the Top Ten. Smokey, Murray, and Riopelle were already over-dubbing their voices for The Parade's first album. To my ear, only "Frog Prince" and "Every Time I Turn My Radio On" were candidates for a possible follow-up hit. But the sound of the summer of '67 was already sweeping onto the radio. The Doors' "Light My Fire," and Procol Harem's "A Whiter Shade of Pale" were telling a different story. The innocence of the early '60s had persisted past the point of relevance and *Sergeant Pepper's Lonely Heart Club Band* was blowing it all away in a flood tide of creative new sound.

Kate was uneasy. Taking John-David and 'Chelle, she left by train for an extended stay in Louisiana. I began to question what I was doing in Los Angeles. A town with that much concrete, steel, and dirty air is no place to raise kids. A combo of events, the Cellar fire, the automation of KTBT, the near break-up of my family, had me asking lots of questions. By day I hunted the streets of Los Angeles and Hollywood, looking for the site of the next Cellar Theatre. We needed 2,000 square feet of space at an affordable price of 10 cents per square foot.

By night I talked the philosophy of life with Smokey, Charles, and Vince. My sister Russie was into reincarnation. She and I spent several evenings delving into her world of mediumship, allowing spirits to speak through her, a practice that took twenty years to become the hot California fad known as channeling. She also claimed to engage in astral projection. Russie's best friend was heiress Deanie Honeywell, a beautiful California girl who was also into Kabala and everything New Age. Their friend and teacher, Carmen Montez, lived in a secluded apartment nestled in the residential area of Highland below Hollywood. Carmen's frequent guest was known by his nickname "Bud." Since Russie and Carmen were sisters in a past life time, Bud kinda looked at all of them as blood kin, since he and his sisters Joycelyn and Frances had grown up with Carmen. She would fix his favorite meals from his boyhood and lay out gold satin sheets where he rested from the intensity of the white hot limelight. Russie had to listen closely when he spoke. Even close up and personal, Marlon Brando mumbled his lines.

I was facing the most unsettling period of my life. No one at home to relate to, no stage on which to step out of my skin into someone else's problems. No groove to slot the needle in, no microphone to turn on.

Hungering for the ride, I wandered around the big town with only the music and the voices of other disc jockeys to keep me company.

"Everytime I turn my radio on
I hear music, lots of crazy music.
Sounds exploding, so exciting to my ear.
Oh oh, I hear love songs,
Move me so strong,
Always someone out there
Playing what I want to hear.

I hear rainbows,
Lots of crazy rainbows,
Bright colored melodies
Come drifting out to me."

"Radio Song," The Parade
(Fred Roberds, Murray MacLeod, Stuart Margolin and Herman Neilds, Inevitable Music/Good Sam Music; Irving Music)

Los Angeles
June 8, 1967

"It's a restless hungry feeling
That don't mean no one no good."

"One Too Many Mornings," Bob Dylan
(Bob Dylan, Special Rider Music)

In less than a week, the Israelis turned the mid-east war into a rout. By contrast the U.S. involvement in Vietnam continued to deepen with no end in sight. The peace movement gained strength and began to sweep the country. The music led the charge with folk singers like Judy Collins, Joan Baez, and Bob Dylan verbalizing in the lyrics what we were all beginning to feel. *Hair* opened in New York. The explicit portrayal of the sixties generation shocked and charmed the audience. Bobby Seale and Huey Newton formed the Black Panther Party. Suddenly the specter of "Niggers with Guns" was real and very scary to white America, and at the same time, militant blacks began to influence and inspire the white radical left.

Link Wyler had a live-in chauffeur's job for Murray McCloud's family at their mansion overlooking the Pacific Ocean. One of his chores was to maintain the pool. A few years later, during the winter rains, that same pool would cave in and fall onto the Pacific Coast highway a hundred feet below, all part of the California lifestyle.

Link would drive the McClouds to the airport in their jammies to catch a Paris flight on a midnight whim. After one particular dinner party, Link drove a prominent attorney's wife home because she'd had too much wine. At sunrise, she got out of Link's car, brushed the sand from her nude body, and walked up her driveway in Bel Air. Allen Wayne, another Arkansas songwriter, was on the payroll, too, for awhile. Until one night, in an attempt to relax, Allen Wayne went down to the wine cellar. He didn't have a clue to the value of a wine label. The bottle he selected and drank was worth $500.

I went to the McCloud's mansion several times to sit around the ill-fated pool and gaze out at the Pacific while Link and Allen Wayne worked at writing country and western. They were trying to put together songs for an album for Milburn Stone, who played "Doc" on *Gunsmoke*. I came up with a couple of lyrics, but it wasn't my bag.

Charles Laquidara and I made another pact to quit smoking cigarettes. On the previous attempt, I had it beat, but Charles gave in once again to the addiction. So, after several months, Charles and I made a second pact. I would smoke until he agreed I was sufficiently hooked, then we'd quit together, again. It was relatively easy for me. Every time I felt the need to smoke, I fired up a joint instead of a cigarette. I canceled my haircut appointment with Peter Pastore. The next morning when shaving time came, the beginnings of the thin wisp of a mustache stayed on.

Charles was working in the print shop at Twentieth Century Fox when he fell in love with a red Mustang, and the beautiful girl driving it through the studio lot. Turns out she was secretary to the studio chief, Richard Zanuck. She was also dating actor Adam West, who played Batman. For awhile Charles was balling Batman's girlfriend. He said only the Joker, Charles's alter ego, could pull that off.

When the deal to shoot *The Boston Strangler* came together at Fox, Charles had the inside story before any other actor in town. When he ran off the script in the print shop, he smuggled out a copy.

Charles was convinced this could be his big break. After all, he was from Boston. He could play the Strangler. Using our video equipment with Charlotte Stewart playing a beautiful, sexy victim, and Vince Donofrio directing, Charles came up with a chilling, haunting portrayal in a scene straight out of *The Boston Strangler* script. Director Richard Fleischer viewed it with mild irritation. How could his script have gotten into the hands of amateurs? Although he thought Charles showed talent, he wasn't about to cast an unknown in the lead. He needed a box office name. Tony Curtis played the Boston Strangler. Charles Laquidara got axed from the Fox print shop.

Charles at the beach, 1965.

Monterey, California
Mid-June 1967

*"I got a dog in my back yard.
Howled the day my baby's gone."*

"Lonesome Dog Blues," Lightnin' Hopkins
(Sam Hopkins, Jewel, Careers BMG Music Publishing)

The record label read "Lonesome Dog Blues" by Sam Lightnin' Hopkins. Recorded on Jewel Records. Address: 728 Texas Street, Shreveport, Louisiana. Even though we were light years apart in lifestyle and cultural background, the old east Texas blues man was hitting me where it hurt. I found myself wandering around our two-bedroom house, trying to figure out how it had become so large. I paused in the kitchen, looking at the little kids' table, that sat by the back door, staring at the empty patio.

One day in June, Smokey came up with a new trip. We'd take a train to Monterey for a concert that was being put together by Papa John Phillips and his record company people. The ride up was filled with anticipation and all manner of prophets. I spent a couple of evenings talking Sufism with a blonde longhaired young man who was very convincing in his belief that Meher Baba was the real Messiah. Through it all, spirituality versus drugs was a common theme. We spoke it with conviction as we puffed grass every night until daybreak.

*"Children danced night and day,
Religion was being born."*

"Monterey," Eric Burden
(Eric Burden, John Weider, Victor Briggs, Daniel J. McCulloch, and Barry Jenkins, Carbert Music, Unichappell Music, Inc.)

Among the fifty thousand that gathered at Monterey were two Los Angeles disc jockeys. The old Top 40 rocker, B. Mitchell Reed and Les Carter, the young KNOB jock voted the most popular jazz air personality in the city. They were meeting with the King of San Francisco radio Tom Donahue. The three of them were planning the next wave of rock 'n roll. This time the *Ether Express* would ride the FM band.

Music, love, and flowers were everywhere. The prototype for all future concerts was being laid out. June 16th and 17th made memories of singers and bands whose names were still brand new. Our heads were filled with images of The Who, Jefferson Airplane, Simon and Garfunkel, the Mamas and the Papas. It was the first concert for the Electric Flag. In a tribute to John Kennedy, The Byrds sang "He Was a Friend of Mine." For the first time, I heard the sexy young blues belter from Port Arthur, Texas. We had grown up a little more than a hundred miles apart. Now, here I sat on the rocky coast of northern California mesmerized by Janis Joplin. A new group featured a guitar player who used his teeth on the strings to make it howl. He played and sang "Wild Thing," "Rock Me Baby," and "Like a Rolling Stone." The Jimmy Hendrix Experience asked, "Are You Experienced?" and we had to respond. Ravi Shankar's sitar and Hugh Masekela's music gave us a preview of how wide and encompassing this new music revolution would be.

One of rock's legends carved his niche at Monterey with performances of songs like "Satisfaction" and "Loving You Too Long." The audience stood on their chairs and gave him a standing ovation when Otis Redding said, "I'll do that song she stole from me. It's my song, you know." Then he sang "Respect" like no one had ever heard it before. It was perhaps one of the best all-time live performances. And when Otis Redding sang "Try a Little Tenderness," the roots of the revolution took hold in Monterey. Six months later Otis checked out in a plane crash.

> *"You want to find the truth in life,*
> *Don't pass music by."*
> (Ibid.)

Louisiana Gulf Coast
July 1, 1967

"If I should call you up, invest a dime
And you say you belong to me
and ease my mind..."

"Happy Together," The Turtles
(Garry Bonner & Alan L. Gordon, Alley Music Corp., Trio Music Co.
Inc.)

Charlotte Stewart's career continued to smoke with steady work on television. Her sexy schoolgirl beauty was way more than skin deep and she always had time for a good deed. When Martin Sheen came out to Los Angeles from New York to take the stage with Patricia Neal in *The Subject Was Roses,* he needed someone to baby-sit his two rowdy boys while he spent evenings at the theatre. Charlotte took the duty of riding herd on three-and five-year-old Charlie Sheen and Emilio Estevez. The little rascals would literally swing from the hotel chandeliers, but they met their match in the girl who knew something about handling boys.

Charlotte talked me back from ego devastation with wisdom on the reality of the new '60s woman that was right on. I rode a train back to Louisiana to reunite with Kate, John-David, and 'Chelle. Our relationship would be patched up and smoothed over. The basic problems were buried for the next five years before finally blowing us apart. In the meantime, we would have an opportunity to develop the nuclear family into a high profile lifestyle, proving you could embrace the revolution and prosper.

One morning at 4:00 a.m., I drove down to the edge of civilization on the Louisiana coast, where the old farm stretched westward from Vermilion Bayou. At this prearranged time, Russie was to visit me via astral projection from Sun Valley in L.A. I walked around under the pecan trees in the cool summer dawn. I looked up into the limbs I used to climb to catch the Gulf breeze and watch the shrimp boats. My mind flashed backward to the '40s and '50s when a day took forever to pass and a year was an eternity. Then fast forward to the freeway pace of fast lane Hollywood. I was caught in some kind of crazy time warp. I tried to live in the moment, to concentrate on the here and now, to receive the universal life energy flowing through me. For a brief moment, I thought I heard Russie's voice. I never knew if it was for real or my imagination, maybe just an echo from 1948 or an even earlier lifetime on the banks of the Rio de Los Lobos.

I drove back into town dodging the blue Schlumberger trucks that had been barreling down this road for fifteen years on their way to the offshore rigs in the Gulf. I visited my step-grandfather and we talked about Vietnam and World War I. He had fought in the trenches in Europe. I had heard the stories before, but once again, he described the horror of hand-to-hand combat. He went into an emphysema coughing spasm, and then he lit another cigarette.

Although the news was still not front page back in L.A., the local papers here in Louisiana were carrying the story. New Orleans District Attorney Jim Garrison had a brand new JFK assassination theory. The fact that Lee Harvey Oswald had lived in New Orleans had always caused speculation about a Crescent City conspiracy, including a Mafioso Carlos

Marcello connection. Jim Garrison had uncovered evidence of a liaison between Oswald and Clay Shaw, the director of the New Orleans International Trade Mart. There were also links to Schlumberger Well Testers of Houma, Louisiana. A phone call to Charles Laquidara fired his interest and his imagination. In a few months, Charles and I would put the Jim Garrison segment of the JFK assassination plot on a Hollywood stage twenty-five years before Oliver Stone shot his film on the subject.

The trip back to the West Coast included a stop over in El Paso for lunch with my cousin, Teddy Cessac. Teddy had lived with my parents after I'd left for California. Almost like a younger brother to me, Teddy was a shy, quiet, introverted young man with a slight stutter. Now he was finishing up an army stint. He'd lucked out, fulfilling his military obligation in a clerical job in El Paso, while he lived with a Mexican girl and learned how to make burritos. He wanted to come to Hollywood. He didn't want to act. He just wanted to meet a real live actress. I told him he was talking to the right guy. As soon as his discharge papers came through, Teddy would catch the first bus heading west on Interstate 10.

Ted Cessac - next stop Los Angeles.

Los Angeles
Mid-July 1967

"The time to hesitate is through..."

"Light My Fire," The Doors
(Robbie Krieger, Doors Music Co.)

Back in L.A., I forgot about throwing in the towel. Whatever I came to L.A. to do was still doable. Rock music was what underscored my daily life. I wanted to play it on the radio. Tim Considine called and dropped a bombshell on me.

"Hey Dave," he said. "There's a deejay out of Detroit named Larry Miller who's pulling a late night shift on KMPX Radio in San Francisco. Get this. The guy is playing rock 'n roll."

"Okay," I said. "What's significant about a rock 'n roll jock on a 'Frisco station called KMPX."

"Think about it, Dave," Tim's voice went shrill on the phone. "MPX stands for multiplex stereo."

"You mean KMPX is FM?"

"That's it, baby. That's what you've been talking about. Now this guy, Miller, is the first one in the country to do it. Playing rock 'n roll in stereo on FM is gonna knock 'em out."

I was burning up inside. I had a head full of songs driving me insane. I had to get in on the ground floor of FM rock. Everything that happened in 'Frisco happened in L.A. and vice versa. Obviously I wasn't the only disc jockey in the country who had a pretty good idea about the future of radio. Los Angeles would have an FM rocker within weeks. The only question was "Which radio station?"

"The time to hesitate is through,
...Try now, we can only lose..."
(Ibid.)

The Doors' first record had gone to number one. Electra Records had released the shorter version, but as soon as the LP came out, the AM rockers stayed on the six minute fifty second version and never got off it. Ray Manzerak's cooking organ was too good to edit out.

Kate and I were beginning to work as a team again. We went after the Cellar project with a vengeance. Within a few days we found a location. I was scanning the *L.A. Times'* classified when the words jumped off the page. "For Lease: 2,000 square feet, 10 cents per foot, 102 Vermont."

John-David was sitting on my lap behind the wheel of the Porsche. We approached the Vermont Exit off the Hollywood Freeway.

"We're getting pretty close to downtown," I said. "But we're still on the edge of Hollywood."

"Go faster, Dad," was all he said.

The building sat on the corner of Vermont and Second, just a few blocks from the Hollywood Freeway. It was everything we wanted, from high ceilings to the kindly looking sixty-year-old landlord, Mr. Sheimer, who had a master lease on the building, and lived in the storage section in the back.

"Y-e-s-s, later we can talk about a lease purchase of the whole building," Mr. Sheimer said. "Since you're obviously an aggressive young business man, you'll probably need the second floor for additional classrooms."

"Hey, Dad, where are you gonna put the stage?" asked the four-year-old, running through the building and sliding on the slick tile floor.

Back in the valley, we held an impromptu meeting in the front yard at 6416 Babcock. Charles, Kate, and I were ecstatic.

"You have to build a separate room for the video," Charles was saying, scratching out a floor plan in the North Hollywood dirt. "We can't go into this thing half ass. It has to be the most beautiful, comfortable workshop theater in Hollywood. We're going to have to spend some money."

"Where are we going to get it?" I asked.

"I don't know. That's your job, David," was Charles' reply.

"Well, I'll tell you what you better do first," Kate said. "You better get Jim Bachman working on a set of plans. You guys don't know jack shit about design. Give it to Bachman. He's an expert, he's got style and taste."

"Good idea," Charles said. "Now I'll start looking for a script. I'll call Bud Tedesco and Pete Pastore. David, you call Karen Valentine. Smokey and Vince might be interested."

"Smokey's pretty hung up with the record business right now," I said. "But it would be terrific to get Vince Donofrio on stage. And I think we can count on Valentine."

"Well, they all gotta get behind us. This is a big deal, David. A hell of an opportunity for everybody. It's our own theatre, man. It's a dream come true."

Blond-headed two-and-a-half year-old baby 'Chelle was standing by my side during the whole conversation. John-David was scribbling in the dirt.

"Lookit, Dad," he said. "You gotta put the stage over here. You and Charles don't know jack shit."

Los Angeles
August 1967

"'Cause the cops don't need you,
And man, they expect the same."

"Just Like Tom Thumb's Blues," Bob Dylan
(Bob Dylan, Special Rider Music)

The long hot summer of '67 was speeding by as the headlines kept the pace. Negro riots in Northern cities. Troops sent into Detroit to quell disturbances. On the other side of the world, 45,000 men were disembarking, pushing toward the goal of 525,000 American soldiers in Vietnam. A U.S. transport was shot down by American gunners in a mishap in South Vietnam.

Back in Hollywood, Jim Bachman had a look at the new Cellar location. His first decision was to put the entrance at the rear of the building. Guests would have to walk through an alley about thirty feet long toward a sign with a big hand pointing around the corner, then walk down a ramp to ground level. In one stroke Bachman had preserved the *raison d'etre* for the Cellar Theatre name.

"Besides, it'll be much cleaner entering from the back," Bachman said. "Hollywood people love this kind of funky, off-beat, out-of-the way place. It has character."

We began working feverishly, putting in the walls that separated dressing rooms, video studio, and control booth from the main stage area that would hold the most comfortable forty theatre seats in Hollywood. Within two weeks we were out of money and the job was just beginning. It was going to take several thousand dollars more to complete the renovation. There was only one place I could get that kind of backing.

We drove back to Louisiana, stole a page from the David Russo book of business and formed two family corporations.

The first company, named Pierce Enterprises, Inc., took possession of the boat docks on the banks of the Bayou Vermilion. Pierce Enterprises, Inc. in turn owned the Cellar Theatre, Inc., licensed to pursue entertainment ventures. I had linked my heritage with my future. Louisiana property would back the L.A. adventure.

In L.A. the Cellar's membership wasn't happy with the new deal. Valentine's new boyfriend, Mac McLaughlin, said he would have nothing to do with a theatre group owned by a corporation, as he walked out the door, taking our ingenue lead with him. The next time we saw Karen Valentine she was acting on television, on her way to stardom in "Room 222." The construction of the new Cellar Theatre continued at a slower and less enthusiastic pace.

Nellie and Casey came out to Los Angeles to look at the Cellar project and see where the investment dollars were going. Down at the theatre, I introduced Casey to our old landlord, Mr. Sheimer.

"We'll look out for the boy," Sheimer assured Casey, with a twinkle in his eye, as I unloaded another thousand dollars' worth of lumber into his building.

At home in North Hollywood, we were all sitting around the patio, enjoying some of Nellie's Cajun cooking, when John-David answered the knock at the front door. He ran back to the patio with this simple announcement.

"Freddy's here," John-David said.

Teddy had arrived from El Paso. The family had all gathered and were reunited with the start of the new theatre project. That night I played some of my favorite Bob Dylan for Nellie. She was not impressed with the lyrics.

> *"Don't put on any airs*
> *When you're down on Rue Morgue Avenue."*
> (Ibid.)

Okinawa
Late August 1967

"Been a soldier for a thousand years."

"Universal Soldier," Donovan
(Buffy St. Marie, Woodmere Music; Caleb Music Co.)

The war build-up included Woodie Bernard. His point of view was a hundred and eighty degrees from the protesters back home.

Sorry I hadn't written, but I've been on the move. I made a three-month trip to Taiwan with an A-Team. Spent the whole time except for two weeks in the mountain areas training National Chinese airborne troops in guerilla warfare. Tough little troops, and tougher little mountains. Not that tall, maybe 2,500-3,000 feet, but damn near straight up and straight down. These Chinese are like Cajuns, they eat anything. Every night that we'd stop near young bamboo, those Chinese would get to digging around and find some big earthworms under that bamboo. They'd throw those worms and bamboo sprouts in that rice pot and chow down. Hell, I figured if they ate it, I could too. Not bad, if you put a little Tabasco on it.

We made a jump at the start of the training and met with the Chinese troops on the side of a mountain. That's a real trip, you ought to try it sometime. At 10:00 p.m. with a rifle and an 80 lb. rucksack. Got-damn brain whirling all the way down, wondering if I'd get a 30 foot bamboo stuck up my butt when I landed. Landed in a tea tree, would you believe it? No problems. Lived on the ground and out of that rucksack for the next two months. Every now and then we'd send a Chinese soldier to buy food in country stores. They'd bring backpacks of rice labeled "A gift of the American People, Not to be Sold." Every time I'd see that, I had to laugh, damn words were written in English. How many Chinese understand English? We got some dumb asses running our foreign aid programs. Those country stores damn sure didn't give it away. I saw some that was milled in Abbeville, LA. I couldn't help wondering if that rice was maybe grown on our property or maybe y'all's property. Wouldn't that be a hell of a note, go half way around the world and have to buy your own damn rice, that you gave away. Kind of makes you wonder don't it?

Not very long after we got back from Taiwan the Colonel on Okinawa that runs our group called everyone in our company together and told us he needed volunteers for four A-Teams. He said that he couldn't tell us where we were going or what we'd be doing when we got there. He did say that we'd be drawing combat pay and earning it. Out of 156 volunteers, they picked 48 men to fill the A-Teams, and I was lucky enough to get a slot on one of the teams. Don't know exactly where we're going, but this is the most intensive training I've seen yet. I haven't slept inside of a building for two months. With practically the whole company volunteering to go and not even knowing where, is a good example of why Special Forces is called the Triple-A Outfit. Three A's or AAA. Anything, Anytime, Anywhere. I know we're headed for Vietnam, cause that's the only place that's paying combat pay, but where in Vietnam, and doing what we have no idea. But with the intense field training we've been doing, it's a safe bet to say we probably won't be used to pour tea and serve cookies in the U.S. Embassy. We'll be shipping out soon I figure, and I'm ready to go. So is everyone else.

How's that Dago gal treating you? You wouldn't believe how good these Asian women treat a fellow. You talk about service with a smile! I don't think these gals know the meaning of the word "No." And I damn sure ain't gonna be the one to tell 'em.

Give those two rug-rats you got a hug for me.

I got to go to sleep. I got another long day tomorrow humping these got-damn hills in Okinawa.

See you Later, Alligator

The Comic Book Kid

Your Pal,
Woodie
Okinawa

Woodie Bernard ready for Vietnam.

KPPC FM
Pasadena Presbyterian Church
October 1967

"Anti-War Demonstrators Try to Storm the Pentagon," screamed the headlines. "U.S. marshals meet them with clubs and beat them back in brutal confrontation."

In Berkley, "Stop the Draft Week" was stopped cold by Riot Police who wiped out the protestors. No draft inductees were turned back. The War Machine rolled on. General Westmoreland needed a million more men. FBI's Hoover said he could not ensure domestic security. Showing the strain he was under, Lyndon Johnson went before the TV cameras to say he would not seek re-election. The really Radical Left became more cut off from the revolution. Most of the anti-war movement realized they had to act in a political non-violent manner. But the more alienated the youth of America became, the more willing we were to up the ante.

Kate had taken a part-time job at KPPC. Al Herion called her regularly to untangle the logs when things got too messy. He would also call me occasionally to fill in an air shift for a sick disc jockey. I was checking over an AP story on California Governor Ronald Reagan, who was trying to balance the budget, when two men walked into the basement studio. One was middle-aged, overweight, thick beard, deep, resonant voice. They talked right through the open microphone, lowering their voices only slightly.

"Excuse me," I said, flicking off the microphone. "This is a radio station. We're on the air here."

The overweight man gave me a disgusted look.

"I'm Tom Donahue," was all he said.

"Hello, Tom. I'm Dave Pierce. Maybe we could step out into the hall to visit," I replied, escorting them out the door.

"Sure, Dave Pierce, anything you say," Tom said, with obvious irritation.

Al Herion came scurrying down the hall to meet us.

"Tom, Tom," Herion said. "Please, come this way. I'm certainly glad to see you. We're so happy you're here."

The way Herion was groveling was very disconcerting. I walked back into the studio trying to remember why I should know Tom Donahue. My question was answered about thirty minutes later when Herion popped his head inside the door.

"Well, what do you think?" he asked.

"About what?"

"Tom Donahue. He's the guy you just met. What do you think?"

"I don't know, Al. You tell me. What's going on?"

All of a sudden, Al had a look on his face like he'd forgotten to tell his blind date he didn't have any money for the dinner they'd just eaten.

"Jesus, Dave. I'm sorry," Al said. "I've been crazy all morning. I got here late and just found out myself. I thought you knew. The Presbyterians just sold KPPC to the people from San Francisco. Tom Donahue is the new Program Director."

"What's the new format?" I asked, as the anxiety began to well up in my stomach.

"Rock 'n roll, jazz, folk, blues. They call it progressive rock. This station is going to finally take off. We'll be the first FM rocker in Los Angeles. It's going to be great. All we've got to do is hold onto our jobs. We'll get rich."

Feeling like I'd just shot myself in the foot, I sat back slowly in the squeaky chair.

"One more question, Al. Do they own another station?"

"They sure do," Al Herion said as he ran out the door in a cloud of cigarette smoke. "It's the FM rock station in San Francisco. The first FM Stereo rocker in the whole damn country. Call letters are KMPX."

Laurel Canyon
November 1967

"Why aren't you on the air at KPPC?" Tim Considine chided.

"I don't know, Tim," I answered. "I've tried everything."

"Well, the station is absolutely great," Tim said. "They're doing everything you said you wanted to do."

I had made several attempts to be a part of the new KPPC. Tom Donahue was almost impossible to get to. I left an audition tape, but got no response. Al Herion had been kept on in the sales department. I suspected his days were numbered but he was a good temporary liaison between Donahue and the church fathers. It would take a few months to find a new location and move the facilities out of the church basement. I hounded Herion to get me an appointment with Donahue. Finally, he succeeded.

"I heard your audition tape, Pierce," Tom Donahue was staring at me from across his desk. "I don't think you're what I'm looking for."

"Why not?"

"Your delivery is too fast. This isn't top forty. Listen to Les Carter or Steve Segal. They're young, bright, sincere. That's what I want on this station."

"Sure, Tom, I understand," I said. "Maybe you could squeeze me in on a shift on weekends or after midnight. It doesn't matter. I'm flexible. Really flexible. I want to learn to do it your way. I believe in what you're doing here."

I was beginning to do the Al Herion grovel.

"I don't have anything for you now," was all Tom said.

I knew he'd never call. Maybe I really wasn't what he wanted. Too slow for top forty, too fast for progressive rock.

North Hollywood
December 1967

*"Messrs. K. and H. assure the public
Their production will be second to none."*

"Being for the Benefit of Mr. Kite," The Beatles
(John Lennon and Paul McCartney, Sony/ATV Tunes LLC)

We were at home in North Hollywood. Les Carter was playing *Sergeant Pepper* on KPPC. It had been another long day at the new Cellar Theatre. Work was proceeding at a snail's pace, but construction had finally reached the painting stage. We had rented a spray paint rig and in one ten-hour marathon, painted the whole interior of sixteen-foot high walls that divided the 2,000 square feet into a myriad of dressing rooms, office, stage, lobby, video studios and control booth. Bachman's design was outstanding. He and Kate's paint selections of rich dark blues, deep reds, and bright yellows were turning it into a show place extraordinaire.

The word was out that Laquidara and the Pierces were creating the ultimate Hollywood showcase theatre. Charles had manned the spray gun all day while Teddy, Kate, and I kept the paint mixed and the supply buckets filled. When it was over Charles looked like the canvas of a new wave painter. Coming out of the shower, he still had specks of blue, red, and yellow on his hands and neck.

"Listen, David," Charles said. "We haven't received an answer from Paddy Chayefsky. Why wouldn't he want his new play performed by our group? We've got a good track record and the theatre is going to be beautiful."

Paddy Chayefsky's new play had been published but so far had been unproduced. In a few years Chayefsky would win an academy award for his screenplay for the motion picture *Network*. Chayefsky may not yet have reached his peak, but he still wasn't returning our calls.

"Listen, Charlie," Kate said. "You can't expect the whole town to fall on its knees because we're building a theatre. Pick another play."

"Like what?" Charles asked. "Another Tennessee Williams' that's been done a zillion times? Or more of that depressing Russian shit that Ken Rose was doing? We're going to have material that is as exciting as our theatre. And we'll need actors who are exciting. David, we have to run an ad in the *Hollywood Reporter and Daily* Variety asking 'Where Are All the Talented Actors?' That should challenge a few good ones to get off their asses and come join us."

"I'll see about it," I said. "We still have at least a couple of months of construction. As soon as we get past the next inspection, I have to go back and pull all that hidden wiring out of the walls."

"Imagine those ass hole inspectors trying to condemn our building," Kate said. "Toughest city building code in the country, and we fooled 'em. By the way, I've got about 400 yards of carpet donated. It's used, but it still looks good."

"I wo-wo-worked as a carpet installer for awhile," Teddy volunteered. "I can, can pu-pu-put it in for you."

"That's go-go-good, Teddy," Charles mocked him. "I knew you were go-go-good for something. You take care of that carpet. And David, you've got to come up with another five grand for the air conditioning. We can't have talent scouts coming into our beautiful theatre being uncomfortable. We also need exhaust fans so they can smoke while watching the show."

"I'll call Louisiana," I said, moving to the stereo. "But we've got to put a lid on this spending. I don't know how we're going to repay all this money."

"One break, David, that's all we need. Any one of us could make it, and we'll all be rich."

I turned up the volume on 106.7 FM. Les Carter was finishing up his shift with a commercial for a record shop called Music Revolution. An integral part of the commercial was the Lennon/McCartney lyrics, "You say you want a revolution." Les followed the taped spot with a live tag.

"Stop by the Music Revolution and say 'Hello' to my lovely wife, Susan," he said.

So Les Carter owned the Music Revolution. What a tie-in. These guys at KPPC were a lot better than Oliver Berliner. They knew how to make money with a radio station. Don't try to force your product on the listener. Sell the product that the listeners want to buy.

Les Carter had a great sound. There was a smile in his voice that made you like him. As a jazz deejay he was known as the Afro American who turned out to be white. He was slick, hip, and knew all the music, black and white, from jazz to blues and all the rock in between. He came out of Detroit and told Los Angeles, "I been to the East to get the Grease, and back to the West to spread the Mess."

Tom Donahue came on after Les. His music selection was excellent. His voice was rich. His delivery sincere. I had decided of all the jocks on KPPC, the one I sounded the most like in style and voice quality was Tom Donahue. But then, I wasn't what he was looking for. Well, screw him. Who needs radio? I've got my own theatre, and when it's finally finished, Charles, Kate, and I were going to blow this town wide open.

"And tonight Mr. Kite is topping the bill!"
(Ibid.)

1967

♦ *Sgt. Pepper's Lonely Hearts Club Band* was the first concept album (a suite of interrelated songs instead of a collection of singles), incorporating electronic collages, a forty-piece orchestra, and a sitar.

The music revolution that was starting in San Francisco and Los Angeles FM radio was also taking roots in a third California city. Down the coast in San Diego, a disc jockey named Ron Middag was playing middle of the road pop music on KDIG-FM, from 6:00 p.m. to midnight. But what Ron Middag really wanted to do was to play rock 'n roll. Every night at midnight he tuned in another middle of the road San Diego station, KPRI, that was experimenting with album rock cuts on FM in the midnight to 3:00 a.m. slot, where the regular audience and conservative community members could not be offended by this kind of outrageousness. Steve Brown, a Navy man by day, was moonlighting as a disc jockey under the air name of "Ocean Beach Jetty" or O.B. Jetty for short. Soon Ron Middag was hanging out with O.B. at KPRI, who put him on the air at 2:00 a.m. Ron also wanted to remain anonymous, so that he could keep his regular gig, so O.B. gave him the name "Inor" when on the air at KPRI. But the bad habit of playing rock caught up with Ron when he signed off at midnight on KDIG with Vanilla Fudge's "You Keep Me Hanging On." KDIG axed Ron Middag, who then became a regular as "Inor" on the now profitable and expanded hours of 6:00 p.m. to 3:00 a.m. on KPRI, thanks to the music lovers' response and the efforts of the disc jockeys that went out and sold ads to local merchants. Ron was also hanging out with Top 40 disc jockeys like Bobby Ocean on KGB the Drake format rocker. Ocean would later come to Los Angeles for a stint at KHJ. Another close friend of Ron's was Jimmy Rabbit, on KCBG. The Rabbit would also come to L.A. to spin records on KLOS-FM and become a top gun on the old Pasadena Rocker KRLA.

From their studios in the basement of the medical building, directly under the drug department, KPRI was playing underground radio to the drug culture of San Diego. O.B. Jetty and Ron "Inor" Middag were riding herd on a menagerie of character voices who were essentially youngsters off the street with no radio background, but a good sense of irony and comedy. The one guy with experience among them, Ron, emerged as a leader of the band of misfits. In order to save the fledgling operation money, Ron went on to get a First Class FCC license so he could double as Chief Engineer.

When Navy Officials realized that "O.B. Jetty" was really Steve Brown, a seaman on active duty, he was immediately shipped out to Vietnam, never to be heard of again. Ron "Inor" Middag became the Program Director of the third FM rocker in America.

> *"But you knew that we would meet again*
> *If your memory serves you well."*
>
> "This Wheel's On Fire," Ian and Sylvia
> (Bob Dylan and Rick Danko, Dwarf Music)

The office was the only part of the Cellar Theatre that was finished. Link Wyler was getting comfortable on the couch, covered with designer fabric left over from a Jim Bachman movie project. I leaned back in the Banker's-style chair and put my feet up on the Wells Fargo desk.

"I know you've got something else up your sleeve," Link was saying. "A smart business man like you can see you can't pay for this facility with a showcase theatre. Whatever you're fixing to do, I'd like to team up with you."

"What did you have in mind?" I asked. Obviously, Link was a couple of steps ahead of me.

"You and Charles Laquidara know how to run the theatre," Link said. "But maybe you and I can become partners in some kind of music business venture. Hell, you got experience doing management and publishing in EPI with Smokey's bunch. And I heard about y'all running songs for Grelun Landon back in '64. Everybody's learned a lot since then. All we need is an office, and right now we're sitting in it. How does the name Pierce Wyler sound to you?"

It had a good ring. More important, I knew I could get along with Link. He was slow-talking Southern boy, but inside he was a hungry dude, willing to dance the Hollywood hustle.

"One other thing," he said. "I need to be involved in your first production from an executive standpoint. Just a title to give me some sort of stroke around town."

"We could do that. Have you thought of a job and a title?" I asked, knowing he had.

"Make me associate producer, I'll stay out of Laquidara's way, and back you up wherever I can. I was thinking, too, with all of your radio background, you could be real valuable to our music business if you were on the air in this town. Why don't you get yourself a job on that hippy station you're always listening to?"

"I've tried. I don't think they want me. After all the years I spent in the bottom of that church, I missed my shot. It's making me crazy."

"Anything can happen. That's why I love Hollywood. Your time will come," Link Wyler said.

"Best notify my next of kin,
This wheel shall explode."
(Ibid.)

1968

♦ New innovations: waterbeds, Jacuzzis, and motion picture ratings.

♦ *Wheels of Fire* by Cream becomes the first platinum album by selling one million copies.

♦ Eldridge Cleaver publishes *Soul on Ice* while on parole.

North Hollywood
February 1968

*"He's fighting for Democracy
and fighting for the Reds."*

"Universal Soldier," Donovan
(Buffy St. Marie, Woodmere Music; Caleb Music Co.)

For several days the U.S. had massed troops at Khe Sahn, 5,000 marines were ready to fight.

Woodie Bernard wrote me from Okinawa. That was his base, but he was making regular forays into the central highlands of Southeast Asia.

This is top secret, of course, David, Woodie wrote. So I can't tell you where, but I'm making runs into places we ain't suppose to be. We take a few Montagnards with us. They're kind of like an American Indian. I'm doing recon work, you know. They drop us off. We walk eight clicks in one direction, then make a turn, walk another eight clicks and then come back to our original point. We make a triangle. We find out stuff. Stuff they want to know. How many trails you cross? Do you observe movement? Are the streams deep? Is the water good to drink? They say we're not going into neighboring countries, but this is the kind of information you need when an army moves into an area. That way they know how to work their tanks. What kind of trees? How high is the first limb? Is it double canopy, triple canopy? Are maps accurate? Many times we're using French-made maps made before the fall of Dien Bien Fu in the '50s. You try to make a capture. That way you can ask your prisoner all kind of questions. What's his age? That tells you how far they have to go down into their teen population to fill their draft. Is he well equipped? Well fed? How's the civilians doing? That way we can evaluate the bombing runs."

I heard about demonstrations in the United States, Woodie wrote, but it doesn't mean anything, because we're isolated here. Yesterday and tomorrow don't matter. I'm totally caught up in the war. Intense fear in the woods. You shoot people. They shoot at you. You kill their people. They kill your people. They kill you, if you're not lucky like I am. But when I get back to Oki or a safe area, the high is better than sex. A lot better than booze or drugs. I thrive on it. I really want it. When my tour is over, I think I'll re-up again. Those draft card burners, and those people running off to Canada, that don't bother me. We all understand it. I don't like it, but I respect it. I'm one of the younger guys in my group, and I'm 25 years old. Most of the guys on the team are 30 years old. That's pretty old for a Vietnam fighter. The older guys understand the protest. Yeah, we've heard the comment that American soldiers are cannon fodder. But that don't mean anything to me. Three million boys will fight in this war. They're rotating them in only one-year tours because it's so unpopular back home. We could lose 60,000 killed, 300,000 wounded. We'll never get over this war.

I guess your hair is down to your butt by now, but that's all right, I understand. You don't fool me, Podnuh, I know where you come from. You ain't no hippy, you're just a displaced Cajun farm boy, and you know right from wrong. What you do is gonna be right. Just like what I'm doing is right for me."

Memoirs from the Comic Book Kid,

Your Pal,

Woodie Bernard,
Okinawa

The toughest part of the war was still ahead. The Tet offensive of early '68 surprised all of America with the strength of the Viet Cong military resistance.

Woodie Bernard was there, he told me later what it was like.

The Cong & NVA hit almost everywhere at the same time. The week of Tet, America lost 3,500 plus men. The North Vietnamese lost 145,000. That's right, 145,000. The Viets hit many places, but they couldn't hold 'em. The North Viets were hurt so bad it was almost two years before they put large units again in South Vietnam. Believe it or not, for the American soldiers that was the best week for the army of the entire war. Somehow, the News Media didn't report it that way. All they reported was that the Viets were attacking large scale. Attacking ain't shit. Being able to take and hold what you attack is what counts. Personally, I spent the Tet offensive in Laos. I went in the day before, the #2 on a 6 man recon team. We didn't see a single enemy the whole time, hell, they were all over in South Vietnam getting the shit shot out of themselves.

Our camp in Kontum didn't get hit, but an American unit close to us did. I think they bypassed our camp, because we'd have made a much tougher target. Four

NVA holed up in a brick post-office in Kontum and the Americans called in "Puff-The-Magic-Dragon." A C-130 with two machine guns that would fire 6,000 rounds a minute each, total 12,000 rounds a minute. They ground down that brick post-office to knee high. Knee high in about 20 minutes! I saw the strike the first night I got back from Laos. Next morning I went to town to see the damage. Amazing, fucking building was knee high, and 4 very dead NVA in the rubble. I still have pictures of those poor dumb bastards.

From the military point of view the Tet offensive was the most misunderstood part of the war. But that was the beginning of the end of the war politically in America. The real Vietnam battleground was changing sets. The next scene was going to be played out in our streets. And on the airwaves.

1968
♦ Police use batons and water hoses to break up riots in Londonderry, North Ireland.

176

*"I got one foot on the platform
the other on the train,
I'm going back to old New Orleans..."*

"The House of the Rising Sun," The Animals
(Eric Burdon and Brian Auger, Brian Auger Music)

The clock radio showed 7:10 a.m. as Eric Burdon's vocal pulled me awake. Then the phone was ringing. Al Herion was on the other end.

"The dumb asses did it," Herion was talking fast.

"Did what?"

"Walked out. The whole damn KPPC air staff."

"What happened?" I asked, trying to get a grip on what Herion was saying.

"Tom Donahue is supporting Lou Avery, one of the owners, but I'm telling you Lee Crosby has more stock. They're trying to bankrupt Crosby. It's a power play."

"Who's left at the station?" I asked.

"Just me. And two salesmen, and Andy Wilson. I'm trying to tell you, it's a walk out. I'm the station manager starting right now. Lee Crosby put me in charge."

I could hear Herion pause to light a cigarette before he continued.

"Listen, I need you. You gotta get down here and go on the air at noon. I gotta guy, Ralph Hull, to take over at 5:00 p.m. The all night kid stayed. He'll come in at 10:00."

"Who's on now?" I asked.

"Andy Wilson."

"You gotta be kidding. Andy, The Flea." I was incredulous. "Andy don't even know who Ringo Starr is."

"Hey, you telling me?" Herion said.

"Jesus, Al, you need some pros on the air."

"I know, I know. I'll find someone else later. I'll give Andy the music business accounts. He's got friends at Warner Brothers. Look, Dave, I need you now, today. I gotta keep KPPC on the air. If we can stay on the air for a week, we win."

"The owners made you station manager?"

"Yeah, ten minutes ago. I'm here. I'm loyal. Who else is Lee Crosby going to turn to except me? I told him I knew the best disc jockeys in town."

"Yeah, right," I said, "And I start today at noon."

"Today, right. There ain't no tomorrow. Get down here right away. And listen, don't let 'em hassle you outside."

"Who?"

"The strikers. The old air staff."

"I thought you said they walked out."

"Yeah, they walked out. They went on strike. What do you think? They walked out and went to Laguna Beach? They're in front of the church carrying signs."

"Wait a minute, Al," I said. "I'm in the Screen Actor's Guild. I can't cross an AFTRA picket line."

"They're not AFTRA. They started their own damn union. The Amalgamated FM Workers, or something. They're not legit. They're a bunch of assholes. They screwed up. Just walk right past them. Get your butt down here. Look the phone's ringing off the wall. The office staff walked out too. I got to go."

My mind was racing as I drove into Hollywood, moved quickly through the interchange and down the Pasadena Freeway. I parked the black Porsche out of sight behind the Pasadena Playhouse. No use being a sitting duck. As I crossed Colorado Boulevard, I could see half a dozen longhairs carrying signs reading "Amalgamated FM Workers, Support Free Radio." Still another sign proclaimed, "Music Belongs to the People." I couldn't argue with that. I didn't recognize any of the mostly young longhairs. No Tom Donahue. No Les Carter. No Steve Segal. Apparently radio stars don't do picket line duty, at least not before noon.

As I approached the pickets, the one with the John Lennon glasses fell in step alongside of me.

"Hey, man. I'm Ted Alvy. You're not going in there, are you?"

Ted Alvy was a tall thin Jewish-Spanish kid from the San Fernado Valley. He had been working as B. Mitchell Reed's engineer, cueing the records, flipping the switches. When B. Mitchell Reed didn't make a shift Ted would fill right in and do the show. It was his first real job and a terrific high. The idea of suddenly being off the air was making him nuts. He was not yet twenty years old.

We reached the flight of steps leading down to the basement of the church. A thin pale girl with scraggly red hair fired up a joint as I walked past. She held it out, offering me a hit.

"No thanks, I'm trying to quit," I mumbled, walking down the familiar steps to the same old door.

It was locked, but a talk box had been installed. Al Herion himself answered the buzzer and appeared fifteen seconds later. He was out of breath, puffing on a cigarette.

"Hurry up, get in here, man," Al Herion panted.

"Hey, Al, who's your new boyfriend?" asked Ted Alvy, with the John Lennon glasses, leaning over from the top of the steps.

"Screw you, Ted," screamed Herion. He flicked his lit cigarette straight at Ted's leering face, but Ted batted it away with his "Keep Free Radio Free" sign.

Inside, Al and I walked across the big empty room where the church had never built the TV studio. The room had been totally redecorated in concert posters and counter-culture slogans.

"They're already falling apart," Al was saying. "Since I talked to you, I got a call from Don Hall. He was doing production."

"He did Saturday nights, too," I said.

"That's right," he said. "As soon as it cools off he'll come back to do weekends."

"Why is he breaking away?" I asked.

"He knows Donahue is just testing his gas. Don Hall can see that it's got nothing to do with workers' rights or free radio."

"Okay, who else you got?"

"Ralph Hull, he's a pro. He'll take over around 5 p.m." Al puffed away.

"Is that it? What about weekend relief?"

"I'm working on that. We'll worry about that later."

When we walked past the On Air Studio, I looked through the window to see Andy Wilson peering at a stack of albums. He looked confused. He kept glancing nervously over his shoulder to see how many grooves were left on the spinning disc that was on the air.

The phone was ringing in the office and Al answered it. I drifted over to a large stack of albums in the corner and started to flip through them. Behind the stack was a dirty ashtray with a half-smoked joint.

"Sure, Les," Al was saying into the phone. "I understand, Les. Well, that's your prerogative. Tell you what I'll do, Les, I'll play your Music Revolution spots the rest of the month at no charge. We'll get together next week to set up a new schedule at a lower rate." Al was silent for a minute. "Sure, Les, I understand. Give my love to Susan."

Al hung up slowly and looked at me.

"That was Les Carter," Al said. "Les has been doing a great job on the air. His wife, Susan, has also jocked some on the weekends."

"I know, I've heard them."

"Well, Les and Susan own the Music Revolution; he's canceled all his ads." Al couldn't hide his disappointment. "He wouldn't even let me give them to him free. He wants off the air. But he'll be back. The Music Revolution can't sell records without this radio station."

Al was digging through his empty cigarette pack, hoping there was still one more hiding inside. I pulled out the dirty ashtray from behind the album stack and offered him the half joint.

"Ever try this brand, Al?"

"Will you look at this shit!" Al was exasperated.

He grabbed the ashtray and dumped the contents in the trashcan. Then he tossed a piece of news copy on top of the joint to cover it up.

"I'm telling you, David, it had gotten out of control around here. The church fathers were going crazy, putting a lot of pressure on Crosby and Avery. I think Avery was egging the staff on to squeeze Crosby into selling out to him. They both want to meet you, by the way. They're here now."

"What do they look like?"

"Well, Lou Avery is the tall one. Thin, genteel, silver gray hair. The short balding guy with the pencil thin mustache is Lee Crosby, the one who looks like a used car salesman."

"Tell me again, Al, whose side are we on?" I asked.

"I work for Lee Crosby," Al replied. "He's going to win."

I met Lou Avery first. Very nice man. Looked like everybody's grandfather. He warned me that anyone going on the air now could not be guaranteed their jobs once he and Crosby settled their differences and the old staff returned. To me that meant that Herion's understanding of the situation was probably correct. Avery, Donahue, Carter, and the staff were squeezing Crosby. Lee Crosby had the appearance of a man who was being squeezed. He looked and acted like a loser whose radio station was up for grabs. And I was standing in the same room with him.

I peeled out of Crosby's office, heading for the control room. "I'll tell you who's not going to win, Al," I said to Herion who was puffing to keep up with me, "the guys who walked away from the turntables. They can't win without the music."

"Get in there and do your stuff," Al said. "Listen, why don't you go ahead and replace Andy now. He looks like he's floundering in there. You know this music, don't you?"

"Sure, Al." I was beginning to smile. "I know this music."

Andy Wilson greeted me when I walked in the studio. He was grateful for the relief and left quickly. I sat down behind the familiar microphone. I felt at home immediately. I'd done this a thousand times before. Only this time I had the music I wanted to play. Slugging it out for control of a radio station wouldn't be a pretty sight. But I didn't have any qualms at all about doing it. Once I opened that microphone, there would be no turning back. I picked up an Amboy Dukes' album that I'd heard Steve Segal playing a few days earlier. After all these years, it was my turn to rock Los Angeles.

"Hello, Angelinos," I said. "This is KPPC FM, 106.7, from the bottom of the Pasadena Presbyterian Church in beautiful downtown Pasadena."

> *"Baby, please don't go...*
> *Down to New Orleans,*
> *You know I love you so."*

"Baby, Please Don't Go," Amboy Dukes
(Joe Williams, EMI Full Keel Music)

KPPC FM
Pasadena Presbyterian Church
April 1968

"Firing 20 shot guns each,
And man, it really hurt."

"40,000 Headmen," Traffic
(Steve Winwood and Jim Capaldi, Irving Music; Universal Songs of Polygram)

I had gotten a few irate calls from fans of the old staff, but most of the feedback had been wait and see. As long as the music was close to what they'd been hearing, the jocks behind the microphone were interchangeable. "Keep playing the music" seemed to be what was important to the KPPC audience. Some calls were very encouraging. There were real people out there who liked what I was doing. The rock music was easy for me, but I also knew R&B, old blues, and a hint of jazz. My biggest strength was my feel for folk music and the message of protest. However, Ralph Hull at night was definitely too Top 40. Andy wasn't anywhere close.

I began to understand that I was a key player. Without me on the air, Herion and Lee Crosby would have a much tougher shot at winning the fight. I didn't think about trying to exploit that option. In a radio war, the fortunes shift rapidly. The wheel was in spin here. Song after song, it was my choice whatever I wanted to play. There were no rules. Just keep it on the edge. Personal taste was all I had to go on. Seldom before in the history of radio had a disc jockey had this much music to select from and this much freedom to decide. Even more so than Donahue's staff. Who was going to tell me what not to play? Not Herion, and certainly not Crosby or Avery. I answered to no one. I decided I was uniquely qualified to take my show in any direction I wanted. My ear was as good as anyone's.

The old staff began calling the rap line to request songs that were weak or overplayed. They hooked Andy like a big fish. I judged that I could benefit from playing some of the newest Top 40 hits, along with the album cuts. A bit of familiar music could be welcome.

Meanwhile, *The Free Press*, led by feature writer John Carpenter became the sounding board for Donahue and the strikers. Their version of events leading up to the strike was printed week after week, along with disparaging remarks about the current KPPC staff. It became apparent to me that the shriller their voice became, the more their hopes were being dashed. Only a few hundred read the Guttenburg Technology of *The Free Press*. I had Marshall McCluen's media message. Thousands were tuned in to KPPC radio. The voice between the rock lyrics was mine.

I had been waiting for this shot a long time. I was the hungriest disc jockey in Los Angeles and KPPC was my station in my town. Being radical and righteous felt real natural. This radio war was already over. They didn't stand a chance.

"I turned around
and knocked them down
And walked across the sea."
(Ibid.)

Los Angeles
Late April 1968

*"Two riders were approaching,
The wind began to howl."*

"All Along the Watchtower," Jimi Hendrix
(Bob Dylan, Dwarf Music)

Martin Luther King, Jr. was shot down in Memphis. The slain minister was carried through the Atlanta streets in a mule drawn wagon. Since whites were suspected, President Johnson urged calm, but violence broke out in Harlem. Curfews were put in place in Memphis, but fire and looting erupted. Stokley Carmichael called for action, saying riots and violence were the only means to black power. In Chicago, seven died as National Guard troops were called out to quell the rioting and looting. In Washington, D.C., army troops had to take control. Two days after King was killed, Bobby Hutton was shot down by police and Eldredge Clever was wounded in the same gun battle. Pictures of young black men, armed, disciplined, and angry, were shown on television news. The Black Panthers began to play the media. Their goal was to come across crazier than they really were. White America was ready to believe them.

Martin Luther King had wanted to build a peace coalition by the time the '68 elections came around. But instead the country was on the edge of anarchy. On April 29, a new group of protestors captured the spotlight with a Poor People's March on Washington. American politics were being permanently altered. With Lyndon Johnson stepping down, Vice President Hubert Humphrey hinted that he would enter the presidential race.

In Czechoslovakia, it was called the Prague Spring of '68 as a new sense of freedom was in the air. In America, the Women's Liberation Movement was gaining momentum. The feminists felt they had the logical conclusion to the '60s question, "How to change our lives?" The answer, they said, was in the kitchen, and in the bedroom.

In Los Angeles, the biggest media news was the fight for control of KPPC. The hip community was divided between the KPPC strikers and the new staff.

I exited the Hollywood Freeway at Vermont, parked in the alley behind the Cellar Theatre, and met Charles coming out of the door.

"David," he said. "I've got an idea for a story. I'm going to disappear for a few days to work on a script. It can be our opening show. By the way, I called the AFTRA office for you."

"What did they say?"

"They said that American Federation of TV and Radio Artist supports workers' rights, and that the Amalgamated FM workers are not associated with AFTRA in any way. What did Screen Actors Guild tell you?"

"SAG doesn't care," I replied.

"Then keep on going for it, David. When the picket line goes down, I'll take you up on that weekend job. I'm ready to try my hand at disc jockeying."

"It's not a picket line. It's a few disgruntled hippies. The old jocks are probably lying around and getting loaded. They're not marching."

"Well, read *The LA Free Press* today. Tom Donahue calls you the scum of the earth."

"Sure he does," I said. "He didn't expect me to screw up his party."

Charles ran off to become a writer and I drove on into Pasadena. I hid the Porsche and prepared to run the gauntlet in front of the church. Four weeks after our takeover, the resistance was starting to fade. The few remaining long hairs were generally friendly. Their radios were tuned to 106.7. They always offered me grass or acid. Ted Alvy fell into step with me.

"Hi, Dave Pierce. Where are you working next week?" he asked.

"Right here, Ted. How about yourself?"

"Oh, I'll be on the air at KPPC, but I don't think that you will," Ted sneered. "The strike is being settled."

"I doubt that, Ted," I said, hurrying into the church basement.

Inside I quizzed Al Herion, "What's this about the strike being settled?"

"It's bull shit," Al replied. "We're winning. Hang in there. The strikers are falling apart. Don Hall will be on this weekend. Another striker, Zack Zenor, wants to come back to work. All that benefit concert money, they're not getting any. Donahue and the inner circle are hogging it all up."

My afternoon was filled with a lot of music and no commercials, punctuated by several phone calls.

"The rap line," I said, into the studio phone.

The girl's voice on the other end was sweet, sexy, and vaguely familiar.

"Hi," she said. "I like your voice, I like your music."

"Thanks," I said. My disc jockey's ego started to inflate. A sexy voice on the request line is always a fantasy.

"You're really great," she continued. "In fact all of us think you're great."

"Thanks again," I said.

"Yeah, my friends and I were just saying that you were a great big asshole."

The phone clicking dead in my ear was like an exclamation mark, and I knew why the voice sounded familiar. It was Susan Carter. The harassment level was heavy all afternoon. The requests for "In A Gadda Da Vida" was designed to suck me into playing a song that was a big hit, but was considered lame by the really hip music lovers, since it was being overplayed on the top forty stations. By the time I got the fifth call for a real downer, titled "Heroin" by the Velvet Underground, I had the feeling at least some of the strikers had targeted me as the jock they wanted to break. I also guessed they were getting desperate. Thirty minutes before my shift ended, I got the call.

"Hey, man," a gruff voice said. "I'm a member of the Hell's Angels. Me and my friends don't like what you're doing. We say you're on the wrong side and you're a loser."

"That's your opinion," I said. "You got a right to it. My opinion is that I got a right to this microphone and these turntables and this music."

"How much is it worth to you?"

I answered his question with silence.

After a moment he continued, "Cause you see, we know you got a family and we know where you live."

Another click. Another exclamation mark.

That night in North Hollywood we gathered our war council. We had to take a Hell's Angel threat seriously.

Link was ready to fight fire with fire. He was working with Randy Boone on an album that would put the young star of the TV series *Cimarron* into the music business. He called Randy and got his immediate cooperation. For the next several days, I arrived in front of the church in Randy Boone's black Cadillac. Link and Randy, dressed like the redneck cowboys they really were, with gun belts strapped to their waist, and a big iron on their hip, escorted me from the black Cadillac to the basement door. At night they arrived to pick me up. The picketers were dumbfounded. They didn't offer any drugs to Link Wyler and Randy Boone. Ted Alvy wanted to know what was going on. He said he was beginning to like me. He wouldn't even mind working with me.

"Tell it to your friends in the Hell's Angels," was all Link had to say.

The message was clear. We wouldn't be scared off. The stakes were too big. Other decisions were being made, but this seemed to be a turning point. The pickets disappeared. The phone harassment stopped. Some of the old weekend jocks drifted back in, along with a few hangers-on like Don Bridges. Tom Donahue had been cutting a deal with Metro Media to put his programmed progressive rock format and the remaining striking jocks on KMET in Los Angeles and KSAN in San Francisco. But it would never be totally free under the watchful corporate eye of Metro Media. B. Mitchell Reed made the move to KMET and the FM Band. His old alma mater, KFWB, switched from Top 40 to All News. KHJ was now the undisputed King of Rock Radio in Los Angeles. It would be three long years before the new sound of FM Stereo-Rock could mount a ratings challenge.

Donahue went back to San Francisco where the antiwar movement was gaining strength. Protesters all over the country were ratcheting up the volume. In New York, at Columbia University, Mark Rudd led a student revolt against the establishment policies.

> *"So let us not talk falsely now,*
> *the hour is getting late."*
> (Ibid.)

Hollywood
Early May 1968

"Some have it nice...flash, paradise
They're very wise to their disguise,
Trying to revolutionize tomorrow."

"She Has Funny Cars," Jefferson Airplane
(Marty Balin and Jorma Kaukonen, Icebag Corp.)

The actress danced and pranced across the new Cellar stage, showing herself off as a multi-talent. Her name was Lynette Winter, early twenties, working professionally for years. Her credits included *Petticoat Junction*, and the running part of Larue, *Gidget's* best friend on the hit TV series, opposite the soon-to-be mega-star and future Academy Award winner, Sally Field. Lynette had seen our ad in *The Hollywood Reporter*, asking, "WHERE ARE ALL THE TALENTED PERFORMERS?" She wanted in the Cellar Group. She had an almost homely, character face with an extroverted, slightly sexy personality. I was impressed.

""She ain't good enough," Charles said, under his breath.

"Thank you, Lynette," I said politely. "You'll be hearing from us."

Lynette Winter made her exit. Charles went into a tirade.

"Dammit," he yelled. "You ready to accept the first actress who auditions for us. What kind of high standards is that?"

"I don't care if she is the first. We just got lucky. She's good. Look at her credits."

"Yeah, all television. No stage. Who says she can act?"

"I s-s-say she can act," Teddy stuttered from the wings where he'd been lurking. "I sh-sh-sure would like to meet her."

"Well we're certainly going to look at a lot of actors and actresses before we make a decision. Anyway, I gotta to do my radio shift," Charles said impatiently.

I walked with him out the back door of the Cellar, up the ramp and into the alley.

"How's the rewrite on your script?" I asked Charles.

"Well, when you write a story in five days the rewrite takes a while. I'm going to title it, *One Hand Clapping*," Charles replied.

"Isn't that a bit Zen?"

"Sure, but Zen's hot. It'll catch people's attention."

"When do I get to read it?"

"Soon, but I can tell you this. It's about a group of young radicals who decide to kidnap the head of the CIA and force him to release information about the JFK plot. Your District Attorney boy down in New Orleans, Jim Garrison, has been talking about a CIA connection for a year. Garrison will be one of the characters in the story."

"Sounds intriguing," I said.

"Intriguing. David, are you kidding me? We're going to blow them away. We'll use all this video equipment live on the stage. We'll be the absolute *first multimedia stage and video production* in Hollywood."

I was seeing his vision. "We can do that," I said.

"And we can cast it from the group. I've already written Bud Tedesco in as the studio casting director. His parody will be super funny. Pete Pastore can do a role. We'll need to bring in some good supporting players, so please make some attempt to keep your standards up. The lead is an unemployed actor like myself. I need Vince Donofrio in the part."

Charles hurried off to Pasadena. I went back into the Cellar to meet Link Wyler waiting in the office with his feet up on the desk. He and I walked out into the adjacent video studio.

"This video studio could double as a recording studio," Link said. "It's already sound proof. We could put the control booth in that dead space above the office. Just knock a hole in the wall and put in a window. Song writers all over town would love a place like this."

From my days in the music business as a tune pusher, I knew he was right.

"Remember Smiley Brunette?" Link continued.

"Sure. Gene Autry's sidekick, Frog," I replied, "I saw him a hundred time in the Saturday afternoon westerns when I was a kid. My folks saw him and Gene in *South of the Border* the night I was born. Me and Smiley go way back."

"Yeah, Frog. That's old Smiley. He'd been working on *Petticoat Junction* lately. He built himself a little recording studio to mess around in. And then he died."

"I didn't know he died."

"Well, he did. Now his family wants to sell the equipment. A complete two-track studio set-up. You won't believe the price!" Link was beaming by now. "Only two G's, it's a steal."

"That does sound like a bargain. Casey and Nellie might front me the money. We'd be thrilled to own Frog's equipment. I don't know if we'd be thrilled $2,000 worth."

"With you at the radio station, it would be a natural for us," Link painted the picture even brighter. "The Cellar would become a total talent center. Stage, video, and recording studio. I even found us an engineer, a young German kid, named Karl. He can wire the whole thing for you, video and audio."

"Is he competent?" I asked.

"When he sleeps, he dreams schematics," Link grinned. "If you ask me, this is the most beautiful theatre in Hollywood. Jim Bachman's design is just outstanding. Is Bachman going to help design sets for Laquidara's play?"

"I hope so," I said. "Bachman just got a job on *Zabriske Point* directed by Michelangelo Antonioni, one of my favorite directors. He directed a film called *Blow Up* with David Hemmings and Vanessa Redgrave. A while back he made a film called *The Red Desert*. He's very hot."

"Yeah, I've heard about Antonioni," Link replied. "He's that Eye-talian communist s.o.b., ain't he?"

I left the Cellar with my head in a turmoil. Taking the Vermont on-ramp to the Hollywood Freeway, which was beginning to stack up, shifting through a pattern on the black Porsche's gearbox, I crept through the downtown interchange, then finally picked up speed northeast toward Pasadena. Kennedy, Garrison, the war, Johnson, RFK, the Cellar, Hollywood, producing, acting. I was trying to quiet it all down and think about what I loved most of all, four hours in a dark studio. The only light aimed on the copy stand for live spots and over the turntables for cueing. There was barely enough foot-candles to read an album jacket pulled from the stacks of LPs that we surrounded ourselves with before sitting down behind the mic.

The black Porsche ate up the Pasadena Freeway and the German Blaupunkt radio put Charles Laquidara in my head. He was winding up his shift and waiting for me to take my turn at the best job ever invented.

"It's a sad day for music, everybody," Charles said, "because the Buffalo Springfield will play their farewell concert this weekend in Long Beach. So we're going to say goodbye to them with a Springfield set that will include the long version of 'Blue Bird,' also 'Broken Arrow,' and the favorite song of my friend, Dave Pierce, who is going to be here at 106.7 in just a few minutes. For you, Dave, and all of you who love Buffalo Springfield, here's 'Nowadays Clancy, Can't Even Sing,' on KPPC FM."

> *"Who's saying baby*
> *that don't mean a thing,*
> *Cause now a days Clancy*
> *can't even sing."*

"Nowadays Clancy, Can't Even Sing," Buffalo Springfield
(Neil Young, Cotillion Music Inc., Richie Furay Music, Springalo Toones, Ten-East Music)

KPPC FM
Pasadena Presbyterian Church
June 6, 1968

*"Somethin' come along and grabbed a hold of me,
And it felt just like a ball and chain."*

"Ball and Chain," Janis Joplin
(Willie Mae Thornton, Bro N Sis Music, Inc.)

The post-strike era at KPPC was settling in. Steve Segal, cut out by the deal Tom Donahue made with KMET, had gone back east to WBCN in Boston. With deejays Sam Kopper and Mississippi, they were building the premier progressive rock station on the east coast. I was on KPPC playing the long rock and blues cuts, while handling Cellar business on the phone with Charles or Link.

A black actor named Little Caesar had responded to the Cellar ad in *Daily Variety*. Caesar did supporting roles in movies. His best credit as a convict playing tackle on Burt Reynolds prison football team in *The Longest Yard* was still years away. What we were doing at the Cellar didn't interest Caesar himself, but Link Wyler and the recording equipment was of real interest to his friend, a blues singer who had paid her dues. She wrote and recorded "Hound Dog" before Elvis and his writers ripped it off her. She was well known in Los Angeles and 'Frisco and was the idol of a new generation of blues singers like Janis Joplin. She needed direction. Someone to baby-sit her finances, pay her bills, buy her a new Cadillac to tour the country from west coast universities to the black clubs of Chicago and Harlem. Pierce-Wyler could provide all that. We put Big Mama Thornton under an exclusive management contract. Link flew to 'Frisco and strong-armed her ex-manager into a co-publishing contract on all her songs. The old manager would keep 50% but we'd administer the copyright. We'd pay Big Mama. The checks would come from the record companies directly to Pierce-Wyler. We'd get first count. It was the only way to see any money.

That evening at our house, Bud and Mel were visiting when we heard the news. Bobby Kennedy had been shot in the pantry of the Ambassador Hotel in Los Angeles. We were numb with shock. Charles arrived a few minutes later. The look on his face was total anguish. He didn't believe we were displaying enough grief. He was wrong, of course, it's just that he was so blown away nothing could console him. We were going to all have to re-live the death of JFK. As Bobby's life ebbed over the next hours, our hopes for the return of Camelot sunk lower and lower until they were no more.

Fifty thousand rallied in D.C. The RFK funeral train took the long ride back east as the people along the way paid their last respects to the man so many of us had decided was our last best hope.

The gruesome nightmare was being replayed. This really wasn't a bad dream. We were wide-awake. This really was the '60s. Turmoil and strife were loose upon the land. What was this great country coming to? Was the establishment involved in a giant conspiracy against the challenge of youth and change? As soon as we placed faith in our leaders, they were shot down by dark forces, wearing the faces of crazy lone gunmen. We felt horrified, betrayed. We didn't know what to say, what to do, how to act. Where did we turn next?

"Where have you gone, Joe DiMaggio?
A nation turns its lonely eyes to you.
...Joltin Joe has left and gone away."

"Mrs.Robinson," Simon and Garfunkel
(Paul Simon, Paul Simon Music)

1968

♦ Lyndon Johnson names a panel on violence and orders guards for presidential candidates.

♦ UC graduate Carlos Castanega, using peyote and psilocybin mushrooms, writes *The Teachings of Don Juan*.

♦ Tom Wolfe writes *The Electric Kool-Aid Acid Test* chronicling the trek of Ken Kesey and his Merry Prankster groupies across the country in a converted school bus.

Southeast Asia
Late June 1968

"He's been a soldier for a thousand years."

"Universal Soldier," Donovan
(Buffy St. Marie, Caleb Music Co.)

Have you gotten a haircut yet? If I didn't know you better, I'd think you were one of those sissy-boys that California is so famous for.

Well, I'm here, only I can't tell you where. And I damn sure know what I'm doing, but I can't tell you that either. I can tell you this though, we're drawing combat pay, and we're earning it.

When we left Oki at 3:00 in the morning, our Colonel surprised us by showing up to see us off. That normally don't happen, Colonels getting up in the middle of the night just to see troops off. When we shook hands, he looked me right in the eye and said, "Give 'em hell, Soldier." I told him "I intend to, Sir." He smiled and said, "I know you will." Then he moved on down the line, and I walked up the ramp of the C130 with a loaded rifle. Ready for bear.

When we got here, first thing off the bat they told us exactly what we were going to be doing. I looked around the room and damn near everyone had a grin on his face. I thought to myself 'I'm in a room full of crazy people.' Then I noticed that I was grinning, too. I figured what the hell, at least I ain't the only crazy one.

This is great work, very, very interesting, but this ain't no game. We playing for keeps here.

We do shit here every day that they lock people up for back home. I love it! I've never felt more aware of being alive. It's easy to see why so many Special Force soldiers keep re-enlisting. I'm thinking about it myself. You remember when we pulled those damn palmettos with Casey? Miserable fucking day, dragging that big ass chain in the mud, watching out for snakes, Casey holding the water jug on that tractor and only letting us drink a little at a time, like we couldn't go get some more? I hated Casey, chains, palmettos, that tractor, and wasn't to crazy about you for getting me into that mess. But you know what? I remember that day. Don't know what I did, day before or after, but I remember that day. So I guess that makes it a good day.

What I'm doing now is kind of like that, I'm scared half the time, tired, sore, and pissed off, but I know I'll remember this as long as I live. If I live.

Most of us do, but some don't. Right now, I wouldn't trade places with anybody. You ought to come over here and get some of this. There's enough to go around! Get a hair cut."

The Comic Book Kid
Woodie

Woodie Bernard.

"Love's got a hold to me, baby,
Feels just like a ball and chain."

"Ball and Chain," Janis Joplin
(Willie Mae Thornton, Bro N Sis Music, Inc.)

The album cover was comic-strip style. On it was a stamp saying "Approved by the Hell's Angels of San Francisco." And right in the center was a caricature of Janis, dragging the ball and chain under a big grueling sun, and the words, "Big Mama Thornton," written plainly on the ball. It might as well have said dollar signs, because that's what was flashing in my mind as I dialed the Cellar number to tell Link that Janis Joplin had put Big Mama's song on the new *Cheap Thrills* album.

"See there, David," Link said on the phone, "I told you our time would come around."

I played every track on *Cheap Thrills* that day, cueing up "Ball and Chain" twice. It was definitely Janis' best work and would propel her further into rock 'n roll stardom. The royalties on "Ball and Chain" would finally bring Big Mama some of the compensation for her talent which was long overdue. Link and I would collect our 20 percent, but Big Mama would make us earn it.

Sometimes I wonder
What I'm a-gonna do,
Lord there ain't no cure
For the summer time blues."

"Summertime Blues," Blue Cheer
(Eddie Cochran and Jerry Capehart, Rumbalero; Warner-Tamerlane Publishing Corp.)

I finished my shift with the raucous feedback of Blue Cheer's guitars. I then joined the rest of the jock staff in the big studio that was used for production.

I had talked Smokey into picking up the night shift, about six weeks earlier, when Ralph Hull left, realizing his Top-40 style was out of step with the laid-back delivery of Free Form radio. Smokey had his own ideas of what Free Form should be, including playing some of his own songs recorded by either himself or other artists. One night I heard him reading *The Prophet* by a Middle Eastern poet and philosopher, Kahil Gibran, about the men at the forefront of human evolution. Behind Smokey's polished actor's voice he played soft and ethereal music. Then he segued into Jimi Hendrix on "Purple Haze." It was as inventive as any programming L.A. had ever heard, and we were just hitting our stride.

Meanwhile, Charles Laquidara would show up at midnight and play twenty minutes of just bird sounds.

"Great to relax and drift out on," he said. Most of his audience agreed.

When *2001, The Space Odyssey* was released, Charles dubbed it the ultimate trip. He was quoted in *The L.A. Times* which further angered *The*

Free Press, all of which sailed completely past Laquidara, as he juxta-posed "The Blue Danube Waltz" and Emerson, Lake and Palmer.

Our theatrical background was bringing a new dimension to Free Form. While FM rockers around the country focused on the music and the revolution, Smokey, Charles, and I looked for the dramatic and the comic. Our sound on KPPC had its roots in '30s and '40s Radio. We were convinced we had the broad based musical background and show biz flair to attract a large audience.

Smokey, Charles, and I took our seats, on one side of the ten-foot ta-ble. In a few minutes, Don Hall, Zack Zenor, and Don Bridges all shuffled in, all obviously stoned. Don Hall and Zack were the first of the pre-strike crew to come back and were working weekend shifts. Don Bridges was a young, brash, bad-complexioned kid, barely twenty. He wasn't on the air. His drug-fried mind made him almost incoherent and even he real-ized he couldn't communicate on the radio. But he did know the music, and in the absence of the old guard, he'd sold himself to Al Herion as the only one in the station with an authentic knowledge of what should and shouldn't be played. He'd become a real pain in the ass, walking into the studio whenever he heard something he didn't like, and asking the dee-jay where he'd found that piece of shit, acting like a program director, but without the authority to back up his opinions. I also suspected he was stealing albums.

"Why the hell did Herion call a meeting?" Bridges asked.

"He's probably going to ask you to leave," Smokey gave Bridges a steely-eyed reply.

"What do you know?" Bridges countered. "'Light My Fire' is one of the best songs the Doors ever recorded and you're playing that lame Top-40 version by that blind Mexican."

"Hey, Jose Feliciano is a great artist. People love his version of 'Light My Fire.' I'm going to keep on playing it," Smokey answered.

"Not if I get my way," Bridges continued to needle. "You don't belong on this radio station."

Smokey was smoldering. "How would you like your pimply, punk ass kicked?" He threatened.

"Peace and love, guys," Charles chortled.

By now Al Herion arrived with a short, blond, curly-haired fellow we all recognized as John Carpenter, who wrote the column "Roach Clips" for The *Free Press*. "Roach Clips" was of course a double entendre, re-ferring to the small alligator clip used in electronic applications to fuse two wires together. It was also perfect for holding a joint without burning your fingers while you sucked out the last potent hit.

"Fellows, you all know John Carpenter," Herion said, "He's got a cou-ple of great ideas for us."

Carpenter went right to the point.

"I hear a lot of talk," he said. "This deejay staff is generally doing a good job, but you're missing on a lot of stuff, and you're playing some cuts that shouldn't be played on this station."

"Well, who died and made you the king of music?" Smokey asked, setting up a confrontation immediately.

"Well, I happen to know everyone in the hip community. I also know all the musicians," Carpenter countered.

"So do I," Smokey shot back. "And I don't remember seeing you at any of the recording sessions."

Herion tried to get the meeting back on his agenda.

"Listen, fellas," he said. "We thought if a man of John Carpenter's standing in the hip community could come in here and act as our program director, it could help defuse some of the flack that we're still taking out there."

"Fuck the hip community," Smokey was hot now, "They're a bunch of sheep following those ass holes at The *Free Press*. Who needs 'em. We have a radio station."

"We don't need a program director," Charles joined in the rapidly heating argument. "This is Free Form radio. The disc jockeys decide what we're playing."

Carpenter knew he was in trouble. He and Herion hadn't expected our reaction.

"Listen, I'm all for you guys," Carpenter said in his best conciliatory manner. "I think you're doing a fine job. It's just when I hear a hard fast rocker backed by a soft folk song, I say you could use some direction."

"And where is it written, slow songs can't follow fast ones?" I asked. "That sounds like a page out of some AM Top 40 rule book that Free Form Radio was supposed to replace. You're going backwards, here, John."

Herion interrupted, "Well, John was also going to help us produce some concerts using his contacts with the bands."

"And where does the money go?" I asked, looking at Don Hall who sat back in a blue haze through the whole meeting. "Hopefully not into just a few people's pockets like the strike relief concerts."

"I don't want any of that shit anymore, everything's a scam," Hall said, getting up and walking out of the meeting.

Bridges started to talk, but the look Smokey gave him changed his mind. Zack Zenor never said a word. He was much too loaded to care. John Carpenter knew he was beat.

"Look, Al," he said, "maybe we could talk about this another time."

There wouldn't be another time. Carpenter would never run KPPC. I always read "Roach Clips" in The *Free Press*. Carpenter wrote about almost every aspect of the revolution. He never mentioned KPPC. I tried to figure his angle. Was he aiming for a cut from the record companies, or was it the concert business that he was after? Surely, Link Wyler and I could promote concerts as well as John Carpenter.

This radio station could be a gold mine. Too many people wanted it. Al Herion was grabbing at straws, but he wasn't going to alienate me and the handful of jocks that kept him on his job. I knew that I had a piece of the power, and I would be able to choose who I shared it with.

At 6:00 p.m. that night, Smokey Roberds opened the microphone to begin his shift.

"Hello, music-lovers," he said. "This is KPPC FM, Free Form Radio for Los Angeles, where the disc jockey is king and you all are loyal subjects. From now on I refuse to play Blue Cheer. Instead I want you to hear the original man who wrote the song, because the original is still the greatest. From the late '50s, here's Eddie Cochran on 'The Summertime Blues.'"

*"Sometimes I wonder
what I'm gonna do,
Lord there ain't no cure
for the summer time blues."*
(Ibid.)

1968

♦ The Doors sold the recording rights to "Light My Fire" to José Feliciano, whose 1968 recording went to number three. The chord progression was inspired by John Coltrane's "My Favorite Things," which Julie Andrews sang in *The Sound of Music*. "Light My Fire" was the last song Jim Morrison performed live. The place was The Warehouse in New Orleans.

Zack Zenor

*"Smoking marihuana is more fun
than drinking beer,
But a friend of ours was captured
and they gave him thirty years."*

"Outside of a Small Circle of Friends," Phil Ochs
(Phil Ochs, Barracade Music)

Like a zombie, Richard Nixon had come back from political death to haunt us, beating out the B-Movie actor Ronald Reagan who was still twelve years away from his turn. Nixon named Spiro Agnew as his running mate, pledged to end the Vietnam War, and vowed to get tough on crime. Since the smoke of my choice made me a lawbreaker, I figured he was talking to me.

Russian tanks rolled into Prague and opened fire on the Czechs, who dared to assemble and asked for a bit of democracy. In California, the fear of Big Brother was ratcheted up another notch.

Chuck Connors was a star from the television hit *The Rifleman.* A former baseball player and super patriot, he was all American to the core. On a USO tour to Vietnam, he learned a Special Forces team was going into Laos. He wanted to go. He pestered the fighters and raised hell to get them to bring him along. Finally, they got him drunk the night before and left without him. Chuck Connors was one ballsy bastard. When producer Freddie Groffe cast Chuck Connors to shoot a western in Bogotá, Columbia, Smokey Roberds and Hank Capps got the call for co-starring roles as outlaw gang members. They would have to ride, shoot, and endure cold Colombian nights. Hank would have to leave Jill Maina and his budding music career behind. Smokey would have to give up his deejay shift on KPPC. They barely paused to say goodbye. In Bogota, Smokey would get Chuck Connors stoned for the first time. He had a silly grin on his face for a week and didn't much care about fighting anybody.

Jim Bachman was working full-time on the movie, *Zabriskie Point.* Antonioni wanted billboards to appear in a shot of a plane taking off over the San Diego Freeway at LAX. Bachman and crew went out and erected billboards with specific ads along the freeway in the exact scale needed to look good as the plane flew over. Expenses on the film were mounting fast. The wife of a Black Panther had been cast in *Zabriskie*, so the FBI had begun to check out activities of all cast and crewmembers, including Bachman. When he drove from MGM to look in on the Cellar's construction progress on Vermont Street the Federales were on his tail. The connection to me, Laquidara, and KPPC was easy to make.

Laquidara had rewritten *One Hand Clapping* and re-titled it, *Alvin P. Peterson*, a thinly veiled reference to John F. Kennedy. Vince Donofrio claimed Charles had stolen his idea for the script and refused to play the lead. Peter Pastore took over the lead role but never created that insane spark that the Detroit Kid most certainly would have provided.

We needed a director, someone who could pull some publicity to our fledgling theatre group. At a Hollywood party, I met Otis Young, a black actor who had just been cast in a western TV series, and would soon co-star with Jack Nicholson and Randy Quaid in the classic film, *Detail*. Otis was ready to have his couple of hours of Hollywood fame. Directing at the Cellar would be good for him, too. I couldn't believe our good fortune. But within days, Charles Laquidara and Otis Young clashed on the script and Otis politely withdrew. Kate said Charles, being a Yankee, didn't know how to get along with a black man.

Charles and Kate had continuing conflicting opinions on the Carlos Marcello mob connections that were part of Garrison's JFK investigation.

"No way," Kate insisted, "the Mafia is untouchable, they don't need to kill the president just because little Bobby Kennedy is making noise trying to prove he's a tough attorney general"

"Okay, Miz Russo, Italian princess of the South, who's Perry Russo?" Charles asked. "Jim Garrison wants to know and I'm wondering."

"How the fuck do I know." Kate shot back. "He ain't kin to me. We got more Russos in New Orleans than you have Laquidaras in Boston or Milford or wherever the hell you're from."

Charles stayed away from that part of the story and focused on the CIA. As writer director he now had complete creative control. Charles and the cast left for a weekend in Tahoe, where they all frolicked at the vacation home of the male second lead. After balling his host's wife, Charles fired the guy on their return to L.A., and brought in playhouse classmate, Jim Reader, to play the part.

Teddy Cessac and Lynette Winter returned from Tahoe holding hands. Teddy was getting into photography. With Cellar funds, I bought him a Honeywell Pentax camera. In the back alley behind the Cellar, using the old bricks and rusty iron buildings as a backdrop, Teddy shot up a roll of film on Mayf Nutter and his guitar. When Mayf's album was released, the picture that appeared in *Billboard* promoting the album was the one Teddy's eye had framed up in the viewfinder of the Honeywell Pentax.

On the air at KPPC, Charles was growing quickly in his musical knowledge. He befriended Don Bridges, who paid him back with tidbits of musical info, and occasionally an exclusive. We never learned where Bridges got the record but one day he gave Laquidara an English pressing of a new artist singing a Beatle song. Charles was the first deejay in Los Angeles to play Joe Cocker's classic vocal of Ringo Starr's "With a Little Help From My Friends."

FM radio stations all over the country were switching to Rock formats. Music fans by the millions were getting their music in stereo, and identifying with the loose rap of the disc jockeys. Politics were a part of the music and the deejay's only position was anti-establishment. Soon the format itself was termed "Underground." Frank Zappa and the Mothers of Invention, who could never have been heard on Top 40 AM, suddenly had national attention. On television, Buddhist monks were seen setting themselves on fire in protest of the war. At the Olympics in Mexico, U.S. contestants thrust their right fists in the air in the black power salute.

Fifteen summers before, Woodie Bernard and I were broadcasting lespidiza seed into the soil of south Louisiana. Now, I was in the basement of the Pasadena Presbyterian Church, broadcasting to the L.A. basin. I took a puff of weed and turned on the mike.

"This is Underground Radio from the basement of the Pasadena Presbyterian Church, KPPC, FM 106.7. I'm Dave Pierce and this is Phil Ochs who sez it all with 'Outside a Small Circle of Friends.'"

"Maybe we should raise our voices,
ask somebody why
But demonstrations are a drag,
Besides, we're much too high."
(Ibid.)

1968

♦ Kitty Genovese was stabbed to death in Queens, NY while her neighbors looked on. Un-involvement mirrored much of American society in the mid-60s. Phil Ochs confronted that do-nothing attitude with "Outside of a Small Circle of Friends," a lively tune with a Dixieland band and stabbing lyrics. Government agencies considered his activities "un-American" keeping a close eye on him. Only underground radio stations played his songs. Phil Ochs helped form the Yippies.

Chuck Connors (somewhat stoned), Smokey Roberds, and
Aron Kinkaid on the set of *The Proud and the Damned.*

Los Angeles
August 29, 1968

With Lyndon Johnson out of the race, his presidency defeated by Vietnam, and Robert Kennedy shot down in Los Angeles, Hubert Humphrey, the old Minnesota war horse, was ready to take up the business-as-usual banner of the Democratic Party at the convention in Chicago.

But the word had gone out from the radical left, to meet the old guard head on. Mayor Daly and the Chicago police were ready. Banned from the convention floor, the new Yippie Party headed by Abby Hoffman, Jerry Rubin, and Tom Hayden converged in the parks and streets outside. While party platforms were being echoed inside the hall, the police and Yippies fought it out in the streets. Tear gas and police batons were barely a match for sticks, stones, and overwhelming numbers of the young street fighters. Television cameras left the hall and went outside to cover the real action. While delegates inside booed the police and fought for the soul of the Democratic party, Americans in their living rooms watched television and saw the youth of the nation slug it out with the aging police state for the heart of our country. Brutality in close-ups did not play well in prime-time. The lawmen scattered the dissenters only to have them reform and taunt the lines of authority with the chant, "The whole world is watching. The whole world is watching."

In North Hollywood, Laquidara, Kate, and I saw it all in a video haze. Only twenty years earlier there had been almost no television. Mass use of color was only three years old. Now the video camera was putting the revolution in front of our faces. When you see this kind of hatred up close, it's a living experience. You never forget it, and you're never the same again. The government's ability to use police to maintain power and control the populace would be questioned from now on.

The next morning in Pasadena, the deejay staff met in Al Herion's office. We were all sick and outraged, but it was Laquidara, who, being the most emotional, and at the same time, the most eloquent, led the radio air attack.

KPPC was the first media voice in Los Angeles to verbalize the emotions of the nation. Charles Laquidara was a real person with real feelings, talking to an audience that was totally tuned in.

"Mayor Daly arbitrarily exercised the use of the police force during the Democratic convention," Laquidara said. "We, the viewers, saw the vicious, violent side of American politics. Chicago is going to trigger confrontations on college campuses all over the country and when it happens, don't ask me who's to blame. You all know who started it. You all saw it on television in Chicago. But the real revolution won't be televised. It'll be live in your street."

This was all the power anyone needed. We knew for sure we could make our voices heard. We were on the radio in the City of Angels.

Smokey had always said, "Don't worry about what you're going to talk about when you open the microphone. When you have something to say, you'll know how to say it."

Don Hall, Zack Zenore, and I were not always as well spoken as Laquidara. We had to say it with music. There was plenty of material to tell our story.

> *"And the words that are used...*
> *will not be understood as they're spoken.*
>
> *... And the ship's wise men*
> *Will remind you once again*
> *That the whole wide world is watchin'."*
> (Ibid.)

Hollywood
September 1968

*"Come on, people,
smile on your brother."*

"Get Together," Youngbloods
(Chester W. Powers, Jr., Irving Music)

Kate was singing the Jessie Collin Young song to John-David and 'Chelle. The Youngbloods' recording was fast becoming the anthem of the '60s. The haunting folk-style message stirred our sense of righteousness that the love generation lived and breathed.

I turned left off Vermont onto Second Street and came through the back alley parking lot, stopping the Porsche against a pile of plywood. It was Saturday at the Cellar Theatre. The cast and crew were building the set for *Alvin P. Peterson.* Jim Bachman was overseeing the construction of the monoliths, the key components to our futuristic set. Bachman had borrowed the idea from the movie *2001.* The tall rectangular monoliths, in the *Space Odyssey* classic, portrayed the kind of look we wanted for the Cellar. Built to rotate for fast set changes, monoliths were practical and gave the impression of somber strength that was a unique part of Bachman's design. The monoliths were a Bachman trademark. This was no studio carpenter crew here, however, and the Cellar cast was still getting the angles down. Kate got right into it with Jim Bachman. She was looking for short cuts.

John-David and 'Chelle were having a ball. To a four and five year old, a theatre construction site was the ultimate playground.

Inside, Charles was fretting over the placement of ashtrays on the rocking, revolving bankers' chairs, which were theatre comfort to the max. Smoking was important to Charles and he felt our industry guests would appreciate that courtesy. To make it all happen, however, I would have to spend several hundred dollars more, to install a cigarette smoke exhaust system. Our goal of building the finest theatre in Hollywood was almost there, but the cost kept climbing.

Link had tried to get construction help from outside the group's immediate circle. He brought in a group of actors he had met, who all applauded our project by grabbing a hammer. One of that group was Victor French, a working character actor who would go on to star in *Little House on the Prairie* and *Highway to Heaven* with his friend and co-star, Michael Landon.

I walked through all the theatre construction activity, making decisions and passing out instructions along the way, before reaching the video tape room in the front of the building. There I was greeted by the smiling face of Danny Truhitte, holding his six-month old son.

"The monoliths are beautiful," Danny said. "You ought to be proud of what you're accomplishing here."

"Yeah, Bachman's got great taste," I said. "So do Kate and Charles."

"And you've got the money," Danny added.

"So far I do. I wasn't sure I was going to make it, but my parents have been very supportive."

"Well, I can't help but wonder why, with all this, this beautiful theatre, a beautiful family, everything you have, that you would still play around with this crazy hippy lifestyle."

"Look, Danny," I said, "I know you're a Mormon now, and family values are important to you, but they are to me, too. I love my family. They are the center of my life. I'm just not as religious about it as you are."

"It's not just religion. It's our American way of life that's on the line," Danny spoke fervently. "You believe you can do what you want. Free sex, free drugs, one hit of acid and you're an instant hippy."

"I haven't done acid," I said.

"You will," he replied. "And the harder stuff. For God's sake, David, I love you man. I love Kate and your kids, and Charles and Smokey, too. I love you as much as I do my family. I can't stand to see you do this to yourself, to our country. This nation will never get over what you're helping to create. The '60s will affect our society for a long time to come. You'll never be able to forget this."

"Hey, I'm doing it the way I think is right for me."

"Is it right to teach your kids not to respect authority, not to respect the police? Just like the bumper sticker says, 'Next time you need help, call a hippy.' Well, I've seen Charles call the police 'pigs.' I've seen John-David repeat right after him 'oink police.' I'm not going to let my kids be around that. Authority is not intolerable. Authority is necessary."

"I understand how you feel, Danny," I said. "You and I are children of the '50s. We were taught to obey authority. Do not question. Do not talk back. But we were also taught we are all free, and I believed that. But we aren't really free, are we? Blacks aren't free to get a good education. And our kids aren't free to breathe clean air. I have to fight for the freedom to play the music I want, or say what's on my mind on the radio. Charles and I had to make a conscious decision to stay out of the military so we'd be free not to have to kill or be killed. This American way of life you're talking about stinks in several places."

"Those people who choose to fight in Vietnam and your parents who chose to kill or be killed in World War II were the heroes," Danny replied. "So butt holes like you and Charles can be on the radio and play whatever dirty rock lyric somebody records. Those heroes are buying time for all of us, so we can beat the commies on the battlefield and then show them our capitalist economy is the only way to organize the world. And buying us time so English, not Russian, can become the universal language, so that you can keep on talking on the radio in your language instead of theirs. That's what authority is doing for you. Wake up, my friend. Free drugs and free sex, letting it all hang out, will leave a bitter legacy for our children."

Danny had run out of steam temporarily. Over at the door to the video tape room, John-David was watching, listening. I looked at him for a moment, then back at Danny.

"I'm teaching John-David to question everything," I said quietly. "Never do anything because someone says to do it. If it doesn't make sense to you, ask why. Don't conform, if it feels real, be different. This era of rebellion might not last. We have to make the most of it to turn things around while we have a chance. I don't mind being a threat to the nation's morals, manners, or values. We'll have to deal with the conflict. We were taught that America was right and good. But now I find out that it's not and I'm outraged. Who's minding the store? Who's guarding the fort? I demand to know. Is it my watch now?"

Danny could only shake his head in silence. He didn't have the answers, of course. Neither did I. Finally he spoke.

"You and I were innocent idealists. Now I see you becoming an activist," he said, "maybe for the wrong cause."

"I thought student demonstrations were something that happened in foreign countries," I said. "Now I find myself cursing authority, and pulling for the long-haired kids."

Danny Truhitte and I shook hands as he left, carrying his baby son through the monolith construction, stopping only to kiss Kate and 'Chelle good-bye.

"You okay, Dad?" John-David had to ask.

"Sure, kid," I said. "What are you doing?"

"I need some paint, Dad," John-David said. "Jim Bachman says the steps to the light booth are supposed to be yellow."

"Come on, people,
smile on your brother."
(Ibid.)

The Pierce kids, 'Chelle and J.D., assisting with the Cellar Theatre construction, 1967.

KPPC FM
Pasadena Presbyterian Church
Late September 1968

"Strap yourself
to the tree with roots
you ain't goin' nowhere."

"You Ain't Goin' Nowhere," The Byrds
(Bob Dylan, Dwarf Music)

I had the Byrds on the turntable, when Link Wyler walked into the studio with a shabbily dressed, long-haired, guitar-playing folk singer, who looked like he'd been sleeping in the streets. I found out later the streets were his only address.

"I want you to meet David Lannan," Link smiled broadly. "He came up to me at the Big Mama concert last night. He's looking for management and his music is right down your alley. Wait till you hear this guy."

I turned the studio monitor down, but David Lannan spoke up.

"You can leave it on low, I'll just sing along. I like that song. That's a Bob Dylan song," he said.

He adjusted the homemade, brightly-colored strap of his acoustic guitar, put one worn-out boot on a chair and fell right in with the Byrds. I was knocked out. He had a beautiful melodic voice. He played chord combos that any folk guitarist would love to master. Every once in a while at the end of a verse, he added something sounding like a yodel that would tear your heart out.

"Ain't that something?" Link beamed. "This guy's a cross between Hank Williams and Bob Dylan."

Link wasn't lying. We agreed to set up auditions with some record company people and put him in the Troubador on amateur night.

Lannan was from Bartersville, Oklahoma. He had an ex-wife and two kids out in Antelope Valley, just over the mountain range from North Hollywood. Moved by the music and the times, he'd gone on the road to see what he might find out there.

Over the next three years, I realized that the freedom to ramble and roam was probably more important to David Lannan than success in the music business. He would stay in Los Angeles a few weeks, get an itch in his boots, and ride his thumb up north to San Francisco and Marin County. Days or weeks would pass before he'd surface and we'd try again to get his career kicked off. When he had any money at all, he'd ride the trains. When he didn't, he would ride with the hobos. He knew more train songs than Jimmy Rodgers. He said when the Revolution was over, and we'd beaten the Establishment, The People would be able to ride trains for free. His vision of America was all of us riding across this great land, stopping here and there to talk, exchange ideas, and then hop a train and roam on down the road searching for whatever it was we were looking to find.

On the way North he'd usually stop in the Big Sur country where the Esalen Shahram group charged guests several hundred dollars to spend a week-end being pampered and bathed in the hot mineral springs that bubbled up from the mountain side. Lannan always crashed their party insisting that he had a right to bath in the ancient waters. He refused to recognize their exclusive ownership. They could keep the pampering, the wine and the rich food. All he wanted was a bath. After awhile they stopped trying to throw him out and listened to his music, 'til dawn.

Lannan finally landed a recording contract in 1971 with David Rubinson who was producing the Jefferson Airplane in San Francisco. Rubinson saw the raggedy tramp playing in the streets, handed him a twenty dollar bill. "How would you like to make a record?" he asked.

"Sure," Lannan replied, accepting the twenty, "but you'll have to talk to my manager in Los Angeles."

It was six months before we got it all together. I located Lannan doing time in a small California town for holding two joints and a few hits of acid. He was singing to the jailer when he got the call.

"Sure, I'll sign a record contract," Lannan said, "but you'll have to bail me out first."

Rubinson put together some of Lannan's best songs with a superb group of musicians and went into the studio. At David Lannan's suggestion they also recorded in a train station. With his producer and the record company geared up to release and promote the album, Lannan left for India. He simply let the deal go.

Rubinson heard the same thing in David Lannan that Link Wyler and I heard, a lot of miles and three years earlier. By that time, the folk era in music was already history. The album he cut was good, but not his best work. Only a few of us had heard David at his best. It would happen late at night, with a few people sitting in a circle on a living room floor, when the wine and the smoke had messed with our heads and played with our hearts, when we'd finished verbally abusing the government and agreed on how we'd do it right when it was our turn to run things. I often wished I could have transferred David Lannan to a recording studio at that moment. But the presence of a microphone in front of him always blew him away.

Most people would say it was the drugs that made David drop out and become the drifter he was. More evidence that the '60s were a bad trip and he was another casualty. That was somewhat true, I guess, but I never thought that was the whole picture. I figured mostly it was just his nature.

That first day I met him in Pasadena, he pulled out a tape that not only described David Lannan, but also captured the restless feeling of the '60s as well as any song I ever heard. I cued up the tape on the reel-to-reel machine and listened to the first verse. It was crudely recorded but KPPC listeners loved raw work.

When the Byrds finished singing Bob Dylans's "You Ain't Goin' Nowhere," I grinned back at the smiling Link Wyler and put David Lannan's song on the radio.

"As soon as it gets daybreak,
I'm gonna move on down the road,
I'll be looking and a'listening,
Where I'm going I don't know.

But I'll remember always,
The way you look right now,
With your breast a'gently moving,
Loose hair upon your brow,

Just brush aside the ashes,
So our fire it will not burn,
You might leave some room for glowing,
Though I probably won't return."

''Loose Hair,'' David Lannan
(David Lannan, Laze Music)

David Lannan, San Francisco Records.

*"The louder they come
the harder they crack."*

"Million Dollar Bash," Bob Dylan
(Bob Dylan, Dwarf Music)

It was my 27th birthday. As soon as the lights went down on this evening's performance of *Alvin P. Peterson*, the cast and crew went into a party mode right on the stage. Kate had kept the whole affair a secret, and I was very much surprised. She broke out the food and a case of champagne.

Charles' original script had received mixed notices. The biggest critique was from those who felt, first, the Kennedy assassination theory should be laid to rest; second, Jim Garrison was just another power-hungry district attorney in the Deep South. And third, no group of radicals would be crazy enough to kidnap a national figure and try to brainwash him. This was still a half dozen years before the Symbionese Liberation Army snatched a screaming Patty Hearst from her boyfriend's apartment. The positive critique came from the Hollywood Reporter who stated the Cellar group "was head and shoulders above any other outfit in town" and Laquidara and I should be applauded for "taking on a bold new work" instead of "doing chin-ups on a door stop" like so many other theatrical groups. Our use of live video in a stage production was correctly termed "innovative." In one scene, the close ups of the action on stage was appearing simultaneously in a monitor on the set. It had never been done this way before. The music, which included the long version of Buffalo Springfield's *Blue Bird* at intermission, was the cutting edge of free form rock. And everyone raved over the comfortable new facility and Jim Bachman's outstanding design and use of space.

For me and Charles and Kate, that wasn't nearly enough. We had worked for over a year, overcome countless difficulties, and I'd spent a small fortune of my family's wealth. Instead of being the big payoff, Alvin P. Peterson was totally anticlimactic. I could feel the let-down in the cast. Charles was already hinting that he would leave the theatre after the show closed and concentrate on KPPC. After all, that's where the money was, or could be, certainly not in an actor's workshop theatre. Bud Tedesco and Peter Pastore would also withdraw. Bud would be a page at ABC and eventually do children's shows before retiring and leaving town, Pete would cut hair in Pasadena before finally getting character work when he was much older. I never again saw Jim Reader, who, with his James Dean qualities, was perhaps the most castable of all of us.

But tonight we were celebrating my birthday. I had started wearing a white hat with a flat brim and a string of beads on the crown. It was my trademark, never taking it off. When the maitre'd' at the famous Fog Cutter Restaurant, suggested I remove my hat, I had left in a huff. Link and Joan Wyler, who were meeting us at the restaurant with director, Bob Tottin, couldn't believe that I could possibly put that much importance on a hat while blowing the opportunity to dine with a hot Hollywood director who could cast me in his next project. Long hair and hat included.

As the party at the Cellar got wilder, Charles brought me some more bad news. A young black actor in a small role was threatening to leave the show. He had given Charles an ultimatum, beef up his part or he was out.

"What should I do, David?" Charles wanted to know.

"Cut the character completely," I replied instantly. "We're not going to let this guy tell us what to do. He's out. In fact, he's out right now. Tell him to get out of my theatre."

By now we had attracted the attention of most of the party, including the young black actor. I approached him swiftly and took him by the arm.

"You want out, man," I said. "Here, let me help you."

In my champagne haze, I never saw it coming. But I felt the crack of his knuckles against my jaw. Only Tedesco and Reader's quick reaction kept me from going all the way to the stage floor. The black kid was hustled out. I then heard all the stories about how he was mixed up with the Black Panthers and was always spouting militant slogans. He called the Cellar Theatre the next morning and left a message of apology. My jaw hurt for three days, long enough to remind me never to lay a hand on a young Black Panther.

Peter Pastore handed me my white hat. The string of hippy beads had been broken and were scattered on the stage. I slapped the hat on my head, downed the glass of champagne, and grabbed the blond girl who worked the light booth. We went into a Watusi dance to the hot rock that Laquidara was playing on the Cellar Theatre's excellent sound system.

> *"Come now, sweet cream,*
> *Don't forget to flash."*
> (Ibid.)

Los Angeles
November 1968

"And they wile away the hours
In their ivory towers...

People walking up to you,
Singing Glory hallelujah..."

"Game People Play," Joe South
(Joe South, Sony/ATV Songs, LLC)

The Joe South hit had been overplayed on the Top 40 AM Rockers, but the lyrics had keyed into the mood of the general public. It was so right-on that, I played it occasionally on KPPC FM. The month had started with hopeful news from Southeast Asia. The U.S. forces had halted the bombing of North Vietnam and wider talks were set to begin. On November 7, Richard Nixon won the presidency by a thin margin over Hubert Humphrey. The Nixon-Agnew era had begun. Lyndon Johnson faded away to Texas with an offer of more than a million dollars for his memoirs. In Hollywood, Smokey Roberds spent four hours every morning getting into monkey makeup for his role in *Planet of the Apes*, a movie about astronauts who came back to earth to find that humans had blown the best deal in the universe. By Christmas, our American astronauts in *Apollo 8* would circle the moon and come back to describe it as a vast and lonely place. On the radio in Pasadena, I played the Moody Blues' lyrics, "Ride my see saw, take my place on this trip just for me."

Meanwhile, Laquidara was again starting to slip into a depressed state. I could tell by his music selection, Arthur Lee and Love singing the suicidal "Signed D.C." and Steppenwolf singing, "God Damned The Pusher Man" a song written by the great folk singer and composer Hoyt Axton.

When barrel-chested, gravelly voiced Hoyt came out to Pasadena, I was happy to meet him and play songs from his new L.P., *My Griffin is Gone*.

Zack Zenor was playing a lot of folk music, including Ramblin Jack Elliot. Don Hall, late at night, would play sets that included sitar solos by Ravi Shankar, followed by Shankar's protégé, George Harrison, on sitar playing "Within You, Without You" from The Beatles' *Sergeant Pepper*.

One evening at midnight, Harrison came down to the bottom of the church to spend a couple of hours talking music and the sorry state of the American government with Laquidara and Hall.

Don Hall was also attracting the attention of Michelangelo Antonioni. Hall's spacey use of Pink Floyd had grabbed the ear of Antonioni, who was sampling the sounds of L.A. radio as he continued shooting *Zabriskie*. Bachman had been down in Phoenix, building the house that would be blown up while seventeen camera crews covered the explosion from every conceivable angle. Thus a five second explosion went on for what seemed like minutes in the final edit. Bachman also had footage of the police riots in Chicago three months earlier, taken when Antonioni had brought in a small camera to shoot without attracting the attention of the FBI agents who were constantly shadowing the cast and crew.

About this time, Les Carter met with Al Herion. They buried the last remnants of ill feeling left over from the strike. After eight months, Les had decided the only thing that mattered in a radio war was being on the air. With Les as our new Program Director, we were all hopeful that we could move ahead with getting more power, a taller tower, and stereo transmitter. Without those three elements, we could never cover enough of L.A. to win any kind of ratings race. Because that's all we could afford, Herion opted for going stereo, which actually cut down slightly on our coverage area. We also moved the On Air Studio into the bigger Production Studio. We put a dimmer on the overhead lights, hooked up the light show monitors that pulsed to the beat of the music we played. Les took us toward a more positive music sound, playing less of Canned Heat's "Amphetamine Annie" and more of Electric Flag's brassy "Grooving is Easy."

At the Cellar, Vince had surfaced with his own project, *Orpheus Descending*, in which he starred and directed. It, too, got good notices, but nothing to bring any income into the theatre's bank accounts. Playing opposite Vince was the heroine of *Alvin P. Peterson*, the beautiful actress Jorjana Kellaway. A tall, brunette, statuesque Cher type, Jorjana was married to Roger Kellaway, a gifted musician who went on to co-author with Carrol O'Conner, the star of *All in the Family*, that hit show's theme song. Roger Kellaway on keyboard and Tom Scott (who later worked as a band leader for late night variety shows) on sax, put together a rock group that sometimes rented the sound-proof video tape room at the Cellar for practice sessions.

Laquidara had fallen hopelessly in love with Jorjana. He had the hots for her real bad, but Jorjana wasn't going to leave Roger Kellaway for Charles. On Thanksgiving, Jorjana and her four year old son had dinner with us in North Hollywood. Roger Kellaway was on the road. Kate was cooking and organizing the kids, Jorjana was confused and vulnerable, and I had a heart full of lust. On the radio, Charles Laquidara introduced his next song.

"Listen, everybody," he said. "This song was written some time ago by Brian and Eddie Holland and Lamont Dozier and it was a big hit by The Supremes. Then last year it was recorded again. This time on ATCO Records and it's an even bigger hit now because we play it all the time here on stereo KPPC-FM. But there's a girl out there who I could have written this song for and she knows who she is. Here's Vanilla Fudge."

"Set me free, why doncha babe,
Get out my life, why doncha babe,
...You don't really need me..."

"You Keep Me Hangin On," Vanilla Fudge
(Lamont Dozier, Brian and Eddie Holland, Stone Agate Music)

Elysian Park
Los Angeles
December 1968

"We better stop, hey, what's that sound?
Everybody look what's going down."

"For What It's Worth," Buffalo Springfield
(Stephen Stills, Cotillion Music Inc., Richie Furay Music, Springalo Toones,
Ten-East Music)

Stephen Stills had written his song about the clash between hippie kids and the cops, at Sunset and Crescent Heights where Laurel Canyon hits the Strip. It was an area close to Schwabb's Drug Store, where in the old days kids from Hollywood High School collected, hoping to be discovered and get into the movies. But these kids weren't interested in Hollywood, their only priority was getting high and hanging out. Property owners were demanding the police do something, and the confrontation was growing. I didn't identify with their hassle. It was just more L.A. excitement to me, and a great song from Buffalo Springfield.

For the past week the Free Press and KPPC had been promoting, as a public service, a picnic in Elysian Park. The Free Clinic would set up a tent and the whole event would publicize fund raising efforts for that organization. It was another bright, sunshiny Sunday in the City of Angels. Kate packed a picnic lunch. Along with Charles, John-David, and 'Chelle, the five of us loaded up the Porsche and headed for what should have been a typical American family outing.

We arrived about 1:00 p.m., pulled into the parking lot, then walked along the top of the hill which overlooked Elysian Park. It was already filled with the bright multicolored costumes of about 5,000 members of the developing counter culture. We spotted an uncrowded area at the edge of the multitude near the Free Clinic Tent.

With the picnic basket in one hand and John-David on my shoulders, I started down the gently sloping hill, followed by Kate carrying the portable radio, locked in at 106.7 FM. Four-year-old 'Chelle, blonde, petite, and giggling, was riding her godfather's shoulders, bringing up the rear. Charles was in a particularly jovial mood, greeting others along the way yelling, "Yay, KPPC, that's my station!" every time the song on our portable radio phased in with someone else's radio.

We found a shady spot, turned the kids loose, and leaned back to soak up the good vibrations. The twin smells of incense and marijuana permeated the setting. John-David and 'Chelle were having a blast. The thought of them getting lost or being accosted by strangers was just not applicable to these surroundings. When Kate began to lay out the picnic lunch, she realized 'Chelle's Linus blanket had been left in the car. Without it, there would be no after-lunch nap for 'Chelle. Charles and I volunteered to stretch our legs and retrieve the blanket. We climbed the hill at a leisurely pace. Charles stopping to talk to people, and proclaiming what a great event this was. I had to agree. It just didn't get any better than this. L.A. was going my way.

As we approached the parking lot we saw them coming. Thirty, forty, maybe fifty cars speeding up the winding road to the park entrance. By the time we got to the Porsche, the first eight or ten cars had come to a quick stop. They were all black Fords, all new, all identical and all bearing the nameplate of a local Ford dealership. Out of each car jumped four fully-equipped L.A. riot policemen. They slammed their doors, adjusted their gear, and began to assemble.

"Something weird is coming down," Charles said in a low voice.

"Let's get back to Kate and the kids," I replied, forgetting about the Linus blanket.

The sound of cars pulling up and doors slamming followed us out of the parking lot. We skirted the top of the hill looking down on the picnic that was now in high gear. The riot police were right behind us, goose-stepping two abreast. Charles and I hurried back to our spot.

"What's the matter? I can't send y'all to get a blanket without y'all screwing it up?" Kate asked.

"Where're the kids?" I was yelling.

Charles was becoming visibly shook as he pointed up the hill. The riot police were now lined up all along the top of the hill. On command, they flipped their plastic visors down in front of their faces, then seconds later, all in unison drew their three-foot long batons from their holsters. We all had seen the World War II movies of Nazi storm troopers surrounding the populace. This was the same scene, only it wasn't a movie. Nothing happened for what seemed like five minutes, while the confusion and paranoia level of the picnickers began to rise. Why were these cops here? They couldn't possibly have a beef with us. What was the deal with all the new cars from the Ford dealership? Were they all loaners, being road tested? Maybe it was some kind of exercise. We didn't want to accept it, but the fear in the pit of our stomachs said these cops weren't out for a Sunday drive.

In a well coordinated move, about a half dozen groups with four storm troopers in each group stepped out of the ranks and began to deploy down the hill. The remaining two hundred strong stood, staring straight ahead in one long ominous line. The cop groups moved separately into the picnic crowd. Soon a chorus of boos erupted from one section. Someone with a six-pack had been arrested and was being hauled away. A murmur ran through the crowd.

"Come on," Charles was screaming, "You can't arrest somebody for drinking in the park."

Then turning to me, he asked, "There's no ordinance against drinking in the park, is there, David?"

"I don't know," I answered, "there may be, but I've never heard of it being enforced."

Another round of boos closer to us and we could clearly see a hapless, long-haired young man being cuffed and roughly led away, his beaded girlfriend following with a barrage of curse words. This time the boos were accompanied by a hail of empty beer cans, bottles and trash directed at the police. That was the cue for the boys on the hill. The next few minutes were a nightmare that would always be branded into us in living, screaming color.

In one unified wave, the riot police swept down the hillside, swinging their batons. Some of the picnickers in outrage tried to fight back. Others were just unfortunate to be in the way. Their heads were busted, men and women alike. Most of the crowd ran screaming in panic. Kate grabbed John-David and 'Chelle, made them lay on the ground, and covered them with her body. Taking her cue, Charles and I dropped down beside her waiting for the wave of terror to get to our spot. When a guy next to us put up his hands to ward off a baton he was dropped from behind by another one. The cop, whose blow had been blocked, immediately began kicking the fallen man, who was writhing defenselessly. I jumped to my feet, screaming at the cop.

"Leave him alone. He's hurt."

My words were echoing in my head as the cop spun around, in what seemed like a slow motion, to attack me. I was face to face with the full force of the establishment and what was behind the plastic riot mask was not pretty. It was not even human. For the first time I saw the hate being directed at my kind. He snarled a low, vicious fear-provoking growl as he raised his baton. Like a running back I faked left, and then stepped back and to the right as his baton missed my head by inches. I kept backing up, throwing up my hands in a gesture that said "I give up."

Someone threw a bottle at the cop. He turned his attention in that direction. Most of the cops had now completed their first sweep and were reassembling at the bottom of the valley.

Somewhere a bullhorn was barking: "This has been declared an unlawful assembly. You are ordered to clear this park immediately."

Kate had John-David by the hand. I picked up Michelle under one arm. Charles had a death grip on the portable radio, still painting tranquility with the Moody Blues singing "Tuesday Afternoon." The picnic basket was left behind. As we ran by *The Free Clinic* tent, a dozen bleeding people were being treated, when several cops began cutting the tent ropes so that it collapsed onto the victims.

"You people get out of here," yelled a six foot four storm trooper. "If you're hurt, go see a real doctor."

We joined the flow of wailing panicked humanity trying to get to our cars while L.A.'s finest mopped up the remaining stragglers below.

On the way through the parking lot, Charles was on a tear. He wanted to burn one of the new Fords. We coaxed him into the Porsche and drove home to north Hollywood in a state of shock. Charles immediately jumped in his car and headed for Pasadena. Thirty minutes later he was on the air at KPPC. He told the whole story eloquently and scathingly, in a ten minute rap.

"I've experienced one of the most incredibly horrible things that I ever felt in my life," Charles spoke into the microphone. "I knew there was a difference between us and them, but I've never really believed the police were 'pigs.' Because 'pig' is about the lowest name you can call a human being. Until today I thought the police were like the rest of us, just making a living, just doing their job. When we arrived in Elysian Park today, there was a celebration of peace and love, with hundreds of people enjoying the day with their families and kids, when these guys, the police, the 'good guys, our protectors,' came there to beat and maim. With helmets on and face masks lowered, swinging billy clubs beating the hell out of people, hurting people, smashing skulls, making the red blood flow on the green grass of Elysian Park. It had been a peaceful gathering. There was no violence, until the storm troopers stormed the crowd. It was horrible. It was horrible and frightening. They beat men, women, husbands, wives, mothers. They weren't just doing their job. These people really, really hated us. And they hate you. And they hate me. They wouldn't care if we died tomorrow, and they wouldn't hesitate to be the ones to pull the trigger. This isn't just a confrontation between two different kinds of people who think differently. This is a real war going on in this city and in this country. These people mean business. You can see that hate in their eyes as they mindlessly obey orders that came down from some untouchable politician somewhere. These are pigs. Total pigs, like an animal with no concept of right or wrong, good or evil. All they know is they hate everything we stand for. They hate your long hair, the way you dress, and what you smoke. They hate your music. You're a communist in their eyes and you deserve to die. We saw their hate today, up close in the tight shot, where their eyes can't lie. This is a major war we're all in, a war we have to win, to lose is unthinkable because of what this nation might become. These pigs represent everything we learned in school that was bad and evil. They gotta be stopped. You have to stop them. I have to stop them. These pigs are not L.A.'s finest. We are! This is one fight we can't walk away from."

The next day the *L.A. Times* carried a paragraph buried on page 53. It said, "A couple of hundred drunk and drugged hippies had rioted and the L.A.P.D. had been called out to restore order."

When one of the top T.V. newscasters at a local network affiliate blamed the riot on the picnickers, Charles called him a liar on the radio, something professional broadcasters just didn't do. The straight media began to realize there were some real radicals in their midst, and we controlled a radio station. There was no one in charge to take us off the air.

We speculated for weeks on who had called in the police to bust up our picnic and why. How early in the week had the battle plans been made? Was it *The L.A. Times* shooting at *The L.A. Free Press*? Was the Chief of Police of the City of Angels making a show of force against the counter culture in order to keep his job? Even more sinister, was the establishment's medical profession trying to shut down the Free Clinic? We never found out. Eventually we stopped talking about it. But the word "pig" for policeman suddenly meant something to me. The lines had been drawn in blood in Elysian Park. I knew I was already on the other side.

When Charles Laquidara ended his speech on KPPC, and turned up the volume on the Buffalo Springfield, Stephen Stills' words had new meaning.

"What a field-day for the heat...
We better stop, hey, what's that sound?
Everybody look what's going down."
(Ibid.)

Los Angeles
January 1969

The U.S./North Vietnamese peace talks in Paris expanded to include the Vietcong and South Vietnamese. It had taken months to get to even this point. Richard Nixon and Spiro Agnew were inaugurated. Nixon announced the first withdrawal of U.S. troops from Vietnam. At the same time, B-52s intensified the bombing of Communist sanctuaries in Cambodia.

In Hollywood, the sanctuary for the Los Angeles hippy scene, crowds began to gather nightly at Ciro's and the Paladium. Sometimes the event was a concert by rock or blues bands, sometimes it was just everybody hanging out.

Charles realized his relationship with Jorjana Kellaway was over. Our dream for the *Alvin P. Peterson* script and the Cellar Theatre had gone nowhere. KPPC was in limbo. No settlement in sight between the two owners, Crosby and Avery. Charles had a superb idea for a script about JFK but it was years ahead of its time, or a little late, depending on how you looked at it. As a disc jockey, his combining rock with an expert knowledge of classical music had pushed the boundaries of free form radio right past anything the Tom Donahue crowd had ever imagined.

Charles Laquidara was the epitome of not quite, but almost, greatness. The trappings of success meant less to Charles than any of us. He would eventually be more successful, and get to enjoy that success, more than all of us.

I had only been dozing a few minutes when Charles called me sometime before midnight.

"David, the damn cart machine isn't working," he said, with that twinge of Boston accent that the best voice trainers could not take away from him. "Tomorrow you need to get that lazy ass engineer, Chester Coleman, to do at least the minimum service around here. And the Beatles *White* album has a click on side one. Get Don Bridges to place a new copy in the control room instead of hoarding it in the library or selling it off for cash."

"Sure, Charles," I said. "We'll handle the problems. Why are you calling me now?"

"Because I'm out of here, David. I'm leaving on a 1:00 a.m. flight to Boston. I'll have someone ship my record collection. I've already called

Zack Zenor to come in early tonight. There's about 20 minutes left on this side of Beatles. I just called to say good-bye. Don't think it hasn't been fun. Kiss Kate for me. Tell John-David and 'Chelle I'll miss them."

With the Beatles *White* album still spinning on the turntable, Charles Laquidara walked out of the church, drove to LAX, and left the keys in the ignition of his '38 Dodge.

More than 30 years later, he would have enjoyed the longest tenure of any disc jockey on WBCN, having been the number one rated morning man. He also became one of the highest paid disc jockeys in the history of radio.

Los Angeles
Early February 1969

It had taken me almost two days to figure out what to say. Finally, I just picked up the telephone.

"Music Revolution," Susan Carter's golden voice answered.

"Look, I'm very sorry about what happened," I said. "Is Les around?"

"Yeah, it's a shame," Susan said putting down the phone and calling for Les Carter.

The sound of the Moody Blues singing, "Timothy Leary is Dead, Oh, no, he's only outside looking in," was playing on the Music Revolution sound system.

"Hey, Dave," Les said quietly in to the phone.

"I was really disappointed to hear you're leaving KPPC," I said. "I thought we had a chance of getting something going. This is a huge set-back."

"I know," Les said. "I think as long as Al Herion's there, nothing much will happen."

"Crosby and Avery are still deadlocked in the courts. There's not too much Al Herion can do," I offered.

"That's probably right," Les agreed. "Anyway, we talked and decided it was best I leave."

"You could always come back," I said.

"I could do that, couldn't I," Les Carter replied.

> *"...He's still stuck on the line.*
> *Come on, give it to me,*
> *I'll keep it with mine."*
>
> "I'll Keep It With Mine," Fairport Convention
> (Bob Dylan, Special Rider Music)

With Charles' exit from L.A., I felt a big hole in my life, and the station had lost some of its edge. Now with Les also leaving KPPC, I moved quickly to fill the vacuum. I met with Al Herion. We were approaching the one year anniversary of his behind the scenes seizure of power. The part I played in making it possible for him to control KPPC was evident to both of us. Al Herion always wanted my thoughts about KPPC as events developed. It was an easy sell to get him to name me as acting Program Director. Don Hall, Zack Zenor, and the new late-morning disc jockey, Bob Sala, all went along with my new title without much enthusiasm, but no opposition.

Needing to boost up the on-air staff, I started listening to a box of air check tapes. One caught my ear. When I called Harry Shearer, he was polite but declined. He had sent the tape to Donahue months before intrigued by the new KPPC sound. By now he was set at KRLA in the news department. I hired Jeff Gonzer as weekend relief jock. Jeff was just another young man with an interest in music. Several, just like him, were always gravitating to the station. Working as a bartender at the most famous jazz club in L.A., Shelley's Manne Hole on Cahuenga in Hollywood, Jeff had an education in jazz that topped most of the applicants, and he had the voice potential to be very pleasant on the air. He had no media experience. Had never been a disc jockey. And he never would have been, except that he loved music, was a KPPC fan, had a dream, and was just pushy enough to get my attention. Just like Charles Laquidara before him, I gave Jeff Gonzer his first job in radio, a weekend gig. Weeknights, Jeff hung out with Zack on his show every night, midnight to 6:00 AM.

On KMET, meanwhile, radio's grand old drop-out B. Mitchell Reid worked out 4:00 to 8:00 p.m. playing the cuts but without the spark. Tom Donahue taped shows in San Francisco and sent them down for delayed broadcast 8:00 to midnight. Same superior voice but somehow you could tell Tom wasn't live. He didn't have the edge and he wasn't residing in the City of Angels. On public radio, KPFK, John Carpenter had wrangled some time to appear at midnight, taking phone calls and playing the music, as he was certain his way was the only way to present it. Shucking and jiving as his ad in The *Free Press* stated. The Program was called "Cocaine Karma."

Since Don Hall was the most prominent member of the original staff currently on KPPC, his 8:00 p.m. to midnight show was the only one listed by *The Free Press*. On Wednesday, February 19, the red headed Aquarian spent four hours celebrating his birthday on the radio by playing only the new Neil Young album. Reprise Records bought ads in the paper promoting the show. When Hall signed off every night, I stretched out on my waterbed in North Hollywood, the radio turned low, with Zack and Jeff in my ear. I knew we were on the right track. Whatever it took to be number one in L.A., what Zack and Jeff were doing was going to be a part of it.

Experimenting with sound, playing a wide array of off-the-wall music and artists, these two young, glib, freaked-out guys were doing most anything that came to mind. Zack's favorite was the Incredible String Band. Jeff leaned to Fairport Convention, mixing in Lothar and the Hand People, a lot of Tyrannosaurus Rex, electronic sounds and jazz. It got very interesting.

Zack would O.D. about 3:00 a.m., and sleep it off till 5. Jeff, less of a druggie, was riding on the high of being on the radio. He was learning fast and chewing up the music library in search of new cuts to play. Al Herion said we didn't have the budget to pay two jocks to do a shift after midnight, so Jeff was working Zacks's shift without pay. Jeff didn't care. He would have paid Al Herion to stay on the air.

Despite the low power and lack of dollars, KPPC was absolutely the most Free Form sound anywhere in the country. I was the Program Director. I didn't have any rules. I wasn't about to make up any.

"And to the rhythm of guitars,
We hope you'll lend an ear.
The man who plays the bass does make
Those low notes that you hear

And the high notes come from you and me
For we will sing so clear.

Come all ye rolling minstrels
And together we will try
To rouse the spirit of the earth
And move the rolling sky."

"Rolling Minstrels," Fairport Convention
(unknow, Public Domain)

Jeff Gonzer

The Midwest
February 1969

"Sunshine on snow white cotton
Nearly makes me blind...
Working my way back home
One row at a time."

"One Row at a Time," Merle Haggard
(Red Lane and Dottie West, Tree Publishing)

Merle Haggard on the country radio station was slightly more audible than the clacking of the snow chains now hanging from around the axle of the Cadillac Brougham easing through the midday haze of the Ohio countryside. The dragging chains on the bare pavement could become pretty annoying, but where the snow built up on the highway the chains swished along quite pleasantly. Teddy Cessac Pierce was taking his turn behind the wheel, driving cautiously. Without the chains in place, the traction often got treacherous. Knowing he was too tired to deal with it, Teddy opted for thirty miles an hour till he could get to a gas station for some help with the snow chains.

From the passenger side of the "Bro-ham," as she called it, Willie Mae "Big Mama" Thornton looked out at the farm houses sliding by in the snow. Tired or tipsy, she always did most of the driving. But the long tour, hundreds of miles, countless shows, and bottles of Ole Grand Dad had her whipped.

"I want to have me a farm house like that one," Big Mama said, closing her eyes, then as an afterthought she remembered out loud, "with a front porch, like where I was raised down close to Montgomery, where Hank Williams grew up."

Big Mama drifted off and began to snore. Along with Hag's lonely lament and the clacking and swishing of the snow chains, her snoring was the only soundtrack for Teddy's thoughts as he tried to concentrate on keeping the Cadillac on the road. Teddy was beginning to know most of Big Mama's many quirks. Like her love for country music or her superstition about whistling. Once at the Cellar Theatre, she jumped all over Charles Laquidara when he whistled in her presence. He forgot and did it again when she stopped in at BCN in Boston to plug a club date.

"What's wrong with you white boy," she cursed at Charles live over Boston radio, "you gonna bring me more bad luck."

It was Teddy's job to get Big Mama to the next town, the next concert, and the next payday, rested and sober enough to get through her set. But Teddy's most important job was collecting the money after the gig. He'd give Big Mama and the band some walking-around change, hold back enough for food, gas, and hotel rooms, then send the rest to Link Wyler who'd pay her bills, put some aside to pay the notes on the Brougham and the band's station wagon. Link always kept a piece for himself and I usually got a taste. Link had figured out the game very quickly. The only way it could work was to put Teddy on the road. A twenty-four-year-old white boy with a group of hardened veteran black musicians and one egotistical, incorrigible, legendary queen of the blues.

When it was time to collect after the show, the man with the money, who would just as soon not pay anybody, would sometime question Teddy's authority.

"I'm Big Mama's white boy," he'd say quietly. "Just give me her money."

Teddy was learning how to blend into the various scenarios they encountered. When Big Mama played at the club in Oakland where Berkeley College kids went to hear the blues, Janis Joplin came backstage to visit her idol. Janis offered Big Mama a shot of Southern Comfort. She refused, pulling out her own bottle of one-hundred-proof Ole Grand Dad. "Give it to my road manager," Big Mama said. "This here's Teddy Pierce from Louisiana."

"I'm from Port Arthur," Janis's face lit up as she handed Teddy the dirty water glass filled with Southern Comfort. "We're practically neighbors."

"We sure are," Teddy smiled back, circling an arm around Janis's waist and exchanging a squeeze.

Months earlier, at the Avalon, Janis told Big Mama she'd be recording her song. They shared a drink, then Big Mama, beaming with pride, went out on the stage and announced to the unruly crowd of five thousand kids that the girl from East Texas was gonna do her song on an album. The young blues fans went nuts as Big Mama belted out her classic "Ball and Chain."

From San Francisco, the group had made its way to the college campuses of the northwest, playing auditoriums, gymnasiums, sometimes an outdoor concert in a baseball park, and usually a joint or two on the outskirts of town before heading east for Chicago, Toronto, Boston, and Harlem.

Finally, they were heading home to L.A. with only a couple more shows to round off the tour, the most successful in Big Mama's career. She was starting to snore loudly now, so Teddy slipped in his own tape of Little Walter on harmonica. Teddy had learned to appreciate the blues, picked up a harp and learned a few licks from George "Harmonica" Smith, who had played with Little Walter and was now backing up his friend and neighbor Big Mama Thornton. Bassman Curtis Tilman was also from south-central L.A. On the stage behind Big Mama, Curtis would play bass while leaning, half-sitting, against a barstool. When he was really tired, he could easily nod out a few seconds at a time and grab a couple winks by the time Big Mama missed the bass line. She'd look over at Curtis but wouldn't jump him in front of the boys because he was the band leader. With eyes still closed Curtis' fingers would come to life and start pulling on those bass strings till he nodded out again.

At a bar in a Toronto dinner club, Big Mama and John Lee Hooker sat laughing and joking while sippin' on the hard stuff. She was finishing her week-long gig; he was coming to town to start his. John Lee kept eyeing Teddy, who was sitting alone at a booth nursing a beer.

"Can that white boy write?" John Lee asked Big Mama.

"Sure he can." She beamed. "Come here Teddy and help this man."

Claiming he couldn't see well enough to write (when in fact he didn't know how) John Lee gave Teddy the address of his manager and Teddy scratched it out on a wrinkled envelope.

Muddy Waters was on stage in Chicago with Buddy Guy, Sr. on piano. After finishing her show at another club, Big Mama breezed into Muddy's set to share a song. The crowd went crazy.

From Chicago there was a side trip to St. Cloud, Minnesota, for another club date where Mississippi Fred McDowell was playing his legendary bottleneck blues guitar. George Smith stepped up to the mic to take the lead on harmonica while the old blues man hung back, took a break, and rested.

A young black man was blowing them all away with harmonica and electric blues dobro. Taj Mahal and Big Mama's band jammed in Boston and other cities along the tour. The crossover between old and young, black and white, blues and country was gathering momentum.

At a Doors concert, Jerry Lee Lewis had the difficult task of opening the show for a crowd restless for the main event. Jerry Lee and other '50s rockers like Conway Twitty and Charlie Rich had already crossed over to country. Many of the younger current rock stars would later do the same, forsaking their roots even before rock peaked. But on this night, the stoned kids didn't want to hear Jerry Lee's new work. When the boos got out of control, he calmed them down by climbing up on the piano one more time for "Great Balls of Fire."

At the Whiskey in Los Angeles, actor Little Caesar would come on stage and sing country with Big Mama, a huge black man soulfully doing Glen Campbell's "By the Time I Get to Phoenix."

The black band from Los Angeles began to treat the white kid from Louisiana like part of the family. Curtis Tilman, carrying a small concealed weapon, began to accompany Teddy on the money pickup from the club owners. The black man packing was good backup, especially in the larger venues like the Avalon, where peace and love couldn't mask the potential for a rip-off that lurked around an exchange of big cash. But Teddy blended in quietly, politely, and he always got the money. His low profile style attracted the attention of Santana's band. They offered him the road manager job, and with it bigger money, better hotels, and a lot more traveling. Teddy passed on Santana, partly to stay closer to home in the Hollywood Hills with Lynette. He was also loyal to me and Link, but I believe the blues harmonica and the low-down bars had grabbed a piece of the boy's soul.

Link Wyler knew that Big Mama, Muddy Waters, and Big Joe Turner on tour recorded live on video and thirty-two track sound would be worth a large deal. If the shows were at two college campuses and a prison in Eugene, Oregon, then you also had the right setting. It's the last known recording by those three giants. The deepest roots of the black blues were there for that last great gig.

Big Mama had a sense of humor that reflected her hard life. When her boyfriend Greene knocked out her front teeth, Kate took her to our dentist, Ed Murachanian, an Armenian artisan who did superb gold work. But after one visit, Big Mama declared that she "couldn't sit still while somebody messed with her mouf." She continued to smile through the spaces in her front teeth, the pain deadened by one-hundred-proof Ole Grand Dad.

At a recording studio in Los Angeles, Big Mama's session was interrupted by the police. In her car was Greene's pistol, which had been traced back four years to a theft during the Watts' riot. Big Mama spent the night in jail before Link could bail her out. The next night she was back in the studio jiving with the musicians.

"Look here," Big Mama told her backup men, "if you all don't act right and play yo music, I'll have the police man come and get you, and y'all have to spend the night in jail like me."

Teddy Cessac was branded with the blues for life. In honky tonk bars up and down the bayou, the band or jukebox may be playing rock, Cajun, zydeco, country, it don't matter what. The man at the table in the corner is blowing the blues, on the harmonica he always carries.

"Workin' my way back home
One row at a time."
(Ibid.)

Ted Cessac

KPPC FM
Pasadena Presbyterian Church
Late February 1969

"A dreamer of pictures
I run in the night.

...chasing the moonlight."

"Cinnamon Girl," Neil Young
(Neil Young, Broken Arrow Music Corp., Cotillion Music)

She had called me on the rap line several times. Play this. Play that. An obvious teenage groupie. Sounded sweet. Sounded sexy. Definitely young. Hundreds of them out there just like her. But she called enough that I began to recognize her voice. Then her name.

"Rap line," I said.

"Hi, David, this is Leslie. What are you doing today?" she asked, as if I had an hour to wait before I cued up the next record.

"Getting it on so you can get off," I said, in deejay-speak.

"Wait till I tell you what happened," she said.

"Okay, but I can't stay long. I've got to get another album cued up."

"Well," she said, "some of my friends said they went down to KPPC and it's in the bottom of this church and all, and it was really groovy. And the deejay let them come in where they play the records."

"Yeah, some of the disc jockeys let people in the studio."

"Well, maybe I could go down with just a couple of my friends sometimes and we could stay and visit for awhile."

"Maybe you could do that sometime," I said, dropping my voice a bit lower, "How about I play a song for you."

"Oh, wow," she whined sweetly. "David, you know I love Neil Young. See you soon. Bye-bye."

The next afternoon about two hours into my show, Don Hall's wife, Cathy, carrying incense and patchouli oil, yelled at me through the open studio door.

"Some fans at the front door for you," Cathy said.

"Let 'em in if you will," I replied, as I headed for the john to take a hit on the half-smoked jay stashed in my pocket.

When I returned, seated politely around the console were two young men about eighteen and a pretty girl looking terrific in overalls and long reddish-blonde hair. I nodded hello, got my next record set up, and then turned to greet them. The handsome California blonde boy close to me reached out to clasp my hand.

"I'm Bob," he said. "And this is Ken."

"And this is...," I paused as our eyes locked, and the buzz from the jay rushed from my head straight down to my groin.

"I'm Leslie," she smiled, a bit shyly.

She was barely legal, I was twenty-seven. I felt like a bastard, but I couldn't help myself. She was from Alhambra, a few miles south of Pasadena, a valley girl, but not from the San Fernando Valley where the KPPC signal was still weak. This was a San Gabriel Valley girl. We were covering this part of town like a blanket and everybody from twelve to thirty-two was listening.

Ken was Leslie's boyfriend. He too was handsome and friendly. He was also leaving town for the summer to travel in Europe. Bob was the most outgoing. He said he would give me some great orange sunshine the next time he stopped by.

"I don't do acid. I hear it messes up your mind," I said, reeling from the impact of the Mexican marijuana I had just smoked.

"Naw, no way, man," they all protested. "This is great stuff, really pure."

"Later," I replied.

"For a guy who don't do acid," Bob cheered me on, "you really play some great music. This is really cool in here. This is a great job."

"I know," I said, smiling at Ken and Leslie. Then I turned to the microphone. "You're on KPPC in Pasadena," I said, "and here's one from Neil Young for the Cinnamon Girl and her friends."

> "A dreamer of pictures
> I run in the night.
> ... chasing the moonlight."
> (Ibid.)

Pinnacle Productions was the most successful concert promoter in the city. They had been at it long enough that radio stations no longer required payment up front for the advertising that brought the crowds out to the well-hyped events. The rock groups didn't always ask for deposits. They were well paid out of the gate receipts. Huge profits were being generated by the new music. Pinnacle Productions was getting a large share.

The smell of easy money kept Link and me on the lookout for opportunities. Link soon found one. A twenty-year-old kid was promoting shows at the Rose Parade Building. It was a large warehouse in Pasadena known as the Rose Palace where the floats were assembled every December for the final application of flower pedals before the big New Year's Day Rose Parade. The rest of the year, it was the perfect place for thousands of long-haired doped-up kids to crowd onto the cement floor and trip-out, while the top groups washed them down with megawatts of over-amplified ear-splitting sound.

Link and I met with the kid who was looking to be the next big promoter. He walked out to meet us in the middle of the Rose Palace. He was accompanied by a dozen youngsters, no older than sixteen or seventeen.

"You Dave Pierce, the guy on KPPC?" he asked.

"That's me," I assured him.

"So, yeah, I could use some partners," he said, "but I need a thousand dollars for the Rose Parade people, I'm behind on my rent."

"We got the grand," Link said, patting his hip pocket, "but we want fifty percent of the profits of this Friday night's concert."

The kid hesitated only a moment before we shook hands on the agreement. Link gave him the cash and he and his dozen juvenile assistants went into an impromptu game of touch football throwing deep passes in the huge Rose Palace warehouse.

"We shoulda done a dope deal," I said, "probably stand a better chance of getting our money back."

"Don't worry about it," Link said, "you just play the hell out of the groups coming to town Friday night, and plug the show every time you open the mic."

> *"A phrase in connection*
> *first with she I heard."*
>
> "Love Is Just A Four-Letter Word," Joan Baez
> (Bob Dylan, Special Rider Music)

The Blues influence on the new music was a very strong primitive embrace. Young lead guitarists exaggerated the raunchy guitar licks first laid down by the Chicago blues men of the '40s and '50s in their economic struggle for survival. Our struggle was against the Empire and the new electric blues men could carry the message.

One night, on a tip from the record company promotion man, I went down to a club on Melrose called the Ash Grove. The surprise guest walked onto the tiny stage with his trademark red bandanna tied around his head. For two hours Jimi Hendrix jammed solo, singing about the tire tracks all over his girl's back on "Crosstown Traffic." The next day the promo man brought me a copy of the unreleased Polydor Track Records English pressing of *Electric Ladyland*, with an album cover featuring twenty bare-breasted maidens. Beside "Voodoo Child," there was a cut titled "1983 A Merman I Should Turn to Be."

Even our gospel roots had a turn as the Edwin Hawkins Singers released "Oh Happy Day" and got enough FM play to climb to number five on national charts by May. Dylan kept everybody guessing, and stayed ahead of the pack when he showed a new optimism in the middle of the turmoil with the lyric "lay lady lay, lay across my big brass bed."

"This is KPPC-FM in Pasadena," I said, "where you can watch the Revolution on the Radio. Tonight at nine o'clock, the taped replay of our interview with Ralph Nader. Ralph's not just questioning the motives of the military, he's the first guy I've heard to take on the American Medical Association. As for the food industry, Nader says there's more food value in the box, than in the cereal inside that box, that we're serving to our kids for breakfast. Meanwhile, down in New Orleans, District Attorney Jim Garrison has come up empty handed in his search for the JFK Conspiracy leaders. Clay Shaw was found not guilty and we'll never know what really happened. Kate, what have you got from the Public Service Department?"

"Well it ain't canned copy for the American Cancer Society," Kate grinned, leaning into the microphone across the turntable from me. "But I do have news about a couple of art exhibits around town, if you'll call me on the rap line, and there's more on *The Free Clinic*. Also my girlfriend Jorjanna Kellaway tells me her mother who has cancer has just gone on the grape cure. If you'd like to talk about the grape cure for cancer, I've got the number."

"Hey, y'all," Kate yelled into the microphone, sending my VU meter banging past the red line, "what we gonna do about the noise pollution in these cities, and guess what folks, the air ain't getting any better in the City of Angels. We use to love to play tennis, but we don't anymore, 'cause we can't breathe. It's real obvious that the environmental quality is goin' to hell, but nobody's doing anything about it. Meanwhile, the whole population is just becoming more desensitized. Can you dig what's happening here?"

Kate and I got out of town every time there was an opportunity. We rode my new Honda-350 motorcycle up into the mountains north of the San Fernando Valley to a commune where David Lannan was living, temporarily, with several hippie families. Lannan's thirsty boots kept him moving and he had counter-culture news from several locales. After the customary round of joints, David handed us a couple of tabs.

"Outstanding Mescaline," he smiled, "very pure, very organic."

Within thirty minutes we were naked, bathing in the cold mountain stream. Several hours later we were still flying as we came down the mountainside on the Honda-350 at eighty miles an hour. My hands glued to the handlebars, with the throttle locked open. My body leaning in and out of curves instinctively making the right moves that kept us from going over the cliff into eternity.

The next weekend we loaded John-David and 'Chelle into the Porsche and took the winding drive up Highway 1 to Big Sur Country, spending the night at the Big Sur Inn. We were overwhelmed by the scenery and the chance to be among the trees. The wood-shingled roof of our simple cabin looked vaguely familiar.

Several days later I was cleaning out the two-car garage on Babcock Street in North Hollywood, when I looked up and it hit me. The garage roof peaking twelve feet above me had the same wood shingles as the Big Sur Inn. I backed the Porsche out onto the driveway, closed the big heavy garage door, grabbed my hammer and nailed it shut. Having built several lofts at the Cellar Theatre, it was an easy task to build this loft thrusting out over two-thirds of the garage interior, giving it a nice mountain cabin effect. We closed in one corner for a bathroom, put an open kitchen in the other, and installed a metal fireplace in the third corner. The plan was for Teddy and Ronnie Linxwyler to move into the new apartment, but they both took offence at having to live in the garage. The more I looked at the apartment the more it looked like home. Especially after laying in rust colored carpet over the oil stained cement. One day I hauled the kids' bunk-bed mattresses up on the loft, filled a waterbed in the last remaining corner, grabbed my stereo and records and told Kate to move her kitchen gear. Our cozy cabin-style apartment, in a garage in the middle of smoggy North Hollywood, became the envy of all who saw it. I decided that the lack of housing in America could be solved overnight. If the government just adopted my idea, all of the homeless could have a great place to live. The automobiles would have to sleep outside.

> *"Complete evaporation to the core*
> *Though I tried and failed*
> *at finding any door."*
> (Ibid.)

Teddy moved with Lynette Winter into an apartment across from Jim Bachman below the Hollywood Bowl. From there he continued to spend a big piece of his life on the road with Big Mamma.

At KPPC the steady stream of artists continued their trek to the bottom of the church. The girl from the Stone Poneys who blew us all out with "Different Drum" was sitting across the turntable from me, flanked by two quiet heavy duty handlers. This wasn't Linda Ronstadt's first trip down to the church. Jeff Gonzer had already interviewed her once when she came, barefoot and cussin', to visit on his Sunday feature "Rawhide and Roses."

"Hey man, this is fuckin' far out," Linda Ronstadt said into the open microphone, "I love this fuckin' place, can you imagine, all this music in the basement of a fuckin' church."

Every other word she said was fuckin' this and fuckin' that. She had the sweetest face and the dirtiest mouth I had ever heard. She was really turning me on. If the FCC came to take me away, it was okay, just lock me up with Ronstadt.

In Chicago, attorney William Kunstler was attempting to mount a defense against the conspiracy charges aimed at the Chicago Seven. Defendant Bobby Seale refused to observe the decorum of the courtroom and was bound and gagged for using "bad words."

For two weekends in a row the turnout for the Rose Palace was smaller than expected. Link and I were out of the concert business, and a grand lighter.

Pinnacle began promoting the biggest concert ever staged. They would fill the Rose Bowl with one hundred thousand music fans. The groups, the radio stations, *The Free Press* would all get their piece of the action. The Sunday afternoon concert started at noon. By two o'clock I knew it was all over. The thirty thousand fans were having a great time, but the old Rose Bowl swallowed them up. Nothing even close to the one hundred thousand expected. No one would get paid. The Pinnacle Promoters would fold their tent and slip out of town in the night. One by one some of the most popular groups of the day made their way to the stage at the fifty-yard line. Mothers of Invention, Janis Joplin, Junior Wells, Wilson Pickett, Buddy Guy, Canned Heat, and Buffy St. Marie played their heart out for their fans. When the sunset over the San Gabriel Mountains, Joan Baez sang to us.

"And I really do not need
to be assured that..."

"Love Is Just A Four-Letter Word," Joan Baez
(Bob Dylan, Special Rider Music)

KPPC FM
Pasadena Presbyterian Church
April 1969

*"She tapes her regrets
To the microphone stand."*

"Blonde In The Bleachers," Joni Mitchell
(Joni Mitchell, Crazy Crow Music)

Joni Mitchell was in town playing at the Troubadour. Naturally, we had heavied up on airplay for the past week. Today the rap line was off the wall with requests for Joni. I didn't mind obliging. I was a fan too, and Kate and I had tickets for tonight's show, courtesy of the record company.

In Boston, Charles Laquidara had called WBCN to praise their sound and stumbled into his next job. Sam Kopper, because he was the only one with legitimate broadcast credentials, was Program Director of a talented air staff that included Steve Segal, Mississippi Brian Wilson, and Peter Wolf. Peter wanted week nights free to sing lead for the J. Geils Band. When Laquidara walked into WBCN a few days later, Sam Kopper put him on the air at ten p.m., turning Peter Wolf loose to become a rock 'n roll star. Segal was wary of Laquidara at first, because he'd followed me into KPPC a year earlier after Steve and Les walked out with Donahue. But Charles Laquidara and Steven Segal quickly began to compliment each other's air work and they went about building the best known Underground Rocker on the East Coast. Charles settled into a regular shift on WBCN, from 10:00 p.m. to 2:00 a.m. Steve Segal, calling himself "Steven the Seagull" was the toast of Boston in the prime shift, 6:00 p.m. to 10:00 p.m. Playing up his knowledge of the California mystique, he had advanced rapidly in the East Coast college town. Boston was a hot bed of dissent, and BCN was fanning the flames. Laquidara fit right in. He wasn't just playing the Rolling Stones, he was reading Mick Jagger and Keith Richards' lyrics into the microphone like it was the work of the great poets.

The kids from Harvard, Boston College, and MIT, even the Wellsley girls ate it up. One night at midnight, Charles put on an album of electronic music and began to read passages from the book, *Eco Catastrophe*. The phone lines lit up in an overwhelming response. Laquidara had blown them away. In the days that followed, he read from Paul Ehrlichman's *Population Bomb*. Digging back into the early '60s, he pulled out the one-time bestseller by Rachel Carson titled *Silent Spring*. He juxtaposed the ecologist's prophecy with the lyrics of the late '60s masters of rock 'n roll writing. The environmental movement was slowly being born.

On the campus of Dartmouth, there were protests against the ROTC. In Vietnam, the casualties mounted with a steady, unending pace. Peace talks with the enemy were going nowhere. The only movement was in the colleges of America where anti-war sentiment was building.

I was studying the album shot of Joni Mitchell's bare buttocks and long bony frame, as she stood nude staring out to sea. She was two years younger than me, having turned twenty-five last November. I took another request, fingered through the stack of albums leaning against the console, and did my best cool smile at Leslie and Bob when they walked in the studio door.

"What's happening?" Bob greeted me.

The Cinnamon Girl and I were exchanging hungry looks.

"Where's Ken?" I asked, glad he wasn't around.

"Gone to Europe," blonde Bob grinned back. "He'll be balling French and German girls all summer."

"No way," Leslie protested.

"Kate and I are going to see Joni Mitchell at the Troubadour tonight," I bragged slightly, as I moved to the rack of albums across the room to file a few LPs and browse for something to segue out of Joni Mitchell. When I sat back down at the board, a small orange tablet was circling around at 33 1/3 RPMs on the empty turntable.

"What's this?"

"Orange sunshine," Bob smiled. "The best. Drop it now. You'll be off the air in twenty minutes before you come on. By the time Joni's show starts tonight, you'll really be rushing."

"I don't know if I'm ready for this," I said. "I'm almost getting weak in my knees thinking about it."

"It's fun," Leslie said, teasingly. "You'll have a ball."

Without any further thought, I gulped down the orange tab with a cup of water.

"You're going to love Joni Mitchell," Bob said.

Within ten minutes I could feel the effects of the acid. By the time my show ended, I was off. I put the needle in the groove for the last record. The tone arm was starting to bend on me, but the groove in the record widened and straightened out like five miles of Interstate 10 in west Texas. I had no problem cueing up.

Kate had wrapped her office duties, so we all walked out of the basement together to where the Porsche was parked in front of the church.

"Cool wheels," Bob complimented.

"I love Porsches," Leslie said. The black sports car was reflecting in her blue eyes and the sidewalk was starting to roller coaster.

"We'll all go for a ride sometime," I said to Bob, while looking at Leslie, and climbing into the passenger side of the black Porsche.

Kate slid behind the wheel, fired the engine, and gunned it down Colorado Boulevard.

"You're doing okay?" Kate asked.

"I guess so," I replied.

The dozens of curves in the Pasadena Freeway rushed up to meet the speeding Porsche, then melted away in my passenger side rear view mirror.

"This is really far out," I said.

"I know," Kate replied.

"What do you know, you've never dropped acid."

"Sure did," she smiled. "Twice with Cameron, two years ago. Sex was fantastic. Made me crazy."

Inside the Troubadour, it was wall-to-wall with opening night music business hot shots. Waitresses with trays held above their heads were plying the crowd with the free booze the record company was pouring. The drinks were just icing. Everyone in the joint was already high on some kind of drug.

Joni came on stage to the roar of a standing ovation. She tossed her blonde mane. Her voice trilled across the crowd and thrilled me to my core. Nothing had ever sounded so beautiful. The shaft of colored lights beamed and bent, waving and washing over her, as she strummed that acoustic guitar and sang like a nightingale. It was an absolutely beautiful performance. The lights, the music, the crowd, were all very high tech. But the drug was working on me at a very primal level. I was lucky, I know, that my first bout with LSD was in such a peaceful, soul-satisfying environment, surrounded by the music I loved, sung by such a great artist.

Others would not be so lucky. They would confront this mind-bending, personality-warping, ragged-edge hallucinogen in much less benign situations. With enough use, they would be crippled for life. I walked away from this first trip in love with Joni Mitchell, music, radio, and the dark-eyed Italian girl who drove me home to the security of our cave in the San Fernando Valley.

1969

♦ Pete Townshend put together a studio group featuring a plump ex-post office engineer named Andy "Thunderclap" Newman and a novice songwriter-drummer called Speedy King. The result was the #1 hit "Something in the Air."

Los Angeles
April 26, 1969

"Call out the instigators
...Lock up the Streets and houses
...We're going to blast our way through here."

"Something In The Air," Thunderclap Newman
(John D.P. Keen, Abkco Music, Inc., Towser Tunes, Inc., Careers BMG
Music Pub., Suolubaf Music)

The Forum was packed. On stage, CTA (The Chicago Transit Authority), later known only as Chicago, was ripping through their cover of Spencer Davis, Steve and Muff Winwood's "I'm a Man, Yes I Am." The long blonde hair on the still unknown boys from the Windy City was reflecting back the white hot light on the bright over-lit stage. When the set ended, the house lights came up. The tie-dyed and beaded in the huge athletic Palace milled and smoked grass. After a few minutes, Jeff Gonzer ran onto the stage with John-David chasing after him. The young long-haired freak and the six-year-old kid traded lines like a couple of seasoned pros as they welcomed the crowd, plugged KPPC and introduced Jimi Hendrix.

This kind of high profile was what every performer's ego craves. The disc jockeys were performers. For that few hours everyday we did our "show" as we were developing a new intensity to what was once just an entertainment medium. We were becoming an integral part of the big battles of the decade that were culminating in the next few months. Record companies pushed product at us in overwhelming barrages. Selecting the best from the wave of newcomers was a fantastic trip, but also quite tricky, as the promo men did their best shucking and jiving to get the lesser talents exposed. Everybody was on the make. Grelun Landon, playing it by ear, surfaced with a public relations party for Harry Nilson at RCA. "Everybody's Talking at Me, Going Where the Weather Suits My Clothes" was the great Fred Neil song now reaching the charts with Nilson's vocals.

English folk group Pentangle was in town and their record company staged a Bangers (English sausage) and Beer publicity party. I took Dwayne St. Thomas with me, and then sent him on events that I didn't want to attend. Dwayne was Kate's high school buddy. He always wore his white suit, impersonating "Cousin Dud," the famous South Louisiana patent medicine man, who rose to fame in the late '40s and teamed up with Hank Williams and Colonel Tom Parker. Dwayne St. Thomas always introduced himself as Dave Pierce at all of these publicity events.

Dwayne was hanging out with a young actress named Mimi Rogers who would later become the first Mrs. Tom Cruise. He joined in with a group of people who were renovating space on Franklin Ave above Hollywood Blvd. Late one night, in a scene straight out of a Ron Hubbard pulp fiction, an entourage arrived all dressed in white jump suits to take over the building that would be known as the Scientology Celebrity Centre.

Doug Kershaw, a talented South Louisiana Cajun fiddler was getting played at KPPC. The record company sent him to visit my show. Doug told me he wrote "Jole Blon," then Kate told him we were from Cajun Country and "Jole Blon" was written before he was ever born. Out of Houston and East Texas came Johnnie Winter on guitar and Edgar Winter on piano. The albino brothers were earthy sounding, strange looking, and were once billed as It and Them. The Winter boys had polished their act as the Great Believer under the genius of "the Crazy Cajun," producer Huey P. Meaux. In their music you could hear the late '40s and early '50s of the old South from New Orleans to Dallas.

Sharing some of the same blues roots, but playing a whole other kind, was Mick Fleetwood along with Peter Green on lead guitar. Mick Fleetwood's long frame was folded over so I could see his eyes below the florescent light that was pointed down at Turntable One. Mick and Peter were seated across from me while Fleetwood Mac's "Oh Well, Parts I and II" preached to the city from the bottom of the church.

> *"Now, when I talked to God,*
> *I knew he'd understand,*
> *He said, 'stick by my side,*
> *I'll be your guiding hand...'"*

"Oh Well," Fleetwood Mac
(Peter Green, Kingstreet Media Music)

We had great hopefulness with "Aquarius/Let the Sunshine In" by the Fifth Dimension going all the way to the top. And everybody was singing "all we are saying is give peace a chance." Then there was also Country Joe's resignation with the neat little poem:

> *"One, two, three,*
> *What are we fighting for,*
> *Don't ask me, I don't give a damn,*
> *Next stop is Vietnam...*
> *Well there ain't no time to wonder why,*
> *whoopee we're all gonna die."*

"The Fish Cheer & I-Feel-Like-I'm-Fixin'-To-Die Rag," Country Joe & The Fish
(Joe McDonald, Alkatraz Korner Music Co)

There was shame and blame. Art Linkletter's daughter committed suicide on drugs. Where was he going to point the finger? At the studio showing of *Easy Rider*, the audience was uneasy. Kate and I felt the vibes, but we resented the unfair portrayal of South Louisiana. The image of red necks and race haters was a long stretch to anyone we knew. The bayou boys don't hate like that and we don't burn things down.

The blacks, under the leadership of Huey Newton and Bobby Seale, were ready to burn anything, putting civil disobedience on the cutting edge. They said whites were just paranoid and sick, because when blacks got together, Whitey thought it was to plan violence. The FBI's full force came down on Huey Newton, and finally, killed him by destroying him a little bit at a time.

The government's paranoia with *Zabriskie Point* continued. Convinced the film was a Communist plot designed to further aggravate the growing rift between American youth and their government leadership, everyone in the film was being shadowed by the FBI. Jim Bachman began to realize the film was not about politics but economics. James Aubrey, head of the

MGM Studios, was fighting Michaelangelo Antonioni over the money due to the Italian director for his box office hit *Blow-Up*. *Zabriskie* was filled with phony accounting, all making it possible for Antonioni to take his fortune out of the United States in a black bag. Never meant to be a great film, the production was filled with theft and waste. In a park north of Las Vegas, among the reddish rock smoothed over by the desert wind, Bachman built nine sets at the cost of hundreds of thousands. When the camera crews came in they shot only stills, then Michaelangelo ordered the sets torn down. A few weeks later, he decided he really did want movie footage, so Bachman rebuilt them all over again. The decadence of U.S. society portrayed in *Zabriskie* was being duplicated in the film's production. KPPC disc jockey Don Hall got into the spirit of the whole thing. When he got the call from Antonioni to coordinate the sound track, Don pulled out the best Pink Floyd his spacey red-carrot topped head could find. Don Hall collected thousands for his musical expertise, and then spent every dollar on a coke binge that lasted several months.

"The electrical dust
is starting to rust...

All the red tape
is mechanical rape
of the TV program waste."

"Plastic Fantastic Lover," Jefferson Airplane
(Martyn J. Buchwald, Icebag Corp)

The disc jockeys were the ears of the city. The soundtrack. Television would become the global community, but for now, the radio was the sound track behind our individual parts in the play. The booming guitar from Don Hall's favorite cut in Pink Floyd's *Zabriskie* sound track echoed in my ears. I had drifted off on the waterbed with Charlotte Stewart and Kate's voices like lullabies in my ear. The electric guitar and birth control pill had arrived at the same time. I was very pleased to be here.

This part of the revolution took many forms, including a brief mushroom period. Charlotte Stewart was starring as Miss Beadle, the sexless school marm spinster on Michael Landon's *Little House on the Prairie*. She was a hell of an actress. Charlotte and three girlfriends had opened The Liquid Butterfly on Melrose. They featured beautiful and hip, hand-sewn wardrobes including my favorite, billowing sleeve buccaneer-type shirts in multiple patterns. They embroidered mushrooms on everything. Their advertisement poster showed the four blonde bombshell seamstresses in a provocative pose with the slogan "We Want In Your Pants."

Sharing lovers was a part of being the love generation. It went with the high of drugs and rock 'n roll. It was another head trip.

I was renting the Cellar Theatre to a group of actors and one evening I stopped in to pick up the rent. After the group left, Kate and Merrily Saks arrived. We all shared a joint in the office. We could feel the tension starting to mount. Bachman's hand-picked designer fabric covered sofa was the only set we needed.

The Cinnamon Girl sweet-talked me into that Porsche ride and a stop over to show her the theatre. A few evenings later she and young blonde Bob showed up on our North Hollywood doorstep. By the time she and I came out of the bedroom, Kate and young Bob were holding hands and smiling Cheshire smiles.

1969

♦ Fleetwood Mac's guitarist Peter Green, who influenced Pink Floyd and Dire Straits, ended up in a mental institution.

Jim Bachman

The Farm
Louisiana Gulf Coast
May 1969

"Just a choogling on down to New Orleans."
"Born On The Bayou," Creedence Clearwater Revival
(John Fogerty, Jondora Music)

Creedence Clearwater Revival came out of San Francisco on Fantasy Records. One listen told me John C. Fogerty had spent some time in the South. Fogerty's bluesy voice was ideal for his version of Screamin' Jay Hawkins "I Put a Spell On You" and "99½ Won't Do." But I also played the hell out of "Proud Mary," "Green River," and "Born on the Bayou." I knew Fogerty was talking to me.

Kate and I were making two or three trips a year to Louisiana. Our roots kept calling and we listened. This trip had been made in record time. Nineteen hundred and fifty miles in twenty-seven hours nonstop. The starter on the Porsche had gone bad, so we seldom stopped the engine. When we did, we had to push it to start it. Not a big problem for such a small car. Kate often pushed it by herself while I jumped in and popped the clutch. Russie gave me flack for being so macho that I would make my wife push the car, but Kate didn't care. She was one tough mama. The small jump seats in the back of the car were spacious for five and six year olds. John-David stretched out on the ledge of the back window. He spent most of the trip there, educating himself on the variety of makes and models of automobiles that we whizzed past at eighty miles per hour.

'Chelle, a quiet, contented child, colored and sang to herself. At night, the jump seat folded down for her bed. John-David crashed on his back window ledge. He felt secure there. If I didn't turn around, the ledge was just beyond my long-armed reach when he was misbehaving.

Kate had packed enough fruit, whole-wheat bread, and avocados to eliminate stopping for food at the greasy spoons along the way. The Porsche sipped gasoline at thirty miles per gallon, so only four pit stops were necessary. Besides, we were in a hurry to cross the desert and get to the green lush tropics of South Louisiana.

Our first night in town, we headed for the old farm, with Hollis Gooch and his wife, Jeanette, all of us sucking on a piece of blotter acid on the way down there. We drove south following the Vermilion Bayou that had turned reddish brown from the heavy afternoon thunderstorms. Livestock and wild animals could be seen in the thick woods along the banks of the Rio de Los Lobos. But only once did I think I saw a wolf. Finally, we turned onto the raised shell road that crossed the flooded marsh to the second chénîer and the giant oak trees. I flashed back, seeing a horse pulling a small sled. The horse was swimming, the sled floating. Casey was standing on the sled, balancing himself with the reins held tightly in his fist. I was holding on for dear life, my tiny hands hooked in Casey's belt.

Tonight the sun started to set with a fantastic display of orange, pink, purple, and every shade in between. The half-wild herd of cattle who grazed this island in the marsh began to gather under the oak trees for the night. We stared at them. They stared back, their ancient animal eyes conveying only confusion by our presence. Then they ignored us, as they stood still, swishing the insects with their tails. If there was any primordial meaning to life, I was probably staring at it.

We tripped away the night in the mobile home camp, talking with the Gooches and listening to music. At dawn, Hollis lit the barbecue pit, and began cooking some steaks he'd brought along. Kate turned cartwheels in the early morning light, her long ankle-length dress falling down over her head, as her legs went straight into the air, revealing that she had quit wearing panties. She was totally natural, flipping cartwheels like a five year old.

The smell of the burning flesh on the barbecue pit made me nauseous. While Hollis and Jeanette wolfed down a T-bone, I nibbled on a papaya Kate had produced from the bag she used for a purse. For the past few months, we had been eating more fruit and less meat. After this night, we became total vegetarians. For more than a year, we ate no meat. We also quit using deodorant. We didn't need it. Our bodies had no odor.

The LSD trip spaced us out for a couple of days, but it still wasn't primal enough for me. A week later, we were back on the farm, sucking on the piece of paper with the light brown dot. This time Kate and I brought only her younger brother, twenty-year-old Peter Russo.

The sunset was just as spectacular, and the full moon was the bonus as it rose over Vermilion Bayou to the east, while the last glow of light faded out on the acres of wavering saw grass in the marshes beyond the edge of the palmettos. Three white palomino horses that Casey kept on the farm were hanging out with the cattle tonight. They galloped around the edge of the herd, generally frolicking, swishing their tails against the insects, which seemed more prevalent tonight. We were all rushing pretty heavily now, and Pete said he was starting to freak out. He was recovering from the accident that totaled his Porsche and damaged his liver.

"Stay cool," I said. "It's only a trip. Go with the flow. Tune into the surroundings. Feel the wildness of this place, nature's finest work, the oak trees, the earth, the moon."

"The mosquitoes," Pete complained with a grin.

"Fuck the mosquitoes," Kate laughed, "I'm taking off my clothes."

We all stripped down to our birthday suits, and ran laughing through the tall oak trees, disappearing in the dark shadows where the Spanish moss hung low, then into the clearings and the full moon light almost as bright as day.

The white palominos began to gallop, swishing their tails to beat off the mosquitoes. Kate breaking off a bushy, three-foot long weed, began to swish it over her back and legs.

"Hey, guys," she said, "Get yourself a tail."

For what seemed like hours, the six of us, three humans, three horses, ran through the woods, chasing the moonlight. We were in tune, we were one.

By sunrise we fired up the Porsche and drove away from the old Cajun farm. The cows and horses would run wild for years. The sun would go down and the moon would rise and sparkle over the lazy Vermilion Bayou forever.

In a few days we were back in the west coast megalopolis and I was in the basement of the Pasadena Presbyterian Church. My stay here wouldn't last that long. I had to make the most of it.

"Hello, Los Angeles," I said into the microphone. "This is under-ground radio, KPPC, and here's John Fogerty."

"Wish I was back on the bayou,
Rolling with some Cajun Queen."
(Ibid.)

In the KPPC studio.

I heard from Woodie again after he left the jungle and returned to Louisiana. He wrote about his trip back to America.

It was in the Frisco Airport. My friend, John Frescura, and I were coming into the Frisco Airport. He was from Lansing, Michigan. He had been doing recon for the Marines at Kason, pulling pilots out of North Vietnam. He brought back flowers from a Hanoi suburb. That's how close he got. So we were in the airport terminal and a guy walks up to us. I can still see his face. A skinny little bearded bastard. Long hair. Got a sign that says "Baby Killers." He spits on me and John both. My first day home. We haven't even walked on American soil yet. We're still on fricken concrete. Anyway, John hits him, knocked him down, and we started kicking the shit out of him. The guy spit on us. Hey, you don't spit on people. A cop comes over rather quickly and proceeds to tell us 'you can't do this to people.' I say, 'Man, he spit on us.' The cop says, 'Yeh, but you can't react that way.' That was my welcome home. I wouldn't give you a dollar for the whole coast of California. But back in Louisiana I find out it's almost as bad. Trying to get in the veterans office, there's peace demonstrators blocking the way. So what I gotta do? I got two possibilities. One, I swallow my pride and go away. Two, I kick my way up the steps to the veterans office. I got no choice. I take number two.

Your Pal,

Woodie

Woodie's fight for his country would stay with him. America was deeply divided, everyone knew they were on the right side. I knew it too. I had searched my conscience. How could I be wrong?

"He's fighting for Democracy,
He's fighting for the Reds."

"Universal Soldier," Donovan
(Buffy St. Marie, Woodmere Music; Caleb Music Co.)

"Ever since I was a young boy,
I played the silver ball."

"Pinball Wizard," The Who
(Pete Townshend, Fabulous Music Ltd.; Abkco Music, Inc., Towser Tunes, Inc., Careers BMG Music Pub., Suolubaf Music)

"Did you get the tape?" Charles was on the phone, he was excited.

"It's on the air right now," I answered. "We've been playing the whole album for two days straight."

"Alright now David," Charles' voice went into a low whisper as though we were in the same room and someone might be listening. "You can't tell anyone where you got it, you hear? There is already a lot of heat on us here in Boston. Decca Records is really pissed."

"I know, they called me. They weren't going to release *Tommy* for two weeks. We're screwing up their marketing plans."

"Fuck 'em, this is what underground radio is all about. KPPC and WBCN are the only stations in the country with a boot-leg copy. How do you like it?"

"Fantastic! The listeners are going crazy!"

Bootleg tapes got recorded in various ways, sometimes with cheap equipment smuggled into live concerts. But the good stuff was usually from an engineer at the recording session who simply dubbed an extra copy, sometimes before the final master, then carried it out of the studio. No matter what the source, the tapes found their way to the underground radio stations. Ripping off The Who's new rock opera was a real coup.

"Don't see lights a flashin',
Plays by sense of smell."
(Ibid.)

On June 9, Richard Nixon announced that he would pull out 25,000 GIs from Vietnam by August 31st. We all suspected that he would sneak in fifty thousand more to replace them. Around the country the television news reported the debate in Congress on whether to build an anti-ballistic missile system across North America to shoot down the Russian nuclear war heads that would come at us from over the North Pole. The ABM, as it became known, would cost billions. Charles told me on the East Coast, bumper stickers were cropping up that read "ABM-America's Biggest Mistake."

"Why shouldn't we have a defense system?" I asked him.

"Because it just escalates the dooms-day mentality," Charles replied. "Come on David, we all saw *Dr. Strangelove*. If we keep building these machines, someone will build a dooms-day apparatus in secret and neglect to tell the other side."

Along with boot-legged tapes, Charles sent a variety of other recorded messages from Boston, which I immediately aired in L.A. One was his own plea for sanity on the drug laws which varied widely by region across the country. While some states tried to crack down and stamp out drug traffic once and for all, others became more liberal. The decriminalization of marijuana looked like a real possibility, which could have limited drug use to the relatively harmless potheads. But it was too good an issue for the politicians and the cops, Charles argued, so it would never happen. The nation's jails would be filled with the easy bust of poor bastards who were holding a couple of joints, while the hard stuff and the criminals got out of control. When we finally lost the War on Drugs after billions of wasted dollars and wasted lives, the politicians and the cops would still be blaming the dope smokers.

Six weeks earlier the counter culture in Berkeley had openly defied the establishment with a show of muscle by taking over part of the University of California property and naming it People's Park. With slogans like "A Culture of Use, Not a Culture of Profit," the long hairs camped out for a glorious month of music, love, and drugs. The young adults and kids plus many older Bay Area residents lived and frolicked freely in People's Park.

In a televised news conference Governor Ronald Reagan laid the blame for this outrage clearly on the shoulders of all the liberal parents and professors who had first allowed any young person the right to question authority.

It was the confrontation that Reagan and the U.C. Regents had been waiting for and had to win. If People's Park was allowed to exist, revolutionary activity like this could spread like wild fire to other colleges and universities.

On May 15th, Reagan sent in the National Guard to retake People's Park. Six thousand citizens took to the street. In the massive fight that followed, many were wounded and protestor James Rector died from an overdose of Double-O buckshot. The superior forces of authority won easily. Fences went up at People's Park and the Guard occupied the city of Berkeley for a month.

Still the Gipper had one more surprise for the kiddies. When the community came back for a peaceful rally, the guard line opened up and let everyone in, but then they wouldn't let anyone out. Helicopters suddenly swooped over and began to drop canisters of nauseous gas into the crowd. The gas-masked police line encircling the park held firm, no one got out.

The future president of the United States sat in his mansion and applauded the work of his troops while the people of Berkeley ate tear gas.

"That deaf, dumb and blind kid,
Sure plays a mean pinball!!!"
(Ibid.)

San Fernando Valley
Los Angeles
July 1969

*"Pay before we start.
I'm the Gypsy- the acid Queen."*

"Acid Queen," The Who
(Pete Townshend, Eel Pie Publishing Ltd.; Abkco Music, Inc., Towser
Tunes, Inc., Careers BMG Music Pub., Suolubaf Music)

I gunned the Honda-350 away from the stoplight, leaving behind the Southern California cult cars, sports cars, luxury cars, and convertibles, up shifting to fifty miles per hour, cruising speed, heading north on Van Nuys Boulevard. The Cinnamon Girl was snuggled to my back, her blonde hair flowing in the wind, and swirling around to tap lightly at my face, and tangle with my own shoulder length hair. The orange tabs we'd dropped fifteen minutes earlier were beginning to put us right. Ahead was Devonshire Downs and the biggest outdoor concert ever staged. I couldn't get much higher. The low moments would come later, in the valleys that counter the peaks of an LSD high, when for a few minutes the reality of what I was doing would pull me up short.

Kate knew I wanted to take this trip. She put it together for me. At our home the three of us had dropped the sunshine together. Kate left for the concert in the Porsche, alone. Leslie and I had straddled the motorcycle and turned west on Victory, out to Van Nuys Boulevard, then up to Devonshire Downs. The traffic into the famous horse racing facility was tremendous, even by L.A. standards. The Honda was able to maneuver close to an entrance. Now Leslie and I were moving our way through the huge crowd getting as close to the stage as possible. We found an ideal spot, near the lighting platform, which was about a hundred feet out from center stage.

The Chambers Brothers were singing, "People Get Ready, There's a train a coming, You don't need no ticket, You just climb aboard."

Leslie and I lay back on the ground looking at the smoggy sky. Helicopters buzzed back and forth overhead, ferrying artists from hotels to the backstage area. Probably a couple of LAPD choppers, keeping a close eye on the happenings down below. A big jet taking off from Burbank turned back heading eastward as Jimi Hendrix came out, attacked his guitar, and made it sing "The Star Spangled Banner."

Then it was the Jefferson Airplane's turn, playing all my favorites. But what was really flipping us out was the light show on the giant screen behind the band. Brilliant colors segued in and out, meshed, then disappeared, only to return in a different form.

"This is really high art," I said to Leslie.

"Far out," she replied.

I could see the lighting director Glen McKay at work on the lighting platform. When the images on the screen began to flutter, I realized Glen was actually vibrating the slides with one hand while flipping switches and rearranging slides with the other hand. I'm sure he had a plan, but it seemed to me he was making up most of his moves in response to the music. It was too frantic to be anything but spontaneous.

By 1:00 a.m. we were all three back at the house in North Hollywood. Kate said she loved the concert as much as we did, she felt our presence among the one hundred thousand music fans there. We were all connected.

We smoked a lot of grass, trying to take the edge off the LSD. Slowly, we took off all our clothes as we lounged on the king-size mattress on the floor next to the glowing fireplace. Kate and Leslie stretched and arched before me, their blonde and brunette beauty contrasting in the candle light. They looked at me and smiled. They looked at each other and giggled. When dawn came creeping through the valley, the girls were ready to start the weekend. I was ready to sleep for a week.

"I'm the gypsy, the acid queen,
I'll tear your soul apart."
(Ibid.)

1969

♦ Pete Townshend wrote "Acid Queen" as an anti-drug song, which is evident from the lyrics. However, U.S. vice-president Spiro Agnew used this song as an example of rock's bad influence on high drug use. Spiro said this was "exactly what we're running against in this country today."

The family homestead in Intracoastal City, Louisiana (above); long haired three-year-old (right); junior high school photo (bottom, right); with my best friend, Woodie Bernard (below).

(Clockwise, from above) my sister Russie
and me - the "Wild Ones;" theatre class at
the University of Southwestern Louisiana;
as Stanley Kowalski in a USL production;
my first ride on the Ether Express at KROF;
all-state half-back at Abbeville (La.) High
School; a south-Louisiana lawn mower.

My California rides (top); ready for Hollywood (above); a Cajun Indian (right); with Smokey Roberds (below, left); the Cellar Theatre (below, right); and on stage at the Pasadena Playhouse (bottom).

The Pierces, a 1960s southern California family: father Dave, mother Kate, and kids John-David (J.D.) and Michelle ('Chelle).

. . . in the KPPC studio.

THE PIERCE FAMILY—A heroic house-hold of master avengers...living for the thrill of the chill!

The Elton John pie fight, which happened outside the KPPC studio a few hours
before his famous American debut at the Troubadour.

Los Angeles Free Press   September 4, 1970   Page 49

A LETTER TO ELTON JOHN FROM KPPC RADIO—

DEAR ELTON JOHN:

WE WOULD LIKE TO THANK YOU AND UNI RECORDS FOR INVITING US TO
YOUR AMERICAN DEBUT LAST WEEK AT THE TROUBADOUR. IT WAS AN
INCREDIBLE EXPERIENCE. YOUR ALBUM HAS BEEN AMONG THE MOST
REQUESTED AND PROGRAMMED RECORDS OF THE YEAR AT "KPPC", AND WE
WERE EXTREMELY ANXIOUS TO SEE YOU IN PERFORMANCE. WORD OF
MOUTH TRAVELS SLOWLY, AND UNSURELY IN LOS ANGELES. STREET TALK
ABOUT MUSIC HAS BEEN SLIGHT RECENTLY, BUT BY THE END OF YOUR EN-
GAGEMENT HERE, THE WORD WAS OUT.

ONE OF THE MOST PLEASANT RECORDING DISCOVERIES OF 1970 ALSO
TURNED OUT TO BE AN OUTRAGEOUS AND EXQUISITE PERFORMER. YOUR
WEEK OF MUSIC WAS A DELIGHTFUL GIFT AND A WELCOME SURPRISE. THANK
YOU AGAIN AND HURRY BACK TO LOS ANGELES.

THE KPPC DISC-JOCKEYS

(Clockwise, from above): Steven Segal and Ted Longmire in the studio; DJs outside the Ash Grove; up all night with Ted Longmire; flower child Deirdre O'Donahue; "Mississippi Brian Wilson" (Joe Rogers); Les and Susan Carter with Steven Segal on the street; the entire KPPC family.

(some of)
The KPPC Family

Zack Zenor

Jeff Gonzer

Joe "Mississippi" Rogers

Joe "Mississippi" Rogers

Ted Longmire

The Pierce Family

Steve Segal

Are you tired of listening to the same old shit?

Susan Carter, aka "Outrageous Nevada"

Les Carter

Steve Segal, aka "Steven Clean," aka "the Seagull"

The Pierce Family

THE CREDIBILITY GAP in the KPPC Studio.
(Harry Shearer, Micheal McKean, David Lander, and Richard Beebe).

KPPC alums: (top to bottom) the late movie critic Joel Siegel; nationally syndicated DJ Jeff Gonzer; Boston's "Big Mattress" DJ Charles Laquidara; and the irrepressible Barret Hansen, aka "Dr. Demento."

October, 1971 - the hammer falls on KPPC: Les Carter, with other DJs, addresses a press conference (above); the infamous Doug Cox (left); the people come to our defense (below).

the /TAFF

Outside 35¢ L.A. County 25¢

ELECTRONIC MIND CONTROL

AGONY OF LOMPOC

NEW LEFT IN CHILE

BEGINNING A NEW STRIP BY THE CREATOR OF 'MOONDOG'

Volume 1, Number 8 (Issue No. 8)   In Two Parts: Part One   Copyright 1971 by The Staff   October 29 - November 4, 1971

GENOCIDE AT KPPC

AUDIO, ART, ASTROLOGY, COCKETTES, FILM, THEATRE, MUSIC, BOOKS, NEWS

A LOCAL ROCKS PUBLIC SERVICE MESSAGE

THEY CUT OFF OUR EARS

BOYCOTT KPPC

"Sign the petition to get the old KPPC DJ's back Or write to Les Carter ¾ KPPC voicing your support. Also, you might try boycotting all companies which are now advertising on KPPC.

After one last Thanksgiving dinner with all our friends (above), we packed up the Crown Coach bus (right), and headed home to Louisiana (below, note bus in background).

Catching up with old friends: (clockwise from above) Smoky Roberds, Charles Laquidara, and Vincent Donofrio at a 1983 Pasadena Playhouse reunion; with Ken Rose; with Dr. Demento and my wife Sarah Fox; with Jim Bachman, Charles Laquidara, and Charlotte Stewart; reuniting with Steven Segal; in the studio with Jeff Gonzer; and viewing footage of filmmaker Cass Paley documentary on KPPC.

Still Riding -
writing original scripts
and producing for
stage and radio.

WOODLAWN PLAYERS
PRESENT

RUN... FOR GOVERNOR

RESERVATIONS
233-8236
893-7824

WRITERS: DAVE PIERCE · SARAH FOX · J.D. PIERCE
©PRODUCTION DESIGN & "MECHANICAL WINDUP CRAWFISH"

Written & Directed
By
Dave Pierce

Co Director
Sarah Fox

This Magic Moment

A Musical Tribute to the Events, Songs, & Singers...1955-75

Live On Stage
"Elvis"
"The Beatles"
"Little Richard"
"Linda Ronstadt"
"Elton John"...and more
All the HITS

Producer
Malcolm St.Romain

Co Producer
Laurie Rowe

Opening
Jan. 11, 2002

©Design: Sarah Fox

ACADIANA
ARTS COUNCIL

North Hollywood
Monday, July 21, 1969

*"Must be those strangers
That come every night..."*

"Mr. Spaceman," The Byrds
(Roger McGuinn, Dimensional Songs of the Knoll, Sixteen Stars Music)

I woke up to the sound of little kids laughing. Slowly I turned over to see John-David and 'Chelle seated in front of the television set, headsets on, laughing at the cartoons. There was no sound coming from the TV. We had fitted them with headphones, so they could get up and watch TV while we slept late. The headsets kept the cartoon sounds from filling the room, but it didn't stop the kids' laughter.

While Kate and I played radio in the bottom of the church, John-David and 'Chelle would spend the day at the Montessori School. Today they would watch Neil Armstrong and Edwin Aldrin walk on the moon and take that giant leap for mankind.

*"Those saucer shaped lights,
Put people uptight."*
(Ibid.)

I filled the airwaves with as many space songs as I could, including David Bowie's "Space Oddity." We'd been playing a ragged copy of the bootleg tape, another gift from WBCN. Bowie got a lot of underground radio play, but "Space Oddity" had to wait till the '70s before it became a hit. First a guy named Elton John would have to pave the way with the song "Rocket Man."

Toward the end of my air shift, Kate came into the studio with a troubled look on her face. "There are some real weirdos out here," she said. "They say they're from 'the family,' they want you to play a tape they brought."

I put Pink Floyd on the turntable. The whole side would play through, giving me enough time to check out the freaks. I met them in the big outer studio, close to the street, where Kate had kept them from entering the hallway leading to the control room. There were four interesting looking young women, one guy and a child the age of my own kids.

"What you got?" I asked.

"A real smash," the guy said.

"Your song?" I asked.

"No," he replied, "it's by the head of our family. A super-talent you'll be hearing a lot about in the music world."

"Oh, yeah?" I said. "What's his name?"

"Charles Manson," one of the girls gushed out, like he was some kind of God.

"Well, I would be happy to keep your tape and give a listen when I finish my show."

"We have a tape machine in the truck, why don't you listen to it now?" the guy insisted.

Kate was hesitant, but knowing I had plenty of Pink Floyd left on the turn table, I followed the family onto Colorado Boulevard, and into the back of a pickup truck parked in front of the Pasadena Presbyterian Church. There was a camper top over the pickup bed with curtains strung across and above the tailgate, closing us off from the street sounds. We all sat on benches along either side of the truck bed, while the guy threaded the tape machine.

"Where are y'all from?" Kate had to know.

"We live on the old Spahn Ranch," one of the girls replied.

Ken Rose had told me about Spahn Ranch. All the Gene Autry movies that I had seen as a kid in Louisiana were shot there. When Rose was a student across the street at the Pasadena Play House, he and classmate Harry Dean Stanton had put together a film project called *Gold at Logan Creek*. Stanton would eventually become a cult hero with a movie called *Repo Man* co-starring Emilio Estevez, but that first time out, he and Ken Rose had struck out at Spahn Ranch. They finally added a couple of porno scenes to their film and tried to market it under the title *Revenge of the Virgin*. Now almost twenty years later, old man Spahn had become weak and feeble, taking whatever tenants he could get. He wound up with the Manson Family.

The girls had become very friendly, "You guys should come visit us sometimes," they said.

One of the girls, named Squeaky, had been pulling hair out of her head the whole time and then embroidering it into a vest.

"Nice work," Kate complimented her.

"Oh, it's something I'm making for Charlie," she replied proudly.

The song by Charlie Manson was nothing I would consider putting on the air, but I wanted to be diplomatic.

"Not bad," I said. "Tell you what, I'll play this tape for the other dee-jays, try to get some excitement going for you."

They liked that idea, and Kate and I kept smiling as we eased out of the camper truck. Back in the studio, I tried to shrug off the contact with these people. We were the pulse of the city. You open the mic, you never know who was listening. Anybody could decide they wanted to be your friend. When Pink Floyd ended, I pulled out an old 45 rpm from the '50s called the *Purple People Eater*, then I cued up The Byrds.

> *"...Won't you please take me*
> *along for a ride."*
> (Ibid.)

Los Angeles
Early August 1969

"Well I'm about to get sick
From watching my TV...
and when it's gonna change, my friend
is anybody's guess."

"That Trouble Coming Everyday," Mothers of Invention
(Frank Zappa, Verve/MGM)

The news came over the wire about the cult murders two nights in a row. The most famous victim was the motion picture star Sharon Tate, pregnant wife of director Roman Polanski. As a child, Polanski escaped the Nazis by walking out of their grasp. He had come this far only to have his life ruined by a freak named Manson, who etched a swastika onto his forehead, dressed in the trappings of the counter culture.

For us on the radio who were fighting fascism with music, it was further proof that the sixties were the black hole of bad idealism. The whole decade would become a cliché, but it was real when it was happening. The protestors against universities' participation in developing bigger and better nuclear weapons at Los Alamos or Livermore Laboratories would be called cowards. America's youth would be charged with violating the government's academic freedom to perpetuate an insane policy that would either blow up the planet, or in even the best case scenario, would cost billions to disarm and dispose. Vietnam became a domestic political war. The opposition would be under surveillance and investigated. Our phone records were commandeered. Nixon and his men would grant no pardons.

The love generation would be mocked and made fun of by people who couldn't understand that making love not war was not about promiscuous sex. It was the triumph of youth and life over age and death. It was a time of great spirituality. Millions seceded from a government of violence to drop out, live on the land and tune in with natural forces.

Drugs, music, and freedom belonged to the young. Bright kids with open faces who were out on the street, riding in the car with the radio on. We were the keepers of the flame of truth. But already the hustlers and the huxters were at work taking over our revolution.

The Top 40 stations had made Mick Jagger's country twang "Honky Tonk Women" number one, and right behind the Stones was Johnny Cash's brawling, fist-fighting tune called "A Boy Named Sue." In Los Angeles the news media were pumping up the unrest coming out of the South Central part of the city. A recurrence of the Watts riots looked like a real possibility. From now on the flickering tube would bring the bad news.

On any street in any town
In any state if any clown
Decides that now's the time to fight
For some ideal he thinks is right
And if a million more agree
There ain't no Great Society
...Blow your harmonica son."
(Ibid.)

Bethel, New York
August 1969

"Well I came upon a child of God."

"Woodstock," Crosby, Stills, Nash, & Young
(Joni Mitchell, Siquomb Publishing Co.; Crazy Crow Music)

When Charles Laquidara called from Boston to invite the Pierces to an outdoor concert in upstate New York, we accepted immediately. We flew east from Los Angeles to Louisiana to drop the kids off with family in Cajun country. Boarding a plane at New Orleans' Moissant Airport, the longhaired kid caught my eye. He was carrying a backpack with the word "Woodstock" scribbled on it. Charles said this was going to be a big happening. He called it right.

Charles was on the air at WBCN when we arrived at Logan Airport, so he sent a limo to pick us up. While KPPC was still virtually underground and struggling, the Boston Rocker was already successful, with a savvy sales staff who knew how to trade for limo service.

Inside WBCN's studio we walked past the group of young people who did all the tedious work of keeping a station on the air. Kate cleared the path with the simple statement, "We're the Pierces from KPPC Los Angeles, show us to Laquidara."

Charles leaped from his chair to greet us. This was our first meeting since he left L.A. eight months earlier.

We collected basic necessities like sleeping bags and drugs. Charles' car was rolling on bald tires, so he borrowed a new Volvo from his buddy, Harold Williams. We drove west on the Mass Pike, then wound our way through the green lush of another New England summer toward Bethel, New York. Traffic got heavier. Finally, by mid-Friday afternoon, it was bumper to bumper, as thick as any L.A. freeway. Thousands were converging on this one speck of earth known as Max Yasgur's farm. When the line of cars, trucks, vans, and hippie buses stopped moving, we parked the Volvo and began the six-mile hike, part of a steady stream of humanity all heading in the same direction. As we approached the site, the flags and banners of the tents on the hillside came into view. There were geodesic domes and tie-dyed teepees looking like the inside of a kaleidoscope. There was something medieval about the scene, much like the KPFK Renaissance fairs in the dry brown of Topanga Canyon, but on a much grander scale, in the green of upstate New York, as green as Louisiana bayou country. My French speaking-ancestors once lived nearby. Here in the land where the last of the Mohicans had hunted, the gathering of the tribes of the '60s was underway. We crossed the fences, or what was left of them, hundreds walking right past the broken up ticket booths at the entrance gates. Obviously, it was already out of control. "Free Concert" was being bantered about. The promoters were going to take a bath, but what the hell do we care. We were all here, let's party. The sea of people on the hillside, rapidly approaching four hundred thousand, was a sight to behold. Down below at the bottom of the hill was the gigantic stage of newly erected timbers, with huge speaker towers on either side. The air of expectation was tremendous.

Picking our way through the crowd, we managed to get halfway down the hill. As we laid out our sleeping bags to sit on, the guy next to us handed Kate a joint and quipped, "Don't stop here, there's plenty of seats down front."

This guy kept eating pills out of a bottle. At first we suspected it was vitamins, finally we decided the guy was chewing speed.

Sound tests were still being made when John Sebastian took the stage. Getting right to it, we all dropped a tab and it began to come on in the middle of Richie Havens' set. Somewhere along, there was a warning about brown acid not being too specifically good, but no problem here, we had carried our lysergic acid from the Coast, straight out of the California laboratory.

It was Charles' first LSD trip. When light rain started to come down, he began to freak. The three of us covered up with a blanket with the music floating overhead.

"What are we doing here, David," Charles asked. "All these people around us."

"They don't count," I replied. "The only thing that matters is who is under the blanket with you."

We all hugged and felt the oneness. Eight years of friendship had laid the groundwork, and the psychedelic experience was bringing it all together as our brain energy worked overtime. The rain stopped and people began moving around, trying to get closer to the stage.

The guy next to us kept repeating, "Plenty of room down front," grinding his teeth and gulping another handful of speed. Each blanket became a single family dwelling. The path between blankets were driveways. The yellow umbrella up the hill was a landmark. Take a left there to get to the port-o-let.

By the time Joan Baez came on stage, it was after midnight and we were really flying. Her clear sweet voice drifted out with "Joe Hill." When she went into "Swing Low, Sweet Chariot," it was very still and almost religious, the three of us could have forgotten there were half a million others. Charles had never cared for Joan Baez before, but now he was a believer.

"Bringing in a couple of keys
Don't touch my bags if you please,
Mister Customs Man."

"Coming in To Los Angeles," Arlo Guthrie
(Arlo Guthrie, Howard Beach Music)

Arlo Guthrie took a guitar ride, sang the final verse, and acknowledged the applause before he began his famous rap, probably the most relevant thing said at Woodstock.

"Yeah, it's far out, man," Arlo said. "I don't know how many of you can dig how many people there are. Like I was rapping to the fuzz, right. Can you dig it man, there's supposed to be a million and a half people here by tomorrow night. Can you dig that. New York State Thruway is closed, man." Arlo laughed maniacally, "Hah, Hah. Yeah, a lot of freaks. Hah, Hah, Hah," he laughed again.

The thump thump thump of the helicopters moved artists into the site. It was reminiscent of Devonshire Downs.

"You can't stage one of these things without a chopper," I observed.

"Just like you can't stage a war without 'em," Kate added.

"You think they'd try to bust all five-hundred thousand of us?" Charles Laquidara asked.

"It would be a hell of a try," I said aloud, wondering just how deep our paranoia ran.

The power of love and music flowed over us until dawn, Charles often repeating, "So it comes down to who's in the blanket with you."

Every time the crowd began to move around, the guy next to us, like a crazed carny show barker, shouted the promise to the multitude of "great seats down front."

Saturday morning daylight came with no sunrise, only a dull gray sky and light rain. Already the mud was becoming thicker than the love and music that had flowed all night. Had there been another band ready to play, we probably wouldn't have moved, but all of a sudden there was a great big empty moment.

Even a good acid trip leaves you tired, worn out, and wasted. As we looked around at the sea of mud and bodies, a kid walked by whose acid trip was obviously of the bad old brown kind. Barefooted, bare-chested, mud in his hair and face, he asked, zombie-like, if anybody had seen Jeannie. The meeting of the tribes was going to have a down side.

"Do you guys really want to be here?" Charles asked.

"I think it's gonna get really crazy," Kate said. "This is a king-size disaster area. I just tried to get to the john, and everybody is relieving themselves anywhere they can. The lines are thirty minutes long. We're going to have health problems here by tonight. There are no phones out of here. I want to call the kids, I feel stranded."

I knew the decision was up to me, so I took a long look at the multi-colored muddy hillside. This was probably the biggest gathering ever of the drugged-out society. Winners and losers all. This was the rise and fall of the counter culture, all in one weekend. I would wash off the mud, the lyrics would fade, but I'd never forget the emotion.

"Well, all the in-bound roads are blocked," I said. "There's not enough food and water to go around. I think I've had enough fun for a awhile. You're not waiting on me."

"You guys find the sleeping bags," Kate ordered.

"Leave them," Chuck replied. "We put a lot of good vibes on them. Some poor bastard's gonna need a place to lay his head."

The rain started again and we walked slowly, mechanically, past the apple trees along the road, heavy with green fruit. Past the miles of vehicles with bumper stickers reading "ABM...America's Biggest Mistake." There was a steady stream of concert-goers still headed towards the big event. Some had tickets in hand admitting them to the Woodstock Music and Arts Festival.

"How much farther," they asked hopefully. "We've walked over ten miles."

"You're almost there," Charles reassured them. "Don't worry, plenty of good seats down front," he chuckled uncontrollably.

We zeroed in on Harold Williams' Volvo by dead reckoning, walking past it at first, before the light bulb clicked on. An oasis in the desert never looked so good. The traffic coming in was indeed a gridlock, but only a few cars were heading out. We stopped after an hour's drive, rented a motel room, and slept until Sunday morning. By sundown Sunday, we were within earshot of WBCN and the news of Woodstock was crackling over the airwaves. It was technologically a disaster poorly organized but overwhelmingly attended. It was temporarily New York's third largest city. Abbey Hoffman was thrown off the stage when he tried to interrupt The Who's performance of "We're Not Going to Take It," and half a million people had responded when Country Joe McDonald led the cheer. The Woodstock nation had been born.

A few blocks from WBCN a tire went flat on Harold Williams' Volvo, but we didn't have the energy to change it, so we rolled in on the rim. For years Harold Williams would brag that his car had gone to Woodstock. He hadn't, but from the looks of his Volvo, he was glad he didn't take the trip.

"We are star dust,
We are golden...
And we got to get ourselves
Back to the garden."

"Woodstock," Crosby, Stills, Nash, & Young
(Joni Mitchell, Siquomb Publishing Co.; Crazy Crow Music)

"What they'd been saying all these
Got dong years has come true,
Now, there's no more morning dew."

"Morning Dew," Rod Stewart
(Tim Rose and Bonnie Dobson, Warner Chappell Music)

Rod Stewart was singing Tim Rose's composition called "Morning Dew," punctuated by Jeff Beck's lead wah-wah guitar with future Rolling Stone Ron Wood on bass. We had just returned to Los Angeles and I was driving through Glendale on my first trip back to KPPC. Rolling around in my head were the goals of the new Woodstock generation. The seeds of the environmental movement were being planted. We had to end the war. We had to fight disease, famine and suffering. The rebels without a cause had found their raison d'être. We knew we really could count. We really could make a difference.

On the radio Don Hall began to play a new album. The first release for Carlos Santana, one month after becoming a hit at Woodstock.

"I'll be damned," I said aloud, "shades of Tito Puente, from KTBT days." I made a mental note to play Santana and Tito back to back. This is one of the great things about being an underground disc jockey, there was no wasted motion, everything you'd ever heard you could play somewhere. The only pre-requisite was it had to be a great song played at the right time. So I'm playing Latin in Los Angeles, and Charles is doing classical in Boston, all on rock 'n roll radio.

When I walked into the studio Don Hall showed me a 45 RPM copy of the song, "In the Year 2525 (Exordium and Terminus)."

"What the hell is that supposed to mean?" Don asked. "It was the number one AM Top 40 song two months ago and now after the world is sick of it, Chester thought we should go on it."

"Chester Coleman?" I asked.

"He's got your job," Don said, "he's our new Program Director."

I stormed in to see Al Herion. He was smoking like a factory and backing up like a crawfish.

"Look man, it's nothing against you, you're doing a good job," Al Herion began apologizing. "It's just that we're in a stalemate here. I need somebody to get us all together on the same team. I think that Chester can do that."

"Chester can barely tune the friggin' transmitter. What the hell you're talking about!" I said.

"Look, don't worry. Everything's going to be all right. You still got your shift, you still got a big influence on this station," Herion broke into a hacking cough before he lit another cig and continued. "The guy that you and Bill Slater wanted from San Francisco, Jack Ellis, he's coming down. He's a good man, he's gonna be real good in the morning spot. Look, the damn church is going crazy they can't stand all you longhairs around here. Chester can talk to them, he still looks straight. You used to look straight, Dave, you could have done it, but your hair is too damned long now. We're in a stand-off here. There's nothing we can do until somebody buys this radio station. We can't get out and find another location. We can't go no where. Meantime, the church is driving me crazy."

I didn't want to hear anymore. In a way I was relieved from some of the pressure of being in the middle. Maybe I could be more effective as just one of the disc jockeys. I didn't even like earning a couple of hundred more every month than the other guys. I had become that socialistic about it. Could have been worse. Herion could have fired me. At least I was still on the air. That was the most important thing. I had to stay on the air. I walked out of Herion's office sore as hell but ready to try something else. Nothing was going to happen with this baby until we could get more power and a tall tower. This interminable holding pattern had been going on for over a year now. The ticket to ride was still just out of reach.

So Chester had the guts to go after my job. Well, let him have it. He'd quickly prove he was in over his head, and like Herion, he didn't quite understand how to put a winning combo together.

Jeff Gonzer had covered my shift for me while I was at Woodstock. I paid him forty dollars cash out of my pocket and he was really pumped-up, looking forward to getting more hours on KPPC. Jeff had an opportunity to interview a crazy spastic white guy who sounded a lot like Ray Charles. It was the first time L.A. had a chance to get inside the head of Joe Cocker. One of the first decisions Chester Coleman made as Program Director was to axe Jeff Gonzer. Jeff was distraught of course, but he was already hooked on disc jockeying. He heard there was a new acid rocker down in Orange County, a station called KYMS. Within a week, Jeff was spinning rock 'n roll down in Nixon-Agnew Country.

> "Lord I wish I had some guitar strings
> Old Black Diamond brand
> I'd string up this old Martin box
> And go and join some band.
>
> To see if I can lose
> Them thin dime hard time..."
>
> "Hell on Church Street Blues," Norman Blake
> (Norman Blake, Happy Valley Music)

KPPC FM
Pasadena Presbyterian Church
October 1969

"Trying to make it real-
compared to what?"

"Compared To What," Les McCann
(Eugene McDaniels, Lonport Music, Inc.)

"From Atlantic Records and the LP *Swiss Movement* recorded live at the Montreaux Jazz Fest, Montreaux, Switzerland, in June of this year. That's Les McCann on piano, Eddie Harris on tenor sax, backed by LeRoy Vinnega on bass and Benny Baily's trumpet, Donald Dean on drums sitting in and stretching you out for eight minutes and eighteen seconds on the track "Trying to Make it Real Compared to What." Got Damn It. Hello out there in the City of Fallen Angels. We're live from the bottom of the church with a play list that's so impromptu I don't know what I'm going to do next. So call the rap line and take your best shot.

Hey, have you heard Jack Ellis, down from Frisco, and in your radio every morning. Bob Sala will be along at noon. Bill Slater from 4:00 to 8:00 p.m., then Don Hall till midnight. If you're up all night so is Zak Zenor, midnight till dawn. And this weekend be sure you call up John Carpenter and welcome him aboard the hottest sound in town. He's on at the witching hour. And me, I'm Dave Pierce, 9:00 a.m. till noon, from KPPC in Pasadena.

The whole city is high and so am I. We're gonna strangle this war with long hair."

"The President he's got his war,
Have one doubt, they call it treason,
Trying to make it real-
compared to what?"
(Ibid.)

Senator J.W. Fulbright had charged the State Department with withholding the facts on Vietnam from Congress. The Nixon White House immediately denied the charge. On October 15, millions of Americans attended mass demonstrations to let the administration know they wanted the war stopped. It became known as Vietnam Moratorium Day. Nixon supporters retaliated by flying American Flags at half-mast.

To me, to be leftist or liberal was certainly not communist or un-American. It was, in my mind, the only correct expression of patriotism. The flag wavers were blindly following an evil and corrupt government. Being a flag burner was more American than a flag waver. We were trying to reform society, starting with the ending of a misguided and politically un-winnable war that was tearing our country apart. To be left or liberal was to stand for the times that were changing. To be a do-gooder, to help the unfortunate, to put right over might, to actually make love instead of war. False patriots were those backing Nixon and Agnew, who stifled dissent. Just as the 1951 House Un-American Activities Committee were the real un-Americans, not those they were investigating, who in some cases were simply trying to help others.

When I left Louisiana for the West Coast eight years earlier, I was a naive all-American boy believing in God and Country. Now I wasn't sure what I believed in, I had seen too much. Laquidara said the corporate capitalism of America had the same rotten roots as the corporate Nazis of Germany twenty-five years earlier. Did some crazed Left Wing Youth spout that out of some deep hatred for America or did Charles simply make it up? Maybe both. But Casey Pierce, the guy with the World War II Purple Heart, was also saying the same thing.

"Where's My God and
where's my money,
Trying to make it real-
compared to what?"
(Ibid.)

San Francisco
Early November 1969

"Oh, I must have killed a million men,
And now they want me back again."

"I Ain't Marching Anymore," Phil Ochs
(Phil Ochs, Barricade Music, Inc.)

On November 7, 1969, a week before the huge antiwar Moratorium Demonstration, The *New York Times* ran a full-page advertisement in support of the Nixon Administration's policy in Vietnam. A similar advertisement appeared two days later. Then on November 15th, The *Times* reported that the pro-Nixon advertisers had blanketed the country with twenty-five million postcards backing the president. The postcards were to be signed and returned to the advertiser's headquarters. The name of the group behind the effort was United We Stand, Inc. Its chairman was H. Ross Perot, a billionaire from Dallas, Texas.

On November 15th we drove to San Francisco with Jack Ellis to join the big march that we knew would be a real happening.

On November 16th a quarter of a million war protestors marched on Washington in the biggest show of force yet against the government. At the White House, the peaceniks held up coffins with the names of American boys who were killed in Vietnam. Rocks and bottles were thrown against the U.S. Federal Building, tear gas was thrown back. That same morning in San Francisco we sat in an apartment belonging to Jack Ellis's friends, firing up Marin County weed. We spent the night there and camped out in sleeping bags. The main parade route was only a block away. When the one hundred thousand strong came singing down the street, we walked down, joined in, and marched the seven miles through the cool gray city to the Golden Gate Park. It was beautiful and peaceful. A thousand people monitored the crowd and kept everything well controlled. Spiro Agnew had charged that there would be "lawlessness" in San Francisco. He was just wrong, just lying, or both.

On November 20th, Congress cleared the bill that would permit the draft lottery.

In Boston, Charles Laquidara spoke into the WBCN microphone, "We didn't give the government the power they have, they took it," he said.

As we always did, Charles and I talked every few days. Now it was by phone, often late at night.

"The U.S. Government is pursuing an obscene military policy," he said, "we can't win in Vietnam."

"After being in the San Francisco march it's more than just a feeling," I said, "I can really see that the tide is beginning to turn."

"Don't think these assholes have any morals," Charles said. "They just as soon shoot their own people. In the '30s a bunch of World War I vets marched into Washington for a protest and a camp-out because they had been promised homes and never got them. The Chief of Staff called up General Douglas MacArthur. He also called up a squad with a machine gun, and when that machine gun stopped, the only veterans still at the protest were dead ones. Guess who was in command of the machine gun squad? Then Captain, later General, Dwight D. Eisenhower. Old Ike himself."

"I never heard that story," I said, totally astonished.

"Look it up, it really happened. But you ain't gonna find it in the National News archives. These are some very evil fucks in control of our destiny. They go to D.C., get power, and forget they're human. We're not going to cave in, David. Just stay on the radio, keep fanning the flames of peace. We need all the help we can get. The battle ground is on the air waves."

"Call it peace or call it treason,
Call it love or call it reason."

"I Ain't Marching Anymore," Phil Ochs
(Phil Ochs, Barricade Music, Inc.)

Santa Monica, California
Thanksgiving Eve 1969

"Stop all that hurrying,
Be happy my way."

"Nothing Is Easy," Jethro Tull
(Ian Anderson, Chrysalis Music)

Jack Ellis pulled the goggles down over his eyes, turned the radio volume up on his '65 Ford and let out a yell. From where I was in the back seat, he looked about twenty feet away. His long bushy hair seemed to stick straight out like antennae. The goggles gave him the bug-eyed look of a six-foot insect. Outside on the San Diego Freeway, eight lanes of traffic sped by at seventy-five miles per hour, going both directions at once. I hoped Jack was on the right side of the freeway. I really couldn't say for sure. Everything was out of control. I knew I had to go with the flow or freak out.

"I am one with the universe," I said silently, and immediately felt more secure.

We had all five dropped acid when we left the North Hollywood duplex. Ventura Freeway west for five minutes to the interchange, San Diego south, climbing the hill, leaving the valley behind, then down past the Sunset Exit, maneuvering into the right lanes to turn west towards Santa Monica. I was definitely starting to rush.

Kate, sitting next to me, was well on her way. On the other side of her, eighteen-year-old Joey Russo, her younger brother, just out of six months in the National Guard, on his first LSD trip, was in a stupor. Jack's wife, Sue Ellis, was locked into Jethro Tull on the radio. Insect Jack maneuvered the heavy traffic on a wild ride out to the Santa Monica Civic Auditorium.

I hadn't been in the hall since the Academy Awards of '65. No elite crowd tonight. No tuxedos. No expensive gowns. The freaks and weirdos streaming in were a colorful, bizarre, undulating mass, jockeying for position in the auditorium as the warm-up band played at full volume. We moved like autobots into five seats, miraculously left open on the right aisle only eight rows from the stage.

Jack, Sue, and Kate boogied with the crowd. Joey and I sat back in our chairs, stunned, stoned, overwhelmed, knocked out.

Ian Anderson had arrived in Los Angeles the day before. At the top of his itinerary was the radio circuit, KPPC-FM was first on his list. He showed up on my shift a little after 11:00 a.m. I was honored. The way the man blew flute and incorporated such a beautiful instrument into hard rock music had gone way beyond the mid-'60s use of the flute in ballads by groups like the Blues Project.

Small, lean, wiry, long bushy beard and hair, he looked like the gnomes that spirited through the British Isles in fairy tales and folklore. Ian was polite, witty, and informative. We talked about the formation of the group: Jethro Tull, being the name of a legendary farmer, plowing the land. We played cuts from his LPs. And I got the impression this was a very intelligent businessman. I wasn't surprised to learn years later, when he'd done everything musically that he could possibly want to do, he became the corporate leader for his own New Age aquaculture company.

After an hour on the air with me, he left for the obligatory stop at KRLA in Pasadena before heading back to Hollywood to stop off at KHJ and KMET. The last thing Ian Anderson did was plug the Santa Monica Civic Concert.

"It's magic," he smiled, with a twinkle in his eye, just before the record company people whisked him out of the darkened church, out into the hazy smog on Colorado Boulevard.

> *"You'll smile in awhile*
> *And discover that I'll*
> *Get you happy my way..."*
> (Ibid.)

Finally it was time. Jethro Tull took the stage and there he was. Ian Anderson conducted the band for the first few bars, then leaned his flute into the microphone, pursed his lips and blew that big room away.

Joey and I were both on our feet now. The acid edge dissipated in a burst of energy. The crowd jumped and bumped, moved and swayed. Jack's goggle-eyed face and wiry hair kept creeping into my peripheral vision.

Ian Anderson alternately led the group with jerky movements of his hands and arms, then singing or blowing flute at the masses. The light show was working overtime, a fantastic array of colors and intensities, pulsating with the beat. I looked closely at the stage, saw the waves of light energy and heard Ian's flute. That's when I realized I was watching a magician. The little long-haired gnome could have pied-pipered us all out into the damned old deep, dark Pacific Ocean a few blocks away.

"Can you see the energy field?" Kate asked.

Yeah, I could see it all right. I know it was lysergic acid distortion, but I also know what we saw. As Ian Anderson flipped his hands outward, the waves of curved colored light bands flowed out from his fingertips. With the opposite motion, he would pull them all back into his body. Absolutely happened. We were totally blown away for the next two hours.

Spent and worn, we walked out into the ocean breeze to realize we had no idea where we'd parked the car. Jack, peering through his goggles, went scouting, while Joey and I, arms around each other's shoulders, went back inside to look for the purse Kate left behind.

Jethro Tull was into the last encore. The crowd was still a soup of freaked-out humanity, as Joey and I meandered down the aisle where everyone was now massed in the first few rows. Easing through on dead reckoning, I turned into a row, leaned down between two dancing, clapping, scantily-clad hippie girls, and put my hand on Kate's purse. I took one more look back at the stage, saw the waves of light energy and heard Ian Anderson's flute. I would never be this high again.

Outside, Jack had taken his goggles off and found the car. We sat silently as he drove us away from Santa Monica's Civic.

The next day was a very subdued Thanksgiving. We did all the rituals of the day, but it was like we had just got back from another planet. Joey was nearly speechless for several days and it seemed his personality had taken a slight turn from that day on.

They say Ken Kesey had gone on the road in 1964 after getting LSD from the government in a student experiment. As the '60s progressed, so did the experimentation with acid. "Turn on, Tune In, Drop Out," was the symbolic slogan. Drop acid and find God. Learn to eat flowers and kiss babies. If LSD could be ten hours of hell with everything more intense, it could also be all the pleasure your brain could produce with spiritual enlightenment thrown in for a bonus.

I decided that if running for the goal line with a football was a rush, carrying an element of risk that could come back years later to haunt you physically, then perhaps this mind expansion business was pretty far out in the danger zone. I wasn't going to drop any more acid.

Joey Russo and I had been to see the greatest rock concert of all time. It couldn't get any better than this. If we quit now we might live to tell the tale of the magician with a flute.

> *"The bad old days,*
> *They came and went,*
> *...We ran the race,*
> *And the race was won*
> *By running slow..."*

"We Used To Know," Jethro Tull
(Ian Anderson, Chrysalis Music)

Los Angeles
December 6, 1969

"Oh, the storm is threatening,
My very life today..."

"Gimme Shelter," Rolling Stones
(Mick Jagger and Keith Richards, ABKCO Music, Inc.)

The Rolling Stones had emerged as the premier rock 'n roll band of the late '60s. On the radio we followed the events of their American tour and played all the Stones cuts. At once hip and revolutionary, they incorporated all the anti-establishment lines, but at the same time gave us a look and a wink at the evolving get-rich-off-the-counter-culture attitude that would evolve into the early seventies.

On November 10th, Bill Graham had brought the Stones to San Diego's Sports Arena. Now he was looking for a location on his home turf in the Bay area.

We heard about the big concert up north before they settled on a site. Finally, it was announced the big show would be at Altamont Speedway. When the weekend was over, the news came back. The Hell's Angels, hired to act as guards and crowd control, had beaten to death a young black man right in front of the band, as Mick Jagger, the new Prince of the Dark Side, pleaded for sanity. It was a prelude of the senseless violence, still to come to the American landscape, in the decades ahead.

"Rape, murder it's just a shot away,
I tell you love, sister, it's just a kiss away."
(Ibid.)

The Cellar Theatre had been going steadily downhill. We sold off the recording equipment after Carl, our engineer, died. The video gear was in my living room. After Vince Donofrio's show closed, I began renting the theatre out to young rock groups for rehearsal. Old man Shimer, the landlord, took on a younger partner who soon squeezed the old guy out. My young aggressive landlord followed my lead and rented the space directly above the Cellar for rock band rehearsal. The big amplifiers roared straight down through the uninsulated ceiling. As a theatre for performing to an audience, the Cellar was now worthless. When water from the top floor leaked down, causing part of the ceiling to collapse onto the stage, I refused to pay rent till repairs were made. The landlord padlocked the doors.

Rather than pay attorneys, Link and I hatched a plan to recover some of what was rightfully mine. On a Saturday night at 2:00 a.m., we pulled up with three pickup trucks and parked in front of the building. Link and I walked around to the entrance in the rear. With the stealth of seasoned burglars, we cut the padlock, never waking our landlord, sleeping in the back unit just a few feet away. Closing the back door behind us, we opened the front door to the crew waiting on Vermont Street. We loaded up all the banker's chairs. All the lighting instruments came down. The velvet curtain, the office couch with Bachman's designer fabric, all went out the front door. While Bill Jensen finished disconnecting the dimmers from the light booth, four of us went up to the second floor, where a group

261

of young longhairs were winding up rehearsal, putting away their guitars and blowing weed. We went through the second floor window onto the first story roof directly over the sleeping landlord. We disconnected the five-ton air conditioning unit, quietly passing it through the window. Then through the hushed cheers of rock musicians and a cloud of smoke, we walked the unit down the long flight of stairs and onto a truck. Finally, Kate went into the ladies' bathroom to recover the piece of marble on the vanity top. It slipped and cracked with a crash. Within seconds the landlord was at the back door and he and I were staring at each other.

"You son-of-a-bitch!" he yelled in disbelief, "I'm calling the cops!"

We all scurried out the front on a dead run, cranked our pickups and hit the Hollywood freeway on-ramp heading north. No charges were filed, no repercussions. Rock bands rehearsed in the old Cellar space for years until Ken Rose briefly revived the space as a theatre. Eventually the whole block of Vermont between Second and Third street was razed and occupied by a Von's Grocery distribution outlet.

The items we took out on the midnight express were passed out to various individuals. The pile of banker's chairs stashed by my back door slowly dwindled down. I still have the velvet curtains. Smokey Roberds, Link Wyler, and I each took a banker's chair. For years Link leaned back in it and put his feet up on the old Cellar desk while he talked Hollywood deals on the phone.

"But what can a poor boy do,
Except to sing for a rock 'n' roll band..."

"Street Fighting Man," The Rolling Stones
(Mick Jagger and Keith Richards, Mirage Music; ABKCO Music, Inc.)

Sun Valley, California
January 1, 1970

Casey and I were standing in front of Russie's new house north of Burbank, snuggled up against the mountains that rimmed the San Fernando Valley. Holidays over, he and Nellie were heading home in a couple of days. I was smoking a joint and passed it to him. He took a brief toke and handed it back. We were silent for awhile, then he asked the question.

"How much longer do you think you'll be out here?"

"Can't say," I replied, "I can't quit now, I know that. I have to play out my hand."

"I'm worried about you," Casey said. "It sounds to me like war could break out in this country. I hate to see you mixed up in all this. You beat the draft, but we could have a battle ground right here. It reminds me too much of World War II."

"I'm already in it," I said, "the music we play, the things I've said on the radio. We're breaking the FCC obscenity laws for months now, but it's got to be done. Up against the wall mother-fucker is what we stand for. It takes dirty words to call bullshit on dirty deeds. The government guys already know who I am. Everybody's playing for keeps."

"It's not worth it," Casey said, "when it's all said and done, it won't mean that much."

"This radio station could still take off," I said. "New owners would give us more power and a taller stick, we could still own this town. We could be a powerful voice."

"But this doesn't have to be your fight," Casey said, refusing the joint when I passed it to him. "I'm fifty years old, my five grandchildren live two thousand miles away. That ain't much of a deal. You come home, your sister will follow you." His eyes misted over and he paused for a moment while we both looked up at the brown L.A. haze, then he continued, his voice starting to break.

"Life is easy in South Louisiana, don't forget that. It's impossible to be hungry in Cajun Country. Maybe I could look around for a home site for you."

"Sure," I said. "Oak trees on the bayou would be just fine."

KPPC FM
Pasadena Presbyterian Church
February 1970

"Trying to make up my mind
Really is too horrifying."

"Sitting On A Fence," Rolling Stones
(Mick Jagger and Keith Richards, ABKCO Music, Inc.)

The request line in the studio was ringing off the wall. I picked it up and barked, "Rap line."

"Hey, Dave! Your old buddy, Steve Seagull," said the voice on the other end of the line.

"Hey, Steve, you in Boston? You calling from WBCN?"

"No, man, I'm in L.A."

"Oh, yeah?"

"Yeah, I'm out here now," Steve said.

"So where you working?"

"KMET, of course."

"Sorry, I didn't know, I'd quit listening," I lied. "What happened in Boston?"

"Nothing. Just got burnt out. Boston's okay, but L.A. is where it's at. You know that."

"Sure, I know that," I said. "Everybody hates L.A., but they all want to be here."

"Yeah, Charles Laquidara told me what's been going on with you. You had some problems out here. How would you like to take over a radio station?"

"What do you mean?"

"You know what it's like, being in the right place at the right time," Steve said, "having God on your side. How would you like to take over KPPC? Again?"

"What did you have in mind?"

"Me and you, and Les Carter."

"I'd like to talk about it."

"Good, I'll come by your place tonight. Where are you?"

"I'm out in the valley. 6416 Babcock, North Hollywood."

"I'll see you there," Steve said. "And, hey, by the way, that's mighty weak Stones you're playing. Put some balls into it. Go back and find some of the early songs. Some of their blues stuff."

Steve showed up at my house that night, with a joint in one hand and a Scotch in the other. He laid out his plan.

"Here's the way we're going to do it," Steve said. "The first thing we're going to do is get me on part-time at KPPC. You get me a part-time job, just one shift, Saturday night, Sunday night, it don't matter. And from there it'll be just a matter of weeks before they offer me a full-time job."

The Seagull certainly had plenty of confidence, he never was short on that.

"And somewhere along there," Steve continued, "we'll get Les Carter hired, and as soon as we do that, then Les is going to gravitate his way to Program Director, and from there on we'll run the radio station."

It seemed simple the way Steve was talking.

"Well, it sounds like you and Les got it all figured out," I said.

"Well, I talked to Les about it, yeah. It's really my idea. Les would like to come back, but he's happy with what he's doing. He's been at KPPC twice already. He's had enough. He really don't care if he comes back or not. But he would, and we need him. He's the one guy who can front as Program Director. He's the guy who can do the job."

"So why do you need me? It sounds like you got it all covered."

"Cause you're already on the inside, you're on the air. You can get me in. Plus, you're the one guy who can do your job like you do."

"What's that?"

"Be the straight man? Suck up to the business guys, keep them at bay. Make 'em feel confident. Even if they think the rest of us are crazy, let 'em know you're not."

"Al Herion says I wasn't straight enough."

"Oh, yeah, you are, Dave. Al Herion is too lame to know the difference. Straight is in your bones, man, you got the instinct for playing it straight."

Steve Segal seemed to be offering me a deal. It was the best one I'd heard yet. I knew Al Herion and Chester Coleman would jump at the chance to bring in Steve Segal. They'd never know what hit them.

"Our fiddler, he just loves to play
and move the rolling sky."

"Rolling Minstrels," Fairport Convention
(unknown, Public Domain)

Steven Segal

Los Angeles
Late February 1970

"When I was a cowboy,
Out on the Western Plain,
I made a half million,
Pulling on the bridle reins.

Oh, the biggest battle,
Ever on the Western Plain,
When me and a bunch of cowboys
Rode into Jesse James."

"Out On The Western Plain," Leadbelly
(Huddie Ledbetter, Folkways Music)

One Saturday night at midnight, quietly, without any publicity or fan-fare, the most radical disc jockey in America went on the air at the last FM Rocker with no rules. It seemed like Steven Segal had never left 106.7. His impact on the sound of KPPC was immediate and profound. He had the knack for finding the tracks that were just enough on the edge to keep us out front. When The Seagull played a song, it was legitimized and the rest of the staff quickly added it to their own personal play list.

Meanwhile the Los Angeles press gave a lot of space to the move of top-rated disc jockey Jimmy Rabbit, who had come up from San Diego to Pasadena, rocked the city from KRLA, and was now going to KABC. Rock music had taken over yet another radio station, this time at the network level, in the Pop Music capital of the world. KRLA continued to present great concerts to the music loving masses, bringing the Jefferson Airplane into Anaheim Convention Center. The back-up group was some of the Airplane's own musicians taking the stage under the name of Hot Tuna. Glen McKay's Headlights did the light show for both groups. Merrilee Saks had become a real groupie hanging out with the Airplane and living with Glen. She brought him over to my show at the bottom of the church where the KPPC listeners heard first hand about life on the road with the Jefferson Airplane.

Randy Newman showed up at the Troubador singing "Mama Told Me Not to Come." The Doors released *Morrison Hotel*. AM & FM Rockers were all playing Led Zepplin. Jimmy Paige and Robert Plant's "Whole Lotta Love" became #1. A month later Sly and the Family Stone owned the top spot with "Everybody Is a Star."

Members of Los Angeles County Medical Association predicted mass mortality rates due to pollution in specific areas of Southern California by the Winter of '75-'76. The *Free Press* ran articles on how to survive in the wilderness.

Rumors of a pending sale of KPPC and KMPX continued to circulate. I decided to take a trip to Louisiana before it all started to come down. After a long day on the road driving east on I-10, we stopped for supper in a small run-down joint in Davis Mountain Junction, Texas. We had to wake 'Chelle, who had fallen asleep with two inches of her security blanket stuffed in her mouth. As soon as she finished eating, she would stand by my side, never saying a word, thus by-passing the rule that kids were supposed to stay seated till everyone had finished. We began to realize how seedy the place really was and hurriedly ate and returned to the black Porsche. I topped off the gas tank, then went to pay the attendant. He took his time filling out the credit card eyeing me the whole time. I tried not to return his cold stare, but it was difficult. He looked to be about fifty years old with lines in his face as deep as the west Texas desert ravines. He walked on a wooden peg leg. On his shoulder sat a black crow.

"Nice looking set of wheels," he said, "built by Krauts, ain't it?"

"That's right," I replied.

"Nazi bullets took my leg," he said matter of fact. "Nice looking wife and kids you got, too."

I glanced over my shoulder where Kate was beginning to give me nervous looks. John-David and 'Chelle had their faces pressed against the Porsche window intrigued by the guy's weirdness. To them, he was another freak, in a continuing sideshow.

"What's a guy like you do?" he asked, finally handing me the ticket.

"I'm a disc jockey in Los Angeles," I said, with a bit of pride in my radio voice.

"Zat right," he said unimpressed in his Texas drawl. "That your excuse for wearing your hair halfway to your ass and looking like a sissy?"

"I guess so," was all I said. I smiled real friendly as I slipped my credit card back in my jeans. I didn't think he wanted to hear that maybe I was anti-Nazi too. I returned to the black Porsche, fired the Kraut engine and laid rubber to the on-ramp heading back on 1-10.

About twenty minutes down the road Kate discovered we had apparently left 'Chelle's security Linus blanket in the restaurant booth.

"Do we have to go back?" I asked.

"Let's not talk about it," Kate said. 'Chelle never asked for her blanket again.

In Abbeville, Nellie was obviously embarrassed by our presence. She took Kate down to the beauty parlor hoping to modify her hippie appearance before all the neighbors and relatives came over. The beautician was able to change the look, but not the attitude.

When we returned to L.A. I began to shop for another vehicle to replace the German-built dream machine with one-hundred thousand plus miles and needing a new engine. I really wanted a Land Rover capable of getting off the pavement and into the woods. The spare tire brackets on the Rover hood was, as I told everyone, the perfect spot to mount a machine gun should such a heavy duty defense system become necessary. I finally settled on a Swedish-made Volvo, tough, built to last, fitting the image of a revolutionary deejay.

We were what we appeared to be. Young and rebellious. This revolution was serious business. If you were involved with the peace movement, they probably had a file on you. But the FBI was used to fighting dumb criminals. Now, they were up against college grads. We were the brightest and the best. The government forces were way over their heads.

We, who had grown up with rock 'n roll, saw it come out of the rural south to the cities of America and ultimately conquer the world with the sound of an electric guitar. Vietnam was blowing away our youth and innocence. We were finding out what life in the mid-twentieth century was about, and we were warming to our role as outlaws. The good guys wear black, not white, like Lash Larue in the old west.

Finally, *Zabriskie Point* was released. The critics thought it was weak and it never caught on at the box office. But the Federales were right to be wary of Antonioni. The image on the big screen sent a clear-cut message.

America was in chaos. The forces of anarchy were loose on the land. Everybody was angry, blacks, rednecks, longhairs, parents, and peg legs. From every city came the cry. Blow it up, burn it down.

> *"When I was a cowboy,*
> *Out on the Western Plain,*
> *I made a half million,*
> *Pulling on the bridle reins.*
>
> *If your house catches fire*
> *And there ain't no water around,*
> *Throw your suitcase out the window*
> *And let the got damn shack burn down."*
>
> *...Shoot low sheriff*
> *We're riding Shetland ponies."*
>
> "Western Plain," Van Morrison
> (Huddie Leadbetter, Beachwood Music Corp.)

KPPC FM
Pasadena Presbyterian Church
Early March 1970

On the drive to Pasadena, I was listening to the Seagull. He liked to play the heavy blues, and he was crazy for Dr. John The Night Tripper, who had brought New Orleans-style rock to national attention. Steve was sounding good, he was definitely leading the station in the right direction. This guy certainly knew his music and he was one of the great radio rappers of all time.

I parked my car in front of the Pasadena Presbyterian Church and took the walk down the flight of stairs to the basement. As soon as I entered the hallway outside the studio, the smell of grass was evident. I walked into the studio and asked Steve if he had heard the news.

"Yeah," he said, "we've been sold. It's perfect."

"Do you know who they are?"

"It doesn't matter. They can't possibly be as smart as us."

"Well, they sure are straight enough," I said. "They're the National Science Network."

"I know. They used to own BCN," Steve replied. "That's the old National Concert Network, NCN. At one time they owned BCN in Boston, WHCN in Hartford, and WNCN in New York City. These guys still own WNCN and, get this, they play classical music in the Big Apple."

"Yeah," I said, "but they also place pharmaceutical ads in medical journals for drug companies. How are they going to react to us?"

"Obviously, the only thing they're interested in is making money, and so are we. We're going to show them how it's done," replied the Seagull. "So we're still on track. As soon as they name a new general manager, we'll get Les in here as Program Director and the rest is going to be easy."

"What do you think is going to happen to Al Herion?" I asked.

"Herion's history," he replied. "So is Chester. These guys are not going to keep Herion in here, and he knows it. It's our turn, Dave."

"It's the right time," I said, "We have to fight hard for free speech. Talking freely to the masses over the radio is essential."

"Just remember this, any time there is a coup in Latin America, the first thing they take is the radio stations. If you want to be a part of the revolution, you need a voice, a loud one. Watching it all happen from a rock radio station at the bottom of a church is like front row seats at a Who concert," laughed Steve Segal.

The blues record ended, the Seagull opened up the mic, did a two-minute rap session, and then hit his next record.

"And I said the right thing,
But it must have been the wrong rhyme,
I've been at the right place,
But it must have been the wrong time."
(Ibid.)

Les Carter, Susan Carter, and Steve Segal.

Pasadena
Late March 1970

"We are all outlaws
In the eyes of America."

"We Can Be Together," Jefferson Airplane
(Paul Kantner, Icebag Corp.)

The National Science Network, the new owners of KPPC and KMPX, had sent their man out to the West Coast to take over their property. His name was Stan Gurrel. He was in his forties, bald, glasses, distinguished looking, impeccably dressed. Gurrel was very New York, extremely corporate. He seemed to take a hands-off attitude, yet had not only promised, but had started bringing in new equipment. He was also looking for a new studio to house the station that we all believed would become the next leader in Los Angeles radio.

"...All your private property,
Is target for your enemy...
Up against the wall, mother fucker."
(Ibid.)

Steve Segal immediately went to work behind the scenes by introducing Stan Gurrel to Les and Susan Carter who easily charmed the East Coast exec, but Gurrel was wary of putting too much power in the hands of the hip broadcaster.

After leaving KPPC in the spring of 1968, Ralph Hull had gone on to become Sales Manager at another L.A. radio station. That made him General Manager material. When Stan Gurrel named him the new head of KPPC, Steve Segal was convinced it was the stroke of good luck we had been waiting for. Steve and I welcomed Ralph Hull into the station and immediately began to explain to him the need for a high powered Program Director that could pull a disc jockey staff together, tune up the sound, and make a run for the top. There was only one guy in town who had the musical knowledge, the stroke with the record companies, the reputation, and the personality to make it all hang together. Ralph's job could get to be real easy. Make the right choice and he would be a hero. We didn't have to lobby hard. In less than a week, Les Carter was the new Program Director at KPPC-FM. Steve, Les, and I had stolen ourselves a radio station. Fate was playing to our hand, and we were holding all the aces.

The pace began to quicken. Chester Coleman found a building at 99 South Chester in Pasadena. It would be our new location and Chester's only legacy. Ralph Hull fired him the next day. We'd finally get out of the underground basement and into the light of day. For the Pasadena Presbyterian Church fathers, it was long overdue. Matt Rubin, the hip young engineer from San Francisco, went to work equipping the new studio with the latest state-of-the-art equipment. Three fast-cueing turntables with Stanton cartridges were just the beginning. Everything the disc jockeys had ever wanted was just a request away.

Les Carter invited Ron "Inor" Middag from KRPI the Power House FM Rocker down in San Diego to dinner at the Carters' home above Laurel Canyon. Inor knew the music. He was also a fanatic about equipment maintenance. He was the only FM Rock Jock around with a first-class FCC license. When the evening ended, Inor was the new Music Director and the 9:00 a.m. to noon disc jockey. Les wanted the late afternoon drive for himself. The only problem was Bill Slater had been in the slot for several months. Les offered Bill late night, but he refused and resigned. On his final shift, Bill Slater played a set of songs that glorified the environment and trees in particular. Susan Carter's comments were that Bill Slater made it sound like his replacement, Les, had to be some guy who hated trees.

> *"Redwoods talk to me,*
> *Say it plain*
> *The human name,*
> *Doesn't mean shit to a tree."*

"Eskimo Blue Day," Jefferson Airplane
(Grace Slick and Paul Kantner, Icebag Corp.)

Don Hall moved to late night, Zack Zenor took weekend relief and became our production man. Les Carter was shaping up a team that could go all the way. This was an all-star staff and I had made the cut. I stayed in my favorite slot, early afternoon. I was comfortable there. Every day I put the new Airplane album, *Volunteers of America*, on the turntable and let Gracie Slick sing out to the city "Up Against the Wall Mother-Fuckers."

> *"Look what's happening out in the streets,*
> *Got a revolution, Got to Revolution."*

"Volunteers," Jefferson Airplane
(Marty Balin and Paul Kantner, Icebag Corp.)

Susan, Les, and Steve entertain a guest in the KPPC studio.

KPPC FM
99 S. Chester
Pasadena
April 22, 1970

"I'd rather be a forest than a street...
I'd rather feel the earth beneath my feet."

"El Condor Pasa," Simon and Garfunkel
(Paul Simon, Jorge Milchberg, Daniel Robles, Paul Simon Music)

"The clear sweet sound of Art Garfunkel and Paul Simon," I said, "George Milchberg did the arrangement of an eighteenth century Peruvian Folk Melody. Instrumental track by Los Incas, English lyrics by Paul Simon. Also, on this LP are a couple of songs that we are going to be hearing a lot. One of them is 'Cecilia You're Breaking My Heart,' a song titled 'Boxer,' and a remake of the Everly Brothers' 'Bye, Bye Love,' and of course the title song, 'Bridge Over Troubled Water.' It's killer.

Hello Angelenos, welcome to Earth Day, it's been a long time coming, but today we celebrate, as we look to the future, when we can get off the concrete and back into the woods. On the concert scene Bill Graham presents Quick Silver Messenger Service and Ten Years After out at Olympic Auditorium, you know where it's at, the interchange of the Harbor and Santa Monica Freeways. Get your tickets at all Wallich Stores, Mutual Agencies, *Free Press* Book Stores, and of course at the Olympic Auditorium. Coming up will be John Mayall, Albert King, and Cold Blood, a Shady Production coming your way here in L.A. The movie *Woodstock* is out, look for the soundtrack. We'll be hearing some more of the new McCartney LP, some people are saying it's under-produced. More music from Mott the Hoople coming along. And later on this evening we will have a report on what's happening up in Berkley with the blazing barricades and that campaign against the R.O.T.C. I don't know if you have seen The *Free Press* article. The cartoon by Neon Park shows a Statue of Liberty with a gas mask. Earth Day is going to take care of that. All inside your radio it's KPPC-FM Pasadena."

The environmental movement now had power. The months of rapping on the radio was bringing results. We had stroke nationwide. Ed Muskie of Maine sponsored the Clean Air Act of 1970. On the last day of the year Richard Nixon signed the bill, not because he, or the business community he represented, believed in it, but Nixon wanted to keep Muskie from being the environmental candidate in the coming election.

Laquidara said, "All those bastards will do nothing for the environment, they just wanted to dull us into thinking they would."

With Bill Slater gone, Jack Ellis became more disgruntled with life in Los Angeles. The smog really bothered him. He and I often talked about how much better the air was in Louisiana or San Francisco. Jack just couldn't wait to get back to the Bay. Some of his friends from up north sent Jack a large plastic bag of high-grade cocaine which he carried around in a leather pouch strapped to his belt. Jack celebrated his last week in Los Angeles by constantly giving away toots to everyone he met.

As soon as Jack Ellis gave notice, Les Carter went looking for a new morning man. There were several Top 40 disc jockeys who were well known in the city with great personality and ratings to prove their audience appeal. Some of them would have made the switch to the new Progressive Rock format at KPPC, but that wasn't what Les Carter had in mind.

Jeff Gonzer had been at KYMS in Santa Anna for eight months. The conservatism of Orange County was beginning to eat at him. These were the people who named their airport after John Wayne. But the revolution was spreading nationwide like wildfire and even the reactionaries in Orange County had to be careful where they tuned their FM radio. They could accidentally lock into KYMS and have Jeff Gonzer spewing that left-wing commie crap music into the innocent ears of their children.

When Ted Alvy arrived at KYMS, Jeff welcomed him like a long-lost brother. Here at last was someone who had been living where Jeff longed to be, the hour's drive north in Hollywood. But it was also depressing for him. Would Jeff, and now Ted, be eternally banned to Orange County? Would Jeff ever get back to Hollywood and Laurel Canyon?

"Don't worry," Ted consoled him. "There are people in Los Angeles who still remember us."

"Well, I wish they'd call sometimes," Jeff could only hope, and keep cueing up the rock albums at KYMS.

One evening Jeff exited the studio to visit a young female acquaintance at her apartment. After some wine and smoke, the girl began taking off her clothes. Jeff wasn't sure what that meant. Perhaps she wanted to get it on, perhaps not. Maybe she just wanted to walk around naked. Who knew? Even the Orange County Board of Supervisors couldn't control this kind of behavior. When the phone rang, the nude body answered and then looked at Jeff.

"It's for you," she said, handing Jeff the phone and taking the joint from his fingers.

"Hello, Jeff," the voice in the phone said. "This is Les Carter."

"Les," Jeff asked, surprised, "how did you find me here?"

"When you're putting together the number one Rocker in Los Angeles," Les replied. "You'll do anything to find the best people. I'm back at KPPC as Program Director, I want you to be our morning man."

> *"Think it's time for a change,*
> *...In that case I'll go underground.*
> *Oh Domino, roll me over Romeo,*
> *On the radio, on the radio."*

"Domino," Van Morrison
(Van Morrison, Caledonia Production Inc.)

"You can't be twenty on Sugar Mountain,
Though you think that,
You leaving there too soon."

"Sugar Mountain," Neil Young
(Neil Young, Broken Arrow Music, Cotillion Music, Inc.)

He hadn't yet reached his mid-twenties. He was a small kid with blonde hair, slightly longer than a page-boy cut. His real name was Joe Rodgers, but to everyone in Boston he was "Mississippi Harold Wilson," using the British Prime Minister as part of his radio name. Mississippi had been a big contributor to the growth of WBCN along with Charles Laquidara, Steve Segal, and Sam Kopper. When "The Seagull" came back to California he never forgot Mississippi.

KPPC's new disc jockey line-up was beginning to catch the ear of the city. Jeff Gonzer's exciting youthful sound was on from six to nine a.m., followed by the steady folk rock mix that was "Inor's" trademark. My own noon to 4:00 p.m. shift, now two years old, made me a steady veteran in the fast changing radio wars. My shift segued into Les Carter 4:00 to 8:00 p.m. and Steve Segal 8:00 p.m. to midnight. Steve and Les were soon to be the two hottest radio personalities in Los Angeles. It didn't take Steve long to convince Les they were working too hard and would benefit from three-hour shifts. Les liked that idea, but gave me the three-hour shift Noon to 3:00 p.m. instead. He then took 3:00 p.m. to 6:00 p.m. for himself and Susan and put Steve in the 6:00 to 10:00 p.m. nighttime power shift. Then he told Steve to make the call to Boston.

If Steve hadn't pushed him real hard, Mississippi probably would have never left New England to come to the West Coast. But Steve kept up the recruitment and eventually Mississippi was on the air late night 10:00 p.m. to 2:00 a.m., a very important shift in a town that cranked up the nightlife around nine.

The first evening he went on the air at KPPC, he dropped Harold Wilson and renamed himself "Mississippi Brian Wilson," in deference to the leader of the California-grown Beach Boys. He was fascinated with L.A., playing the intro to the old Dragnet TV show when Jack Webb's voice intoned "This is the city, Los Angeles, California." From there he segued into a '50s Little Richard, and his show was off and running. I tuned him in again around midnight, and was immediately impressed with his choice of music and low-key laid-back delivery. He was perfect. In his rap session I began to hear his sound effects. Everything he said was orchestrated, punctuated, exclamated by various sounds. I thought I detected the tapping of pencils, the rustle of paper, and striking the microphone, along with other varied noises I couldn't pinpoint. He was another whole piece of entertainment when he opened the mic. Other radio personalities would copy his style, and in the future, even the far-right conservative Rush Limbaugh would rip off elements of this technique. But Mississippi was the first disc jockey to do it this way, no one did it better. "Mississippi Brian Wilson" was a master of radio sound.

It wasn't long before Mississippi hooked up with Diedre O'Donahue. The hip, hot redhead was a great contrast to his young school-boy style. Most FM radio shows were the product of the disc jockey and his "old lady" who pulled and filed records for him, thus developing a musical knowledge of where to find a particular song. Which shelf in the record library, which album, and which side. Sometimes you had a brainstorm, brought on by a particular note or lyric. With your mate's help, it was possible to get a song on the air, with less than fifteen seconds to go. The girls often suggested songs for airplay and most knew the board well enough to handle a shift. Years later, Diedre O'Donahue became a radio star on her own, doing a 10:00 a.m. to noon show on KLSX called "Breakfast with the Beatles," listened to by all the old aging L.A. hippies.

"Ain't it funny how you feel,
When you're finding out it's real."
(Ibid.)

1970

♦ Neil Young wrote "Sugar Mountain" on his nineteenth birthday just after leaving Buffalo Springfield. When Joni Mitchell heard "Sugar Mountain" she wrote "Circle Game."

Dierdre O'Donahue and "Mississippi" Brian Wilson.

...SOUNDS LIKE A MIRACLE... BUT IT ISN'T !!

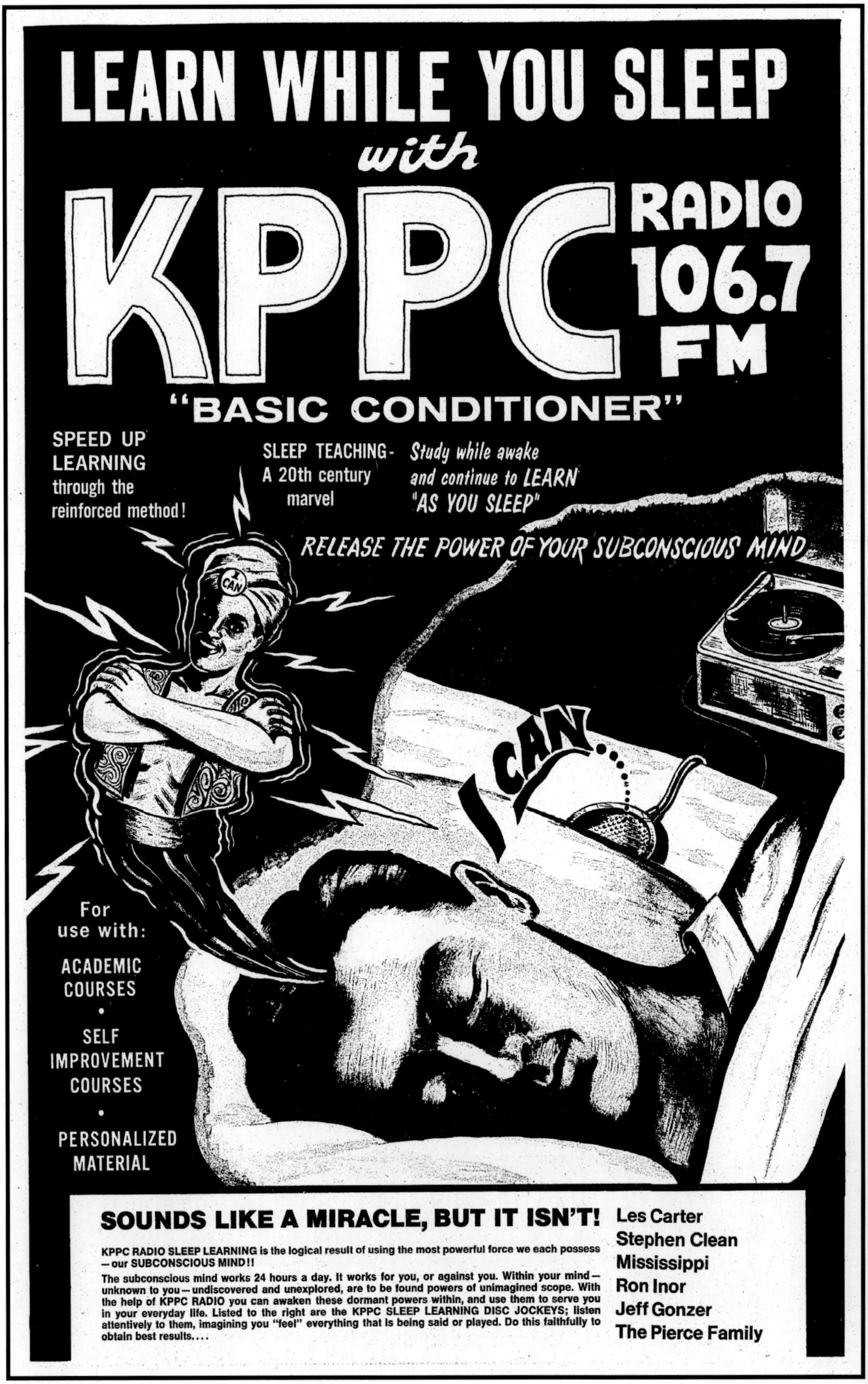
LEARN WHILE YOU SLEEP
with
KPPC
RADIO
106.7
FM
"BASIC CONDITIONER"
SPEED UP LEARNING through the reinforced method!
SLEEP TEACHING - A 20th century marvel
Study while awake and continue to LEARN "AS YOU SLEEP"
RELEASE THE POWER OF YOUR SUBCONSCIOUS MIND
I CAN
I CAN....
For use with:
ACADEMIC COURSES
•
SELF IMPROVEMENT COURSES
•
PERSONALIZED MATERIAL
SOUNDS LIKE A MIRACLE, BUT IT ISN'T!
KPPC RADIO SLEEP LEARNING is the logical result of using the most powerful force we each possess —our SUBCONSCIOUS MIND!!
The subconscious mind works 24 hours a day. It works for you, or against you. Within your mind—unknown to you—undiscovered and unexplored, are to be found powers of unimagined scope. With the help of KPPC RADIO you can awaken these dormant powers within, and use them to serve you in your everyday life. Listed to the right are the KPPC SLEEP LEARNING DISC JOCKEYS; listen attentively to them, imagining you "feel" everything that is being said or played. Do this faithfully to obtain best results....
Les Carter
Stephen Clean
Mississippi
Ron Inor
Jeff Gonzer
The Pierce Family

MORE DUCK RUSH FROM KPPC 106.7 FM · ALL DAY CHRISTMAS EVE AND ALL DAY CHRISTMAS DAY
48 HOURS WITH NO COMMERCIALS AND ALL REQUESTS · DIAL A DEE JAY · REQUEST LINE 681-4501

MERRY CHRISTMAS FROM LES CARTER · STEVEN CLEAN · MISSISSIPPI · INOR · JEFF GONZER · THE PEIRCE FAMILY
JOHNNY AND SHUGGIE OTIS · TED ALVY · ZACH ZENOR · HARRY SHEARER · ELLIOT MINTZ · MISS OUTRAGEOUS NEVADA
RICK STAEHLING AND NEON PARK

¿HEY ELLIOT-
YOU WANA TED?
KPPC 106.7 FM
TED ALVY 9AM to 1PM
(ALMOST EVERYDAY)
ELLIOT MINTZ SUNDAYS
6PM to 9PM (NEW TIME)

AN ALBUM BY THE PEOPLE WHO BROUGHT YOU THE RADIO SHOW:
THE CREDIBILITY GAP PRESENTS
"WOODSCHTICK AND MORE"

Capitol.

MORE CREDIBILITY GAP WEEKDAYS AT ONE, SIX, AND ELEVEN PM ON KPPC 106.7 FM

SOUNDS LIKE A MIRACLE....BUT IT ISN'T!!
KPPC 106.7 FM
"THE RADIO STATION THAT PLAYS SWELL RECORDS
AND LAFFS ALMOST CONSTANTLY."

JEFF GONZER-DON HALL-TED ALVY-THE CREDIBILITY GAP-LES CARTER-THE PIERCE FAMILY-MISSISSIPPI FATS
TED LONGMIRE-A.J. THE D.J.-MISS OUTRAGEOUS NEVADA-"MR. GULLIBLE"-THE OBSCENE STEVEN CLEAN
JOHNNY OTIS-DR. DIMENTO-NEON PARK-ZACH ZENOR-SHUGGIE OTIS-JEFF BARRON-THE PERSUASIONS
HARRY "DESTINATION MUSIC" SHEARER-SUSAN CARTER 'N' PENNY NICHOLS-WALLY COYLE
LITTLE JULIAN HERRERA — **PLUS** — THE HOLY DELIVERANCE PENTECOSTAL CHURCH
(THE OLDEST CONTINUING RADIO PROGRAM. 11-12 AM 11-12AM ON SUNDAYS ONLY)

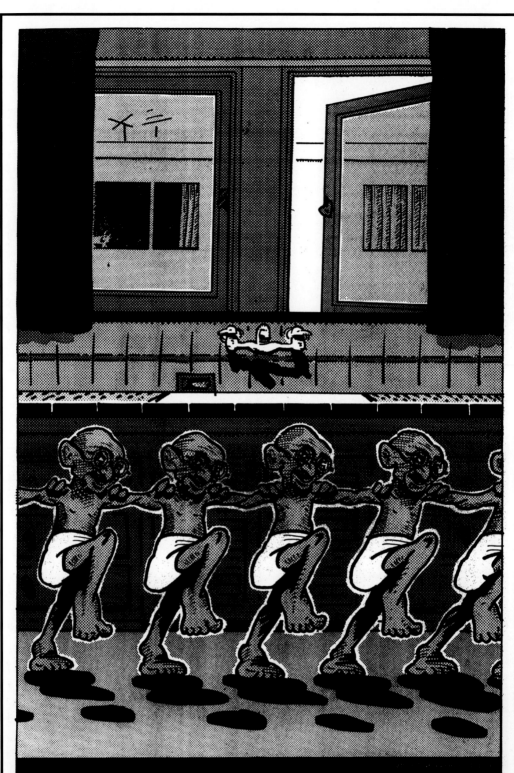

STRONGER THAN WATERBEDS!

THE CREDIBILITY GAP
DAILY AT 1,6,11 P.M.
KPPC/ 106.7 FM

HEY KIDS   A WEDDING IS COMING TO YOU FROM THE PLUME OF
NEON PARK !!! KEEP LISTENING FOR DA DEE TAILS

KCET-TV AND THE
KPPC DISC JOCKEYS
PRESENT
CAT STEVENS
IN STEREO SIMULCAST

8:30 PM - JUNE 8th & 12th
CHANNEL 28 KCET-TV
AND KPPC 106.7 FM

© 1971 NEON PARK

**COMING SOON - ONLY SEVEN MILES MORE - ON THE LEFT
RIDE DUTCH FREIGHT - MERMAID AND NOD - A SPECIAL OFFER
FROM THE STUDIO OF NEON PARK**

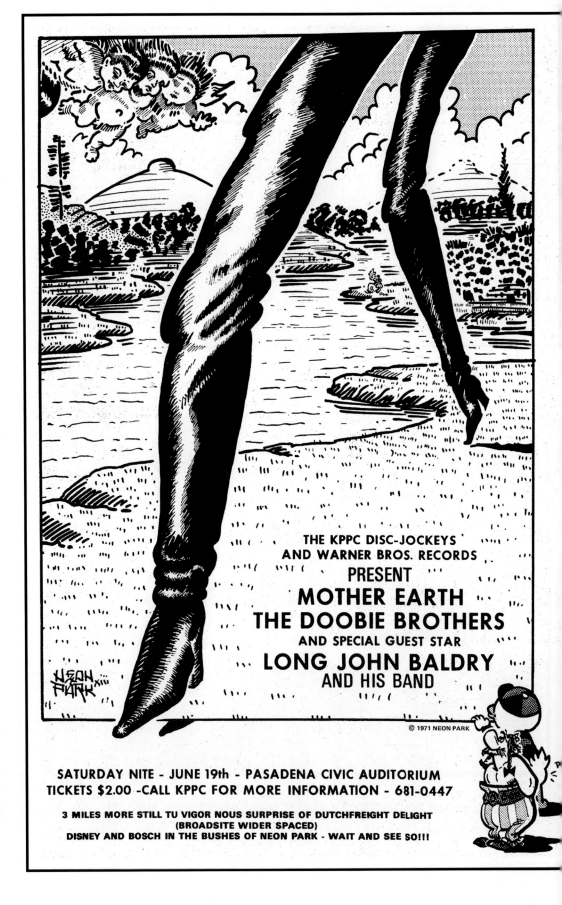

FRANK ZAPPA
AND THE MOTHERS OF INVENTION

PAULEY PAVILION, UCLA

SATURDAY, AUGUST 7 - 8:30 PM

TICKETS: $5, $4, $3 - *RESERVE YOUR SEATS NOW* AT THE UCLA CONCERT TICKET OFFICE, 10851 LE CONTE, WESTWOOD; MUTUAL AGENCIES; WALLICHS MUSIC CITY & TICKETRON. FOR INFORMATION PHONE 825-2953.

Presented by UCLA COMMITTEE on FINE ARTS and the MERLIN CO.

AVAILABLE SOON ON BIZARRE/REPRISE *(MS 2042):

THE MOTHERS LIVE AT THE FILLMORE EAST, JUNE 1971

*"There's a woman that you ought to know,
And she's coming...
Singing rock and roll..."*

"Rock and Roll Woman," Buffalo Springfield
(Stephen A. Stills, Cotillion Music, Inc., Richie Furay Music, Springalo
Toones, Ten-Ease Music)

To say Susan Carter's voice was drop-dead sexy would be an understatement. She was a good enough singer to have a record company back her album, although it was not a commercial success. The framed photograph on the album cover was a nude girl reclining. The body wasn't Susan's but everyone thought it was, which only added to the allure. With long brown hair and killer eyes, she could intrigue any guy. But in a sex-charged atmosphere, she could quickly become an ice queen. When an over zealous record promoter at the radio station asked her the come on of the decade, "What's your sign?" Susan Carter replied, "clitoris," leaving him open-mouthed and shut-down.

Les met Susan when she guested on his jazz radio show to promote her album. By the time we met them, they definitely shared a similar off-beat sense of humor. Knowing there was a popular San Francisco underground disc jockey using the radio name "Reno Nevada," Susan went on the air as "Outrageous Nevada." The great voice, the attitude, and the knowledge of music and musicians, along with the new name, made her another star among a rapidly growing menagerie of KPPC radio characters.

The late '60s and early '70s were sunny optimism and sullen irony. Kate knew how to express both. As soon as she realized PSAs could be something other than announcements for the Cancer Society and the March of Dimes, Kate began to heavily promote Zero Population Growth and Planned Parenthood, which were her favorite causes. All manner of social issues were given space in the Public Service Fact Sheets that she created and the deejays used to weave in and out of their between-record rap. The conscience of the community was being gently prodded along to pay attention to all the issues that needed help. It was a short step for the disc jockeys to speak out with apparent authority on everything from politics to philosophy.

When the Rolling Stones promotion man came by the station, Kate demanded that the best coke available to the Stones, should also be sent over in large quantities to the KPPC deejays.

Kate got into ad sales because she didn't like the quality of some of the commercials on the air.

"What's this crap?" she demanded of Les, when she heard an ad for Gulf Oil. The ad was telling Los Angeles that Gulf Oil was doing a lot for the environment and people of Louisiana.

"If you don't like Gulf Oil, go sell something else," Les challenged her. Kate called Gulf Oil and told them their commercial was a lie.

"We stand by our advertisement," the First Vice President asserted, "but in the interest of good will and public relations with your radio station, I'd like to send you a gift certificate for one-hundred dollars of free gasoline for your vehicle."

"You can take your ad dollars and your gift certificate," Kate told the First Vice President, "and shove 'em up your ass."

The next day she started calling agencies and advertisers in Los Angeles and around the country telling them what a great advertising opportunity they could have on the soon–to-be number one radio station in Los Angeles.

"Could it be, she don't have to try."
(Ibid.)

Susan Carter,
aka "Outrageous Nevada."

Kate

Los Angeles
Early June 1970

It was the first simulcast ever produced. Radio and television married together for a one-hour special, *An Evening with Cat Stevens.* The superstar was in L.A. to record for A&M Records. Tonight, the music fans could see him live on KCET-TV and simultaneously hear Cat Stevens in the superior sound of stereo FM on their friendly local pioneer Free Form Radio, KPPC.

The whole show was being directed by Taylor Hackford, who would later direct *An Officer and a Gentleman, Against All Odds*, and *Ray.* Tonight's emcee was Jeff Gonzer.

The disc jockeys were all gathered in the television studio, along with an audience of insiders, to witness the premiere event, as Cat Stevens ran through his repertoire of familiar hits including "Hard Headed Woman," "Wild World," "Miles from Nowhere," and "Longer Boats."

Inside the studio we sensed that we were making history, but for those in front of their television sets with FM radios tuned to 106.7, it was just another great musical high.

For John-David and 'Chelle it was one more chapter in a fairytale existence. They roamed the TV studio at will, savvy enough to stay out of the way, but with kid curiosity, stopping to ask questions about how some piece of equipment worked and what exactly was that technicians' job. They always got an answer. John-David was a total extrovert with macho-bravado to match the young deejays that he emulated. 'Chelle was much quieter, listening intently, but followed her older brother's lead and was ready to go on his cue. At the radio station, she often amused herself reading, painting, or filing records for the disc jockeys. John-David liked playing one-on-one basketball with Steven Segal under the hoop they had set up in the vacant lot with the avocado tree next door to the studio.

John-David had become adept at chess. When Charlotte Stewart brought Academy Award winner Jon Voight over to our garage apartment late one evening, Kate and I were finding it hard to be natural in the presence of such an actor's idol. 'Chelle crawled into Jon's lap, John-David challenged him to a game of chess and check-mated him in a few minutes.

Our garage apartment and the radio station were the two main centers of learning for John-David and 'Chelle. The third was the highly experimental Montessori school where they continued to grow at their own pace, 'Chelle in a wide range of subjects, John-David in social skills. Amidst all this activity, Kate was still able to take them out to the Griffith Park merry-go-round to ride the beautiful hand carved wooden horses. Mother and children were a striking trio and the old merry-go-round keeper let them ride for hours without payment. It was the same story at Kabakian's Bakery where the old Jew always gave them his bread sticks for free.

"Well you roll on roads,
Over fresh green grass,
For your lorry loads,
Pumping Petrol gas."
(Ibid.)

I was experiencing a mild crisis of confidence. Surrounded by disc jockeys with overwhelming talent, I began to question if I could keep pace. In my own mind I began to develop a fall-back position. I would jump into sales full time. Maybe do back-up air shifts on weekends. Lower the pressure to perform at radio-star levels everyday.

The station needed talented sales people, sympathetic to the disc jockey's cause. Perhaps I would be more valuable that way. The sales manager slot was still wide open. I outlined my plan to Les Carter in a heart-to-heart smoke-filled session. "Besides, Les, I am concerned about having the kids in the studio," I was concluding, "I don't want to keep them out, but they just can't stay quiet when the mic is open."

Les took his characteristic puffs on his pipe before answering. "I know what you're taking about," he said, "I've been listening to your show, and I came up with an idea. First of all forget about deejaying just on weekends; we need you right where you are. You've been in that early afternoon slot for a long time now, and you mix them up as well as anyone. If you want to help Kate with sales, go ahead, but get her to come in and do some live PSAs for you. Maybe give out some of those Cajun Cooking Recipes she's always fixing up. As for the kids, quit worrying about them. In fact, put them on the air, they sound great. From now on, we'll bill you guys as the Pierce Family. You'll be another first for KPPC."

Les had just solved all my problems, fulfilled some dreams I didn't know I had, and laid out a new challenge. I now had security in an ego-draining environment, plus an opportunity to rack-up the bucks in the sales department. Best of all my family was working with me, and my children were playing on the radio. Les Carter was one hell of a brilliant program director. I tried not to act too grateful.

"I know we've come a long way,
We're changing day to day..."
(Ibid.)

The Pierce family (with cheesy smiles), 1970.

Laurel Canyon
Los Angeles
Late June 1970

*"About the good and the bad and the poor,
...So I'm keeping on top,
Of every fat cat who walks in my door."*

"Space Cowboy," Steve Miller Band
(Steve Miller and Ben Sidran, Sailor Music)

It was the Pierce family's night to be up at the Carter's home for dinner. Over wine and grass, Les was telling us how it happened. He and Ralph Hull had flown up to San Francisco to meet with Stan Gurrel and the KMPX management team. During an expensive dinner, at one of San Francisco's finest old hotels, they discussed the future of the two hot West Coast broadcast properties. When dessert arrived Ralph Hull jokingly made a crude remark about the texture of the chocolate mousse. Les's quick glance at Stan caught the almost imperceptible wince. A few days later, Ralph got the ax. He was stunned, dumbfounded, and out as General Manager of KPPC. Les waited a respectable few days before applying for the job. But Stan said it wasn't in the cards. In the meantime, we could feel the power gravitating to Les Carter. As the head of programming, he began running the station, making day-to-day administrative decisions. Steve Segal and I shared in the additional stroke.

Stan Gurrel's firing of Ralph Hull was indicative of his management style. We should not be surprised if he wanted to fire any or all of us on a whim. None of this seemed to matter to Kate, who never danced around Stan's feelings. She referred to him familiarly as Uncle Dad, and they often sat down and talked about recipes together.

Kate was on a tear in the Sales Department, running her rap past local sponsors and agency buyers, painting the picture of opportunity—a chance for them to reach the hard to impress new counter-culture community, who still bought, but didn't want to be sold. Simply give the copy to the KPPC deejays and let them ad lib it live in sincere hip jargon, or put the latest hit rock songs under the copy. The disc jockeys could move product. On the sales staff was a young, pseudo-hip, overly laid-back salesman named Spencer St. Clair who was having trouble understanding the fast moving out-landish cartoon world that the disc jockeys were creating on the radio. I could identify with Spencer. I was having trouble keeping up myself. But unlike other sales people who resisted Les's taking control, Spencer was totally loyal. Even though he was something of a slacker, we made Spencer the Sales Manager. We figured the Sales Manager had to be in tune with the Program Director and Music Director as much as the disc jockeys. Through Spencer and Kate, the disc jockeys now controlled the Sales Department, too. Les, as an after-thought, told Stan Gurrel about the new Sales Manager appointment some weeks later.

Les Carter in a momentous positioning stroke, asked his friends, the Persuasions, a soul group who were remaking '50s hits a cappella style, to cut a KPPC ID. The result was a funky, happy, positive, soulful sing-out of a slightly extended legal ID "KPPC-FM...The Sound of Stereo...Pasadena...Ster-ee-oo." No music, no stingers, no reverb and echo. Nothing boss. Just the Persuasions out there harmonizing. A confident upbeat statement of who we were. No matter how crazy, outrageous, or radical the disc jockeys and the music would get, every half hour the Persuasions sang out, reminding everyone this was, after all, just a show on the hell-raising end of the FM band.

Under news reports of U.S. bombing air raids over North Vietnam, you would sometimes hear Eric Burdon's plaintive "Sky Pilot" lamenting organized religion's support of Corporate America's war. General Waste-moreland was loose in South East Asia. The free fire zone stretched from the Mekong Delta to the American airwaves. Rock 'n roll was subversive, always was, and always will be. So was chaos, bedlam, and anarchy by America's elected officials.

"The boys in the military shirts..."
(Ibid.)

The fall of Saigon was still five years away, but the war was already lost. No matter what side you were on, sooner or later we'd all have to share the guilt. Only weeks after it had happened, Neil Young's recording of "Four Dead in Ohio" was on the radio, stating the fact that Nixon and his soldiers had finally got down to it, shooting our young at Kent State. The Temptations, one of the great rhythm and blues and soul groups of the past decade went to number three with the song titled "Ball of Confusion, (That's what the World Is Today)."

Even though the calendar said summer of 1970, we were still trying to wrap up the chaos of the '60s. Locally, it was the end of Pacific Ocean Park in Santa Monica when the old pier burned down. Leon Russell made his first appearance and the Who came to California for a performance at Anaheim Stadium. In London the Beatles got together at the old Abbey Road Studios and recorded their twentieth and final number-one song calling it "The Long and Winding Road." It was also the summer of Mungo Jerry's number one hit "In the Summertime." John-David and 'Chelle got right into the spirit, their little kid voices singing Mungo's "Somebody Dropped the Bomb" live on Steve Segal's show.

With the Steve Miller Band playing behind him, I heard the Seagull open the mic and speak, "We are not a bunch of crazy students in some Latin American country, we are the youth of the United States of America. We will set the standard of protest for the whole world for the rest of this century. I bet you weren't ready for that."

"All you backroom schemers,
Power trip dreamers...
you got some heavy dues to pay."
(Ibid.)

KPPC FM
99 S. Chester
Pasadena
July 1970

Nothing was sacred to the KPPC disc jockeys. Any and all of the American lifestyle was fair game. On close examination, there was a lot to criticize. Kate was going after the food industry. Almost every week she dug up new information, exposing the callousness of the men who reaped the profits. They fed their own greed by serving up fat to the populace, seasoned with near lethal doses of sugar and salt, in a low level of nutrition common to most processed foods. At this time, few people had thought about food value. But the thousands out in KPPC Radio Land listened up and believed. No one was surprised to learn that the moral decay of Corporate America spilled over into the food we ate. The Pierces became well known for hammering the food giants including Del Monte and Campbell's.

When King Crimson's new album, *In the Wake of Poseidon*, was released, Steve Segal's ear for the absurd locked onto "Cat Food." Before he put it on the air for the first time, he called us at home to make sure we were listening. We knew then we weren't alone on the food issue. Now we had a song to take our message to the masses. "Cat Food" became a hit on KPPC and King Crimson was a break-out group in the L.A. market.

During one of my air shifts, John-David and Steve came in from a game of one-on-one. John-David squiggled up onto my knee, while Steve shuffled through the albums in his keyed-up nervous, manner. The log called for a live promo for El Monte Legion Stadium, a famous concert site in the city of El Monte, not far from Pasadena in the San Gabriel Valley.

"Johnnie Otis will be playing the "Hand Jive" this Saturday night at El Monte Legion Stadium. You know about El Monte don't you, John-David?" I said into the microphone, bouncing the long haired seven year old on my knee.

"Sure I do," John-David said, speaking with assurance to the city, as Steve and I looked at each other, choking back our laughter with disbelief, "they're the people who can the bad food."

North Hollywood
Early August 1970

"If I can just get off this L.A. freeway,
Without getting killed or caught
Down the road in a cloud of smoke
For some land that I ain't bought."

"LA Freeway," Jerry Jeff Walker
(Guy Charles Clark, World Song Publishing)

Around 6:00 a.m. every weekday morning, I would begin to feel the vibration. Since our waterbed was lying on the concrete slab, only a half block off Victory Boulevard, we were wired to the rumble of the cars that were heading to the clover leaf, to climb the on-ramp of the Hollywood Freeway, heading south past Universal Studio through Cahuenga Pass and into the L.A. Basin. The intensity of the vibration would continue to increase and peak three hours later, at which time we were usually up and about. This morning the telephone jangled me out of the low rumble at eight o'clock.

"I found your place, man." It was Casey on the other end of the line. It was 10:00 a.m. in Louisiana and he couldn't wait any longer to call.

"What place?" I asked, still waking up.

"Your home site," he replied.

"Say goodbye to the landlord for me,
Sons-a-Bitches always bored me."
(Ibid.)

Maybe someday we would like to have a place in Louisiana. Even if we were still in L.A., it would give us something to look forward to later in life. A sense of security that we wouldn't be trapped in the city, that the kids could maybe grow-up where the air was fresh, away from the brown L.A. haze, even if we only went there to visit and camp out.

It wasn't just our dream. Just about everyone we knew in the City of Angels had the same idea. Just a little piece of land, you know, to call your own. A bit of earth somewhere with trees, so that when you cashed in your chips you would have some place to go, or if the fighting in the streets got too heavy, and this town started burning, you could always get out. If you had that farm tucked away, you would feel a lot better about the whole city thing.

"Throw out them old L.A. papers,
...Adios to all this concrete,
Gonna get me some dirt road back street."
(Ibid.)

After I told him what we wanted, Casey worked pretty quickly and followed through on a lucky chain of events. He heard there were a bunch of local hippie kids smoking dope and getting laid at the old pumping plant site, three miles south of Abbeville. Curious, he pulled in one day, and failed to find any naked stoned kids, but did see a For Sale sign with a phone number. Within weeks he had bought the sixteen-acre tract for himself and Nellie, with the idea to build a retirement home for them.

Casey had his dream, too. When the sale was completed, the former owners, Acadia Vermilion Rice Irrigation Company, informed Casey they had another piece of property for sale.

This too was a former pumping station, no longer used to lift water from the Vermilion Bayou into the network of irrigation canals that fed the rice farms of northern Vermilion Parish. Naturally, it was located at the highest point in the area, so that once the water was lifted it would flow by gravity down to the farms throughout the area. Being that high, this property was also a former Indian campground.

"Are there any trees?" I asked, getting excited.

"Full of oaks and gum, some cypress, too," Nellie was also on the phone describing the land.

"Live oaks?" I wanted to be sure it was perfect.

"Live oaks, white oaks, red oaks, water oaks. It's beautiful," she replied. "If you don't want it, I do," her mouth seemed to be watering.

"How big is it, and how much money?" I asked, afraid it was beyond my budget.

"Twenty-seven and one-half acres, fifty-five thousand dollars," Casey said.

"Fifty-five grand!" I exclaimed, "we barely have four thousand saved up."

"The local bank will probably back you," Nellie offered. "It's two grand an acre. It'll never be this cheap again."

Kate was awake by now. "What's the deal?" she asked. When I repeated the numbers Kate had only one other question, "Is it on the river?"

I nodded yes, and she said, "Buy it."

A few weeks later, we finally broke away from KPPC long enough to visit and camp out on the property. It was a fantastic dream come true. The place was definitely mystic, and perhaps a little sacred. Standing in the woods, I could feel the spirits of the Indians who had surely camped there and painted their faces with the dye from the old walnut trees. The wolves must have howled at the moon when it rose over the Rio de Los Lobos. In the years ahead, when people asked me how I could have been so fortunate to find such a paradise, my answer would always be the same. "I willed it," I would say. It is the only answer that seemed appropriate.

"We got somethin we can believe in
Before you know it's time we're leavin'.

If I can just get off this L.A. freeway
Without getting killed or caught..."
(Ibid.)

"We'll be fighting in the streets,
With our children at our feet,
...They decide and the shotgun
Sings the song."

"Won't Get Fooled Again," The Who
(Pete Townshend, ABKCO Music, Inc., Career BMG Music Publishing,
Suolubaf Music, Towser Tunes, Inc.)

"*Who's Next,*" 'Chelle said, reading the album cover.

"Okay, John-David," I said to the longhaired seven year old sitting in my lap, "you back-announce this one. You got the song title?"

"Sure," he said, with total confidence. He began to sing along with Roger Daltry, "Meet the new boss, same as the old boss."

Kate had already left the studio to set up a sales call for us after the show. I was wrapping up the three-hour shift.

"Come on in here, 'Chelle," I said to the tiny blonde doll standing in between my disc jockey chair and the two turn tables on the right. I put on my headphones. "Mic opened," I said, before sliding the microphone pot up and hearing the final thrust of Pete Townshend's guitar in my headset. Then, I nodded to John-David.

"The Who on KPPC," he said, "We Won't Get Fooled Again."

"And from what album?" I asked.

"*Who's Next?*" 'Chelle chimed in on cue.

"Meet the new boss, same as the old boss," John-David sang behind me, as I went into my disc jockey rap.

"Pierce family, from Pasadena," I said, "for another ten minutes, followed by Les and Susan Carter stepping into your radio till Steve Segal time, tonight at 6:00 p.m." I punched up the commercial in the cartridge when in walked Les and Susan. "How did it go with Stan Gurrel?" I asked.

"Not so hot," Les replied. "I told him I felt that it was time that I stepped into the GM position, that I was uniquely qualified and had the backing of the staff. Well, Stan just looked at me and said he had just hired a GM."

"Wait until you hear this," Susan interjected. "We're so disappointed."

"Who?" I asked.

"A fellow named Doug Cox," Susan said with a sneer.

"I know Doug Cox," I said. "Met him in the record business a few years ago, nice guy as I remember."

"Yeah, too nice," Les was hesitant. "I don't trust him."

"Neither do I," Susan added. "We're so disappointed."

"I know," I said, gathering John-David and 'Chelle into the microphone to sign off. "But Doug Cox may be okay, we could have done worse."

"I'm not so sure," Les Carter said.

*"I'll move myself and my family aside,
...I know that the hypnotized never lie."*
(Ibid.)

"Doug Cox is a snakey-eyed son-of-a-bitch," Steven Segal was say-ing into the telephone. "I told Les we needed to all sit down with Cox, the whole disc jockey staff, and take the offensive. Tell him how we're gonna run it. And, if we don't get what we want, we'll tell Stan Gurrel right now, Cox is unacceptable. So Les is going to set-up a meeting. What do you think?"

"Sure Steve," I replied, "but let's give the guy a chance."

"No compromise," Steve was adamant. "Nobody tells us what to play."

"Hey, I'm with you, we'll just have to make it work."

"The meeting is early next week," Steve said, "at Les's house, make Cox meet us on our turf."

"What time?"

"Twelve noon. Maybe Kate can open your show, you gotta be there. We all gotta be united."

The disc jockeys took the drive up to Laurel Canyon to Les's house. At the appointed time Doug Cox arrived, smiling, friendly, shaking hands all around. Les opened the meeting. The purpose was to set ground rules, to avoid any future misunderstanding with management.

"Great idea," Doug said enthusiastically, "but believe me, guys, we won't have problems, I am here to work with you and for you, to get you everything you need to make this the number-one station in Los Angeles. I'm totally thrilled to be here. You guys are the greatest, I want to be on your side. We're going all the way to the top."

"You're right about that Doug," Steve interrupted. "We're the people who are doing it. We know what we are doing. We can't tolerate any in-terference with the sound we've created."

"No problem," Doug smiled, "I absolutely agree, I'm only here to run the business part of it."

"Commercial policy is already established," Les stated firmly. "Eight spots an hour, no clutter, no exception."

"Fine," Doug agreed.

"That's eight spots, not eight minutes," I clarified, "no playing thirty-second spots sixteen times for a total of eight minutes. It's eight units, thirties or sixties."

"I understand," Doug said, continuing to smile.

"Les negotiates for us," Mississippi said, "we work for him, not for you, not for anyone else."

"This is going to be a totally successful relationship," Doug assured us.

After a few minor issues and small talk, Doug Cox shook hands all around once more and was gone.

We all looked at each other.

"That wasn't so bad," I volunteered, "Doug doesn't act like he's ready to fight for corporate America. We acted more like butts than he did."

"Yeah, but we're honest," Jeff Gonzer said, "that's the difference."

"Doug Cox is a snakey-eyed son-of-bitch," Steve Segal said.

Zack Zenor didn't say anything.

Doug Cox, with Ted Alvy in the background.

"I took myself a blue canoe,
...Dirty was the daybreak,
Sudden was the change."

"Where To Now St. Peter?," Elton John
(Elton John and Bernie Taupin, Dick James Music; Universal Songs of Polygram, International Inc.)

The Pierce family had finished the afternoon shift at KPPC. We were driving into Hollywood to talk advertising with one of our sponsors, when we first heard Elton John on the Les Carter Show. We were blown away. The young piano player was already a hit in England, but still unknown in America. Uni Records who had the U.S. rights, was looking for a rock star to help its floundering label. Elton was their pick. Now it needed a radio station to make sure Elton John got enough airplay to kick off his American Tour. Someone at Uni was hip enough to believe Les Carter was the right Program Director to get the job done. Since the Uni copies would not be released for another two weeks, they drove out to Pasadena with an arm full of copies of the English pressing.

The record company had come to the right town. Les and Susan Carter chewed up the air waves all afternoon with both sides of Elton John's first album.

The next day, Les called the disc jockeys together and gave us the scoop. We had exclusivity for ten days, and would have promotion rights for the first live show at the Troubador. If we did our job, we would also have bragging rights for breaking a new artist.

I had heard all of Les's show the day before, and I knew it was a hell of a deal. There wasn't a bad cut on the album. Over the next few days, we worked Elton John into our daily radio shows. When we learned this chubby English kid, whose real name was Dwight Reggie, had borrowed the back-half of his show biz name and just a taste of his style from British blues piano player, Long John Baldry, a copy of an old Baldry LP miraculously appeared in the studio. Suddenly, KPPC listeners were hearing sets that included back-to-back Long John and Elton John.

By the time Elton came to Los Angeles, we already had an advance copy of his second LP, *Tumbleweed Connection*, not yet released in London. The day Elton John flew into LAX, the City of Angels had a bad fever for his music. He limoed directly out to Pasadena, where hundreds of fans were waiting at KPPC for the pie fight between his band and the disc jockeys, which we staged in the vacant lot next to the studio. Jeff Gonzer did the play- by-play of the pie fight. We broadcast live to the whole city Elton John's first hour in America slinging pies.

"Behind four walls of stone,
The rich man sleeps,
It's time we put the flame torch
To their keep."

"Burn Down The Mission," Elton John
(Elton John and Bernie Taupin, Dick James Music; Universal Songs of
Polygram, International Inc.)

It was another great night at the Troubador, overflowing with record company, radio, and PR people. Kate and I, sharing a front row table with Les and Susan Carter, had a couple of drinks while John-David and 'Chelle polished off orange sorbets. The KPPC disc jockeys had the best seats in the house. By putting Elton in this small intimate club, Uni Records had chosen well. The select crowd would see him at his best and take the message to print and to the air waves. The big halls and stadiums would come later, as the album, and the single "This Is Your Song" moved up on the charts. The big crowds were down the road, so was the big money.

From the opening song, Elton John and his group had won over the crowd. Backed by a lead guitar and drummer Nigel Olson, who would go on to establish himself as a rock star for the Seventies, the three musicians laid out a huge rock 'n roll sound. But it was Elton on piano, playing everything from boogie-woogie to classical licks that led the way instrumentally. Then there was the incredible voice. And the lyrics.

"Burn down the mission...
Watch the black smoke fly to heaven
See the red flames light the sky."
(Ibid.)

All the lyrics were written by Bernie Taupin, the word man counterpart to Elton's melodic composition on piano. They were destined to become one of the most successful song writing teams of the next two decades, like Lennon and McCartney, and Jagger and Richards before them, two guys from the English suburbs, capturing the imagination of the American Youth movement. Echoing the cry of the Black Panthers and the Yippies, burn it down, it's rotten to the core, no part of the establishment worth saving. Not the government, not the churches, nothing. Burn it all down, because sooner or later they're coming to get us, even if we left the city and tried to hide in the mountains of northern California, or the woods of the Deep South. We might as well stay here and fight in the streets and on the radio.

"Deep in the woods the squirrels are out today,
My wife cried when they came to take me away."
(Ibid.)

The crowd was really cranked now. I could see Jeff Gonzer leading a standing screaming ovation. The booze was flowing, the drugs of choice were firing off in our heads. Surely, Elton John had been in front of a frenzied crowd before, but never in America. This was his first time. His maiden voyage to the colonies. His fingers were flying on the keyboard twenty feet away from me. The look on his face was total amazement. Somehow, I don't think he had expected this kind of overwhelming response in L.A. The record company executives were flashing dollar signs in their eyes. I looked across the table at Les Carter puffing slowly on his pipe, a very self-satisfied look on his face. It was no accident that everyone in the Troubador knew all the lyrics to all the songs. The KPPC disc jockeys had burned them in. Les Carter had tested our gas, and it was straight ahead rocket fuel. On the stage, the look on Elton John's face segued from amazement to ecstasy. The chord that his songs had struck, deep down inside of us, would soon sweep the nation. But it was on this night in this small room on Santa Monica Boulevard he had become a star. He knew it. We all watched it happen.

> "I may not be a Christian,
> But I've done all one man can,
> ... So where to now St. Peter,
> Show me which road I'm on."
>
> "Where To Now St. Peter?," Elton John
> (Elton John and Bernie Taupin, Dick James Music; Universal Songs of Polygram, International Inc.)

The Elton John pie fight outside of the KPPC studio, September 1970.

Los Angeles
Late September 1970

"I'm a country station,
...Broadcasting tower,
...And I'm sending you out this signal here,
I hope you can pick it up
Loud and clear."

"You Turn Me On, I'm A Radio," Joni Mitchell
(Joni Mitchell, Crazy Crow Music)

The *Free Press* labeled KPPC the *Mad Magazine* of radio. We were proud of the compliment, and kept working to earn it. The Fire Sign Theater, who was known to millions through their recordings, became our Sunday night 6 to 8 p.m. weekend wind-down, going on live for an intense off-the-wall smorgasbord of sound and humor. They were masters at the use of stereo, bouncing voices and sound effects from corner to corner in living rooms and pads all over the city. Elliot Mintz followed 8:00 p.m. to midnight. His insider interviews with the celebrities from the music and entertainment world gave KPPC another niche with the in-crowd.

Les's direction of the KPPC sound was probably the most laid-back but effective of any Program Director's power. His penchant for jazz was not too big a stretch for me, since I had deejayed under jazz purist Walt DeSilva. Paul Desmond's "Take Five" still worked, as did Vince Guaraldi's "Cast Your Fate To the Wind" and Bobby Scott's "A Taste of Honey." When the South African ex-patriot Hugh Masekela released "Grazing in the Grass," we helped break it into mainstream rock's play list. I had the feeling that music would never be fragmented again. No more folk, rock, jazz, blues, or country and western stations. The lines would be blurred. More crossover hits. More people liking a variety of music. We were paving the way with the Free Form format.

"If there is no good reception for me,
Then tune me out...
Who needs the static...
...From 'Breakfast Barney,'
To the sign off prayer."
(Ibid.)

I'd begun doing research for a possible radio feature and found out that the first disc jockey was Dr. Lee deForest. He had the idea of sending a singer's voice through a pickup device from one point to many receivers. The most descriptive term he could find was the phrase he borrowed from the farmers. He called it broadcasting. After World War I, deForest sold out to Am Tel. David Sarnoff, who founded RCA, had also absorbed Marconi's wireless telegraph and the work of Howard Armstrong. Armstrong had widened the broadcast band and invented FM Radio. By 1939, Sarnoff knew FM would make AM obsolete, so he shelved it and concentrated on the development of television. Armstrong went on to build his own Yankee network, but his FM band remained a step-child. He became depressed that RCA and the FCC had made a failure of his life's work. As a young man, Howard Armstrong loved to climb towers.

In 1954, at age sixty-three he stepped out of a thirteenth-story suite. If he had lived, Howard Armstrong would have had the great joy of hearing the disc jockeys prove him right, as we took that incredible FM radio ride on the Ether Express.

> *"If you're lying on the beach,*
> *With a transistor going,*
> *Call me at the station,*
> *The lines are open."*
> (Ibid.)

"Turn off the television and turn on the radio, the picture's better," Jeff Gonzer's voice floated out of the Volvo speaker while we made our early trek into Pasadena. Jeff had played a Purple Haze tribute to Jimi Hendrix, who OD'd on September 18[th.] Three weeks later, on October 4[th,] Janis Joplin would take the same way out; both were twenty-seven years old. Society was taking a drastic turn with drugs in the years that followed Woodstock. Speed, cocaine, and heroin gradually came to replace or augment marijuana as the drug of choice. Some people were no longer seeking highs of consciousness, delving instead into lower depths. They became twisted from these new paranoid drugs. No one could have imagined the next generations of "legal drugs" would come from the laboratories of the pharmaceutical giants, as the pusher psychiatrist moved into our educational system to destroy lives with Ritalin and Prozac.

Jeff Gonzer and Zackary Zenor had done some fancy editing on Merle Haggard's country and western hit, so the redneck right-winged conservative singer-songwriter now sang out, "We Smoke Marijuana in Muskogee; we take our trips on LSD. We make a party out of loving, like the hippies out in San Francisco do."

Jeff followed up "Muskogee" with Ray Charles singing "Let's Go Get Stoned" and Bob Dylan's "Everybody Must Get Stoned." If "Drinking Rum and Coca-Cola" was one of the themes to World War II soldiers, dope songs would be remembered as the soundtrack for the Vietnam War.

After dropping John-David and 'Chelle at school, we arrived at the station and could immediately feel the creative buzz that was happening on this quiet residential street in rich old Pasadena. Almost like a team of athletes, we were living, playing, and working together, going out to compete for the top of the heap. To be number one and still climbing.

I recorded commercials and auditioned new records. About forty-five minutes early, I went into the studio. Listening to Inor, I methodically thumbed through the library looking for the older classic cuts that would be a big part of the mix. Planning ahead, I set aside several two and three record sets that I could put on any time the creative juices failed to come up with something that would blow the listeners' minds. Finally, it was my turn.

"Hello out there in radio land," I said. "Turn your radio up and listen to the music in the air. Keep those cards and letters coming in and call me on the rap-line, 'cause we got the sound of the city, the sound of the revolution."

"You know I'd go back there tomorrow,
But for the work I've taken on,
Stoking the star maker machinery,
Behind the popular song."

"Free Man in Paris," Joni Mitchell
(Joni Mitchell, Crazy Crow Music)

1970

♦ "Free Man in Paris" was written by Joni Mitchell for David Geffen of
Electra Records after the two of them spent several weeks there.

With the kids in the studio.

Pasadena
October 1970

"I pulled into Nazareth,
Was feeling about half passed dead."

"The Weight," The Band
(J.R. Robertson, Dwarf Music)

Levon Helm, Garth Hudson, Richard Manuel, Rick Danko, and Jamie Robbie Robertson came to Pasadena. The Band had delivered the music scene a wallop, as big as the pink house on Overlook Mountain in West Saugerties, New York, where the five musicians honed their act before releasing their first album. The record was filled with their unique sound and the lyrics of Jamie Robbie Robertson and Bob Dylan. Dylan himself painted the album cover for *Music from Big Pink* before going on to do his own *Self Portrait* and create some really funky country tunes.

The Pierce Family was back stage at the Pasadena Civic Auditorium, along with the other disc jockeys. Les Carter was dressed in a gorilla suit and would carry Susan out on the stage as King Kong and Fay Wray. The show was a total sell out to KPPC fans. Since we were the promoters, the only way you could get a ticket was through the station, another Les Carter coup. The disc jockeys were all here to meet our audience. When it was our turn, John-David ran onto the stage followed by Kate doing a cartwheel, this time wearing panties. I carried 'Chelle hanging on my hip, my left arm around her. We looked out at the sea of cheering smiling faces. This was a happy crowd. Nothing but peace and love. No revolution here tonight. Just mellow folk. The stage seemed huge. We looked up at the beautiful ornate architecture of the old Pasadena landmark.

"Hey everybody," I said into the microphone at center stage, "what's the greatest radio station in America?"

"KPPC," the crowd roared out.

"This here is Sister Kate," I said, introducing her to a fresh round of applause, cheers, and whistles. Kate did a Southern Belle curtsy to more whistles.

"You guys know this kid, this is John-David," I said, as he lifted up his right hand in a peace sign, "and this here is blonde baby 'Chelle," while she giggled into the microphone," and me, I'm Dave Pierce. We're the Pierce Family."

The applauding and cheering crowd went crazy. You could have sworn we were the main act. The adoration was overwhelming.

"When I saw Carmen and the devil,
Walkin' side by side."
(Ibid.)

The paradox of The Band's lyrics echoed the contradictions of the counter culture. On the one hand, it was a big pleasure freak-out; on the other, it was deadly serious. Only days before, the FBI had broken into Jane Fonda's and Donald Sutherland's homes to steal phone books looking for Black Panther connections. A SWAT team had opened fire on a house where the Black Panthers served breakfast. It was supposed to be a center of radical lawbreakers. The cops found no arms, no revolutionar-

295

ies, only some canned food. The follow-up investigation included an FBI visit to the KPPC control room where Kate was questioned. It seemed that running PSAs for the Black Panthers' feeding program had put us under suspicion.

"What the hell's the matter with you people?" I exploded. "We're more American than the FBI, we play music here."

The federal agent only sneered at me and pressed on.

"What were Kate's Black Panther connections?" the government men wanted to know.

"What old hard luck Panther connections?" Kate asked incredulously. "The only black man I know is Shabby, my Dad's cook in Louisiana."

John-David and 'Chelle handled the paranoia well. They figured it was part of growing up. If you hung around a rock FM radio station, the FBI would come to see you. It was a lesson in the workings of the U.S. government.

John-David had a habit of singing Bob Dylan's lyrics.

"Look out kid it's something you did,
God knows when, but you're doing it again."

"Subterranean Homesick Blues," Bob Dylan
(Bob Dylan, Special Rider Music)

He usually had a grin on his face when he sang it. Improvising on the old upright in the garage apartment, John-David composed a short piano piece. I taped it, Steve Segal heard it, and was soon playing the tape on his show.

Steve and his girlfriend Delana were living next door to us in the duplex in North Hollywood. We didn't see much of each other at home during the week. He was usually in Pasadena before my shift ended, then he'd get home late. But on weekends we hung out, all dining together, listening to music, smoking, talking radio. At any time Steve could bounce through the door.

"Let me see," Steven would say aloud in mock wonder, "I'm working, [meaning he was employed, had a job and a pay check] but not today."

He also had the maddening habit of bringing over an album he wanted me to hear and putting it on my stereo. Then he'd crank up the volume to the pain threshold and leave. Steve's taste in music was a lot farther out than mine, but I always gave him a listen. He was finding more than his share of the hits, setting a hot pace. But Steve, like the rest of us, felt his own taste was more right on than anyone else. He began to hint that perhaps Ron "Inor" Middag wasn't playing the right music. Steve said Inor was a little light, a little too folksy. Actually, I kind of liked what Inor was doing, particularly in the late morning slot, but I took the cue from Steve Segal, made sure I rationed the folk, and the protest, and included some jazz in the early afternoon.

"I said, 'wait a minute Chester,
You know I'm a peaceful man.'"

"The Weight," The Band
(J.R. Robertson, Dwarf Music)

Within a few days I got a call from Les Carter.

"Dave, I wanted to tell you, I'm calling a deejay meeting this afternoon," Les said, "I'm going to announce that I fired Ron Middag. Inor is off the air."

I was stunned, "What happened?"

"Several things. Basically, I didn't agree with his music he was playing. And I had some problems with his job as a music director."

"Hate to loose one of our original team," I said, "especially now that we are starting to roll."

"It's a decision I had to make; I think we will be stronger now. I'm going to put Zack Zenor in late morning. He'll flow out of Gonzer and into your show really well."

"Yeah, he and Gonzer used to share an after midnight shift," I reminded him.

"That's a good idea," Les was quick to respond. "They can overlap each other; do a half hour or so together every morning when they change shifts."

"Great," I said, then after a pause, "Steve Segal going to be music director?"

"No," Les said slowly, "Steve is a great disc jockey, a highly creative personality, but the Music Director has to take care of business. *You* have to do it."

"Take a load off Fannie,
And...(and)...(and)...you put the load right on me."
(Ibid.)

Les Carter made some more changes. He brought in Joel Siegal to be our entertainment reporter. Joel was Jeff Gonzer's neighbor, who gave Jeff tapes of Shondoo the Magician to play at 7:30 a.m. every morning. Since I had given Jeff his big break to get into radio, he was eager to pass the favor on to Joel. Jeff introduced Joel to Les and lobbied hard to get him on KPPC. Later, Joel would write for the *L.A. Times*, move to New York City, and begin reporting for the ABC owned-and-operated Channel 7. Joel Siegal would eventually become the film critic for ABC News on *Good Morning America*.

Jeff and I speculated on what exactly had brought Ron Middag down. We finally agreed that Ron had over-played his hand. When the record companies asked for talent to do voice overs for record commercials, Ron always took the job and the hundred dollar bill that went with it. From this point on, that perk would get passed around to everyone on the disc jockey staff. Les's connections with the record companies got tighter. Perhaps Ron had been in the way of that happening. Les wouldn't have that problem with me. The relationship between the disc jockeys and music reps evolved to a new era of mutual respect and good will. There was never any pressure to play a particular song, just a need for information. We played only the records we really liked. We gave the record companies straight info on hit songs, new releases, upcoming artists, and how much airplay they were getting. They paid the station back with ad dollars to promote the latest winners paying us with tons of product. If there were any extra goodies, Les Carter did the collecting, although most of the cash and the cocaine was going to the Top 40 Jocks. But albums were the same as cash. Individually, we made our weekly trek down to Aaron's

Record Shop on Melrose. An unopened LP, still in its wrapper, fetched a couple bucks. Since the record companies delivered cases of product to the radio station, there was always some extra walking around pocket change.

From Aaron's, the LPs were bought back by the record companies as part of a return policy. As an artist, Smokey Roberds objected to this policy, because those costs were charged against the artist royalties. But since most of the LPs involved were by artists whose final product had not proved commercially viable and received no air play, the money was really coming out of the record companies' budget to develop new artists. The dollars had just been moved to the promotion department's use and no cash had been passed from promo man to disc jockey. Even Smokey had to agree it was a slick deal. Another example of American ingenuity.

From the rear of the Pasadena Civic, I was looking at the backs of the fun-loving flower children. It was a sea of tie-dye, the colorful costume of the New Age. On stage, Les Carter could not resist taking the gorilla head off to reveal his true identity. With his long hair flowing onto the gorilla fur, he carried the scantily clad Susan towards the exit as the five Band members hit the stage. Garth Hudson on organ, Rick Danko on bass, Richard Manuel's piano, Levon Helm's drums exploding, and Jamie "Robbie" Robertson's weird wavering vocals filled the old classic music concert hall, reverberating off the hand-carved sculpture.

I was really going to miss Inor, but I wasn't going to talk about it.

"Catch a cannon ball now,
t' take me down the line,"
(Ibid.)

Joel Siegal

"Didn't I see you down in San Antone,
On a hot and dusty night,
Weren't you eating eggs in Sammy's there,
When the black man drew the knife,

...You'll still be in the circus,
When I'm laughing, laughing in my grave."

"Memo From Turner," Mick Jagger
(Mick Jagger and Keith Richards, Gideon Music; ABKCO Music, Inc.)

Back in Louisiana, David Russo was preparing for a hunting trip in south Texas as he, Carlos Marcello, and other members of the family did every fall. His friends convinced Russo he should go in for an annual check-up. The spot on the x-ray was lung cancer.

I wondered what, in David Russo's lifestyle, would make him vulnerable at age fifty-two. Was it the alcohol and nicotine, or the four hours sleep per night? A string of bad luck and fires had destroyed his gambling camp, the Club Four, and his home; Kate's mom and brothers barely escaped the flames at 4:00 a.m. Three years earlier, under suspicious circumstances, his boat blew up in the boat shed when he turned the ignition key. Russo survived the fire by diving into the water, but he was badly burned. Had the smoke and flames seared his lungs or simply lowered his immune system to make him vulnerable to the Big C?

Was the sequence of fires and explosions the way the families jockeyed for position? And who would profit the most from the coming drug running and dope busts?

Kate's immediate reaction was to be at home with her father, but there was no way I would leave Los Angeles, not when my radio career was really starting to happen. So Kate settled for making the fight via long distance. She researched cancer cures on both sides of the Mexican border, including the controversial drug Laetrile, which many swore to be the answer. Kate became even more radicalized toward the American Medical Association and conventional methods of treating cancer. The link to food and other environmental poisoning was investigated and reported between rock and protest lyrics.

Mick Jagger went solo on the big screen in a movie titled *Performance*. The soundtrack's "Memo From Turner" was all over 106.7 FM. James Taylor's "I've Seen Fire and I've Seen Rain" got to be number five on *Billboard's* Hot One Hundred. Both James Taylor albums, including the single "Rock-a-Bye Sweet Baby James," were getting heavy play at KPPC-FM along with Free's hard rocking "Alright Now."

Meanwhile, the Top 40 AM's were playing Richard and Karen Carpenter's "We've Only Just Begun," a song that Smokey Roberds had recorded, and was headed for the top when the Carpenters' covered it and stole his thunder. The song was so good, that even when it was picked up by the Bank of California as a commercial jingle and over played more times than any other song had ever been, "We've Only Just Begun," still continued to be a classic song from the early '70s.

Jeff Gonzer celebrated his twenty-third birthday on the radio. Fans came down to the station from all over the city to wish him well. Many showed up with live ducks since "Duck Rush" was the name we'd put on an off-the-wall promotion. A beautiful girl from Sierra Madre carried cupcakes to the party, then brought Jeff back to her house. She immediately asked him to take a shower with her, but since Jeff was engaged, he declined. Besides, her commune house was full of people, and although he was an extrovert on the radio, Jeff was still a shy Jewish kid. The Gonzer was a big fan of the Bonzo Dog Band who had recently split up. As a result of his on-the-air encouragement to get them back together and the record sales caused by heavy KPPC airplay, the Bonzo Dog Band re-formed and went back into the studio to record another album. Jeff got the public recognition and the KPPC deejays got the satisfaction of knowing that we could make it happen.

"We're your new voice in the revolution," Les Carter said into the microphone with only a slight smirk. "And tonight at 6:00 p.m., we're going to become the most powerful Rock 'n Roll FM Radio station in Los Angeles."

The long awaited power increase was about to happen. Being a superb showman, Les had picked 6:00 p.m. to make the switch. Not only was it the break between his show and Steven Segal, it was the time when the most automobiles would be jam-packed on the freeways from San Bernardino to the Pacific Ocean. As the promos for the big event had increased for the past several days, Les had instructed Matt Rubin, our engineer, to systematically decrease our power slightly, but imperceptible. So while our reception got worse during the last week, the impact was even greater than it would have been... when we finally flipped the switch to the new high powered transmitter pushing the signal up to the new antenna on a taller tower. It was a terrific publicity stunt. At 6:00 p.m., I fired up a joint, stretched out on my waterbed and tuned in the stereo in my garage apartment in North Hollywood. The signal in my Jensen stereo speakers was excellent. I smiled as Les, Susan, and Steven congratulated the KPPC *fans* on making *their* radio station available to everyone.

We'd pay 'em back Les promised, by making KPPC number one. Another room in radio heaven had just opened up in the City of Angels.

"So Rosie dear, don't you think it's queer,
So stop me if you please...

You're the great, gray man whose daughter
licks policemen's buttons clean.
You're the man who squats behind the man
who works the soft machine."
(Ibid.)

With success being evident, the disc jockeys felt justified in asking for a raise in salaries. Representing management, Doug Cox and Stan Gurrel stalled only briefly before agreeing to meet Les Carter for dinner and discuss the possibilities. The three met in a Melrose Boulevard steak house, ordered drinks, explained to the waiter exactly how they wanted their steaks cooked, and got down to the business discussion. Les Carter had done a superior job of orchestrating the KPPC disc jockeys, resulting in a great sound, and an upbeat, cohesive, creative pool of talent. Les had done it all with very little hands-on, but as much style as John Phillips had used tuning and playing with the Mammas and the Papas. All the disc jockeys trusted him to bargain for us. It was a great deal of power for Les to wield. Management knew it.

Stan Gurrel set up his defense with the need to show advertising sales growth, and thus profits, before talking about more money for any staff members. Les countered that the investments made in equipment, studios, and tower space had to be followed by the next logical investment, in talent.

When the drinks arrived, Doug Cox raised his glass and said, "Here's to the KPPC management team. Look Les," Doug continued his obvious come on, "it's impossible for us to make across-the-board raises, but we can invest in more rewarding salaries for management. We are the brain trust here; without me, you, and Stan, nobody out there has jobs. We can see this radio station develop into a real cash cow. There will be plenty of room for modest raises later on. Right now we need to pay ourselves for making a good start. Congratulations, you've earned it."

"You got it mixed up Doug," Les replied, "without the disc jockeys none of us have a job."

Les slowly put his napkin on the table, pushed back his chair, and walked out of the restaurant. The outcome of the meeting spread quickly. We all were disappointed but supported Les unanimously, while hardening our attitude toward Doug and Stan.

Next pay period saw a small increase in salaries for disc jockeys and office staff. We felt better, but suspicions remained. The age of enlightened management was on us, but these guys were still busy trying to re-invent Simon Legree. With great difficulty, I tried to see their side of the issue. Only briefly did I wish Les Carter had stayed at the table long enough to taste the steak.

> "Weren't you at the coke convention,
> Back in 1965..."
>
> Come now gentlemen,
> I know there's some mistake,
> How forgetful I'm becoming,
> Now you fixed, your business straight."
> (Ibid.)

1970

♦ The "Memo From Turner" recording session featured the sound of Ry Cooder's guitar. Steve Winwood and Al Kooper were probably also on the session.

"The jungle is a nice place... hell,
Except it's got a yellow face... well, well,
Stoned in Saigon,
The gooks are dying easy."

"Stoned in Saigon," Fresh
(Simon Napier-Bell, Ray Singer, Alan E. Gorrie, EMI Unart Catalog, Inc.)

Fresh Out of Borstal was the title of the album. Borstal was the English reform school for juvenile delinquents. The record company pitch was that these guys were tough-ass teens turned musicians, natural-born rebels, therefore worthy of airplay. The very least we could do is give 'em a listen, and take the promotional denim shirt, with "Fresh Out of Borstal" stenciled on the back. Since the shirt matched my jeans, I wore it regularly, but my long hair covered the word Fresh and most people who saw it asked only about Borstal.

Steve Segal did turn me on to a couple of cuts and Fresh got enough play to be a familiar name. I was on the air when the promo copy for their second LP hit the station. Steve put it on the audition turntable in the production studio. I could see him through the glass window, fidgeting with his thick glasses, looking like a young Bolshevik out of the Russian Revolution. Then he broke into a smile and came into the studio waving the album.

"I told you to watch these guys, Fresh," he said. "Play this next, first cut on side two. It's outta sight!"

"Stoned in Saigon" kept reminding us that no matter what happened in our daily lives, no matter what progress we made with the revolution, the war still raged in Southeast Asia. "Stoned in Saigon" became a part of the consciousness of the KPPC listener. After it had been burned in, we used it as a sound track played under the war reports that we read on the air.

By now Woodie Bernard had been discharged and was back in Louisiana going to college. I wrote him asking about drugs in the military. The Comic Book Kid wrote back telling me a story that went much deeper than the newspaper headlines.

"A stoned success
of all the best,
I passed the test,
But like the rest,
I'm feeling kind of queasy."
(Ibid.)

You can get into the Army with a seventy test score, Woodie wrote, you'd be a cook, a grunt, whatever. The Army's best, those that become officers, need a score of one-hundred ten, you want to be pilot and an officer, you need to score one-hundred eighteen. With a score of one-hundred twenty-four, you're in the top three percent. Then you can get accepted by Special Forces for training. Sixty-five percent of that three percent wash out. Those who are left don't have to be told twice. Tell 'em once and they got it.

Here is the gospel. If you lose one-third of your fighting force, the enemy will flatten you, if he's not hurting. Part of our training was military history. The first people who refused to run from the British bayonet were the Gurkhas from Nepal. When the British couldn't whip them, they hired the little sons-of-bitches. From then on, for over a hundred years, the Gurkhas have fought in the British Army. World War I, the Gurkhas were there. When the British had Hong Kong, the guards were Gurkhas. British officers, Gurkha troops. When the battles were the bloodiest, British sons were held back, and the Gurkhas were thrown into the breech. The Gurkhas always bled, they went in first. In World War II German airborne troops held a heavily fortified cliff. The English assault lasted one week before hitting twenty-five percent losses and pulling back. The Americans in a few days were up to thirty percent losses and pulled back before their unit was destroyed. The Gurkhas followed with forty-five percent losses and never broke, never ran. The Rangers at Normandy took seventy percent losses, but it was pitch black night, they were working as individuals and didn't know they had been devastated as a unit. There is a long military history of up to thirty-five percent maximum losses and you can still be successful. Above that thirty-five percent, the spirit of the unit is broken, the human psyche starts to fray.

An eighteen-year-old American recruit is walking through the jungle. He is part of a platoon, that's part of a company, that's part of a battalion, seven-hundred and fifty young bad asses along with officers, chopper people, artillery people, you're talking one thousand people. If this kid takes a toke he's no longer aggressive. I think it's been well documented that marijuana does not make people go berserk and shoot-up stuff. One kid don't hurt you. Not if you got one thousand bad-asses. But if a hundred are smoking, now you got ten percent of your force too laid back to fight. It's the same as if they'd been a casualty. Stoned or shot, the effect on your ability to fight is the same. That unit gets into a combat situation and boom, boom, boom, boom, boom, lets rock 'n roll. You're already ten percent down, and you can't be successful past thirty-five percent loss, but that unit could take another twenty to twenty-five percent casualties before it reached thirty-five percent. You still got a lot of fight left if only ten percent of your unit is stoned.

Now suppose you and I would have been on a Special Forces Recon team. Two Americans, me and you, and four Montagnards. Six men, but the sub-group is two Americans. Me and you.

You get down to the nut cutting, we're two men. If one of us is stoned, we're at fifty percent casualty and can't be successful. Remember, we've studied military history as part of our training. There is no way I would gamble our lives on a toke. Would you? I doubt it.

Suppose we dropped into someplace we're not supposed to be. We've got leave papers already signed but not dated. If we get caught, guess what old buddy, we're on leave. Have been for two weeks. We are wearing Asian boots and gear. There are no serial numbers on our rifles. No dog tags. We could be civilians, for all anybody knows. If we get caught nobody is going to claim us. Our job is to dance with the devil, and live to tell about it. We're looking for men and supplies moving on the Ho Chi Minh Trail. I said a trail. Remember David, when we were kids in Intracoastal back on the farm looking for rabbits on Coon Island, we'd see a path where the cows had been walking? Then it would split into two. Over there would be some more paths running parallel. Expand Coon Island a couple of thousand times and you get the Ho Chi Minh Trail. Thousands of enemy troops moving south over a complex of trails. Our job as a six-man team was not to kill people, but to find them, back off, follow them until they camped, then we call in the B-52s coming out of Thailand or Okie. We'd find guys in the morning and put B-52s on 'em right after midnight. If we'd made contact we had fucked up. We were illegal, thirty to seventy kilometers inside Laos. We couldn't ask for backup. We didn't exist. If we were spotted we had to run. Would you want me stoned in that situation? Think I'd want you stoned?

When our fathers fought in Europe in World War II, they could be one hundred, two hundred strong, stand behind rocks, in the trees, hold the ground, bang... bang... bang play shoot-out. We didn't have that option in the jungle. Not with six people.

We had two drugs we carried, besides morphine, of course. Little white pills that looked like aspirin, good for about six hours. Keep you awake. And the green hornets, time-released capsules, good for twelve hours. Take 'em when you had to run. Take 'em before, and you'd burn-up forty percent of your body's resources and be depleted when all hell broke loose. When you took a green hornet you were so alert you could hear the grass grow. I know you'd love the feeling. Your muscles would twitch. You could run for eight to ten hours. We weren't carrying very much food but had eighty pounds of ammo and water.

About 2:00 p.m. one day the six of us bump into a hundred fifty guys. We had to run. The only way to get away was to out run 'em. So we drop a green hornet even though the price on your body was terrific. We lost one Montagnard to rifle fire, but kept running through hard brush, up and down hills. Me and the other American got our big hip pockets stuffed with Vietnamese money. Every now and then we'd reach down and grab half a hand full and throw that son-of-a-bitching money behind you. If Charlie wants to keep up with me he's got to watch that money as he goes by it. I'd like to think we slowed him down with it, we weren't just throwing money to the wind. In any case, we got far enough ahead of the bad guys to stop for an hour or so around midnight. Our bodies begging for a rest but our brains still wanting to run. When we heard them coming, we got on our feet, popped another Green Hornet and boogie. Around 4:00 a.m. we came to a stream and turned up instead of down. Wound up in a blind canyon looking up at a waterfall. No way to climb out. It's dark, rocks are slippery. Double back. By the time we'd back-tracked, the bad guys are at the stream. They start pouring fire at the sound of us trying to climb a ridge. A second Montagnard gets hit. He's still breathing. We carry him an hour, but he's slowing us down too much. It's him or the radio, we can't carry both. We got to leave him. We can't get captured. We can't even prove who we are. No ID, remember? No name, no blame, makes the game hardball. If you get captured, you think they gonna get you back, if you're not even there? Think about it. In the '50s, the Vietnamese had captured the French and worked 'em till they dropped. It wasn't going to happen to me.

By the following afternoon we got far enough ahead to let the choppers come get us out of there. The Vietnamese pilots are paid thirty-five dollars for each Montagnard and one hundred dollars for each American they carry out. Those sweet little bastards would kick bullets out of the way to come get us. After the de-briefing I slept for thirty hours. My body was bruised black and blue from being beat-up by the underbrush. But as a guerrilla fighter you live to fight another day.

In '61 we signed in Geneva that we had pulled out of Laos. The North Vietnamese were violating that treaty and so were we. Our government just didn't have the balls to say 'fuck you, we're in there, what are you going to do about it' like the Vietnamese did. That was the only difference. We didn't exist. Our unit didn't

305

exist. My army record showed I was digging water wells in Okie. Then I was supposed to be in Da Nang, on an agricultural advisory committee. That's how I was spending the war. In actuality, I was at FOB-2, Forwards Operations Base Two at Kutom. Lots of beautiful French architecture here in Kutom. So where does all the money to pay for this part of the war come from? Every month two different guys like me fly to Saigon.

"The Sergeant here is so kind... nice,
He's out of sight and out of mind...
Twice, twice,
Stoned in Saigon the gooks are getting lazy,
While we can laugh about the past,
Red necks print our photograph,
Without the grass I think we'd all go crazy."
(Ibid.)

In Saigon we go to the CIA Headquarters in the business district. You go behind the tailor shop through the little rabbit horn thing, cross the back alley, and there's the CIA guy. He gives you the satchel case full of money. That's to pay your troops, your bonus to the Montagnards, and buy your groceries in the local economy. All of it is Vietnamese cash. Montagnards get about twenty-five dollars a month. That's a lot of money for them. They get another extra month's pay for every gook they kill during the operation. Kill three men, get three extra month's pay. Made tigers out of them. Common sense approach.

So every month two of us are in Saigon. This was the deal. You picked up cash money in a satchel in a city of beautiful whores in a war torn land. Those three days were too precious for sleep. That's when we'd take the little white pills non-stop.

What a temptation for men in their prime. The agreement is you reach down in the satchel with one hand, wad it up and whatever you pull out you can spend over the next three days. We were picking up about seventy-thousand dollars per month. The handful of Vietnamese money was maybe twelve hundred bucks each. A hell of a party for two Green Berets in Saigon.

"The company is good here...kind,
And mescaline is food out here...fine, fine,
Stoned in Saigon,
The gooks are dying easy."
(Ibid.)

For kick-ass kids, smoking marijuana was the same all over the world. It was the number one brand name for the eighteen-year-old American recruits in the jungle or chasing the girls in Saigon, for *Fresh Out of Borstal*, and for Charles Laquidara, Steve Segal, Jeff Gonzer and the rest of the FM disc jockeys who were fighting the war on the airwaves.

But it was different for Woodie Bernard and the professional soldiers who went into the woods to face the mud and the blood. The Comic Book Kid and his buddies only asked for bullets, water, and a couple of green hornets for the job ahead. And if you could stay alive, maybe some whites for Saigon.

> *"The jungle is a nice place hell,*
> *Except it's got a yellow face well...well,*
> *Stoned in Saigon,*
> *The gooks are dying easy,*
> *Stoned in Saigon,*
> *The gooks are getting lazy."*
> (Ibid.)

Pasadena/North Hollywood
January 1971

"Took a look around,
See which way the wind blows,
Where the little girls,
In their Hollywood Bungalows.

Are you a lucky little lady,
In the City of Light
Or just another lost angel,
...City of night."

"L.A. Woman," Doors
(Robert A. Krieger, Raymond Manzarek, John Paul Densmore, Jim Morrison, Doors Music Co.)

"Hey, rock 'n rollers, that's the Doors and I'm Sister Kate, your L.A. woman on KPPC-FM. The rest of the Pierce family will be along later. Meantime, I got music and news about the city of lights, and your piece of it. Was that the earth moving last night or was I just having a good time? Credibility Gap at 6:00 p.m., Les and Susan, Steve and Mississippi, all coming up later. The West Coast Record Promo Man sez to me Santana's 'Black Magic Woman' is number five in the country and we gotta play it more and I say 'Man I got yo 'Black Magic Woman.' What do you say? Call me on the rap line, tell me what you wanna hear, and I'll try to stick it in there."

Like the rest of the voices at KPPC, Kate's on-air personality was developing. At once hip and cynical, she was already what the women's movement of the '70s and '80s would strive for and lose sight of. Mother figure, business woman, talent, she was doing it all.

We witnessed her creating one of the most used expressions of the early '70s. Kate went with Jim Bachman to see the Italian movie *Mondo Cane* from which came the Academy Award winning theme and love song, *More*. "Mondo" became a favorite and more accurate response than weird or far out, and since Kate felt most of life was bizarre, it was a short step to "Mondo Bizarro." Used to describe a wide array of happenings, "Mondo Bizarro" found its way into the headlines of Rolling Stone Magazine. Sister Kate was certifiable.

"L.A. woman Sunday afternoon,
Drive through your suburbs,
Into your blues."
(Ibid.)

Jeff Gonzer's girlfriend Valerie moved into one of the duplex apartments next door, so we were seeing a lot of Jeff. Smokey and Raula were living in the other apartment. It was very much like our own little commune. Our waterbed on the floor of the garage apartment was surrounded by several hundred albums stacked on shelves all the way up to the wooden shingle roof. When the waterbed sprang a leak, we pulled it outside and started sleeping up on the loft with the kids, while I looked around for the best deal on a new waterbed.

Some waterbed merchant would probably do a deep discount in return for the Pierce Family touting his business on the radio. A few free plugs were not frowned on. Of course, if Kate could sell the merchant a schedule of live sixty second spots, that sixty seconds would probably stretch into a couple minutes or more. So long as it was loose, natural and entertaining, no problem.

There were other opportunities to bend the radio rules. Some more serious than others. The practice of double billing was rampant with media all over the country, until eventually laws were passed that could cost a station its license if caught. I had been approached by Ron Johnson of the Sound Factory in Beverly Hills. I would give him the blank form, he'd enter the double billed numbers and the money would roll in. Meanwhile, the blank billing forms had been stashed on the top shelf of the record albums...waiting.

> *"I see your hair is burnin',*
> *Hills are filled with fire,*
> *If they say I never loved you,*
> *You know they are a liar."*
> (Ibid.)

Sleeping with the kids in the loft wasn't really comfortable. John-David slept badly, tossing, turning, and kicking most of the night. At 6:00 a.m. the kicking was so insistent that it woke me out of a fitful dream in which a giant was at the back door shaking the entire house. Consciousness clicked in after I was already standing, only to be thrown violently, bruising my left shoulder against the six-by-six post that supported the roof. John-David and 'Chelle woke up as the loft shuttered and shook. Kate was already comforting them.

"It's okay," she said. "Lay down, don't try to get up."

The sound of breaking glass and falling objects were all around us. Next door Jeff's voice rang out yelling, "Earth-quake!" It was over in less than thirty seconds, but it seemed longer. Much longer. Amid the after shocks, the news slowly came in. At 6.5 this certainly wasn't "the big one." The epicenter was in the northern part of the San Fernando Valley just a few miles away. There were a dozen deaths. Freeway overpasses had collapsed and crushed automobiles. Wide spread damage, but a lot to be thankful for, including the hour. At 6:00 a.m., commuter traffic was still light. But the big fear was there. Smokey, Jeff, and I sat around the apartment talking about the possibility of the Big One coming within days or weeks, and what would be the best possible escape routes from L.A. in a worst case scenario. Each time an after shock rumbled the floor, we'd tighten up.

When I finally got around to picking up the pieces, I started with the pile of record albums that had crashed onto the exact spot where the leaky waterbed was once located. I imagined the headline: "Disc Jockey Killed By Falling Rock 'n Roll Records in L.A. Quake." At the bottom of the pile was the blank forms to double bill the Sound Factory. I threw 'em out with the broken glass.

"Drivin' down your freeways,
...Cops in cars, the topless bars,
Never saw a woman,
So alone, so alone."
(Ibid.)

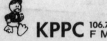

KPPC 106.7 FM

99 SOUTH CHESTER AVENUE, PASADENA, CALIFORNIA 91106   213/681-0447

RATE CARD NO. 3
EFFECTIVE 6-15-71

MONDAY-SUNDAY **AA**   12:00 NOON-12:00 MIDNIGHT

TIMES PER WEEK	1 WEEK	13 WEEKS	26 WEEKS	52 WEEKS
6	32.00	31.00	30.00	29.00
12	30.00	29.00	28.00	27.00
18	28.00	27.00	26.00	25.00
24	26.00	25.00	24.00	23.00
36	24.00	23.00	22.00	21.00

MONDAY-SUNDAY **A**   6:00 A.M.-12:00 NOON / 12:00 MIDNIGHT - 2:00 A.M.

TIMES PER WEEK	1 WEEK	13 WEEKS	26 WEEKS	52 WEEKS
6	27.00	26.00	25.00	24.00
12	26.00	25.00	24.00	23.00
18	24.00	23.00	22.00	21.00
24	22.00	21.00	20.00	19.00
36	20.00	19.00	18.00	17.00

MONDAY-SUNDAY **B**   2:00 A.M.-6:00 A.M.

10.00 FLAT

TOTAL AUDIENCE PLANS

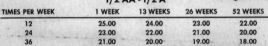

TAP ONE
1/2 AA • 1/2 A

TIMES PER WEEK	1 WEEK	13 WEEKS	26 WEEKS	52 WEEKS
12	25.00	24.00	23.00	22.00
24	23.00	22.00	21.00	20.00
36	21.00	20.00	19.00	18.00

TAP TWO
1/2 AA • 1/3 A • 1/6 B

TIMES PER WEEK	1 WEEK	13 WEEKS	26 WEEKS	52 WEEKS
12	23.00	22.00	21.00	20.00
24	21.00	20.00	19.00	18.00
36	19.00	18.00	17.00	16.00

GENERAL

Rates commissionable to qualified advertising agencies who provide copy, are financially responsible and who do not work for competing media.

Rate protection to continuous advertisers from effective date of increase 90 days.

All copy must be in 48 hours prior to broadcast date, or 96 hours required for Monday start.

Programming will exercise creative freedom in all spots produced at KPPC. All spots produced outside KPPC subject to approval by programming.

Los Angeles
February 1971

The idea first hit me when I saw an ad in the *L.A. Times* announcing the giant mobile home show to be held in Dodger Stadium. Kate, John-David, 'Chelle, and I headed over to Chavez Ravine where over a hundred motor mobile homes were on display. We checked out several models, the kids were having a grand time running through the miniature homes. Kate was somewhat more skeptical.

"These things cost thousands of dollars, we can't afford something like this," she said.

"Wouldn't it be great to get out of the city, go up to Big Bear or Arrowhead, even up to the Sequoias in Yosemite, get out of this smog, get a breath of fresh air for the kids?" I was selling hard.

"Drive it to Louisiana and camp out on our property," she added, "but we don't have the money."

"No we don't," I had to agree, "not yet anyway."

Over several months the idea kept gnawing at me, I wanted a motor mobile. Maybe it was the '60s syndrome, maybe it was being in the car culture of Southern California. The ability to keep moving became an obsession, the flexibility to get out of town became a real need. By the time The Who's song came out I was ready.

Still being no closer to having the several thousand dollar price tag on a motor mobile, I began to consider alternatives. The conversion of VW vans to campers and semi-livable units was wide spread. School buses, in particular, were a favorite, but these front engine nose vehicles were not very attractive. Now a Greyhound Bus, or some of the rigs that rock bands toured in, that would be the way to go. Then one morning on the ride from North Hollywood to Pasadena, I spotted a school bus in Glendale. I had seen these buses hundreds of times before, grinding their gears through block after block, hauling kids through the L.A. streets. They were thirty-five feet long, flat nose, with mid-mounted Hall-Scott gasoline powered truck engines. They were great looking buses. Engineered for safety, they had heavy duty frame work inside three skins of top grade steel. Across the front was the name of the manufacturer, Crown.

While I went on the air, Kate got on the phone and came back ten minutes later, "It's the Crown Coach Company," she said, "they build only two vehicles, both for the city of Los Angeles. One is fire trucks, the other is school buses."

"Great," I said, "do you think they will trade air-time for a bus?"

"I asked the guy," she said. "He wasn't sure what he would want to advertise on a hip rock station, but I told him it would be good for his community image. I don't think he's buying it."

"We could live in it Kate," I blurted out.

"I was afraid you would say that," she said, "Are you sure you wouldn't rather have a fire engine?"

> "Keep me movin', over fifty,
> Keep me groovin', just a hippie gypsy."
> (Ibid.)

A few days later Les Carter and I met with Doug Cox. "Dave has this idea," Les began, "he would like to trade some radio time for a bus."

"A bus? What would you do with it, Dave?" Doug wondered.

"Convert it to a motor mobile and live in it," I said.

"With your family?"

"Sure, why not?"

"Well, it seems a little crazy, but that's your business," Doug said as he segued into being a manager. "The only problem is if we trade air time, the station would have some ownership."

"Well, we thought we could use it for promotions," Les was trying to help, "drive it around town, show up at concerts."

"Yeah? Yeah?" Doug was beginning to catch on, "Where would it be parked?"

"Out back in the parking lot, under the avocado tree," was my answer. "You guys know how we love this place, I would always be available, never be more than fifty feet away, it's a hell of an idea."

"Yeah, Yeah," Doug said slowly. He wanted to think about it some more, he didn't want to say no just yet.

A few days later a call came from the Crown Coach salesman. We drove to downtown L.A.

"Mr. Pierce," the salesman said, "here's your bus," pointing to the big yellow one with the Rialto School District written on the side. "Just got it in this morning, I was looking out for you. It's a 1952 model, been in service ever since."

"How many miles on it?" I asked.

"Well, the speedometer says seventy-seven-thousand, of course that could be one-hundred-seventy-seven; or...perhaps it could be two-hundred-seventy-seven, I have no way of knowing."

"Well, can we do the paper work now?" I was getting eager. "I'll sign for it, and when you're ready, I'll run some commercials."

"Can't do it," he said, bursting my bubble. "The President of Crown didn't want any ads on your radio station, but he did want me to make you a generous offer, only eighteen hundred dollars."

That did sound generous. Perhaps he was just trying to avoid any bad press from a hippie disc jockey. So while John-David, 'Chelle, and I explored the interior, Kate wrote the check. Within minutes I was wheeling out my very own Crown Coach. Sitting forward of the front wheels made steering weird, and the whole system seemed a bit loose. But I was soon following the Volvo as John-David and 'Chelle looked out the back window of the car, their eyes huge with excitement. I was hugging the right lane, occasionally scraping the guardrails of the Pasadena Freeway. Finally, I parked on the tree lined street across from KPPC.

Kate went on the air, "Listen up radio fans," she said. "Here's your chance to get your own seat out of the bus that will become the Pierce Family's home, so bring a couple of wrenches and meet me at 99 South Chester Street in Pasadena."

When my air shift ended three hours later, I walked across the street. The last happy long hairs were unscrewing the final seat, bolted to the floor. They thanked us profusely, and scurried away, carrying their prize. The interior of the bus was now stripped bare and ready for conversion.

The next day a trip to Camper World with Bill Jenson secured electrical and plumbing parts, stove, fridge, sink, shower, and john. The long process was ready to begin. I was determined to travel light, stay loose, and be mobile.

"I don't care about pollution,
I'm an air conditioned gypsy,
Watch the police and the tax man miss me."
(Ibid.)

Interior of the the
Crown Coach bus.

"James Dean, James Dean,
You said it all so clean,
And I know my life would look alright,
If I could see it on the silver screen."

"James Dean," The Eagles
(Jackson Browne, Glenn Frey, Don Henley, and John David Souther,
Asylum Records; Swallow Turn Music)

"Hello David, my name is Alan Gerstal, I'm a big fan of KPPC and I listen to the Pierce Family. I'm taking a break from CBS-TV City and I would like to produce a film on the Pierce Family." The voice on the telephone had my attention.

"What format are you going to shoot on?" I asked.

"Sixteen millimeter," Alan answered. "It's not like a feature or anything," he said, lowering my expectations slightly.

"How long will it be?" I asked.

"Fifteen, twenty minutes, maybe."

"You'll want to shoot in the KPPC studio?"

"Yes," he replied, "but not just your work at KPPC. I want to show your home life, the relationship within your family. You know what you're doing on the radio is unique."

"It's been done," I said. "Ozzie Nelson got rich on this idea."

"Kids as part of a family of disc jockeys on an underground radio station is brand new," he said.

"I'll talk to Kate," I told Alan, getting his phone number and thinking that we needed to do it. Sixteen millimeter could be blown-up for theater distribution. As an actor, I would have some good film on myself which could lead to acting roles. Disc jockey Bob Crane from KLAC had made it big on "Hogan's Heroes," KRLA's Sam Riddle was hosting music specials and doing voice overs. I could do all of that. Kate agreed the film could have possibilities. It would be a great pulpit for our ideas and lifestyle. At the very least, it would be a well-made family movie.

"Magic mirror won't you tell me please,
Do I see myself in anyone I meet,
Magic mirror if we only could,
Try to see ourselves as others would."

"Magic Mirror," Leon Russell
(Claude Russell Bridges, Skyhill Publishing)

We shot inside our showcase apartment, setting up a lifestyle just from the look of the space. The kids on the piano, Kate on the phone selling airtime, I was on the waterbed, headsets on my long shaggy hair, as I auditioned LPs and marked the album covers for future reference. There was a shot of the Volvo, bike racks loaded, climbing the mountain road, the thick brown haze of the Los Angeles Basin in the background. We were always on a mission to escape the bad air, so Alan and two crewmembers simply came along on one of our frequent camping trips in the nearby mountains. There were no big trucks filled with movie equipment. No honey wagons, no teamsters and no production assistants and script supervisors, but they shot enough film to capture the adventure.

On John-David's eighth birthday, Kate staged a party in the back yard on Babcock. The colorful tie-dye affair rolled for the camera. When a Cajun song played, Jeff Gonzer and I danced each other around the party of hyper kids and spaced-out adults, our long hair bouncing off our shoulders.

"To policemen I'm suspicious,
Just am the way I look...
To the censor I'm pornography,
With no redeeming grace...
The sellers think I'm merchandise,
They'll have me for a song,
Left ones think I'm right,
The right ones think I'm wrong."
(Ibid.)

The scenes in the studio were probably the best, an authentic look at what really happened during the Pierce Family Show: the kids on my knee leaning into the microphone to insert address or telephone numbers in the live commercial copy, or introducing a record because they knew the artist from having memorized the look of the album cover, turning on Kate's mic across the turntable from me so she could do a PSA or get down on local authorities for the latest counter-culture grievance. Throughout it all, my fingers danced on the control board, moving the slide pots up and down, selecting the volume on the mics, stopping and starting turntables, firing off the cartridge tape machines, one eye on the VU meter, the other on the clock. Circling an arm around 'Chelle to keep her from falling off my constantly bouncing knee, with my mind racing to the next sequence and thinking this has to be the absolute best job in the world. The homemade sound of KPPC was right there on the audio track, The Persuasions singing out, "KPPC-FM, The Sound of Stereo, KPPC-FM Pasadena Stereo..." The tape cartridges ready to declare, "Mistake, mistake. This disc jockey has just made a mistake." Another tape reminding everyone to "segue" and perhaps our most famous announcement which played off the Avon make-up commercial. It featured a doorbell, the announcement "A-Bomb Calling," followed by the nuclear explosion trailing off into the next rock record.

The biggest obstacle to the Pierce Family film was getting rights to the music. A film about disc jockeys had to have a sound track filled with the music and lyrics of the late '60s and early '70s hits. To get through the legal hurdles would be a nightmare, way out of our league. So I called Don Hall, who by now had sent most of his *Zabriskie Point* wages up his and Kathy Hall's collective noses. If Don Hall could score Antonioni's film he could certainly do mine. Not as well, of course, with only three musicians and limited studio time, which was all we could squeeze from Alan's production budget.

Don Hall did a good job of capturing the feel of what we were about, but it wasn't the kind of sound track I'd heard in my head where a million tunes were running around. When we viewed the final product I didn't think it would ever make it to the big screen. It was, after all, a well-made family movie.

Its real value would be as footage in the future documentary on KPPC.

"Magic mirror, won't you tell me please,
Do I see myself in anyone I meet,
Magic mirror if we only could,
Try to see ourselves,
As others would."
(Ibid.)

1971

♦ Claude Russell Bridges, "Leon Russell," was from Tulsa, Oklahoma, which was also the home of Bob Wills, the king of western swing, who launched his career with a live show on KVOO radio. Bob Wills' most famous line to his steel guitar player, Leon McAulliff, was "take it away Leon." It is supposed that's why the young piano and guitar player, Claude Bridges, took the name "Leon Russell."

'Chelle at J.D.'s birthday party, part of Alan Gerstal's Pierce Family film.

Early April 1971

"Say, when this is all over,
You'll be in clover,
we'll go out and spend
All a your blue money."

"Blue Money," Van Morrison
(Van Morrison, Caledonia Productions, Inc., WB Music Corp.)

The Troubadour had become a shrine. Our regular pilgrimages there were a ritual. When Van Morrison booked in for an evening, so did the Pierce family. I had heard of Van Morrison's legendary reluctance to face his audience, but his music, his words, his wavering, bleating voice would make it a memorable evening. Still, looking at his back while he conducted the band, which included a seven-man brass section, was disconcerting. Surely Van did not have stage fright. Maybe he just didn't like playing in clubs. The KPPC disc jockeys did. Concerts and clubs gave us an opportunity to either emcee or just mingle with the music-loving public. John-David and 'Chelle were natural born show folk. Like Van Morrison up on that tiny crowded stage, Kate and I could have turned into our inner dialog after the initial rush of being recognized and greeted. But the high energy Pierce kids were all over the crowd, stopping to visit and rap with everyone who saw them. When Jeff Gonzer emceed the Tim Rose Concert in the Valley Theater, a huge in-the-round arena much like Melody Land, he took John-David with him. The kids were much too cool for school. Going out to the movies or even in the supermarket, people would hear their voices, stop to smile and nod in recognition as they realized who these four not-quite-average-looking folks were. I was convinced there was some marketable talent here. Even in a town that walks over gifted people, being on the radio made us different enough to get noticed.

Les Carter had brought to KPPC four of the most talented individuals in the city known as the Credibility Gap. The Gap had been working out in a shack behind KRLA but they jumped on the chance to be our news team. They were led by Harry Shearer, whose forté was voices. He could do Richard Nixon so well that casual listeners would have thought it was the president, until they realized he was saying all kinds of outrageous, outlandish things. Harry Shearer got inside the man's soul. Shearer went on to success on Saturday Night Live and later the Simpsons, creating the voice of Homer Simpson's boss, Mr. Burns, who seemed to share some of Tricky Dick's psyche.

David L. Lander and Michael McKean were off the wall, too, in their characterizations. Both were just a few years away from stardom as Lenny and Squiggy on *Laverne and Shirley.*

The great KRLA newsman, Richard Bebe, was the voice that legitimized their wild spin on the events of the day. His straight intros and outros sounded like a real news cast, until the boys from left field took the story over the edge.

The Creditability Gap's 6:00 p.m. news helped catapult KPPC to over three hundred thousand listeners, a huge share of the number two market in America. Billing was on the rise, increasing fivefold to over a half million dollars annually.

The whole staff was concentrating on the job at hand, winning the ratings race. Like a professional team of athletes we sucked up the star status, never forgetting who we were in our relationship with the city who loved the music as much as we did. It was a lot of talent and a lot of ego in one building. We couldn't imagine any other life. You knew you couldn't exist if you heard a killer song and couldn't go on the radio to share it with the music fans out there who tuned in. We played everything, and listeners ate it up, demanding more variety from their local deejays.

Five months after her death, Janis Joplin went to number one, haunting us with Kris Kristofferson's wayward tale of "Me and Bobby McGee," the immortal ode to their brief romance. Santana sang "I Ain't Got Nobody, I Can Depend On." Paul McCartney proved there was life after the Beatles with the group he called Wings. Steven the Seagull's favorite was Ike and Tina Turner singing "Young, Dumb and Full of Come on Tell Me." Jeff Gonzer was playing the Andrews Sisters from the '30s and '40s on "Bie Mir Bist Du Schoen." Jeff said the only reason the Credibility Gap's half-hour newscast sounded better than our disc jockey shows was because they rehearsed. We didn't. Leslie "Frog Man" Carter did a live interview with Barry McGuire and the Dr. He played one cut from the new LP, broke into the middle of the song, claiming that the phones had been lit up by listeners all over Los Angeles demanding that he play the whole album. Les was happy to oblige, and called in his marker from the record company.

In the KPPC production room Zack Zenor created a jingle for Jeff, who's favorite new radio expression was "Hooahh." When Kawasaki asked Zack to produce a commercial, he filled it with Japanese words like "Hah Sonh" and various motorbike sounds. Strange, but right on. Jeff liked to put John-David and 'Chelle on the waterbed commercials. At the customers' request the whole sales staff was asking to use them more. In fact, they spent almost as much time with Zack Zenor in production as they did on the air with me. The Pierce kids were just shy of demanding a talent fee. They quickly caught the big money vibe from the grown-ups. We were the best. We would soon be bullet proof. We had a huge influence on the music industry in the global musical Mecca of Los Angeles. This was big business.

On this day, John-David was leaning over the tape machine by the sign that said, "logs to be corrected." The stack of incorrect broadcast logs was over a foot high. I was on the air, running through my rap, "Hey everybody, Pacific Stereo has on special, this week only, the new Spectro Sonic AM-FM receiver that can bring in FM stations all over the dial in every kind of difficult reception condition. Your price, $299.95. No man, I'm not jiving, that's the deal at Pacific Stereo, in Torrance, Costa Mesa, LaHabra, Santa Monica, and North Hollywood."

"Here's what's happening on the music scene," I continued to lay out the info. "On Friday, May 8, Bill Graham is bringing Country Joe to Olympic Auditorium. Little Richard, Albert King, and John Hammond will also be playing a set."

Through the glass that looked out onto the courtyard I could see them coming. As they entered the studio building, I saw them crossing by the studio window looking into the hallway, and I realized it was Sha Na Na. They had broken the protocol of letting me know they were coming. The group stormed into the studio and two of the '50s styled ruffians pulled me out the door. One of them sat behind the mic and pointing to John-David said, "Hey you, kid, how does this work?" I realized I had been set up and sat back to listen to Sha Na Na and John-David do the rest of my show.

"Doot, dooya do, doot doot,
Doot dooya do, doot doot,
Blue money, blue money."
(Ibid.)

Kate, John-David, and 'Chelle were singing along with Van Morrison, on the radio joining in on the Doot Dooya Dos. The Volvo was in 60 mph bumper-to-bumper on the 134 West riding through Burbank. Sometimes I felt like it was already over and we were just playing out our hand. But then, there was the Blue Money. How much was the number-one station in Los Angeles going to be worth? A bundle to the people who owned it. To the disc jockeys who built it and ran it, it would be worth sticking around for.

"Photographer smiles,
Take a break for awhile,
...Take five honey,
When this is over,
You'll be in clover,
We'll go out and spend
All a your blue money."
(Ibid.)

The Credibility Gap (Harry Shearer, Michael McKean,
David Lander, and Richard Bebe).

Los Angeles
Late April 1971

"The triangle tingles,
And the trumpet plays slow,
Farewell Angelina,
the sky is on fire,
And I must go."

"Farewell Angelina," Joan Baez
(Bob Dylan, Special Rider Music)

The rumblings of the '60s were slowly, uneasily, settling into the '70s. The nation would calm and try to forget. Then quickly get down to this country's real business, making money, leading to Ronald Reagan's trickle down vision for America in the '80s. The spirit of Revolution would not be seen again until the late '80s, turned upside down in Eastern Europe when the ideals of communism and much of '60s American Radicalism would go down in one large flush.

On Sunset Boulevard, a giant billboard appeared. We heard it had been placed by John and Yoko. It said simply, "The War is Over." Even though bullets were still flying and American boys were dying, somehow that definitive statement rang true. After all those years, maybe it was over. All we had to do was believe. It was as though a whole generation, and then a whole nation, had willed it. Now, it was so. In our hearts the fight was over. But for four more long years, till the fall of Saigon, the war with no integrity would drag on, leaving us with few heroes on either side.

"There's no need for anger,
There's no need for blame."
(Ibid.)

In the dictionary, radio and radical are on the same page. Charles Laquidara and I played out those roles longer than most of the disc jockeys. I still played John Lennon's "Working Class Hero." The voice of Spiro Agnew that I had recorded off television news months before continued to sing out, "That's exactly what we're running against in this country today." When kids' voices, or happy music, or anything positive found its way onto the air, somewhere in the background, sometimes almost imperceptible, you could hear our vice-president stating what he and his republic would fight against.

We had better scripts than the old guard. Jim Morrison was the revolution's premiere post-beat writer. Influenced by Kerouac and Ginsberg, his words led us down psychedelic lanes looking for self-awareness and fulfillment. What was seeded in Tibet and Galilee was finally sweeping the North American continent in a new spirit of life. But the strange new disciples were guitar heroes. George Harrison underscored Lennon and McCartney's gospel. Eric Clapton made our inner beings sing with joy. Hendrix pulled political and sexual power out of a guitar string with his teeth. When Mr. Fender electrified the guitar and Les Paul built the solid-wood body, they created a monster. The weapon that couldn't be stopped. The message was so right on. Love was really better than hate. Peace had to be better than war. How could we be wrong about drugs or sex or rock 'n roll. It was all part of our affirmation of life.

The fact that we were real people behind the radio characters was one of the keys to the popularity of KPPC. The airwave anarchy was led by clowns and pirates. But these were people with highly developed communication and entertainment skills. Steve Segal, the Seagull, changed his air name to the "Obscene Steven Clean." That name covered all the bases. "Clean here at 106.7," he would say after rapping a well verbalized statement of where a particular issue was really at. Somewhere along there, the small skinny school boy known as Mississippi Brian Wilson became "Mississippi Fats" stealing the visual personage of Jackie Gleason's pool shark in *The Hustler*. Joel Segal played Jack Benny bits on "Ha Ha Theater" on Saturday mornings as Uncle Joel. Then on Sunday night he did the mystery shows as Uncle Noel. The sound of radio became like a good comic book. When you listened, your mind created the scene in animation. Sound invites the imagination. That's what radio is all about. Radio was still listened to in living rooms. People gathered around the speakers to get loaded and listen. Like little kids again, hearing without seeing. The *Free Press* called KPPC the most imaginative programming anywhere. Groucho Marx and Carmen Miranda mixed in with Bonzo Dog and the Mothers of Invention. An ad policy that said *no* to over-produced Madison Avenue stretched our listening base and increased our billing. We were all young, talented, and confident, full of the excitement that only comes around when there are no limits. To our fans out there, the music and the radio station contributed to their life style. For those of us inside the station, it was our *whole* life style. It was magnified tens of times.

Being on the air was intense. We gradually quit smoking before going on, preferring to ride a natural energy high. The physical act of cueing tapes and records on a top rated radio station demanded sharp wits. We longed for the technical break-throughs that would allow disc jockeys to spend more time creating. We imagined how the computerized control room would put all those songs, thousands of them, all of the comedy bits, political sound bites, a painter's palette of sound at our finger tips, instantaneously. Think of it, call it up, put it on the air. But it would never happen. Instead, the corporations' computers took radio's soul and imagination, and much too big a piece of its fun.

> "In the space where the deuce
> And the ace once ran wild."
> (Ibid.)

Maybe this country would never again be this restless in the same way. The awesome technology of future shock would prevent us from taking the time to just get stoned, listen to hours of music, reflect and protest. Who would care so much about simple rights and wrongs for all God's chillens and critters? Larger issues would demand our attention. Walking the earth in thirsty boots would be left to a handful, while the national psyche got on with survival for the fit only. The Cyber Space Race would come calling.

"The fiends nail time bombs,
To the hands of the clocks,
...Farewell Angelina...
I must go where it's quiet."
(Ibid.)

The Pierce family in the KPPC studio.

*"Don't try to stop me girl,
I'm movin out today..."*

"San Francisco Girls," Fever Tree
(Scott Holtzman, Vivian Holtzman, Michael Knust, Uni)

The April ratings results were in. For adults eighteen to thirty-four in Los Angeles, KPPC-FM made a dramatic rise to the number three spot. We weren't at the top yet, but we were close, and the growth was already in place. It was just a matter of time. Under Les Carter's steady influence as Program Director, we all blossomed. Jeff Gonzer in the morning set up our day with comic wit, laid-back Zack Zenor put his own spaced-out style into the late morning airwaves before disappearing into the production room to create the best radio advertising in the country. After handling the album distribution and record company business, I sat down 1:00 to 4:00 p.m. for the best time of my life, playing rock, country, folk, and old blues. I generally started the show solo but sometimes with Kate. Later, John-David and 'Chelle would skate in after school to blow the city away with their seven and eight-year-old energy. Les and Susan's drive time from 4:00 to 7:00 p.m. was a strong mix of rock, jazz, and R&B. Steven Clean's tremendous creative energy made him the star of L.A. radio and that fed his hungry ego as he constantly redoubled his efforts in the 7:00 to 10:00 p.m. power shift. The Boston expatriate, Mississippi, came in late night at 10:00 and stretched our imagination with a smorgasbord of sounds that created a whole show between the records. Allowing deejays to work only three-hour shifts, as Zack, Les, Steve, and I did, was unheard of in radio. No disc jockey had ever worked only fifteen hours on the air per week, but we were proving that it was worth the investment. We paid back the audience with the best three hours a day they could possibly hear. We never got tired, we never got bored or boring, we were at the peak of our performance every time we were on the air. And most important, it put more voices and music variety into the rotation. Our weekend staff included backup from old pros like Don Hall, Ted Alvy, and Sam Kopper, who came west from Boston's WBCN, plus the outstanding work of the Fire Sign Theater doing live off-the-wall radio theater of the mind Sundays at 6:00 p.m., followed by Dr. Demento with the most complete record collection of oldies available anywhere. Elliot Mintz did interviews both in the studio and via phone with show biz personalities, laying the groundwork for a new talk radio format. Mintz cut his interviews into segments and plugged them in on Saturdays and Sundays. And of course, the Credibility Gap was live every night at 6:00 p.m. Though we had the freedom to pick and choose, we were very cohesive in our sound. Listening to each other's shows constantly, we had a feel for whatever tracks were being over-played or what might be neglected. No rules, no format, self-policed, self-regulated. The ability to pick the right song at the right time, the only rule a disc jockey really needed. When one of us discovered a good cut or a new artist, we all got on it, and burned it into the audience for instant familiarity, hitting them in a totally spontaneous flow. On those occasions when Les decided to go on an LP in return for record company support, we mixed it in smoothly and enthusiastically. It didn't get any better than this. We all knew it, the big money was on the way. KPPC sales were climbing steadily. Our new rate card with artwork by Neon Parks featured cartoon clips of Esther Williams in a swimsuit in a diving pose, Ghandi was deep in meditation and ducks marched in locked step. Ad agencies didn't know what it meant, but they did know that KPPC was on a meteoric climb and they could still dominate the young adult L.A. demographics for a low ball rate. Doug Cox began to show up at work in Buddha robes, disappearing into his office, converted to a temple with incense and candles. We never knew what he did. We suspected he did nothing, which was just fine, because he never talked to us; he let us do what we wanted to do. The Free Form format that we were pioneering was popping up at FM stations in markets big and small all over America. No one did it with more style and flair than the disc jockeys in Pasadena. Many Free Form stations were hampered by big brothers looking over their shoulders, corporations like Metro-Media, stations like KMET in Los Angles and KSAN in San Francisco. ABC's seven station radio chain, including KLOS in Los Angeles, WPLJ in New York City and KAUM in Houston had gone to the rock 'n roll stereo sound, which played the right album cuts, but was as tightly formatted as Top 40. Already some FMs were evolving into what would become the album oriented rock of the '70s and '80s and eventually the AAA format of the '90s. Only Charles Laquidara in Boston, with the WBCN disc jockeys, continued to enjoy the kind of autonomy that was working so well in Pasadena.

In San Francisco, KMPX had not been so successful. The disc jockeys had commandeered the station, locking out the management and sales staff. Jack Ellis and Reno Nevada were among the radicals who had held out for three days, while the hip community cheered them on. Finally, they gave up, walked out, and went looking for other jobs.

"Out there it's summer time,
Milk and honey days
Ohh, San Francisco girls..."
(Ibid.)

At 4:00 p.m. Les Carter came out of a meeting with Stan Gurrel and Doug Cox. As he and I switched positions behind the microphone, he asked Kate and I to meet him and Susan at their home later that evening. When we arrived, Les's first question was "How would you like to move to San Francisco?"

"Are you kidding?" Kate said. "Give me three hours to pack."

"You mean KMPX?" I asked.

"That's it," Les said. "Stan Gurrel is tired of the walk-outs and strikes, we've shown stability, they're pleased with our progress."

"What's the deal?" I wanted to know.

"I'll be Program Director in both cities," Les beamed.

"That was Tom Donahue's plan," I reminded him.

"I know," he said, setting his pipe down and firing a joint.

"What about Doug Cox?" Susan asked.

"They didn't say," Les replied, "but I think he stays in Los Angeles, at least that's the way I want it."

"Would you guys go up there?" Kate asked.

"Oh no," Susan replied, "Los Angeles is our home. Besides we'd miss L.A. Les will be going up there regularly and I will come up to visit you guys, but we really don't want to move. But it's ideal for the Pierce family," she smiled. "You're ready to leave town anyway. You've already sold your house."

"Anyone else from KPPC?" I asked.

"Well, Steve Segal wanted to go as soon as I told him the news about an hour ago, but he'll change his mind and I think he needs to stay here. Jeff Gonzer might want to go or maybe Don Hall or Ted Alvy, I don't want to break up the regular KPPC air staff too much."

Kate and I were ecstatic as we drove back to the Valley to tell John-David and 'Chelle the big news. For anyone trying to escape the smog and the spreading megalopolis of Los Angles, San Francisco was a Shangri La, a dream come true.

> "Do what you wannna do,
> And play what you wanna play,
> I just gotta go
> And get back to the Bay."
> (Ibid.)

The KPPC Family

North Hollywood
Late May 1971

*"Leave your stepping stones behind,
something calls for you...
Stike another match, go start anew."*

"It's All Over Now, Baby Blue," Bob Dylan
(Bob Dylan, Special Rider Music)

Smokey and I were sitting under the tree at Babcock, a spot where we had smoked and talked many times over the past eight years, especially during the period when he and Raula had lived next door. Jimmy Rabbit, now on KABC, had just slammed through Ringo Starr's "It Don't Come Easy" and Rolling Stones "Brown Sugar," both mega hits in the summer of '71. We were taking a break, after moving the last of the Pierce Family's belongings into the big yellow Crown Coach, parked by the curb a few feet away. Not all of our possessions would fit in the bus. A lot of accumulated material goods had been given over to Goodwill. The U-Haul trailer parked in the driveway had been loaded and locked. I had paid an extra service charge to rent the U-Haul because this year more people were moving out of California than moving in.

We had left a four-by-four foot stack of boxes in the middle of the garage apartment. We'd deal with it later, after enough harassment by the blonde soap opera star of General Hospital, who had bought our former home. In a few weeks Smokey and Al Schmitt would be all over her and take her mind off the problem.

*"My foot's in the stirrup,
My pony won't stand.
Goodbye ol' partner,
I'm a leaving Cheyenne."*

"Leaving Cheyenne," Ian Dawson Tyson
(Public Domain)

"Well Brother Dave, we are sure going to miss you," Smokey was saying. "L.A. won't be the same without you guys."

"It's time to go," I said.

"I know, I feel it too," Smokey looked up at the smoggy sky. "I've been thinking about Nashville lately. You and I grew up on country music. Some of the best tunes I've ever written were country. Maybe I've been in the wrong town for ten years."

"You could do well in Nashville," I said. "You know the music business."

"It's only a day's ride from Louisiana, partner," Smokey smiled. "God do I miss the South. L.A.'s changing. I don't like the direction. Maybe it's just 'cause the '60s are over. Anyway, good luck up north. I hear Frisco's a hell of a town."

I watched Smokey drive away. Two years later, he'd be living in Nashville.

"I'm goin' to Montana
For to throw the Hoolahan."
(Ibid.)

Although the bus was still missing some necessary equipment, like a plumbing system, it was road worthy, so we decided to road test it on a trip down to San Diego. I adapted to handling the thirty-five feet of length, but the loose steering was still disconcerting. About halfway down the San Diego freeway, we were pulled over by the California Highway Patrol.

"What are you doing driving a school bus down the road?" the CHP officer wanted to know.

"It's not a school bus sir, it's my home," I replied, showing him the waterbed and the kids' bunk in the back. Kate, John-David, and 'Chelle were all trying to look as normal and American as they possibly could.

The CHP officer was nice enough, considering the length of my hair. "I've seen a few conversions on the highway," he said, "but this one is big and roomy. Gonna live in it, you say?"

"Yes sir," I replied proudly.

"Well, get it painted before you put it back on the highway. In California yellow is reserved for school buses. You wouldn't want to confuse anyone."

"No sir," John-David said loudly from the back of the bus.

The lawman exited the bus with an amused look. I spun the bankers chair that we had taken out of the Cellar into forward position, facing the windshield. Then gunned up the Hall-Scott truck engine and we were rolling down the road.

Ted and Lynette had moved onto a small farm outside San Diego. We parked in their yard, had dinner with them, and slept in the bus overnight. It felt like home. The next day we were back in Los Angeles. Because he was always advertising on TV, we gave Earl Schieb the job painting the bus for three hundred and fifty dollars. The blue color we picked was not nearly as deep and rich as we had imagined. Our new home was a light bright blue. On the highway, it would be as visible as any yellow school bus.

"...Smokin' in to New Orleans.
Somebody help me get out of Louisiana."

"The Promised Land," Chuck Berry
(Chuck Berry, Arc Music Corp.)

Leaving the bus behind at Babcock, we hooked the Volvo to the loaded U-Haul containing some furniture and my most prized possession, my record collection, all bound for Louisiana, where we would vacation before moving up north to San Francisco. We'd have an opportunity to visit with Kate's dad, David Russo, whose condition was deteriorating. Before leaving Babcock, I walked back into the garage apartment I had designed and built. I would carry this floor plan in my head for seven years before re-building it in the middle of twenty-seven acres of oak trees on the banks of the Vermilion Bayou. In the meantime, we had no address.

"Los Angeles, give me ...
Tidewater four ten oh nine
Tell the folks back home
This is the Promised Land callin'
And the poor boy is on the line."
(Ibid.)

South Louisiana
June 13, 1971

"Well I don't have much to say...
Walking to and fro beneath the moon..."

"Watching The River Flow," Bob Dylan
(Bob Dylan, Big Sky Music)

"There is nothing like a full moon in Louisiana in June, is there?" I asked.

"We have the same moon in Massachusetts, David," Charles Laquidara replied, "and these mosquitoes couldn't possibly compare with a full moon over the Cape. So will you just get out of here?"

Charles had come down from Boston to meet us. We were walking in David and Barbara Russo's backyard as it sloped down to meet the Vermilion Bayou, the moonlight ricocheting off the muddy river in a wavering pattern.

Charles and I had already covered the news on Daniel Ellsberg. The *New York Times* published the classified Pentagon Papers about U.S. involvement in Vietnam. Ellsberg, who had disclosed the papers, was indicted for unauthorized possession of secret documents. The Pentagon Papers revealed years of covering up by the government, validating many of the arguments put forth by the anti-war movement. We felt vindicated. In less than two months the White House would authorize the illegal break-in of Ellsberg's psychiatrist's office looking for incriminating evidence.

Also visiting out at David Russo's this evening was our old dare-devil friend and agri-pilot Hollis Gooch, Kate's brother Peter Russo, and Peter and Hollis's friend Reece Place. Along with Kate, the three of them returned from their walking excursion at the edge of the moonlit bayou. The talk centered on the growing demand for high-grade marijuana and cocaine. Buy enough ice for the local heat, and satisfaction could seep in through the south Louisiana coastline by the barge load. Everyone passed around a joint and then we went inside.

Kate and Peter's organizational skills, their inherited disdain for corrupt law enforcement, along with Hollis and Reece's get it done attitude would become the brain trust of a marijuana and cocaine smuggling organization that ultimately employed two hundred people, flowing millions of dollars into the local economy over a ten-year period. It would take a similar investment by the government to finally shut them down in Operation Bulldog.

David Russo was now bald from the cancer treatment. He seemed to be speeding through an old age he would never have.

"How you feeling?" Charles asked.

"About as good as a man with cancer can," David Russo replied.

When we drove out of the white shelled driveway later that evening, we were all very quiet.

"I've been through this before with my mother," Charles said in a low voice, "I won't be seeing David Russo again."

The next day Charles bought a handgun from Peter Russo at the Sportsman, the Russos' sporting goods store. Kate drove Charles to New

Orleans where she took him shopping. He updated his wardrobe with super-stylish *Superfly* threads and for good measure put an ornamental coke spoon on a gold chain around his neck. Then he boarded a jet for Boston.

On the plane, he struck up a conversation with a young man who was similarly attired. The talk led to the revolution, music, and drugs. Charles' new found friend was a high rolling coke dealer. On arriving at Logan Field in Boston, Charles deplaned into the arms of several FBI and DEA Agents. Although the search of his bags revealed no cocaine, Charles was charged with transporting an undeclared weapon on a passenger airline. As he was being cuffed and led away, the real dealer walked, winking at Charles and strolling leisurely for the exit.

After several hours behind bars, and a lot of explaining that he was not a coke dealer but just a paranoid disc jockey who wanted to own his own gun, Charles was released.

"It would be funny," he said to me on the phone, "but there is something else going on here."

"You mean the FBI?"

"That's it, David, the damned old FBI didn't care about any cocaine, that's not their job."

"What did they ask you?" I wanted to know.

"They were curious about Jim Bachman and *Zabriske Point*," Charles said. "They seemed to have a real deep interest in any left-wing activity. I am looking out from behind bars and I'm thinking, it's hard to figure out if we're the good guys or the bad guys."

"We're not the bad guys," I said, "Nixon's the bad guy."

"I know," Charles said. "What he's done to this country is unforgivable. He and his kind have turned it upside down so that we've become the outlaws. Nixon is a mean spirited vindictive man. We're probably on his enemy's list right now. They're the ones who subverted the Constitution. And we're being wired tapped, investigated, audited, and arrested. Watch out for the FBI parked in your neighborhood and don't think you're safe in Louisiana either. They'll probably just reassign the agents watching Carlos Marcello and the Russos to keeping an eye on you and Kate. And just try to ignore that chill creeping up your spine."

If the federales were wire-tapping David Russo's line, all they got was Kate sitting on the banks of the Rio de Los Lobos in Louisiana, selling air time on KPPC in Los Angeles to ad agencies in New York. Our subversive efforts were focused on getting the establishment ad dollars to pay for our revolutionary radio. Meanwhile, the establishment was co-opting the revolution to sell the same old corporate America themes of produce and consume. We were all getting too cynical too soon. The real revolution was in the consciousness of America that had been irrevocably changed. The deeper changes that could have been were fast becoming lost opportunities that would have to wait for some other future decade.

While the restless wind off the Gulf of Mexico blew through the oak trees, I contemplated the task still ahead. The stakes were huge in the two cities on the West Coast, but the green leaves of summer kept us from moving on. Les Carter called every day for a week. The Pierces had to get back. We just weren't quite ready.

"Oh this ol' river keeps on rollin' though,
No matter what gets in the way,
And which way the wind does blow."
(Ibid.)

1971

♦ "Cocaine Blues" writer Luke Jordan was a blues guitarist and singer out of Lynchburg, Virginia. He was 37 years old in 1929 when Victor Records took him to New York to record. "Cocaine Blues" was one of the songs on that session.

San Franciso
Late June 1971

Les Carter and I flew into San Francisco and checked in the Miyako Hotel in late afternoon. We tuned in the radio to KMPX, Les pulled out the record industry's finest promotional product and we each did a couple of king-sized lines. After awhile, we dialed up KSAN. Metro Media owned KSAN was the sister station of KMET in L.A. and just like down south, here in San Francisco, Metro Media would be our main competition for the heart and soul of the hip community. After losing KPPC, Tom Donahue had retreated to KSAN and though he was no longer on the air, the KSAN staff was Donahue's. Now his one time protégé, and the nemesis he never knew, had come to invade Tom Donahue's turf. Everyone in radio knew we were in town. The word had leaked from KMPX that we were due at the studio early the next morning.

Les sat quietly, smoking his pipe. Occasionally, we did a line and I smoked a couple of jays. We segued between KMPX and KSAN, taking note of the deejays' styles and music they played. We had very little conversation. Around midnight, Les tuned in a jazz station, left it playing softly, and then we turned in.

The next morning, around 10:00 a.m. we took a cab to Momma's Restaurant on the square. We had a large breakfast without talking. It would be our only meal of the day. When we left Momma's we walked across the square enjoying the cool sunlit morning. Hippies in colorful dress were all over the park. An occasional businessman in paisley tie with handmade leather briefcase strolled by. No Los Angeles pace here. This was one laid back hip city. Across the square we took a cab. Les told the driver our destination was the Miyako Hotel.

"We're not going to KMPX?" I asked surprised.

"Not right away," Les replied.

At the Miyako Hotel the day passed doing lines, smoking, and listening to the radio. Occasionally, we strayed to the top forty stations or the jazz stations, but it was mostly KMPX and KSAN. We were beginning to get the feel of Frisco's radio. We never left the Miyako.

"Jump out of bed, run downtown,
Take along the money,
And look all around.
Cocaine, aw you ol' cocaine."
(Ibid.)

The next morning, we repeated our trek to Momma's for breakfast and then back to the Miyako. The phone was ringing when we arrived. Susan Carter wanted to know if we were okay, and what had happened to us, because the KMPX staff was on edge in anticipation of our arrival.

"We're fine," Les said, "let them wait."

We repeated the previous day's activities. By afternoon, the legendary disc jockey Reno Nevada came on KSAN doing a relief shift for the regular jock. Reno was a veteran of at least two KMPX walk-outs. He had been banned from the station. Probably in his mid-thirties, he was one of the oldest and the most knowledgeable deejays in Underground and Free Form Radio. Now, he was scratching out an existence doing weekends and relief on KSAN.

After about one hour of Reno's show, Les spoke up, "What do you say we hire Reno Nevada for late night, 10:00 p.m. to 2:00 a.m.?"

"It would be a nice coup," I agreed, "bring the old warrior *and* his listeners home to KMPX."

Les called Reno on the KASN request line and offered him the job. Reno accepted. The next night, he was behind the mic on KMPX.

Later that evening, we cleaned out the last of the white powder from the brown colored bottle and talked more than we had in two days. The young disc jockey doing all night was a Jeff Gonzer type. Les was betting he could be as successful as Jeff in the morning drive. Don Hall and I would cover the rest of the daytime. The only other major shift was from 6:00 to 10:00 p.m., prime time in FM-Rock Radio. Les finally shared with me what he had, obviously, been thinking about for sometime. He would bring in Dr. Demento from Los Angeles to play his off-the-wall oldies show five nights a week in the city by the bay.

"That's pretty unorthodox, that's quite a long shot," I offered.

"This whole deal is a gamble," Les said. "I think this town is going to love Demento."

Once again, the only part of San Francisco we saw was from the window of the Miyako Hotel.

"Get out of here, Man,
I thought you understood
You got no connections
then you're no damn good.
Cocaine, aw you ol' cocaine."
(Ibid.)

Our third morning in San Francisco, we finally arrived at KMPX. Les called a meeting with the disc jockeys and let them know who was part of the team and who was going to have to look for a job. A couple of jocks were in limbo, maybe they would get a weekend shift, maybe not. We would decide later. Then we sat down Indian-style in the corner of the record library with the sales manager. He was forty, balding on top but long hair to his shoulders, wearing an expensive jacket.

"Glad you guys are here," the sales manager said. "It's about time this station is run by professionals. We can all make some big money here, but let me warn you, this isn't L.A. This city doesn't like outsiders, especially those from Tinsel Town. L.A. is a melting pot. San Francisco is a much thinner slice of the American Pie. It's much more hip and introspective."

Les and I exchanged glances. This guy was not only talking about the city, he was speaking about himself, too. "Well, that's fine," Les said slowly, firing up his pipe. "We will make some changes, the first one that effects you is the music business. As Music Director in L.A., Dave Pierce handled all the record companies' advertising dollars, he is going to do the same job here."

"Wait a minute," the sales manager protested, "that's my territory."

"Not anymore," Les said flatly.

"Why should I give up my relationship with the record industry so Dave Pierce can line his pockets?"

"That's not what it's about," I said. "We want a direct pipeline from the disc jockeys to the music advertising dollars, that's what the record companies want, too. It's the best way to keep the flow of information and dollars traveling down the same corridor. That's what I do."

"I'm not going to yield on this," the sales manager said, getting to his feet. "Stan Gurell told me personally that I was going to continue to handle the sales department. You guys are here to get listeners."

"We're here to run this radio station," Les countered.

"We'll see," the sales manager said, going out the door.

I stood up, and walked around the big record library room. Les continued to puff on his pipe.

"That guy will have to go," Les said, "as soon as you and Kate have the sales department figured out, fire him."

"Do we have that authority?" I asked.

Les smiled slowly. "Let's act like we do," he said.

> "Take me down, little Susie, take me down,
> I know you're the queen of the underground,
> ...Send me dead flowers by the U.S. mail."

"Dead Flowers," Rolling Stones
(Mick Jagger and Keith Richards, ABKCO Music, Inc.)

Los Angeles/San Francisco
Early July 1971

"Oh, hello, Mr. Soul
I dropped by to pick up a reason
For the thought that I caught
That my head is the event of the season."

"Mr. Soul," Buffalo Springfield
(Neil Young, Cotillion Music, Inc., Richie Furay Music, Springalo Toones,
Ten-East Music)

Finally, everything was in place for the Pierce family to move to San Francisco. The last night in Los Angeles, we spent the evening in Laurel Canyon at Les and Susan's home. After the dinner and wine, we sent John-David and 'Chelle up to bed, along with Kate's youngest brother, Carlos Russo, who had come back with us from the Louisiana visit. We rolled up some joints and Les pulled out the heavy stuff. We had an occasional bump of coke and talked about the 'Frisco expansion. That holier-than-thou attitude that the northern California city had for southern California in general, and Los Angeles specifically, was most rampant in the hip population of San Francisco. It wouldn't be easy to crack. Although we had blitzed L.A. in a year, we couldn't take that long this time.

Around midnight, Susan excused herself and reminded Les he had a show to do the next afternoon. After a while, I dragged myself upstairs to crash on the guest room floor where the kids were asleep and Carlos Russo was tossing and turning.

By 2:00 a.m., Carlos was talking in his sleep. At one point, he woke me up with the words, "You stupid son-of-a-bitch."

Where in his Russo family subconscious had that come from? Was he talking to me?

I lay there for several minutes, then I eased on down the stairs to find the louvered doors to the living room were closed. From the other side, I could hear soft jazz and hard breathing. Being something of a gentleman, I knocked lightly.

"Kate, Les, you guys still up?" I asked.

"Come on in," Les' voice came back through the doors. They were sitting together on the sofa. Kate was straightening her ankle-length frontier dress. Les was smiling sheepishly.

"Just having another little bump," he said.

"Couldn't sleep without you," I told Kate.

"I know," she said.

Suddenly, Susan appeared in the doorway, borderline fuming, her hands on her hips.

"If you think you can act like you're sick tomorrow afternoon and I'll do your show, you're crazy," Susan said to Les, as she exited up the stairs. "Now I think we should all say good-night."

If I had known Susan was awake, I would have gone to her room, I thought to myself as I grabbed Kate's hand. She kissed Les on the cheek. He poured himself another line and got a far-away jazzy look in his eye.

By 10:00 a.m., we had all hugged the Carters good-bye and started up I-5. No leisurely cruise up Highway 1 through Big Sur this time. We were over the Grape Vine, ten lanes wide, the Volvo picking up speed down into the San Joaquin Valley, the Santa Suzanna mountains to our left in the western sky. We bypassed the old Highway 99 route through Bakersfield, and continued up I-5 side-by-side with the California aqueduct, flowing the precious northern California resource to the water-starved Los Angeles basin.

"Don't waste the water," Casey had kept saying in the '40s and '50s. "We could run out."

I decided if he was right, I'd have to bet the faucets would go dry first in the L.A. basin.

We drove into San Francisco and went directly to KMPX. Don Hall was on the air. He was glad to see us, but seemed more freaked and spaced than usual.

"I don't know, man," Don Hall said. "I get bad vibes from the people up here."

"KMPX staff?" I asked.

"Yeah."

"Jocks, sales people?"

"Office staff, everybody. Not real obvious, you understand. Just bad vibes."

"I hear you, Don," Kate said. "I can feel it and I just walked in."

"Hey, they're just paranoid like the rest of us," I said. "We're coming into their town. What are the listeners saying? What about the community?"

"Everything's cool, man. Except for Demento. He's too L.A. for this town."

"What are you saying, they don't like oldies?" I asked.

"Not like we do in L.A. Demento's oldies are just a little too far out, too diverse, too much stuff that ain't rock 'n roll."

"I thought this was a hip town," I said.

"It ain't Los Angeles," Don snorted, as he cued up his record.

That evening we all checked into a motel where we lived for the next three nights. Days were spent at KMPX. I took over a 10:00 a.m. to 2:00 p.m. shift. The control booth looked out into the long twenty-by-thirty record library room. Kate had set up her office in a corner of the room. As I worked the show I could see her on the phone, burning up the wires to the advertising agencies in New York, Chicago, and L.A. She had figured out how to work the phones and deal quickly in information about the flow of advertising dollars, record product, music trends, and the latest drifts in the world of counterculture politics.

She fed it all back to me and I dispersed what I thought the KMPX audience cared to hear about.

The kids weren't feeling any bad vibes. They quickly won over the KMPX staffers. They spent all of my shift in the library, so I watched them color, snack, nap, and learn how to read the album covers stacked in the library shelves around the three walls of the library room.

"Hey, Dad, what does this say?" 'Chelle wanted to know.

"Read it," I said. "Sound it out."

"K-e-e-e-f Hart-ley Band," she pronounced slowly.

"Boy, KMPX has albums KPPC don't even have," John-David said, running back in the library room to thumb through the rows of albums for more new treasures from the world of music. From the KMPX Studio, it was a steep descent to the health food store on the corner for carob peanut butter bars. The kids always bought three bars, ate two and stashed one for later.

We liked the energy here in San Francisco. The Pierce family was going to fit in real good. After the third night at the motel, we put the word out that we were a homeless family available for adoption on a night-by-night basis. One of the weekend jocks graciously made the invitation. We followed him over the Golden Gate Bridge out to Marin County to spend the night at his home. But there was something missing in this northern California hospitality. After several weeks in Louisiana, we were having trouble feeling completely at home.

Of course we were total nomads by now and it became obvious by the end of the week that housing was both scarce and expensive. The bus was really our only immediate alternative. The total conversion to functioning livable space was going slowly and would not be completed by itself. We would have to split up. Kate, 'Chelle, and Carlos would drive back down to Los Angeles. John-David and I would remain at KMPX.

In the few minutes alone in the alley outside KMPX, I told Kate what had been bothering me for a week.

"Look, about this thing with you and Les, the night before we left Los Angeles..."

"It wasn't anything," she protested. "We were talking. We did a few lines, and in between he kissed me a couple of times, and put his head in my lap."

"What if I hadn't come down to get you?" I asked.

"I don't know. We were pretty turned on. But nothing happened, okay."

"Look, I know we're all free spirits, and..."

"...And you are a double standard, double dealing, rolling minstrel," Kate smiled at me. "Who can't even sing!"

> "She said, 'You're strange,
> But don't change.'
> And I let her."
> (Ibid.)

Now John-David and I were really on our own. One night we went home with Reno Nevada to his home in Marin County, a one-bedroom pad. After dinner, Reno apologized for the small quarters and showed us to the cellar space down a half flight of stairs. John-David and I rolled out our sleeping bags and crashed on the dirt floor in an area under the kitchen with only about three feet of headroom.

After that night, John-David and I lived at KMPX for a few days, rolling out our sleeping bags at night in the traffic office. Somewhere along the way, my wallet was lifted from our bags. It turned up later minus the American Express and Carte Blanche charge cards. For weeks after that, the vouchers came in: luggage, clothes, restaurants, car rentals, airline tickets. It didn't cost me a dime. I had reported the theft. Of course it could have happened anywhere, but I took it personally that someone at KMPX had targeted me. Maybe Don Hall was right. To me it was one more sign, the hip community and the revolution had big cracks in the armor of self-righteousness.

I decided it was time to weed out some of the opposition. I fired a particularly negative and not very talented weekend jock, replacing him with Jack Ellis. Not only was Jack an outstanding disc jockey, he was a native and very in tune with local politics. It was a brilliant move, or so I thought.

The local station manager, the National Science Network's personal rep and Stan Gurrel's protégé, was a thirty-five-year-old woman from New York City. She called me into her office.

"What do you mean hiring Jack Ellis? He was one of the strike leaders who took over KMPX last spring. He's persona non-grata at this station. Stan Gurrel will go nuts when he finds out."

"Frankly, I'd forgotten about Jack's role in the strike," I said, truthfully. "That's old history. We need Jack. Just like we need Reno Nevada. If we're going to turn KMPX into the kind of success we're enjoying at KPPC, we've got to get on with it. Jack's a bit of a radical, but he's just what this city loves. Besides, he's good people. I lived and worked with him in Los Angeles. Don't tell Stan just yet. Give Jack a chance to get in here. He's not going to lock me out of the control room."

"Don't tell Stan?" the corporate girl from New York City was outraged. "You people have no sense of company policy and protocol. You claim to advance a new way of doing business, then ignore all the rules. Like Les Carter down in Los Angeles, raving about free speech so he can play the Mothers of Invention with Frank Zappa singing, 'Rub an enchilada up a donkey's ass until he comes.' What's the point?"

"You got me there," I had to admit. "I would have passed on that lyric."

"Just because someone recorded it doesn't mean you have to play it," she said. "There's a difference between free speech and bad taste."

"Sure," I agreed. "But it's just a transition. In the big picture, the fight against censorship of the airwaves is what it's really all about, and I need Jack Ellis."

"All right," she said finally. "He stays for now. But no problems, okay?"

"Fine."

"Good. You know, Dave Pierce, I can't figure you out. You're obviously a talented broadcaster with the background and the smarts to work at any level in this industry and make some real money for yourself. But what I see in front of me is a man with hair to his shoulders, needing a shave. You're wearing faded jeans, worn boots, sleeping on the floor in a sleeping bag, your family split up, no home, planning to live in a bus. What's your goal?"

"The wheel's still in spin," I said. "Radio is my life. Disc jockeying is the greatest high there is. Sure, it's revolutionary, and it's right, but I also intend to cash in. We're on our way to the top in Los Angeles. We can do the same thing at KMPX. The National Science Network can own the two top stations on the coast. What's that worth?"

The girl from New York City looked at me like she had only now understood Les Carter's plan.

"You really believe you can do it, don't you?"

"That's what I'm here for," I replied.

"Is it strange I should change?
I don't know
Why don't you ask her."
(Ibid.)

San Francisco
Late July 1971

"I'd pay any price just to win you,
Surrender my good life for bad,
I call that a bargain,
The best I ever had."

"Bargain," The Who
(Pete Townshend, ABKCO Music, Inc., Careers BMD Music Publishing,
Suolubaf Music, Towser Tunes, Inc.)

The next weeks moved fast in both cities. Progress, however, was slow. Grasping control of KMPX was no easy task. Les and I talked daily by phone.

One weekend, Jack Ellis drove John-David and I over to Berkeley where the Mothers of Invention were playing in a small auditorium. Courtesy of the record company, we had seats close to the stage. I would have preferred to be in the back. The giant speakers on either side of the proscenium arch were totally overwhelming. With enough power to play an outdoor stadium, the decibel level in the small room was borderline painful. After a while the band took a break, and we all walked to the men's room. We stood in line outside a stall, and one by one stepped inside for a long snort of some first-rate coke, courtesy of the record company.

John-David waited for us outside. He was having a great time, delighted to see Frank Zappa up close and personal. He'd been singing "My dick is a monster" since he was four years old. Zappa was as big a hero as Batman.

"Come on, guys," he said. "Hurry up, we're going to miss The Mothers."

Down in Los Angeles, Kate was selling radio ads during the day and working on the bus at night, beating on Bill Jensen to finish the plumbing. One night she had a line of crystal meth, was wired for hours, and painted the entire bus interior in one evening. Charlotte Stewart was working on curtains with special backing material to insulate from the outside. The inside, however, was a soft velvety look from the '40s.

Kate was spending a couple of nights with Jeff Gonzer up in Laurel Canyon. One day Carlos Russo found a package stashed in the water softener container on Babcock. Kate took it on up to Jeff's house where the two of them sampled it, deciding it was high-grade coke. They went back for seconds and thirds to make sure they weren't deceiving themselves about the quality. Two days later, they returned the unused portion. By this time, however, the true owner, a renter of one side of the duplex at Babcock, had discovered the misappropriation and traced Kate to Jeff's house via a phone call to KPPC. For several days, Jeff was in a panic, convinced the Babcock renter was a Charles Manson-type killer who would come for them in the night.

Living on reds, and vitamin C, and cocaine was an exaggeration for most, but the casual use of coke was widespread. There was no perceived danger behind this slightly recreational involvement. It was just icing on the drug-culture cake.

I was on the air at KMPX when Nixon's wage and price decree came down. I picked up the feed and cued in the story.

Nixon's voice went out on the air, "We must stop the upward spiral of wages and prices, therefore, I have ordered a wage and price freeze."

Then I pulled out the Drifters with Clyde McPhatter singing lead on the '50s hit.

> *"You know the landlord rang my front door bell,*
> *I let ring it for a long long spell,*
> *...asked him just to tell me,*
> *What was on his mind."*

"Money Honey," The Drifters
(Clyde McPhatter and Gerald Wexler, Hill & Range; Unichappell Music, Inc., Warner-Tamerlane Publishing Co.)

San Francisco/Los Angeles
Early August 1971

"I'm going to inject your soul,
With some sweet old time rock 'n roll,
Shoot you full of rhythm and blues."

"Steamroller," James Taylor
(James Taylor, EMI Blackwood Music, Inc.)

When James Taylor went on the road in the spring of '71, his opening act was Carole King, who wrote his only number one song, "You've Got A Friend." By now, everyone knew who this beautiful singer-songwriter was with "It's Too Late," at the top of the charts and "Earth Move Under My Feet," at number three. John Lennon was preparing to release a song he titled "Imagine" and John Denver made the whole country homesick for a place that most had never seen with "Take Me Home Country Roads." John-David and I flew to Los Angeles for a visit and a conference with Les Carter. Though the calendar said we had not been there that long, Les and I were both impatient to show progress at KMPX. The networks, notably ABC, were already ripping off our Free Form approach with a tighter formatted Progressive Rock. The window of opportunity was steadily closing.

"Look, Demento's floundering up north," I said.

"I can't understand it," Les replied. "Demento has actually out-hipped San Francisco."

"Could be," I said, "but perhaps he's overexposed. Maybe we ought to play him only on Sunday nights, like we did in Los Angeles."

"Let's give him a little more time," Les insisted.

That night we all went to see Randy Newman at the Troubadour. We were seated on the right side of him where his piano didn't obstruct our view, and Randy had the satisfying habit of turning his head and throwing each lyric over his right shoulder. He also kept his right foot tapping throughout the entirely entertaining show.

The Pierces and Carters were high rolling, having a great adventure. We had spent enough time together to understand and genuinely like each other. We felt totally capable and in control. The heady aura of power followed us around Los Angeles, to the 2:00 a.m. parties where the Persuasions on the radio were telling you it was on "Pasadena Ster-r-e-o-o," through the clubs and restaurants, to the promotional meetings in the record company conference rooms, where the decisions were made and deals were cut. A new band's career and thousands of dollars depended on how many times the disc jockeys put the needle in the groove on their record. When you broke a song or an artist in Los Angeles with San Francisco as a bonus, every disc jockey and program director in America would take notice.

The next morning John-David and I flew back to San Francisco. When I went on the air at KMPX at 1:00 p.m., I called Susan Carter who had taken over my old shift from 1:00 to 4:00 p.m. at KPPC. We put our conversation live on both radio stations. We talked for five minutes about Randy Newman's music and his performance at the Troubadour, then came out of it with a three-record Randy Newman sweep in both cities simultaneously.

The radio fans loved it. The record company knew how to be grateful. Les Carter and I knew it was only the first of many such two-city hookups.

"I'm going to inject your soul,
With some sweet old time rock 'n roll,
Shoot you full of rhythm and blues."
(Ibid.)

San Francisco/Los Angeles
Late August 1971

"I started out on burgundy
But soon hit the harder stuff
...But the joke was on me,
There was nobody even there to call my bluff."

"Just Like Tom Thumb's Blues," Bob Dylan
(Bob Dylan, Special Rider Music)

Kate got in touch with Glen McKay who had a house in San Francisco where he kept all his materials for the Jefferson Airplane light show. For the next few days we had a place to crash since Glen was still holed up on the Oregon border. He did come down one evening to show John-David and 'Chelle how to put his light show together, using a complete library of hand painted slides projected onto the screen behind The Airplane.

Glen McKay was a master artist. In thirty minutes, John-David and 'Chelle learned more about lights and projection than they would have learned in two weeks of public schools.

We continued a pattern of weekdays in San Francisco, flying to Los Angeles on Friday afternoon to work on the bus, keeping tabs on KPPC sales, and talking strategy with the Carters, before flying back to Frisco on Monday morning. Since we had a trade deal on Pacific Airlines, no one cared about the cost. We started doing a show on Saturday afternoon at KPPC while we were in Los Angeles. For several weeks the Pierce Family was on the air in both cities and loving it. Through constant phone contact with Laquidara in Boston, we had a great deal of input and a terrific overview of what was going on in all three cities.

Right after Labor Day, the family stayed in L.A. while Les flew north with me to look in on KMPX. Again, we stayed at his favorite hotel, the Miyako. The next morning with the KMPX staff waiting for us to arrive for a general meeting, Les took his time getting dressed, then we went down for a leisurely breakfast. When we had finished a second cup of coffee, Les leaned back and lit his pipe.

"I'm going to resign as Program Director of KMPX," he said, dropping the bombshell.

"When?" I asked.

"This morning."

I was stunned silent.

"I know this is a surprise," Les said. "I don't think we can make it happen up here. Because we're from Los Angeles we're getting more resistance than normal."

"We've built an audience," I said.

"I know, but not fast enough," Les said. "I thought we could take the city by storm like we did in L.A. That's the only way it could have worked. We don't have enough momentum. It was always a gamble. We lost."

"I think you're bailing out early. Stick with it through the end of the year. I've only been here two months."

"You can stay if you want to," Les said. "But I'm going back to Los Angeles. I think I went one radio station too far. I'm worried about KPPC. Stan Gurrel has spent a lot of time in Los Angeles this summer meeting with Doug Cox. When he was in town last week, he wouldn't take my calls. Something's up."

"If there is, we'd just weaken our position by leaving KMPX," I argued.

"That's possible. But now I've got to gamble the other way. You and Kate stay here with Don Hall. I know you love San Francisco. You'll do fine."

"It doesn't add up, Les. I'm your guy. If you leave, I'm a dead Cajun hippie at KMPX. I'm out too."

We finally arrived at KMPX around 11:00 a.m. Les gave the staff the news and then talked with Don Hall.

Jack Ellis and two weekend jocks were in the library doorway.

"It's just like Bob Dylan said, man," Jack was loud enough for all to hear. "We're only a pawn in their game."

I walked outside into the alley to sniff the fresh, foggy air. No smog up here. My dream of having 'Chelle and John-David grow up in this enlightened city had just been crushed. I was bitterly disappointed. It wasn't smog that was burning my eyes. It was my own tears streaming down my face.

"Mr. Pierce, you okay?" the voice asking belonged to one of the young weekend relief jocks.

"I'm okay, man," I replied. "It's just that I was beginning to like it here."

I wasn't quite thirty years old, and this kid was calling me Mister.

By the 2:00 p.m., Miyako check out time, Les and I were in a cab schlepping our few bags back to the airport. When the game is over, you get out of town fast.

> *"A thousand miles away from home*
> *Sleeping in the rain...*
>
> *I'm on my way from Frisco*
> *Goin back to Dixieland."*
>
> "Waiting for a Train," Jimmie Rodgers
> (Jimmie Rodgers, APRS)

Los Angeles/Louisiana
September 1971

"And the thing that you're hearing,
Is only the sound of..."

"The Low Spark of High-heeled Boys," Traffic
(Steve Winwood and Jim Capaldi, Warner-Tamerland Publishing Corp.)

Back in Los Angeles, the Carters and the Pierce Family licked our wounds and tried to consolidate our power at KPPC. The legendary Pasadena Free Form Rocker was becoming more mainstream as the radio audience continued to grow. We knew the ratings that were due in November were going to be huge. We were already acting like we were the number one radio station in L.A. We sounded smooth and professional with all the attitudes that said we were on the leading edge of the early '70s hipness. But the old uneasiness of the '60s was haunting us. For Steve Segal, now known as the "Obscene Steven Clean," it took the form of going on the air one Saturday night and doing a very down rap about being sick and having diarrhea. Poor taste, but fascinating in the depths of the despair that he vocalized.

Susan Carter continued to work my old afternoon shift from 1:00 to 4:00 p.m. Some on the staff felt she should have stepped aside and let me do my show. It seemed evident that the big loser on the KMPX gamut was the Pierces, not the Carters. However, Kate was still selling. I did a couple of weekend shifts, filled in for Zack late mornings so he could do extra production, and put the finishing touches on my bus. I drew my salary and enjoyed the feeling of success and power that was flowing into KPPC.

"If you had just a minute to breathe
And they granted you one final wish
Would you ask for something like another chance?"
(Ibid.)

In Louisiana, David Russo's condition was deteriorating quickly. On September 19, Mike Russo called Kate.

"If you want to see our daddy while he's still alive, you'd better come now," Mike said.

Kate, John-David, and 'Chelle flew out immediately. I piddled around the bus all day, then crashed early that evening. At midnight, Kate called me from Louisiana. She had raced from the airport to the hospital. While John-David and 'Chelle waited in the back seat of the Russo's black Cadillac with Carlos, she hurried to David Russo's hospital bed. He came out of his near-death coma long enough to say, "Kato, my love," then he cursed and passed on.

I took the 2:00 a.m. flight from LAX, arrived in Abbeville that morning at 9:00 a.m. totally worn out and spaced.

David Russo had always said he wanted to be carried to his grave by six black men wearing diapers and led by a jazz band. Kate was trying for a jazz combo at least. But the Catholic church hierarchy was already straining to allow even the very basic church sacraments to this notorious personality. The church choir of a dozen young people sang, "Blowing in the Wind" at the gravesite.

The sky was heavy. Great black clouds pillared from horizon to horizon punctuated by flashes of lightning. It was, of course, the first cold front of the season coming down from the Pacific Northwest over the Rockies and across the Great Plains, passing over our heads to the Gulf of Mexico. But on this day, we knew this sky had been ordered by the Great Spirit. Men who leave their mark do not pass from this earth without the universe taking note. A king was dead.

The days that followed were somber, but included the feeling of relief that always comes to the family when the struggle is over for someone who has suffered with cancer.

We were not in a hurry to return to Los Angeles. Charles Laquidara called from Boston. He was putting together a local TV show to capitalize on his radio popularity. Vince Donofrio had come east from California to direct the episode. Charles wanted us to help with the show.

Kate and the kids took his offer and appeared in several sequences. It was a good move. She needed the diversion. I elected to stay behind in Louisiana, feeling the need to spend some time with my own parents. Casey was hopeful that I would come up with more concrete plans to come home to my roots.

By contrast, Nellie was not at all eager to have us return. "You've got your career," she said. "What will you do around here? A big-time Los Angeles disc jockey, you'll be bored in South Louisiana."

I appreciated Nellie's concern. She'd always been the one to inspire me to think big. There was more going on here, however. She knew what she'd have on her hands would be a bunch of longhaired, pot-smoking, left-winged radical hippies in a conservative small town. Worst, she'd have to admit they were her family.

There was still another factor working its way out of my subconscious into the new reality. My long twelve-year competition with David Russo was over. Had he survived, the two of us would have disagreed on several fronts. He thought very little of the lifestyle I'd chosen for his daughter and grandchildren. Only the physical distance between us had kept that issue from boiling over.

I drove up to our twenty-seven acres on the Vermilion River and walked around. There was a great healing presence that I felt among those oak trees. The same boyhood feeling I'd had in Intracoastal City, without the wildness and loneliness. This place was calmer. A great spot to raise kids, feel the oneness with nature that the concrete and smog of the L.A. basin made us crave.

With the '60s finally over, was the future in the cities going to be dictated by the rat race and riots? The fast track of Los Angeles was still there, but the tug of autumn in the woods was calling me back to this place of oak trees on the bayou. The only question was when.

> "And the man in the suit
> Has just bought a new car
> From the profit he made on your dreams."
> (Ibid.)

"When are you coming home?" Les Carter said on the telephone.

"I was beginning to think I was home," I said.

"Well, we need you out here," Les continued.

"What's cooking?"

"The station's doing great. Everything sounds really good. I want you guys back. Sales have to increase. Our nut keeps growing. Kate's the only one who can have an immediate impact on our income."

"Well, I'll tell her you miss her when she gets back from Boston," I said.

"I need you, too. Susan and I have talked it over. She and I are over-extended doing back-to-back shifts. She still wants to do a few shows, but you should get back on the air from 1:00 p.m. to 4:00 p.m. Things are getting weird with Doug Cox. You gotta get back out here. We all want the Pierce Family back in Los Angeles."

"We'll get on the airplane one more time," I said. "Thanks for calling me."

"And the thing that you're hearing,
Is only the sound..."
(Ibid.)

"Hello, Los Angeles," I said into the microphone. "Pierce family back from the radio wars in San Francisco, back from the country roads of South Louisiana. Kate, John-David, and 'Chelle back from a television pilot for Charles Laquidara on WBCN in Boston. Back to play radio with you on KPPC in Pasadena, the number one rock 'n roll station in Los Angeles playing Stevie Windwood and Traffic for you on a Tuesday afternoon. The smog level's high but so am I, and there's no place I'd rather be. Stay with us. Les Carter, the Obscene Steven Clean and Mississippi, all coming up later, at 106.7."

When I turned off the microphone, I heard the buzz of the intercom phone.

"Stan said he's coming down to see you," the secretary said.

A couple of minutes later Stan Gurrel walked in, his collar as stiff and tight as ever, with a perfectly matched tie, crisp looking.

"You wanted to see me?" he asked.

"Yes, I did, Stan. I appreciate you taking the time. I just want you to know I didn't want to leave KMPX. After going up there, I think we should have finished the job. It's my belief that we bailed out early."

Stan said nothing. He only stared back at me from behind his thick glasses. I knew this was the way you wielded corporate power. Say nothing, let the other guy talk. But I got the feeling he just had nothing to say to the longhaired guy in front of him. I kept talking.

"Now that I'm back in Los Angeles, I'm very enthused about KPPC. This station is definitely on a roll. We can feel it all over town. We have arrived. When the ratings come out in November we have a lock on first place. I don't know what angle you're looking from, Stan, but it's payoff time in Pasadena. All we have to do is stay the course. Don't let anybody mess with the combination. What we've got going here can't be re-created. This is a once in a lifetime situation. It'll never happen again. I know what ultimately happens out here is your decision. Don't let this one get away."

Stan still didn't answer.

"Look," I said. "We're not anarchists here, even though on the air we act a little crazy. These are all smart broadcasters. You know my background. I'm not just another hippie off the street."

I had run out of things to say. I didn't know exactly why I was saying them. I just felt the need to try to communicate with this man who showed no comprehension, no emotion.

"I'll get back to you," Stan said, as he left the control room.

> *"But today you just said*
> *That the man was shot dead*
> *By a gun that didn't make any noise."*
>
> "The Low Spark of High-heeled Boys," Traffic
> (Steve Winwood and Jim Capaldi, Warner-Tamerland Publishing Corp.)

Los Angeles
October 1971

"Did you see them in the river,
They were there to wave to you."

"Broken Arrow," Buffalo Springfield
(Neil Young, Cotillion Music, Inc., Richie Furay Music, Springalo Toones, Ten-East Music)

Susan Carter wanted to work my Friday afternoon shift, so I took the day off to put more final touches on the blue bus. We were living in it now, parked at the curb in front of our old home on Babcock in North Hollywood. The bus was beautiful, all systems worked. Compact, but totally livable. For me, a dream realized, for the kids, high adventure, for Kate, another challenge to keep it all together for her family.

I was at a camper shop on Ventura Boulevard out in Encino, having a towing hitch welded to the frame. I would be able to tow the Volvo easily, if we wanted to roll out of Los Angeles. All we needed was a reason and a place to go.

"You, the guy with the blue bus," the shop secretary was saying, "a lady wants to talk to you."

Kate was on the line, she'd just heard from Les Carter. I should call him at the station. When I got through to Les at KPPC, his voice was strained.

"It's all over, Dave," he said. "They're gonna take us out."

"Who, what? What are you talking about?"

"Our traffic girl is going out with a disc jockey from San Diego. Doug Cox hired this guy to go on the air at KPPC Monday morning. Steve also got a call from some friends at Warner Brothers, the word is out, Doug Cox and Stan Gurrel have put in the fix."

"I can't believe they're that crazy," I said, knowing that they were, and this really was for real.

"We're all going to stay on the air as long as we can," Les said, "you need to come on down and help us out."

"What's your plan?" I asked.

"Well, we'll just play music and rap," Les replied, "We'll stop plugging anymore sponsor messages, we'll tell our story. Let the whole city know what's going on. Galvanize the public opinion while we still have a voice."

"Doug's new staff will be dead before they walk in," I said.

"That's it exactly," he replied. "We'll go out in a blaze. We built this station. We created this sound. When we go, KPPC goes with us, there won't be anything left to steal."

"I'll be there," I said, "but I've got a couple of things to get done first."

The Pierce family didn't go to the station that night. The four of us listened to the radio, intermittently, for the next day. Catching smatterings of how it was going. The disc jockeys were taking turns doing a couple of hours at a time. Retelling the history of KPPC, the tapes, the live recollections, and the music. It was authentic and professional. The last look at Free Form Rock Radio.

On Saturday night, Kate and I went to dinner with Charlotte, Smokey, and Al Schmitt. I had turned thirty earlier in the week and this, my birthday celebration, had been planned for several days. In an old home in the hills above Sunset Strip, some young people were serving Greek cuisine in their living room. You booked the home for the whole evening. Tonight was our night courtesy of Smokey and Al Schmitt. The dinner was superb. Afterwards, Smokey pulled a small brown bottle, and passed it around. Just a couple of sniffs after dinner to brighten our senses. The only way the drug should ever be used, in an intellectual fashion, on special occasions. The talk turned to KPPC. The whole city was buzzing. Never in the annals of radio history had a disc jockey staff this popular gone out this way. The number one rocker in town was breathing its last gasp and all its listeners knew it. The station that I helped build. Monday morning I'd be unemployed. The events of the last six weeks had prepared the Pierces well for the final blow. The '60s had proved to be the ground school we would need for the future decades. You only turn thirty once. Once would be enough.

Around dark on Sunday evening, we unplugged the bus and drove it to Pasadena and onto 99 South Chester Street. It looked like a war zone. People and cars were streaming up to KPPC. When the bus appeared, some people moved a couple of vans so I could maneuver it in close to the studio, and plug into the same power source as the turn-tables. Sam Kopper's production bus was already parked. I pulled in behind him. Several members of the staff came into the bus, to check it out. I lingered outside the studio making small talk, greeting people. The way you do at a funeral home, reluctant to go inside and face the deceased. Finally, I went into the control room. It was overflowing with people. Jeff had been on the air, but Steve was now sliding in behind the microphone, as the Persuasions sang again a cappella "KPPC-FM Pasadena...Ster-ee-ooo." The rap line was ringing off the wall. Les and Susan were in one corner of the studio. Les was leafing through a large box of telegrams. He handed one to Steve who read it live on the air. It was a message from one of the faithful fans, thanking us for the many years of great music. Other telegrams cried out for vengeance.

"We got hundreds of them," Les said.

"The Hell's Angels have offered to put a hit on anyone from the station ownership or anyone of the new staff that's coming in," Steve was saying on the radio, "but everyone knows, that's not us, that's not the KPPC family. We represent the future. We are not just peace and love. We are what's right."

Susan looked at me, "We were beginning to think you weren't coming."

"We've been here in spirit," I replied.

The air of apprehension was heavy. Would Doug Cox come down to the station with storm troops, enforcers, demanding that we return the broadcast property we had commandeered? It wasn't like we had locked ourselves in the control room. Anyone could walk in, including Doug Cox. It was only a few minutes later when the On the Air monitor went dead.

Steve turned to Les, "They pulled the plug," he said.

"Must have killed the signal at the transmitter. Good strategy on Doug's part," Les had to admit.

I walked out of the control room into the record library. Ted Alvy was there. "Any of this look familiar?" I asked him.

"We're only a pawn in the game," Ted replied.

I pulled a joint from my pocket and passed it to Ted. "You were always offering one of these when you were on the strike line," I reminded him.

"Yeah, I remember," Ted Alvy smiled.

We were pretty high ten minutes later when Doug Cox walked in with one policeman. The first thing he did was turn on all the lights.

"Can everyone hear me?" Doug announced loudly. "You're all fired. You may be a commercial success but frankly, I don't like you."

In a quiet and orderly fashion, we began to disburse. Les cornered Cox about severance pay. He quickly assured Les that everyone would be dealt with fairly. After all, this was just business. Everything was very civilized. In a few minutes I had disconnected the cables to the bus, and we were heading west on the new 210 freeway north of Glendale.

"Very weird tonight," Kate said. "Right after Doug Cox walked in I swear, I heard my Daddy laughing."

Just like David Russo, I thought. He would take the last hand and laugh about it. Suddenly, the bus lost power, it just didn't pull properly. We crept back to the North Hollywood curb and crashed.

The next morning the news of the KPPC firing was all over Los Angeles radio and TV. Les Carter called a news conference and in front of the TV cameras he dumped the box with hundreds of telegrams of support.

The S.D.S., Students for a Democratic Society, sent the message, "say the word and KPPC would be bombed into oblivion." In a long article, The L.A. Times named the ex-staff. Les had listed Kate and me twice, both in sales and as air staff. The Pierce Family were listed as air staff, plus Kate and I, John-David, and 'Chelle as individuals. With that kind of accounting, the staff numbered twenty-seven fired.

I dropped the bus off at the Crown Coach Company in downtown Los Angeles. The six cylinder Hall Scott truck engine had overheated, and would cost one thousand dollars to rebuild. By tilting the fan blades we could avoid a future problem. It seems that school buses were made for hauling kids up and down streets, at thirty-five to forty miles per hour, tops. Fifty on the freeway was more than the cooling system was built to handle. No one at Crown Coach had thought about telling me that. Now our bus would be in the shop for a week. But since it was our home, we had no place to live.

Kate picked me up in the Volvo and we drove over to KPPC for a ten-minute meeting with Doug Cox. He was conciliatory, apologetic, and offered us our jobs back.

"I know you guys have put your balls into this place," he said to me and Kate. "Stan Gurrel is not a bad guy, he is a business man, he specifically told me to ask you guys to stay on."

"Obviously, we couldn't work here with you Doug," Kate was quick to reply. "Tell Stan Gurrel he can suck my dick."

I looked at Doug for a long moment then began to speak, "You know Doug, I've been in and out of this station several times. The last time, in the turmoil of an ownership fight. It's actually very fitting that I leave this way, and, for the final time."

"I know that," Doug Cox said. "I want you to know that I could work with you, this is still a great station."

"No, it's not, Doug," I said. "Last night you killed a great station, what you have on the air is a pretty lame imitation. You are right about one thing, though, you could have worked with me, we could have all been winners. This is the best shot you and I will ever have, this way we all lose. You, me, Les, the disc jockeys, and Stan Gurrel."

When the ratings came out, two weeks later in November, KPPC-FM was the **Number One Rock 'n Roll Station in Los Angeles**, in eighteen to thirty-four-year-old adults. The next rating period was in April 1972, after six months under Doug Cox's new staff. KPPC-FM did not even show up in the rating book. It had literally fallen out of the book. Doug Cox was fired a few days later. The National Science Network of New York City eventually sold KMPX San Francisco and KPPC Los Angeles for several million less than their estimated values in October of 1971.

> *"The lights turned on*
> *And the curtain fell down,*
> *And when it was over,*
> *It felt like a dream."*
> (Ibid.)

Los Angeles
Late October 1971

"You don't need no gypsy
to tell you why
You can't let one
precious day slip by."

"Ain't Wastin Time No More," Allman Brothers Band
(Gregg Allman, No Exit Music Co.)

Duane Allman went out for a motorcycle ride and never came back. "Eat a Peach" zoomed on the charts, but it was the last time we'd hear Duane and Dickie Betts trading lead guitar lines, snaking in and out of a continuous tangle of sound that soothed the soul. And from now on, Greg Allman's husky haunting solos would always evoke the memory.

KPPC wasn't just the end of another radio war. For us, and all the radio fans, it was the symbolic end of the great experiment. It was the failed expedition of a new lifestyle, the end of the Woodstock generation. The end of the desire to do right and good, while we simultaneously embraced all the same sins that always keep movements from living up to their potential. We had fought the monster, and the best we could settle for was a draw.

All over America it was ending, co-opted by the establishment. The flower children selling out for adulthood, responsibility, and a piece of the promise of the '70s.

"Look up at the stars above,
Go on down town baby,
Find somebody to love."
(Ibid.)

I had the feeling that in the future, nostalgia for the sixties would run rampant. Rock historians would wax poetic about this era. Future rock musicians would return to these roots. Music from the heart, they would call it. But the rallying cry of sex, drugs, and rock 'n roll would never be as sweet. '60s drugs would be blamed for society's ills while the Pharmco giants, backed by big government buddies, bankrupted America on prescription insanity. Free sex would become dangerous to your physical health as well as your spirit. And a lot of rock 'n roll would bore you to death.

I knew that I would often think back to this time, but it would be hard, painful. It's not just the lost youth, it's the lost opportunity.

"Meanwhile, I ain't wasting time no more."
(Ibid.)

Los Angeles
Thangsgiving 1971

"Well you ask how much I love you,
Why do ships with sails love the wind."

"Ships With Sails," The Doors
(Robert A. Krieger, Raymond D. Manzarek, John Paul Densmore, Alchemical Music Co.)

At Mississippi and Dierdre O'Donohue's house in Altadena, the ex-KPPC disc jockeys and their families gathered for the holiday meal. We drove the blue bus over. It was totally road worthy and we had adapted to the small quarters. The Pierces were living a perpetual campout. We parked next to Sam Kopper's production bus. He and I talked about how it would be possible to put together a complete radio staff and tour around the country in these buses and do radio shows in different cities. Cross pollinating the counter culture, the way we had done in Frisco, L.A., and Boston.

Les Carter had negotiated to move the entire disc jockey staff and supporting sales people to a new position on the dial. KBIG came very close to taking the deal. But they were corporate owned and leery of these disc jockeys who now had the reputation of being anti-business, even though our ratings had proven that we were the best at the business of radio broadcasting. KMET had immediately gone after Jeff Gonzer and Steven Clean. They were the two highest rated performers from the KPPC staff because of their morning drive and 6:00 p.m. power shifts. They could fit very easily into KMET's operation. Finally, we all agreed that Jeff and Steve should take the KMET jobs while the gig was available. Again, I thought we dialed out early, because that ended any possibility of all of us continuing to work as a team that was as pro at radio as NASA was at moon shots. On Thanksgiving Day, we knew it was the last time all of us would be together.

Jeff, Mississippi, and I were sitting in the living room looking through the open window. We could see John-David and Steven having one more game of one-on-one under the basketball hoop. 'Chelle was helping Kate and the girls complete dinner preparations.

"I wonder how these kids might remember the '60s?" Jeff said aloud. "Will they follow in our footsteps?"

Mississippi thought a minute before he snickered, then smiled, "They'll probably grow up to be right-wing Republicans," he said. He was right.

"You seem pretty calm through all of this," Jeff said to me, "almost philosophical."

"I'm on automatic now," I said, "too much has come down too fast. There is nothing left to feel."

"What will you guys do now?" Jeff asked

"I think I would like to go down South and plant some corn, maybe grow a little grass between the rows."

"You're not leaving Los Angeles for Louisiana?" Mississippi found that hard to understand.

"My problem is that I really believed what we said on the radio," I answered. "I sang all the lyrics in my head so many times, I believed them."

"Please don't ask me my direction,
Let my tracks be buried in the sea."
(Ibid.)

All the good-byes to all our Angelino friends were tempered with "We'll be back." Jim Bachman was most optimistic about our future.

"The entertainment industry is diversifying," he said. "Hollywood is not the only center anymore. Runaway productions are the future. You'll probably have as good a chance of acting in New Orleans and Lafayette as you would here in Los Angeles."

Inside, I knew the old red-haired German's heart was breaking, so was mine.

Link Wyler and I had already drifted apart, too much ideology had gotten in the way. He would hear later that I was gone.

I had one more phone call to make, this time to Charles Laquidara.

"So, David, this is the big move," Charles said. "You'll get used to it. Look at me; there's something nice about being on your home turf."

"Yeah, I've been craving that part a long time. It's just that after riding on the Ether Express, after the high of the last couple of years, I'm afraid everything from now on will be anticlimactic. I love this town. Who knows, I can always come back."

"Sure you can, and you don't have to quit radio, you know. If you're desperate to go back down South with all the bigots, you could work in New Orleans or Houston, or if you want to come to Boston, I know I could get you on here," Charles offered.

"Yeah, you could, and I might. Then again I would like to move into television. A whole other world."

"No music on TV, David."

"Not yet. Anyway, you're my voice now. As long as you're behind the mic and cueing up records, I'll feel like I'm on the air."

"Look at it this way, David, we *were* the '60s, the first step in crying out for a better world. That cry is going to echo around the planet and into the '70s and '80s. Who knows how far into the future, 'cause every society is going to have to keep fighting for their freedom. In the '60s, in America, our generation showed them how to do it. Just because it's over don't mean it was a bust."

"It all got turned around, didn't it," I said. "Civil Rights, Women's Rights, the fight against an imperialistic foreign policy. From personal issues all the way to planetary changes."

"I don't think this country will ever fight another Vietnam War," Charles said. "To every American boy that turns eighteen from now on, we can say we did our part. I feel pretty good about that."

"When would you say was the beginning?" I asked.

"I don't know when exactly, but I'll tell you where. Where revolutions always start. With a handful of students who keep talking until it sweeps the country like a wild fire. Later, people will write volumes about the politics that powered the revolution, but that's how it started. Rebellion is a young man's game."

"So is disc jockeying," I said.

"I'll tell you, David, you may be right, but they're going to have to pry my cold dead fingers off the microphone. There's nothing else I wanna do. Hell, there's nothing else I'm capable of doing."

"You think a time like the '60s will ever come again?"

"I'd bet on it; the job's not finished. This country is still fat, lazy, and greedy at the core. The powerful and wealthy will always find ways to divide and conquer us. Tell us that a piece of the pie is more important than doing what is right. The job's not finished."

"You're saying that sometime in the future there will be another awakening?"

"Absolutely, only this time with even greater awareness. It will build on the '60s. The next generation will pick-up where we left off. It's evolution."

"Want to pick a time frame?" I asked.

"No, but I'll tell you this. You will hear it first in the music. Listen carefully for the signs. It will be on the radio in the lyrics."

> "Well, you asked how much I love you,
> Why do ships with sails love the wind."
> (Ibid.)

Los Angeles, I-10 East, Louisiana
December 1971

Hollis Gooch flew to Los Angeles to meet us. The dare devil agri-pilot was not about to miss the upcoming adventure.

Our last night in the city, Charlotte Stewart came over to spend the evening. She and Kate cooked dinner for all of us, which included Russie's kids: Lisa, Leslie, and Michael, all hitching a ride in the Blue Bus for Christmas in Louisiana.

The next morning we said goodbye to Charlotte. Towing the Volvo, with our few remaining worldly possessions stashed and lashed down, I maneuvered the blue Crown Coach away from the curb at 6416 Babcock in North Hollywood. Dodging traffic we left-turned onto Victory Boulevard for a block and a half then up to the Hollywood freeway ramp. One last glance at the Capitol Records building, through the downtown interchange, and then east to San Bernadino. The brown L.A. haze followed us all the way to Indio. By dark, we were in Yuma where we docked at a KOA campground.

On day two, Hollis, who was still on Louisiana time, where he was usually in his airplane at the crack of dawn, woke up at 4:00 a.m.

Thirteen-year-old Lisa got up with him to roll his jay supply for the day and talked to him about Louisiana. Hollis unplugged the bus and was rolling east on I-10, before we ever woke up. We passed through the familiar towns of Gila Bend and Tuscon. Somewhere in South Arizona, we drove through the tail end of a winter snowstorm, the big Blue Bus tracking through the white stuff. We stopped long enough for the five kids to have a snowball fight, then we were on the road again. The Blue Bus drew a lot of looks from passing motorists. After a decade of very weird and colorful conversions of vans and buses, this was still the first Crown Coach they had ever seen to hit the road as a motor mobile home.

That night we made camp in El Paso. After dinner, Hollis slipped out to make a run over the border into Juarez. It was after 3:00 a.m. when he stumbled in, smelling of cheap tequila and bad women. The next morning, Hollis did not wake early. We were halfway through Texas when he finally regained consciousness, but he did wake up grinning.

I-10 was virtually complete now, as was I-40 further north, changing forever the American landscape, killing off the Old Spanish Trail, Route 66, and all of the small towns which would be replaced by off ramps to fast food franchise sameness. We had passed through Vanhorn and Fort Stockton, rolling past the exit for Marfa to the south, where James Dean had swaggered around Little Reatta in his last role as Jett Rink. On the radio, Don McClain's "Bye Bye Miss American Pie" was heading for number one. The five kids and three adults on the bus sang along on "The Day the Music Died." Hollis and I singing the loudest on the line "with the coat he borrowed from James Dean."

I thought about Casey, traveling this same route after the horrors of World War II and convalescing in Santa Fe, with a bullet hole in his shoulder trying to get back to the bayou. Now I was coming home with everything I had to show for the past ten years, all loaded into a 1952 Crown Coach.

> *"Who should be sleepin',*
> *But is writing this song,*
> *Wishin' and a-hopin*
> *He weren't so damned wrong*
> *...Who's saying baby,*
> *That don't mean a thing."*
>
> "Nowadays Clancy Can't Even Sing," Buffalo Springfield
> (Neil Young, Cotillion Music Inc., Richie Furay Music, Springalo Toones, Ten-East Music)

There was one last campground in Austin. The western landscape began to give way to the southern belt, where the green of another growing season was turning to December's golds, yellows, and browns. Finally, we crossed the Sabine River out of east Texas into Louisiana. An hour later we were east of Lake Charles in the flat prairies that mechanized Germans and industrious Cajuns had turned into rice country.

Just before dark, we turned down the old familiar tree lined street to Casey and Nellie's house on the Vermilion Bayou.

I had left this sleepy little town ten and a half years ago, a bright-eyed kid with a dream. The '60s had changed us all. I was returning with a family and an uncertain future. I could not even think about what life would be like here. The smog basin dream factory would be hard to forget. My days with the disc jockeys would haunt me forever, but for now I felt good on this Christmas season. The banks of the Rio de Los Lobos were peaceful. The journey was over. We were home.

Epilogue

In April of '72 John-David, 'Chelle, Kate, and I joined Les and Susan Carter, Sam Kopper, and Spencer St. Clair in Denver to try and win control of an FM station for an owner who was about as honest as a Denver man can be. We lost. In August, shot too high at BCN trying to get involved in a piece of their record company business, Laquidara couldn't help me that big. In '73, Jeff Gonzer sent my air check to the KLOS sister station in Houston, KAUM FM. I played rock 'n stereo for the ABC affiliate until my ears hurt from the repetition.

Restless, I went back to the bayou country again to try and make my stand. When I got tired of cleaning out the barns on the old farm in Intracoastal (I had actually gone from radio star in L.A. back to shoveling shit in Louisiana), I went full circle and deejayed Top 40 at KROF for a year before turning off the microphone and turn tables.

Ted Cessac had followed me home to the bayou. His wife, Lynette Winter, easily convinced us that we knew how to run a theatre. The Abbey Players sprang out of the Cellar Theatre roots. With professional productions and superb promotion, we quickly became known from New Orleans to Houston.

When Kate and I split up, she and Reece Place got the kids and the Mercedes, and the franchise to smuggle and distribute. I got an old pickup truck and a rate card and started selling television advertising.

As sales manager at KADN TV-15 in the mid-80s, my job was to keep enough money coming in after the oil industry went bust. There was no blood on the streets, but after the Wild West gold rush-type spending binge that preceded this downturn, Lafayette, Louisiana, was drowning in red ink. Channel 15's survival was not a done deal. A twelve-hundred foot stick and 2.5 million-watt transmitter would do the job. I had to find the money in a depressed market. We called it guerrilla television. Down the road, Rupert Murdoch (who was the best strike buster ever, getting his start by out-slugging the London newspaper unions) would be going after the ultimate media prize, global domination. The old Metromedia television station group in the major markets, along with small town UHF indys like us, would form Murdoch's Fox Network. At Fox 15 our fortunes would change rapidly. We'd become a top rated Fox affiliate and cut out our share of the local ad dollars. Doing television advertising deals would, on some days, become almost as much fun as playing music on the radio.

I was adding to our sales staff when Shelly Brown, twenty years old, blonde, polite, and confident with a slightly punk attitude walked into my office. Her dad was in the Orleans Parish Sheriff's department and had worked for Jim Garrison. In the fifteen years we were married, we helped build the Abbey Players into one of the most successful community theatres in the country, directing and co-starring in shows that set box office records. She lived in Los Angeles months at a time, learning show business and hanging out on the set of *Cheers* and *Frazier*.

In 1999, she walked out with all the enthusiasm of a new Divinity student chasing the siren call of the Scientologist to their gilded Celebrity Center on Franklin Avenue in Hollywood. Intrigued by the technology of Dianetics, I took several courses, but declined their advice to sell my home to finance going clear.

In the '80s I started to write screenplays, fleshing out ideas John-David brought to me. The lead characters were two young men based on J.D. and a composite of buddies.

"Hey Dad," he told me one midnight as he ran out of the house to report to the Intracoastal docks for his job as a diving assistant, "you and your buddy are on a diving boat heading out into the Gulf of Mexico, but you don't know where you're going or why."

Six years later that story made it to the Abbey stage when *90 MILES OUT, 90 FEET DEEP* opened to enthusiastic audience approval, and a promise to myself to get it on film.

In '97, I accepted the role no actor could refuse, John Proctor, the righteous farmer with the wandering eye who got crossways with the hanging judges in colonial Massachusetts. *THE CRUCIBLE* was Arthur Miller's Pulitzer prize-winning shot at the 1950s House Un-American Activities Committee. I figure he had written it for me. The Abbey production put me opposite Sarah Fox wearing her hair in a tight bun, the epitome of a Puritan wife.

I learned she was an artist, as well as a costume and production designer on several movies shot in Louisiana. Defintely knew her way around a film set and had indeed designed the costumes worn by Armand Assante and Robert Duvall in *Belizaire the Cajun*. The tight bun was really waist-long auburn hair, just like the flower girls from the '60s. Miz Fox became my mate and partner. My house was once again filled with youngsters and teens, as grandchildren and step-kids decided the place to hang was where there was a tolerance for a variety of bad music and the parental authority was most lax.

With Sarah's expertise and John-David's leadership skills, we formed the WOODLAWN PLAYERS, writing and producing comedies with local settings and characters, filled with music selected by the old hit-maker's ear. Audiences turned out to see themselves on stage. In the heat of a Louisiana political race, we wrote and staged Boudreaux & Thibodeaux Run...for Governor. Our actor portraying Boudreaux, the mythical comic Cajun folk hero, entered the race and ran eleventh in a field of seventeen. My original script THIS MAGIC MOMENT delved into the record company/disc jockey/ad sponsor relationship while a talented cast of impersonators ripped through the hits from 1955-75. In JUKEBOX JACK, I portrayed a Cajun farmer's mistrust of the oil companies drilling on his land and spoke my late father's words asking once again "who's counting the barrels." The oilmen in the audience chuckled knowingly and stopped the show with a round of applause.

Took the edge off my unsatisfied need to anchor the news by hosting *UP ON THE STAGE*, a half-hour show, produced by Sarah, promoting local community theatre on the access cable channel. All of this longevity was recognized by *The Times* Reader's Poll Award for "Acadiana's Favorite Actor."

Glendale, Claifornia
June 27, 2005

Today I was seated on the sofa in the house of film writer Stephen Moos who sat behind the cameraman in front of me. To my right, award-winning documentary filmmaker Cass Paley peered into his monitor, voicing approval at the progress of the shoot. To the left, Sarah Fox had her digital video camera tight on my face so we could later critique my reactions. Outside a few blocks south, traffic on the 134 crisscrossed Glendale at 75 mph running parallel to Colorado Blvd. where forty years ago I sped to Pasadena at 5 a.m. to fire up the KPPC transmitter.

Steven Moos had contacted Charles Laquidara in Maui for info to make a documentary on KPPC. Charles' reply was "call Pierce, he wrote a book about the whole story." As I emailed *Ether Express* to Moos and Paley, one file at a time, I learned they were for real. Stephen Moos was part of the Los Angeles cult following that still wondered what happened to KPPC all those years ago. He was at The Band concert in October 1970 at Pasadena Civic when he was thirteen. Cass Paley had spent his youth in Boston listening to WBCN and Laquidara. With the skills of a good detective, necessary for a documentary maker, he hunted down the disc jockeys. Paley put the phone to my ear when he got Jeff Gonzer on the line at Westwood One. He found film maker Alan Gerstal anchoring the news in Florida. Alan's original *Pierce Family* footage would be in the documentary. When he reached Steven Clean in Milwaukee, the Seagull's response was "How come it took you thirty-four years to get to this story?"

With the light bouncing off my silver grey hair, Steven Moos fired the questions. When did you first go on the air as a deejay? Where did you meet Les Carter? How did you manage to do that kind of radio from the basement of a church? What do you remember of the summer of '71 in San Francisco, and the final days on Chester Street in Pasadena?

I was trying to re-create the word flow from my most recent read of the book. I had sat on *Ether Express* for over fifteen years. Except for several typo cleanups and updates of the epilogue, it was pretty much the same as it was when I wrote it out, in those all night sessions in the deep woods of Vermilion Parish when the memory was still strong and the ink flowed from the pen. The mechanics of publishing were in place. *Ether Express* was ready for the ride.

In a Cajun joint no bigger than Berro Bernard's 1940s Fais Do Do Club, I was inducted into the local fraternity of "Living Legends." With my family and friends gathered, I was proud and humble. From far away I could hear the tingle of the triangle and the clackity of the spoons.

"Jole Blon,
Tu m'as quitte'
Moi, tout seul
Pon t'en alle
Avec ta famille."

"Jole Blon"
(Joe Falcon and Cléoma Falcon)

Bobby Charles

Wrote and sang with members of The Band, Neil Young, Willie Nelson, and Kris Kristofferson. His music often shows up on movie soundtracks. His "Walkin' to New Orleans," written with Fats Domino fifty years ago, has more meaning than ever. He lives alone on a stretch of beach on the Louisiana Gulf Coast.

Woodie Bernard

Is still punching holes for the oil industry in the Gulf of Mexico. He built a home on the banks of Vermilion Bayou a few miles north of where his Grandpa Berro Bernard's Cajun Dance Club once stood. When the season opens each September, he hunts alligators.

Woodie Bernard's letters from Vietnam were never mailed. He put them in my hand years later when the war was over. He was very much a patriot and would never have disclosed that he was in fact a member of SOG, a highly classified unit which conducted operations in North Vietnam, Laos, and Cambodia.

Smokey Roberds

Became a Doctor of Chiropractic in Nashville. Dr. Roberd's clientele included some of Music City's most treasured residents. His syndicated talk radio show "Second Opinion" played in several markets. Now in the Arkansas Ozarks, I drive or fly to Fayetteville regularly to visit Smokey and his family. He e-mails me concerns about the size of America's national and personal debt. And the price of gold and silver.

Vince Donofrio

Raised his son as a single parent, and worked on the fringes of the entertainment industry. He visited Louisiana to direct and act in Abbey Players productions. While working for the Los Angeles Lakers, he won an Emmy for sports broadcasting. The Detroit Kid continues to write and record music. When in L.A., I always stay at his home off Topanga Blvd.

Ken Rose

Was a lighting man for CBS news in Los Angeles. Ken built and produced several theatres at the Padre Hotel before retiring to his home in the Hollywood Hills above the Capitol Records Building.

Charlotte Stewart

Lives in Studio City, and continues to act in character parts in television and films. She is now married to David Banks, Jr.

Stuart Margolin

Lives on an island off Vancouver. He acts, directs, and reprises his role as Angel on new episodes of *The Rockford Files.*

Danny Truhitte

Runs a dance studio in North Carolina.

Link Wyler

Became a focal point of the busing controversy in Los Angeles when he refused to bus his children from Sherman Oaks to downtown L.A. He acted in and directed titles for several movies, including *Splash* and *Elec-*

tric Horseman. Link fulfilled his dream of becoming a producer in the summer of '94 with a *Grizzly Adams* sequel shot on location in Mammoth, California, his favorite fishing spot in the high country...then he was shot down with a brain tumor.

David Lannan

As a vehicle delivery driver, he travels all over America's highways. David brings along his guitar and writes and sings cutting-edge environmental songs. His work is available on his web site.

Ron Adkins

Became a corporate troubleshooter reversing the fortunes of floundering companies.

Jim Bachman

Continued to work in the motion picture industry until the early '90s. After convalescing in the VA hospital from a stroke, he became a recluse. His voice on an answering machine was all that was left of his contact with the outside world. When he died on his birthday, December 12, the answering machine also expired from input overload.

Jim Garrison

Died in New Orleans in 1992, still the only man to bring the murder of John F. Kennedy to trial.

Carlos Marcello

Was finally convicted of mail fraud, and spent his final years operating the elevator at a federal prison. Soon after his release in 1993, he died at home with his family.

Carlos Russo

Grew up to design ladies' fashions and manage his own clothing store. He abruptly went into the ministry and operated The Well, a shelter for the homeless in Lafayette, Louisiana. One of his sons, Frankie Russo, is a singer-songwriter.

Joey And Mike Russo

Joey heads an agency dispensing home care to the aged.

Mike runs the family business, The Sportsman. His son, Joseph David Russo, is a unit production manager in Hollywood.

Peter Russo, Hollis Gooch, And Reece Place

All did three years in federal prison, charged with smuggling on the high seas, for their part in Operation Bulldog, one of the largest drug cases in U.S. history. They all became model citizens in their community. Peter Russo died at forty-seven, five days into 1996 when his damaged liver failed.

Hollis Gooch is still an agri-pilot, dawn to dusk.

Reece Place hot shots drilling equipment to the oil patch, riding the interstate highways and back roads blacktop as an independent trucker.

Kate Russo

Kate Russo and I were divorced in 1973. She married Reece Place in '74. In December 1982, Kate was run off the road a half-mile from her home in south Louisiana. The hit men were Noriega agents involved in the Bulldog conspiracy. For the next eighteen years, she was slowed down only slightly by the wheelchair from which she conducted her life, her business, and her family. Forty days into the new millennium, her liver failed.

'Chelle Pierce Campisi

Worked at my TV station while studying for a Masters Degree in Sociology specializing in dysfunctional families. She now works and lives in Houston, Texas, with her son Andrew, daughter Sarah Elizabeth, and husband Kevin Campisi, who builds drilling equipment for the booming oil industry. Michelle lines up financing and insurance for Pierisi Properties, a company that renovates housing for low-income families in Louisiana run by John-David. I collect the rent and make a show of hobbling into the bank with hundred dollar bills where I'm know as Mr. Pierisi.

John-David Pierce

Dropped out of college to work in a pizza parlor. He became the youngest general manager in the Bennigan's Restaurant chain and supervised T.G.I.Friday's restaurants in Lafayette, Baton Rouge, and New Orleans. J.D. launched locations for Hops Restaurants in Louisiana, Mississippi, and Tennessee. He lived with his wife Lauri Beaver and the Pierce girls Jill, Jessie, and Julia across the woods from me. We lost Lauri the summer of '04 to breast cancer. Somehow the Pierce girls all remind me of Kate.

Dr. Demento

Went on to share his collection of weird oldies on his syndicated show that played to audiences all over America, including San Francisco. "KMPX was the weirdest gig I ever had in radio," Dr. D recalled recently. "I quit my job with a record company in L.A. to move up there and work for Les Carter. Being on the air full-time was part of the deal . . . I couldn't have afforded to move North for just a weekend shift, since there wasn't much record industry work in the Bay Area. Les told me to just play great music and let it flow, improvise, experiment. I wound up playing lots of new music hardly anyone had heard of, mixed with blues, jazz, folk, a little classical, hardly anything funny. If anything I was too serious. I couldn't listen to the other KMPX jocks much because the signal was terrible in the little valley where I lived . . . so I was pretty much on my own. Les gave me enough rope to hang myself. After Les left I followed him back to KPPC, just in time to get fired along with everyone else. I found another record company job in L.A., Steven Segal got me a weekend gig at KNET, and the Dr. Demento saga got back on track."

Ron 'Inor' Middag

Was in the production department at KRON television in San Francisco. He now works in Hawaii.

Joe "Mississippi" Rodgers

Was a restaurant broker in Boston, before becoming a teamster.

Zack Zenor

Works in electronics in Santa Fe, New Mexico.

Ted Alvy

Lives in Los Angeles, keeping alive the KPPC memory on his web site.

Don Hall

Always a film lover, he was last known to be a projectionist at a theatre.

Jeff Gonzer

Was a disc jockey at KMET and KLOS in Los Angeles, then in Miami and Boston. He went back to L.A. doing talk radio at KLSX. He is now the Program Director for one of the Westwood One Rock channels. He's on the air deejaying every morning in thirty-eight markets.

Steve Segal (The Seagull/Steven Clean)

Helped put together a super star staff at KMET that included Raechal Donahue, Jimmy Rabbit, and Mississippi. Steve worked in several major markets as a top rated deejay for many years before turning off the mic. He's a single parent in Milwaukee, and works as a fund raiser for the arts. His son Alex is a rock musician.

Les and Susan Carter

Wrote scripts for television including *Charlie's Angels*. Continued their career from Ojai northwest of L.A. where Les died in '98. Susan is still writing.

Charles Laquidara

Charles Laquidara played to a third generation of listeners at WBCN and WZLX in Boston. Presiding over a staff of producers, directors, music selectors and gag writers for his 6:00 to 10:00 AM show (dubbed the Big Mattress), Charles enjoyed one of the longest and highest paid runs in radio. Now retired, Charles currently kayaks, hikes, swims and works on his blog http://www.bigmattress.com from his home overlooking the whales that frolic off the southern coast of Maui. "It was all luck." he says, "I'm glad Tony Curtis got the part."

Crown Coach School Bus

The blue paint is peeling to reveal the yellow school color underneath. The Hall Scott engine is frozen, rusting away underneath an oak tree. When I walk the woods, I never pause to go near the bus. It's been over ten years since I've been inside. The California license plates once visible through the Spanish moss have been stolen by Cajun vandals.